THE MAPS OF THE BRISTOE STATION AND MINE RUN CAMPAIGNS

An Atlas of the Battles and Movements in the Eastern Theater After Gettysburg, Including Rappahannock Station, Kelly's Ford, and Morton's Ford, July 1863 - February 1864

Bradley M. Gottfried

SB

Savas Beatie
California

The Maps of the Bristoe Station and Mine Run Campaigns: An Atlas of the Battles and Movements in the Eastern Theater After Gettysburg, Including Rappahannock Station, Kelly's Ford, and Morton's Ford, July 1863 - February 1864

First edition, first printing

Library of Congress Cataloging-in-Publication Data

Gottfried, Bradley M.
The Maps of the Bristoe Station and Mine Run Campaigns: An Atlas of the Battles and Movements in the Eastern Theater After Gettysburg, Including Rappahannock Station, Kelly's Ford, and Morton's Ford, July 1863 - February 1864.
p. cm.
ISBN 978-1-61121-152-8
1. Bristoe Station, Battle of, Va., 1863—Maps. I. Title.
G1294.B79S5.G6 2013
973.7'35—dc23
2013018573

SB
Published by
Savas Beatie LLC
989 Governor Drive, Suite 102
El Dorado Hills, CA 95762
Phone: 916-941-6896
(E-mail) sales@savasbeatie.com

Savas Beatie titles are available at special discounts for bulk purchases in the United States by corporations, institutions, and other organizations. For more details, please contact Special Sales, P.O. Box 4527, El Dorado Hills, CA 95762. You may also e-mail us at sales@savasbeatie.com, or click over for a visit to our website at www.savasbeatie.com for additional information.

The fifth volume of
The Savas Beatie Military Atlas™ Series

To William P. Griffiths

A man who was like a brother to me. May you rest in peace, Griff.

Contents

Contents (continued)

Map Set 3: Approach to Bristoe Station (October 6 - 14, 1863)

Contents (continued)

Contents (continued)

PART 2: THE MINE RUN CAMPAIGN

Contents (continued)

Contents (continued)

Contents (continued)

Map Set 11: Confrontation at Mine Run (November 27 - December 2, 1863)

Map Set 12: Winter Interlude, 1863 -1864 (December 2, 1863 - March 1864)

Contents (continued)

Introduction

As readers of this series know, and newcomers will soon discover, I developed an idea several years ago to better visualize and understand the battle of Gettysburg and the major campaigns in the Eastern Theater. The idea has since developed into multiple volumes that are now part of the Savas Beatie Military Atlas Series—a significant effort to research and illustrate the major campaigns of the Civil War in an original and useful manner.

The first effort in 2007 resulted in *The Maps of Gettysburg*, which spawned a second book two years later entitled *The Maps of First Bull Run*. Soon after the Gettysburg volume appeared, my publisher expressed an interest in expanding the series to the Western campaigns. I was flattered and agreed it was a good idea, but because my interest lies in the Eastern Theater, other historians would have to be brought aboard to assist. The first two were David Powell (text) and David Friedrichs (cartography), who collaborated to produce *The Maps of Chickamauga* in 2009—the same year my First Bull Run study appeared. Other Western Theater campaign studies for this series are in the works, as are atlas books dealing with Napoleon's 1812 invasion of Russia and campaigns dealing with both world wars. This is personally pleasing because, as so many people have shared with me, the only way you can really understand a military campaign (besides walking the ground) is through good maps, and the unique presentation of the Savas Beatie Military Atlas titles *unlocks* other books on the same subjects and makes them more usable and accessible. My third title, *The Maps of Antietam: An Atlas of the Antietam (Sharpsburg) Campaign, Including the Battle of South Mountain, September 2 - 20, 1862*, appeared in 2011.

My fourth title is the book you are now reading: *The Maps of the Bristoe Station and Mine Run Campaigns*. I am currently working on *The Maps of the Wilderness and Spotsylvania*. Although I am not producing these books in chronological order, it is my sincere hope that I will one day complete the major Civil War campaigns in the Eastern Theater of the Civil War from 1861-1865.

Like all my books, *The Maps of the Bristoe Station and Mine Run Campaigns*, which includes the ancillary cavalry fighting and several other operations, is intended to be neutral in coverage. The text and maps cover the movement of the armies from the end of the Gettysburg operation through the fascinating fall campaigns and into early 1864. Although these operations were not as complex as the Gettysburg fighting, Bristoe Station and Mine Run have been largely overlooked by historians and cartographers, and there are substantially fewer primary and secondary works covering this overlooked portion of the war in the Eastern

Theater. As anyone who is familiar with this series will attest, the purpose of these atlas books is to offer a broad and full understanding of the complete campaign, rather than a micro-history of a particular event or day.

No other single source has pulled together the movements and events of this slice of the war and offered it in a cartographic form side-by-side with reasonably detailed text complete with endnotes. Like the books that have come before, *The Maps of the Bristoe Station and Mine Run Campaigns* dissects the actions within each sector of a battlefield for a deeper and hopefully more meaningful understanding and reading experience. Each section of this book includes a number of text and map combinations. Every left-hand page includes descriptive text corresponding with a facing original map on the right-hand page. One of the key advantages of this presentation is that it eliminates the need to flip through the book to try to find a map to match the text. Some sections, like Map Set 1 covering July of 1863 required only three maps and three text pages to set up what was coming. Others, like the fighting at Payne's Farm on November 27, 1863, required a dozen complex maps and their corresponding text pages. Wherever possible, I utilized firsthand accounts to personalize the otherwise straightforward text. I hope readers find this method of presentation useful.

As I have written in previous introductions, the plentiful maps and sectioned coverage make it much easier to follow and understand what was happening each day (and in some cases, each hour). The various sections may also trigger a special interest and so pry open avenues ripe for additional study. I am hopeful that readers who approach the subject with a higher level of expertise will find the maps and text not only interesting to study and read, but also truly helpful. Hopefully someone will place this book within easy reach and refer to it now and again as a reference guide while reading other studies on these campaigns. If so, the long hours invested in this project will have been worthwhile.

A few caveats are in order. *The Maps of the Bristoe Station and Mine Run Campaigns* is not the last word or definitive treatment of these topics, the various engagements, or any part thereof —nor did I intend it to be. Given space and time considerations, I decided to cover the major events of these campaigns and combats, with smaller transition sections to flesh out the full story of these six months of overlooked war. As a result, many aspects have not been as deeply mined as possible. For example, although I discuss in various places the prickly relationship between Maj. Gen. George Meade and the authorities in Washington (the politics of which played a key role in both of these campaigns), the nature of this presentation does not allow for an in-depth examination of this topic. The important point to keep in mind is that Lincoln and Maj. Gen. Henry Halleck had doubts about Meade's ability to defeat Lee, and consistently pressed him to act. The endnotes offer additional avenues of study on this and other interesting but tangential matters.

Original research was kept to a minimum. My primary reliance was upon firsthand accounts and battle reports, followed by quality secondary scholarship. Therefore, there are no new theories or evaluations of why the campaign or battles unfolded as they did. I am also familiar with the battlefields described in this study and have visited them over the years, often in the company of other students of the war. Whenever a book uses short chapters or sections, as this one does, there will inevitably be some narrative redundancy. I have endeavored to minimize this as much as possible.

Sources can and often do conflict on many points, including numbers engaged, who moved when and where and why, what time a specific event unfolded, and of course, casualties. No one knows the exact location of every unit at all times, and in many cases I have pieced the evidence together to come to a educated conclusion. I am sure some of my conclusions are subject to debate, but they represent my best effort to get them right. It is also important to realize that the time a particular action occurred is always approximate. Not only did various participants disagree, but watches were not synchronized and memories were not always reliable. It is common to be confronted with multiple recollections of when events occurred, even by those who were present making the history we so enjoy reading today.

Inevitably, a study like this makes it likely that mistakes of one variety or another end up in the final text or on a map, despite endless hours of proofreading. I apologize in advance for any errors and assume full responsibility for them. Any mistakes discovered will be fixed in subsequent printings.

*   *   *

This book could not have been written and produced without the assistance of a host of people. As always, Theodore P. Savas of Savas Beatie heads the list. A good friend and effective editor, he has always championed my efforts. Because Ted is also a distinguished historian and author in his own right, he understands the researching and writing process and is always supportive. His probing analysis identified questions and inconsistencies in the text and maps and tremendously improved the book's accuracy and clarity. Ted also happens to be an expert in his own right on the Mine Run Campaign in general, and Payne's Farm in particular. Together with his friend Paul Sacra of Richmond, Virginia, Ted played a key role in mapping out the true boundaries of the Payne's Farm battlefield in the 1990s and turned over his research to the Association for the Preservation of the Civil War Sites—the precursor to today's outstanding Civil War Trust. Ted's efforts helped assure the preservation of that sacred field. I would also like to thank everyone at Savas Beatie for their assistance in producing and marketing my work.

I am also indebted to Robert Orrison, Historic Site Manager with the Bristoe Station Battlefield Park. Rob organized a tour for me of the Bristoe Campaign, has read several sections of the manuscript and has been an important sounding board when I have questioned conflicting accounts of the action. His generous spirit helped in any and every way that he could.

Todd Berkoff, another expert on the Bristoe Campaign, read several sections of the manuscript and we had several long discussions via email on what happened at various portions of the campaign. We did not always see eye-to-eye, but had some thought-provoking interactions.

John Pearson helped me better understand the confusing action at Auburn during a tour of the battleground and provided me with some wonderful resources.

Mike Block toured the Rappahannock Station and Kelly's Ford battlefields with me, which proved extremely helpful.

Donald Pfanz, Staff Historian (recently retired) at the Fredericksburg & Spotsylvania National Military Park, allowed me access to the tremendous bound resources collection housed at the Chatham House. He was always accommodating of his time.

And finally, I would like to thank Linda, my friend, my partner, and my wife, who traveled with me on my many trips to the battlefields, patiently listened to my endless stories, and allowed me the time and space to complete this important effort.

Bradley M. Gottfried
La Plata, Maryland

THE MAPS OF THE

BRISTOE STATION

AND MINE RUN

CAMPAIGNS

An Atlas of the Battles and Movements in the Eastern Theater After Gettysburg, Including Rappahannock Station, Kelly's Ford, and Morton's Ford, July 1863 - February 1864

Map Set 1: End of July, 1863

Map 1.1: The Army of the Potomac

The Union Army of the Potomac that emerged after the bloody fighting at Gettysburg was much weaker in several significant ways. Maj. Gen. George Meade's army fielded about 94,000 during the battle. When it ended, casualties totaled more than 3,100 dead, 14,500 wounded, and 5,300 missing or captured. These staggering losses not only reduced its strength but also its fighting ability and leadership. Some of Meade's most capable veterans were among the dead and wounded, and they could not be easily replaced. Field officers had been hit hard, and by the time the fighting ended, many regiments were the size of early-war companies.

Attempts to swell the ranks with the draft (the Conscription Act passed Congress in early March 1863) sparked riots. Bounties were added to bribe men into service. These efforts increased enlistments, but the new men were untrained and not as motivated as early-war enlistees. Many deserted, and large numbers never reached their units in Virginia. Meade employed firing squads in an effort to improve discipline. For example, the First Division of II Corps watched the execution of five deserters from the 148th Pennsylvania. In many cases the condemned were foreign-born. Conventional thinking held that new recruits would become more effective soldiers if they were added to existing units. As the officers learned, however, Anglo-Saxon veterans did not mix well with newly arrived German- or Irish- born troops.[1]

Losses throughout the officer corps crippled the army's effectiveness. Three of the seven corps commanders fell at Gettysburg: John Reynolds (I Corps) was killed, Winfield Hancock (II Corps) fell seriously wounded and would not return until the spring of 1864, and Daniel Sickles (III Corps) lost a leg and would never return. John Newton, who had taken over for Reynolds during the battle, was elevated to lead I Corps and William Henry French replaced Sickles. Gouverneur K. Warren was given II Corps during Hancock's prolonged absence. How these men would perform with the added responsibility was unknown. Of his remaining corps leaders, only VI Corps' John Sedgwick showed real command promise. Meade's former command, V Corps, remained under George Sykes, who many believed never grew into his role as a corps leader. XI Corps' Oliver Howard, who turned in another questionable performance at Gettysburg, remained as the head of his corps, as did Howard Slocum with XII Corps. Neither man inspired real confidence.[2]

Meade's own reputation was called into question once the campaign ended in mid-July. His elevation from commander of V Corps during the waning days of June was accompanied by high expectations. His victory at Gettysburg seemed to justify President Abraham Lincoln's faith in him. Questions about his aggressiveness and judgment after the campaign ended soured the president's and public's initial elation when the crippled Army of Northern Virginia, trapped for days against the swollen Potomac, slipped across. Lincoln considered removing Meade, but none of the corps commanders appeared to be better suited for the job and the president was not ready to replace him with any of his successful generals from the Western Theater. To Meade's credit, he was the only field commander who had stood tall and defeated Robert E. Lee in a face-to-face battle. Removing him for another risked triggering a backlash. Meade remained in command.[3]

When July ended, the Union army was back in Virginia on the northern side of the Rappahannock River in Fauquier County, with Lee's Army of Northern Virginia camped to the southwest protecting the Orange & Alexandria Railroad. The Federal VI Corps was near Sulphur Springs and I Corps at Rappahannock Station, with III Corps deployed between them. V Corps was at the opposite end of the line at Kelly's Ford, with XII Corps between it and Rappahannock Station. II Corps was camped behind in reserve. XI Corps was deployed along the vital Orange and Alexandria Railroad. The area had been picked clean by the opposing armies during previous campaigns, so a steady outside supply of food and other materials was required to maintain the new position.[4]

The three Confederate corps held positions protecting the Orange & Alexandria Railroad. James Longstreet's First Corps was in camp near Stevensburg, A. P. Hill's Third Corps was north of Culpeper, and Richard Ewell's Second Corps was in deep reserve behind Robertson's River near Madison Court House.

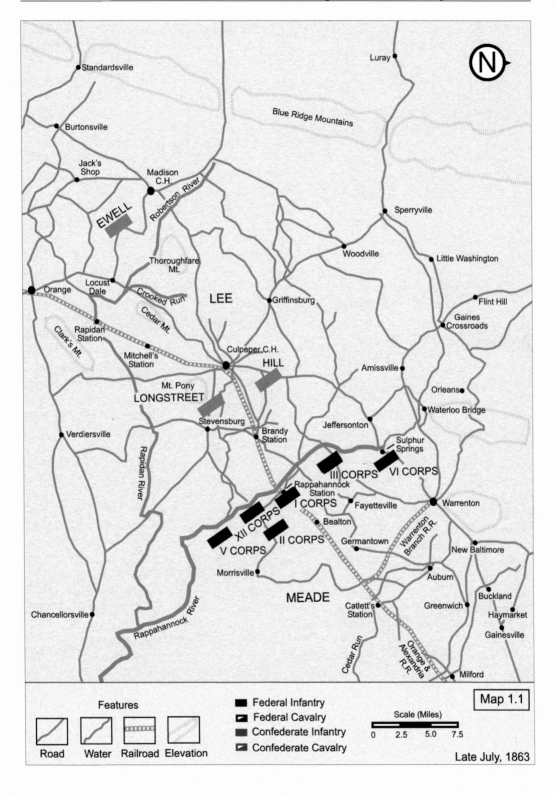

Standardsville

Luray

N

Blue Ridge Mountains

Burtonsville

Jack's Shop

Madison C.H.

Robertson River

EWELL

Sperryville

Thoroughfare Mt.

Woodville

Little Washington

Locust Dale

Orange

Crooked Run

Cedar Mt.

LEE

Griffinsburg

Flint Hill

Gaines Crossroads

Clark's Mt.

Rapidan Station

Mitchell's Station

Culpeper C.H.

HILL

Amissville

Orleans

Waterloo Bridge

Mt. Pony

LONGSTREET

Verdiersville

Rapidan River

Stevensburg

Brandy Station

Jeffersonton

Sulphur Springs

III CORPS

VI CORPS

Rappahannock Station

I CORPS

Fayetteville

Warrenton

XII CORPS

Bealton

II CORPS

Germantown

Warrenton Branch R.R.

New Baltimore

V CORPS

Morrisville

Auburn

MEADE

Catlett's Station

Greenwich

Buckland

Haymarket

Chancellorsville

Rappahannock River

Gainesville

Cedar Run

Orange & Alexandria R.R.

Milford

Features

Road   Water   Railroad   Elevation

■ Federal Infantry
◣ Federal Cavalry
■ Confederate Infantry
◣ Confederate Cavalry

Scale (Miles)

0   2.5   5.0   7.5

Map 1.1

Late July, 1863

Map 1.2:
The Army of Northern Virginia

If the Army of the Potomac was in rocky shape, Robert E. Lee's Army of Northern Virginia was in even worse condition. It lost 23,231 at Gettysburg, or about one-third of its strength. Although none of the corps commanders had been killed or wounded, the army sustained heavy losses at the division, brigade, and regimental levels. Replacing these valuable officers was getting harder as each month of the war passed. According to one modern source, three months after Gettysburg the Army of the Potomac was back to about 90 percent of its former strength; in contrast, the Army of Northern Virginia was smaller by more than 40 percent than what it had been when it left Fredericksburg in June to begin the invasion.[5]

Desertion was rampant among many of Lee's less ardent troops. The general wrote to President Jefferson Davis on August 17, "the number of desertions from this army is so great and still continues to such an extent, that unless some cessation of them can be caused, I fear success in the field will be seriously endangered." Lee implemented a system of furloughs to help improve morale. Southern authorities also turned to religion to reignite Confederate ardor for the cause. President Davis, for example, designated Friday the 21st of August as a day of fasting and prayer. Baptisms became commonplace as religion threaded its way into the everyday life of the soldiers. The religious revival, wrote John Worsham of the 21st Virginia (John M. Jones' Brigade, Edward Johnson's Division), "spread so rapidly over the entire army; and the converts were so numerous that they numbered not by tens and hundreds, but by thousands."[6]

A lack of adequate supplies continued to plague Lee. The grueling campaign just ended sapped the army's strength and drained the wagons of supplies in general, and food and clothing in particular. The dramatic reduction in the quantity and quality of horses was especially concerning to Lee. The campaign and score of engagements killed, wounded, or simply wore out many thousands of animals, including those consumed by disease. Lee could not remedy this dire situation without the help of others, and if left unaddressed, it would have a major impact on his artillery and cavalry arms. On August 24, he wrote to Davis that "nothing prevents my advancing now but the fear of killing our artillery horses. They are much reduced, & the hot weather & scarce forage keeps them so. The cavalry also suffer, & I fear to set them to work."

Ironically, Meade won the campaign but lost the trust of his commander-in-chief, while Lee lost the campaign but Davis continued to hold him in high esteem. Lingering health concerns, however, including likely bouts of angina pectoris (heart problems), convinced Lee that he was no longer able to satisfy the rigorous demands of running an army in the field. His stamina was waning. Lee tendered his resignation after Gettysburg, but Davis would have none of it. Who else could possibly command the Army of Northern Virginia as well as even a weakened Lee?[7]

In addition to thinned ranks, supply issues, and his own health problems, Lee worried about the growing pressure on him to transfer to the Western Theater to assume command of Braxton Bragg's Army of Tennessee, or for part of his army to reinforce it. With Tennessee hanging in the balance, Davis decided to transport Lee's most experienced commander, James Longstreet, together with most of his corps, to reinvigorate Confederate fortunes beyond the Allegheny Mountains. Longstreet's men began their journey on September 9, and arrived just in time to help Bragg win a decisive victory at Chickamauga over William Rosecrans' Army of the Cumberland on September 20. With the defeated Rosecrans bottled up in and around Chattanooga, Washington transferred XI Corps and XII Corps away from Meade's Army of the Potomac to help break the siege. The Federal troops began hopping on trains on September 25, and reached the Chattanooga theater a few days later.[8]

The transfer of Longstreet west, however, was still in the future that July. The short supply of livestock forced Lee to disperse his army during the latter part of the month. Longstreet's First Corps camped between Pony Mountain and Stevensburg, about three to six miles southeast of Culpeper. Richard Ewell's Second Corps camped about ten miles southwest of Culpeper in eastern Madison County, while A. P. Hill's Third Corps camped a few miles east of Culpeper.[9]

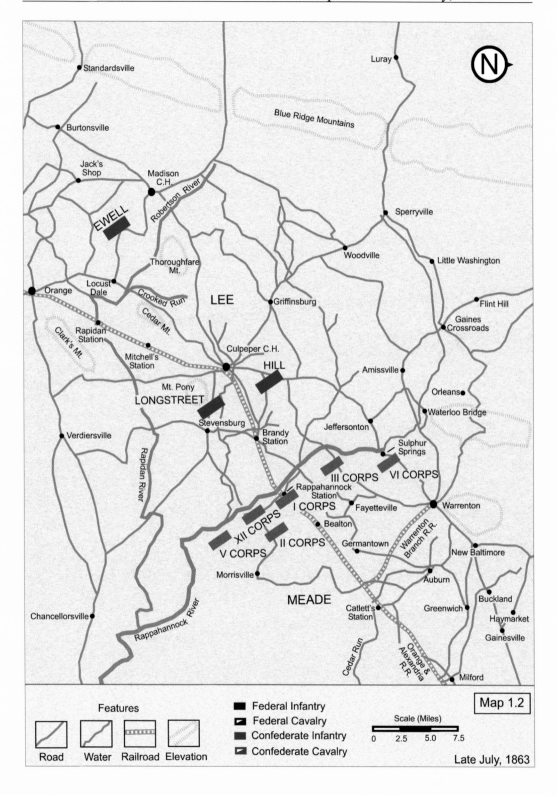

Standardsville

Burtonsville

Jack's
Shop

Madison
C.H.

Robertson River

EWELL

Thoroughfare
Mt.

Locust
Dale

Orange

Crooked Run

Cedar Mt.

Rapidan
Station

Clark's Mt.

Mitchell's
Station

Mt. Pony

LONGSTREET

Verdiersville

Rapidan River

LEE

Griffinsburg

Culpeper C.H.

HILL

Stevensburg

Brandy
Station

Chancellorsville

Rappahannock River

Blue Ridge Mountains

Luray

Sperryville

Woodville

Little Washington

Flint Hill

Gaines
Crossroads

Amissville

Orleans

Waterloo Bridge

Jeffersonton

Sulphur
Springs

VI CORPS

III CORPS

Rappahannock
Station

I CORPS

Fayetteville

Warrenton

Bealton

XII CORPS

II CORPS

Germantown

Warrenton
Branch R.R.

New Baltimore

V CORPS

Morrisville

MEADE

Catlett's
Station

Auburn

Greenwich

Buckland

Haymarket

Gainesville

Cedar Run

Orange &
Alexandria
R.R.

Milford

Features

Road   Water   Railroad   Elevation

■ Federal Infantry
▱ Federal Cavalry
■ Confederate Infantry
▱ Confederate Cavalry

Scale (Miles)

0   2.5   5.0   7.5

Map 1.2

Late July, 1863

Map 1.3: The Battleground

Most of the operations conducted between July and November of 1863 were in or near an area referred to as the "Iron Triangle." The confluence of the Rappahannock and Rapidan rivers constituted the eastern tip of this triangle. The area opened and broadened to the west (about a 25-five mile line) between the Robertson River and the Rappahannock River, with the Blue Ridge Mountains defining the triangle's western boundary. One contemporary described the region as "well wooded and watered; it abounds in practical roads; a railroad [Orange and Alexandria Railroad] intersects it from end to end; while from its gently undulating surface occasional hills or knobs, rising from hundreds of feet above the general level enable considerable areas of the surrounding country to be observed and afford rare opportunities for the operations of the Signal Service, which were fully taken advantage of by the opposing com- manders." Culpeper sits roughly in the center of the "Iron Triangle."[10]

The terrain south of the Rapidan River differed from that found in the "Iron Triangle" because it was "more or less rolling, and wooded with dense groves of pines and hardwoods, mostly oak." Lee would take refuge here twice during the fall of 1863. Roads were fairly plentiful in the "Iron Triangle," but there were fewer south of the Rapidan. Those that existed in 1863 primarily ran in a north-south or east-west orientation. Because they were composed of mainly clay or sand, it did not take much moisture to make them all but impassible. A few of the roads were corduroyed or planked to allow faster troop movements, particularly during wet periods.[11]

Both the Rappahannock and the Rapidan posed major obstacles to the armies because they were too deep to cross except at fords and bridges. This simple fact influenced the strategic and tactical plans of both leaders. The two waterways also differed in their topography. While the north bank of the Rappahannock commanded the south shore, the opposite was true of the Rapidan, where the steep southern bank towered over the river in some places by as much as 100 feet. Lee would make good use of both advantages during the fall campaigns.[12]

How a commander evaluated the "Iron Triangle" depended upon whether he was on the offensive or the defensive. For Meade, who was pressured by Washington to take the offensive against Lee's army that fall, the region "abounded in military positions and [was] in every way favorable for the development and maneuver of large bodies of troops." On the defensive, Lee probably viewed the area differently, for it "afforded Meade the chance to maneuver around either of his flanks."[13]

On August 10, Meade reported that his Army of the Potomac numbered 90,000. Lee's strength, after Longstreet's departure, was just more than 54,000. Despite the disparity in numbers and supplies, the Confederates had several intangibles working in their favor. A British officer visiting the Federal army during this period concluded that Meade faced "a fine army commanded by a first rate general in his front, and an uncertain, interfering, yet timorous government in constant communication with him in his rear, while his own army is chiefly composed of undrilled, undis- ciplined conscripts."[14]

The "fine army" Lee commanded was still stunned by its loss in Pennsylvania. Many of the units had fought exceptionally well at Gettysburg, only to be turned away and forced to retreat back into Virginia. Adding to their discomfort was the news that two important bastions had fallen to the enemy. As one North Carolinian put it, "the news of the fall of Vicksburg and Port Hudson has startled us like a clap of thunder on a cloudless day. We were not prepared for such intelligence." Another soldier wrote that "our whole army was very much depressed by the news from the west." A Virginian agreed, adding that the news "has had a very depressing effect on us all & some seem to be almost in despair."[15]

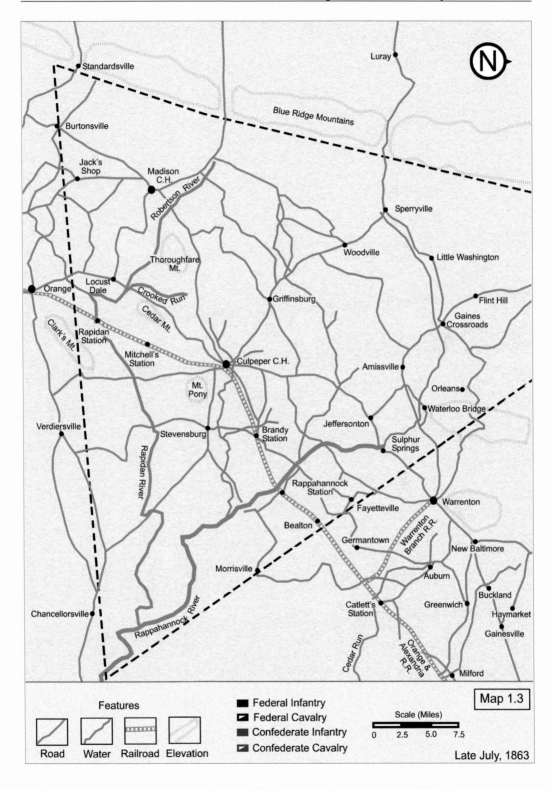

Luray

Standardsville

Blue Ridge Mountains

Burtonsville

Jack's
Shop

Madison
C.H.

Robertson River

Sperryville

Woodville

Little Washington

Thoroughfare
Mt.

Locust
Dale

Orange

Crooked Run

Cedar Mt.

Griffinsburg

Flint Hill

Gaines
Crossroads

Clark's Mt.

Rapidan
Station

Mitchell's
Station

Culpeper C.H.

Amissville

Orleans

Waterloo Bridge

Mt.
Pony

Verdiersville

Stevensburg

Brandy
Station

Jeffersonton

Sulphur
Springs

Rapidan River

Rappahannock
Station

Fayetteville

Warrenton

Bealton

Germantown

Warrenton Branch R.R.

New Baltimore

Morrisville

Auburn

Buckland

Chancellorsville

Catlett's
Station

Greenwich

Haymarket

Gainesville

Rappahannock River

Cedar Run

Orange & Alexandria R.R.

Milford

Features

| Road | Water | Railroad | Elevation |

■ Federal Infantry
◨ Federal Cavalry
■ Confederate Infantry
◨ Confederate Cavalry

Scale (Miles)
0   2.5   5.0   7.5

Map 1.3

Late July, 1863

Map Set 2: Cavalry Actions
(August 1863)

Map 2.1: The Second Battle of Brandy Station (August 1: 6:00 a.m. - noon)

Knowing that President Lincoln expected action against Lee's wounded army, Gen. Meade decided to conduct a reconnaissance in force on August 1 by pushing his cavalry, with strong infantry support, across the wide Rappahannock River. His plan involved a multi-pronged approach. Brig. Gen. John Buford's cavalry division at Rappahannock Station, supported by I Corps, would spearhead the advance to ascertain the location of the Confederate army. Twelve miles farther north, Brig. Gen. David Gregg's cavalry division would cross at White Sulphur Springs, supported by the foot soldiers of VI Corps. Brig. Gen. Judson Kilpatrick's division, temporarily under Brig. Gen. George Custer, would remain in reserve near Warrenton Junction. From that point, it could reinforce either division. Meade's five other infantry corps could also cross and provide support, if needed.[1]

The bridge spanning the Rappahannock was not ready when Buford arrived at dawn on August 1, so he rode three miles north to Beverly Ford. When he determined this crossing was unacceptable, he rode south to Kelly's Ford, which was spanned by a pontoon bridge. Buford's troopers quickly crossed the river and rode north (No. 1) along the waterway to the Orange and Alexandria Railroad opposite Rappahannock Station. There, engineers from Maj. Gen. John Newton's I Corps were putting the finishing touches on a pontoon bridge; the infantry would soon be crossing. Buford turned his riders southwest and followed the railroad toward Culpeper. Farther upriver, meanwhile, David Gregg slipped his troopers across at White Sulphur Springs and headed for Jeffersonton (No. 2). He sent some of his men as far south as the Hazel River to reconnoiter. Everything seemed to be going well for the Federals.[2]

There was not much Confederate cavalry in front of the Yankee horsemen. Because of a lack of forage for the horses, and not knowing where the enemy would cross the Rappahannock, Lee had scattered his handful of cavalry brigades from Fredericksburg to the Hazel River—a distance of about 25 miles. Only two brigades were available to contest the Federal troopers: Brig. Gen. William (Grumble) Jones' near Rixeyville and the Hazel River (No. 3), and Wade Hampton's, now under Brig. Gen. Laurence Baker, south of Fleetwood Hill at Brandy Station. The latter brigade numbered fewer than 1,000 men because of the heavy losses it had sustained at Gettysburg on July 3 at East Cavalry Field. Many of those present were demoralized by the loss of so many comrades (including Hampton, who had been severely wounded) and the possible loss of their mounts, which were ridden to exhaustion during the Pennsylvania campaign and suffered from inadequate food and the intense heat.[3]

Baker's men were up and in the saddle shortly after dawn on August 1. Scouts brought word that a large enemy force of cavalry (Buford's division) had crossed the river and was heading for the Orange and Alexandria Railroad. Gen. Baker led his veterans northeast along the railroad and formed into a line of battle across the tracks about one-half mile from Rappahannock Station (No. 4). The 1st and 2nd South Carolina, together with a horse battery, occupied the north (left side) of the tracks, while Cobb's Legion, the Phillips Legion, and the Hampton Legion formed on the right side of the line. Hart's horse battery formed on their left. These troops had to be dispersed before Buford could accomplish his mission of determining the location of the Confederate infantry. It did not take him long to realize that his division outnumbered his Rebel opponent, but he probably did not realize that he held a four-to-one advantage.

The fighting began about 10:00 a.m. when Buford's artillery opened on Baker's guns. The bombardment forced Hart's pieces off the field. Buford's troopers, who overlapped Baker's men on both flanks, advanced and the Southern horsemen grudgingly gave ground. For the next four miles, Baker repeatedly halted his men to face the enemy in an effort to slow or halt the Federal advance. Buford's overwhelming numbers, however, nearly surrounded the overmatched Confederates, who managed to withdraw just in time, each time, before suffering heavy losses (No. 5).[4]

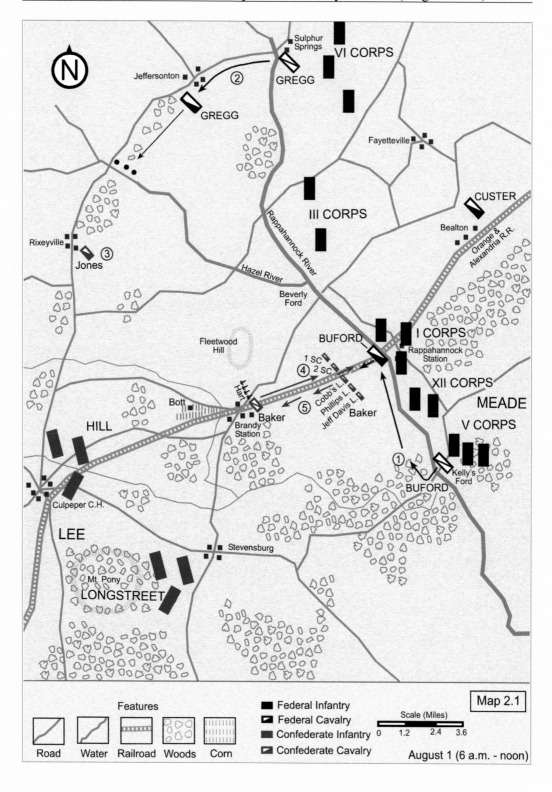

Map 2.1

August 1 (6 a.m. - noon)

Map 2.2: The Second Battle of Brandy Station (August 1: noon - 7:30 p.m.)

The situation looked bleak for Hampton's Brigade. Gen. Laurence Baker had conducted the four-mile fighting retreat well, but Buford's heavy force men showed no signs of relenting. Baker halted his men just northeast of Brandy Station and prepared to give battle yet again (No. 1). As before, the Union tide nearly surrounded the Confederates. Baker called upon his horse batteries to fire at the enemy, who were by this time fewer than 50 yards away. After a few rounds, Baker saw an opening in the Federal lines and quickly led his men to safety.

The worn-out gray troopers rode southwest before halting on the Orange and Alexandria Railroad with Buford's men in hot pursuit. The large mansion owned by Union-supporter John Minor Bott loomed behind the Confederate makeshift line. Buford did not know that A. P. Hill's Third Corps was camped nearby. Jeb Stuart, riding at the van of Jones' cavalry brigade, arrived to provide support (No. 2). These troopers had been watching Gregg's cavalry ride to Jefferstonton and Amissville, but when the Federal cavalry halted, Stuart turned Jones' men south to face Buford. Although it was still a mismatch, the odds were not as heavy as they had been.

The Confederates counterattacked about 4:00 p.m., Jones' men striking from the north and Baker's from the west and south. The assault rocked Buford's division (No. 3). Much of the fighting was centered in a large (and soon-to-be-destroyed) cornfield stretching half a mile from the Botts mansion to the railroad tracks. Attacked on three sides, and occasionally in their rear, Buford's troopers began giving ground. Chew's horse battery was particularly effective against the Federal troopers, changing position five times to exert maximum pressure on the enemy. Buford's men were confused, not only by the sudden turn of events, but also by the change in Southern tactics. In the past, the enemy had extensively used pistols. Today, the charges were more determined and sword thrusts much more common. After Gettysburg, Stuart ordered more shock charges with sabers flashing. Some troopers did not have horses but remained with their units using infantry muskets, while others

simply dismounted to fire into Buford's men with muskets.

Buford's situation took a turn for the worse when Confederate infantry from Maj. Gen. Richard Anderson's Division rushed from their camps and arrived on the scene (No. 4). William Mahone's Virginia brigade was in the front, closely followed by Carnot Posey's brigade of Mississippians. Buford slowly and stubbornly fell back toward Rappahannock Station on the river (No. 5). Anderson was so intent on getting his infantry into the fight that his division followed the Federals about five miles to the Rappahannock River.[5]

Once near the river, Buford saw that the pontoon bridge was complete and a number of Gen. Newton's I Corps troops were on the southern side. The realization angered Buford, who believed that if Newton's infantry had smartly advanced, the combat may well have turned out differently. Together, his cavalry and I Corps numbered about 15,000 against about 6,000 Southerners.

Gen. Meade was generally pleased with the outcome. Strategically speaking, John Buford accomplished his mission: Meade now knew that Rebel infantry was camped near Culpeper. Buford, however, believed Newton let him down and noted it was a "severe day upon men and horses." Federal losses totaled about 270 men killed, wounded, and missing.

The Confederates paid a heavy price for their sharp tactical victory. Baker's (Hampton's) already-decimated brigade lost about one-half of its remaining men in dead or wounded, which in turn reduced the unit to the size of a field regiment (about 500 men). No fewer than five men led the brigade that day, for Baker and three others fell in succession to enemy lead.[6]

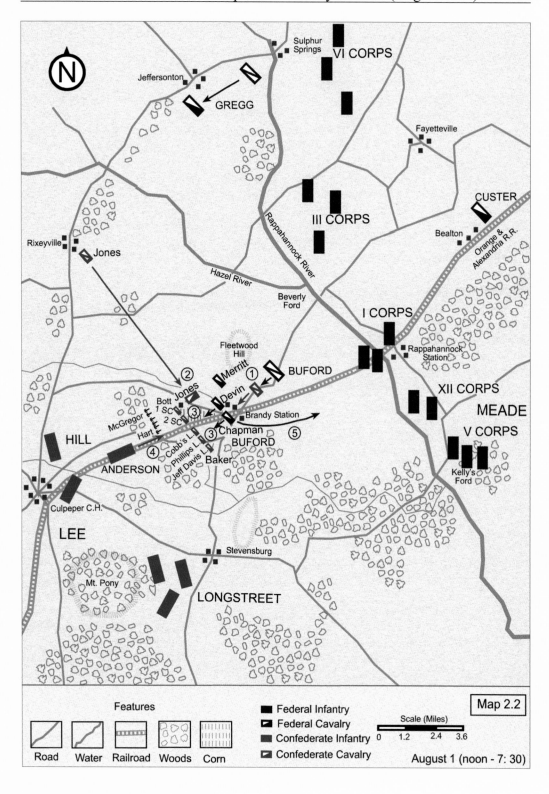

Map 2.2

August 1 (noon - 7: 30)

Map 2.3: Lee Pulls Back Across the Rapidan River (August 2 - September 12)

A number of cavalry skirmishes were fought on August 3, 4, 5, 8, and 9. Every case included Stuart's troopers probing the Union strength south of the Rappahannock River. Perhaps still feeling uncomfortable in his new post, Meade continued to seek advice from his senior officers. He wanted another opportunity to coax Lee into attacking him while he remained on the defensive, much like what had transpired at Gettysburg. His adversary, however, refused to cooperate. The idea of taking the offensive during brutally hot weather gave Meade pause. Lincoln and General-in-Chief Halleck expected Meade to attack Lee.[7]

Lee, meanwhile, sought council from Jefferson Davis. The general was troubled by his position south of the Rappahannock River with the Rapidan River in his rear, and his ongoing supply problems. Davis suggested that Lee fall back below the Rapidan and use Orange Court House as his supply base. The high ground there was perfect for defense, and there were fewer places for the Federals to cross. Lee also knew that Meade would follow him farther south, which would lengthen the Union supply lines and make his flanks more vulnerable to being turned.

While Stuart's troopers distracted the Federal army, Lee began to pull back across the Rapidan River on August 3. The rumor mill shifted into high gear as Lee's foot soldiers tried to ascertain what was underway. Speculation ended when the troops crossed the river and took up defensive positions. Most of Hill's Corps moved to the railroad north of Orange Court House, but some continued northeast of the town. Longstreet's men crossed at Morton's Ford, about 15 miles northeast of Orange Court House, and camped from Verdiersville east to almost Chancellorsville. Lee ordered Richard Ewell to maintain his corps' position in Madison County, within striking distance of the main line of the Orange and Alexandria Railroad.

While Fitz Lee's cavalry brigade patrolled the south side of the Rapidan and Rappahannock rivers from Germanna Ford to Fredericksburg, Stuart sent Col. Pierce Young (who was now commanding Hampton's/Baker's) Brigade and Jones's Brigade to patrol the Rappahannock from the Rapidan to Waterloo Bridge. Gen. Lee knew that if he removed all of his troops from the ground between the Rappahannock and Rapidan rivers, Meade would quickly advance and capture Culpeper.[8]

For a variety of reasons, Meade appeared content with the stalemate through August 13. Raiding Confederate guerillas plaguing Meade's rear forced him to deploy XI Corps along the Orange and Alexandria Railroad. He did not trust the new recruits that had swelled his army, and many of his veteran regiments had been sent away to help quell draft riots in northern cities. Meade also knew that crossing the Rappahannock would only make his supply problem that much more difficult. Like Lee, his horses were inadequate in number and food sources were insufficient to keep them well fed and fully healthy. Still, his mounted arm remained active. Gregg's division patrolled the upper Rappahannock River from Fauquier White Sulphur Springs to Jeffersonton and as far north as Thoroughfare Gap, while Kilpatrick's division patrolled from Rappahannock Station to Kelly's Ford. Buford's division operated on Meade's left flank, from Ely's Ford to Fredericksburg.

Meade's infantry corps maintained their positions. III Corps and VI Corps held the right, II Corps and V Corps the center, and I Corps and XII Corps formed the left.[9]

After William Rosecrans' Army of the Cumberland flanked Braxton Bragg's Army of Tennessee at Tullahoma and thus exposed Chattanooga, Tennessee, to capture, President Davis decided he had no choice but to send reinforcements from Lee's army. On September 8, most of Longstreet's First Corps (two divisions, a brigade from a third, and a battalion of artillery) boarded trains at Orange Courthouse for northern Georgia. This left Lee with only about 54,000 troops and a good dose of anxiety. This emotion was compounded by Lee's ongoing heart condition, which tired him and often forced the general off his horse and into a wagon for transportation.[10]

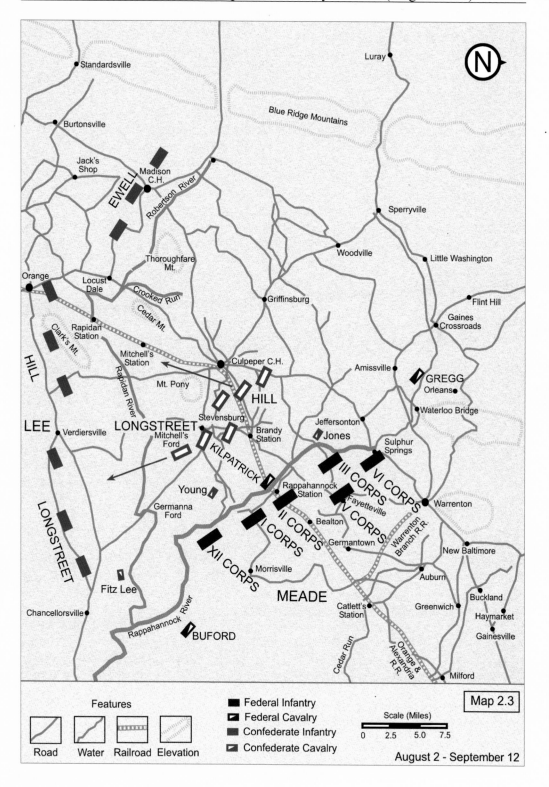

Standardsville

Luray

N

Blue Ridge Mountains

Burtonsville

Jack's
Shop

Madison
C.H.

EWELL

Robertson River

Sperryville

Woodville

Little Washington

Thoroughfare
Mt.

Orange

Locust
Dale

Crooked Run

Griffinsburg

Flint Hill

Cedar Mt.

Gaines
Crossroads

Rapidan
Station

Rapidan River

Clark's Mt.

HILL

Mitchell's
Station

Mt. Pony

Culpeper C.H.

Amissville

GREGG

Orleans

HILL

Waterloo Bridge

LEE

Verdiersville

Stevensburg

LONGSTREET

Mitchell's
Ford

Brandy
Station

Jeffersonton

Jones

Sulphur
Springs

KILPATRICK

Rappahannock
Station

III
CORPS

VI CORPS

Warrenton

Young

Germanna
Ford

Fayetteville

V CORPS

LONGSTREET

II CORPS

Bealton

Germantown

Warrenton
Branch R.R.

New Baltimore

I CORPS

XII CORPS

Morrisville

Auburn

Buckland

Greenwich

Fitz Lee

Chancellorsville

Rappahannock River

BUFORD

MEADE

Catlett's
Station

Cedar Run

Haymarket

Gainesville

Orange &
Alexandria
R.R.

Milford

Features

Road	Water	Railroad	Elevation

■ Federal Infantry
◗ Federal Cavalry
▬ Confederate Infantry
◤ Confederate Cavalry

Scale (Miles)

0   2.5   5.0   7.5

Map 2.3

August 2 - September 12

**Map 2.4: Meade Tests Lee's Strength:
The Fight at Culpeper
(September 13: 5:00 - 7:30 a.m.)**

When Washington caught wind of rumors that some of Lee's troops were heading west to reinforce Braxton Bragg, Henry Halleck requested confirmation from Meade, whose headquarters were in the village of Germantown. He was unable to immediately confirm or deny the news. Meade soon received an article in the New York Herald dated September 9 confirming the information. Lee also saw the paper and complained to President Davis that, "I fear that there has been great imprudence in talking on the part of our people."[11]

After Longstreet's departure, Lee decided to review Ewell's Second Corps on September 10 and Hill's Third Corps the next day. These reviews provided Lee with an opportunity to assess his army's physical state and overall morale. The pageant-like events took place in a large field with an adjacent hill, which Lee used as a grand viewing platform.[12]

Shortly after midnight on September 13, Jeb Stuart received a visitor who told him Federal cavalry was planning to attack within five hours. Stuart had but three brigades in the sector to stop the enemy's thrust: Hampton's (led by Col. Pierce Young), Jones's (under Col. Lunsford Lomax because Grumble Jones had been arrested for insubordination), and W. H. F. Lee's (under Col. R. L. Beale). In total, Stuart's cavalry (most of which was stationed in and around Brandy Station) mustered only 5,000 troopers. In contrast, Maj. Gen. Alfred Pleasonton's Federal cavalry totaled about 11,000.[13]

As predicted, Federal cavalry crossed the Rappahannock River at dawn in a reconnaissance in force to ascertain the position and strength of Lee's army. Gregg's division splashed across at White Sulphur Springs (No. 1), and Kilpatrick's at Kelly's Ford (No. 2). Buford's division crossed at two places: Beverly Ford and over a shaky pontoon bridge near Rappahannock Station (No. 3). II Corps infantrymen also crossed to provide support while V Corps waited in reserve.[14]

Gregg's division splashed across the river just after daylight. The Pennsylvania units in the lead almost immediately encountered a company of the 11th Virginia Cavalry on picket duty. The company was no match for an entire division and began drifting to the rear. The rest of the Virginia regiment quickly arrived and the two sides blazed away at each other for about half an hour (No. 4). The Federal cavalry pushed the Virginians back across the Hazel River, with the Southerners trying to set the bridge on fire as they crossed. The attempt was unsuccessful, and Gregg followed on the Rixeyville Road. Stuart grasped the seriousness of the threat to his left flank and sent the remainder of Lomax's brigade—the 7th and 12th Virginia Cavalry—galloping northwest to contest the enemy approach (No. 5).[15]

Meanwhile, Kilpatrick's men crossed the Rappahannock River downstream at Kelly's Ford at about 6:00 a.m. Col. Henry Davies's brigade led the column, followed by Custer's brigade. The division turned north toward the Orange and Alexandria Railroad. Along the way they encountered the 6th Virginia Cavalry (Lomax's Brigade) and a squadron of sharpshooters from the 9th Virginia Cavalry (Beale's Brigade) forming a picket line under the command of Maj. C. E. Flournoy. The two sides exchanged carbine fire for about an hour (No. 6). Realizing the enemy's strength was growing, Flournoy ordered his command to fall back. Most withdrew toward Brandy Station, while others headed for Stevensburg. The major portion of Kilpatrick's division headed toward the former, but the 1st Michigan Cavalry was sent southwest toward Stevensburg. Buford's division crossed at Beverly Ford, and when it encountered little opposition there pushed west to Brandy Station and formed a supporting line behind Kilpatrick about 7:30 a.m.[16]

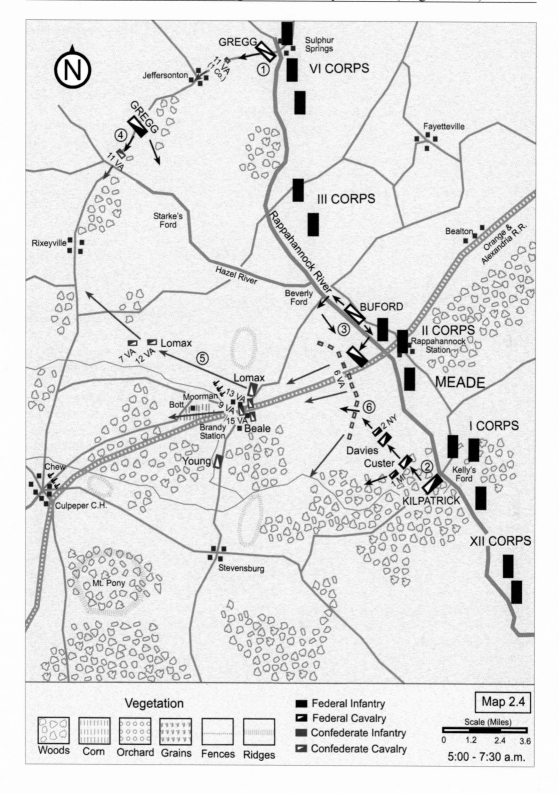

N

GREGG
Sulphur
Springs
VI CORPS
①
11 VA
(1 Co.)
Jeffersonton

GREGG
④
11 VA

Fayetteville

III CORPS

Starke's
Ford

Bealton

Rappahannock River
Orange &
Alexandria R.R.

Rixeyville

Hazel River

Beverly
Ford
BUFORD
②
Rappahannock
Station
II CORPS

Lomax
⑤
7 VA 12 VA

6 VA

MEADE

Lomax
13 VA
Moorman
9 VA
Bott
15 VA
Brandy
Beale
Station

I CORPS

②
2 NY
Davies
Custer
1 MI
Kelly's
Ford

Young

KILPATRICK

Chew

Culpeper C.H.

XII CORPS

Stevensburg

Mt. Pony

Vegetation

Woods Corn Orchard Grains Fences Ridges

■ Federal Infantry
◪ Federal Cavalry
■ Confederate Infantry
◪ Confederate Cavalry

Map 2.4

Scale (Miles)
0   1.2   2.4   3.6

5:00 - 7:30 a.m.

Map 2.5: The Fight at Culpeper Continues (September 13: 7:30 a.m. - noon)

The 1st Michigan, following a portion of Flourney's men toward Stevensburg, ran into Hampton's/Baker's Brigade (under Col. Young) within a mile of the town. Despite the inequity in numbers, Col. Peter Stagg calmly deployed his Michiganders and ordered them forward, driving the Rebel skirmish line before them (No. 1). According to Stagg, his regiment was "met by a shower of shell and musketry, and [was] obliged to retire with the loss of 1 man wounded." When he requested orders from Custer, he was called back to the brigade, which was now approaching Brandy Station.[17]

While Stagg's Wolverines pressured the Rebels falling back toward Stevensburg, the 2nd New York Cavalry led Col. Henry Davies's brigade in pursuit of Flournoy's men who retreated toward Brandy Station. According to one of the New York troopers, "our advance was rather slow and cautious till we reached the forest bordering on the old Brandy Station battle-field. Here we first struck the enemy in some force." In its haste to engage the retreating Confederates, the regiment far outpaced the rest of the division. The New Yorkers impulsively attacked Beale's skirmish line, driving it back. Col. Davies later reported that the regiment was "met by two regiments of rebel cavalry, who made a brisk attack on them." The two regiments were likely the 9th and 13th Virginia Cavalry stationed just outside of Brandy Station. During this time, the 15th Virginia Cavalry arrived to add its weight to the Confederate attack (No. 2).

Davies noted in his report that the New Yorkers initially repulsed the attack, "but being nearly surrounded and at some distance in advance of the brigade, Colonel [Otto] Harhaus fell back gradually, keeping the enemy in check, to the piece of wood on the left of the railroad near the station" (No. 3). Davies's modest account notwithstanding, it appears that his New Yorkers were all but surrounded and forced to mount a desperate charge to save the unit from being captured. Reaching a wooded area southeast of Brandy Station, Harhaus dismounted his men and ordered them to open fire on the dogged enemy, who seemed to realize that one more determined attack could spell the

end of the 2nd New York. Before that happened, however, bugles sounded in the distance announcing the arrival of the rest of Kilpatrick's division. Buford's division was also approaching and would eventually link up with Kilpatrick's right flank.[18]

While two Federal cavalry divisions headed due west and southwest to overwhelm Beale's brigade, Gregg's division continued its approach from the north. The 7th and 12th Virginia Cavalry of Lomax's Brigade, along with Griffin's Battery, stood in the way of what were overwhelming Federal numbers. The Southerners grudgingly gave up ground by adopting the usual delaying tactics. Their efforts slowed, but could not stop, Gregg's determined advance (No. 4).

When he received word that Union troopers were approaching from three directions, Jeb Stuart wisely pulled Beale's men back from Brandy Station (No. 5). Knowing he needed to buy time for reinforcements to arrive, Stuart called up Chew's battery of horse artillery from near Culpeper. The gunners deployed along the road to Brandy Station and threw an accurate fire into the pursuing Federal horsemen. Beale's grayclad cavalrymen also periodically halted their retreat toward Culpeper, dismounting to fire into the enemy before remounting to fall back again. In some cases they launched mounted charges with sabers when least expected. Such tactics helped slow the Federal pursuit. The aggressive Federal troopers also launched their own assaults, and in one case captured a number of men from the 15th Virginia Cavalry. The 9th Virginia Cavalry counterattacked, recapturing many of the 15th Virginia prisoners.

Stuart regrouped in front of Culpeper with Chew's Battery on his left.

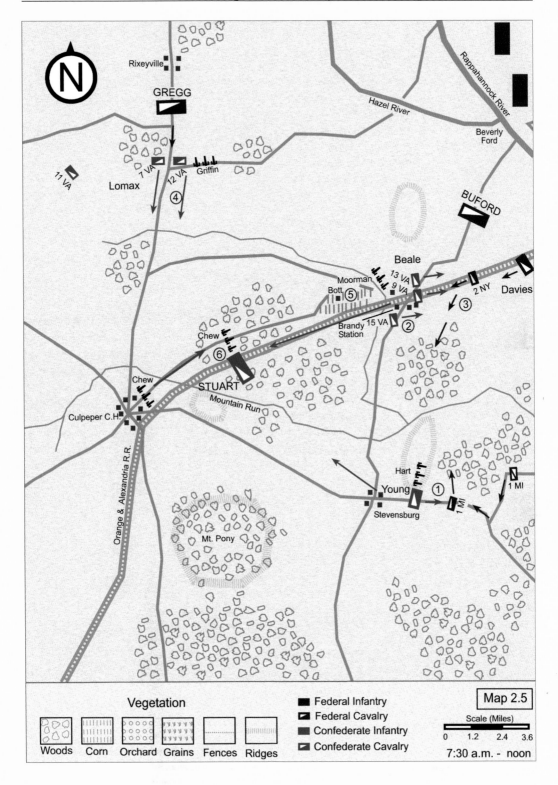

Vegetation

Woods   Corn   Orchard   Grains   Fences   Ridges

■ Federal Infantry
◪ Federal Cavalry
◼ Confederate Infantry
◪ Confederate Cavalry

Map 2.5

Scale (Miles)

0   1.2   2.4   3.6

7:30 a.m. - noon

Map 2.6: Stuart is Driven Back
(September 13: 7:30 a.m. - 2:30 p.m.)

Despite heavy numbers of Federal cavalry pushing in from the north and along two converging roads from the east, Jeb Stuart decided to make a strong stand against Kirkpatrick's thrust. He did so by dismounting his troopers in a large woodlot stretching more than two miles toward Culpeper. Although his reasoning is unclear, it appears that Stuart was trying to buy time for one last railroad train of supplies to be loaded and moved to safety.

The Confederate position was a good one on high ground behind Mountain Run, a steep-banked stream swollen by recent heavy rains; a Federal crossing here would be difficult. The three guns of Chew's Battery unlimbered on high ground on Stuart's right. The portion of Mountain Run north of the railroad was narrower and did not pose as much of a problem for the Federals to cross should they attack that section of the stream. (See Map 2.5 for more detail on this position.)[19]

While Stuart's men waited for the enemy to arrive, Kilpatrick dismounted the 1st Michigan Cavalry of Custer's brigade and sent them forward about 1:00 p.m. After clearing out a group of Confederate sharpshooters, the rest of the division proceeded toward Stuart's position. One Federal trooper wrote in a letter home that the "cavalry moved across the plain in perfect order . . . it presented one of the most brilliant spectacles of the war." Despite the inherent strength of his position, the mounting Federal pressure forced the outnumbered Stuart to pull back his command about 2:00 p.m. to high defensible ground just east of Culpeper Court House (No. 1).

About this time, the last train from the south chugged into the station along the Orange & Alexandria Railroad. Enlisted men immediately began loading it with supplies lest they fall into the hands of the advancing Federal cavalry. Kilpatrick, meanwhile, brought up a pair of six-gun batteries under Lts. William Fuller and Jacob Counselman to help neutralize Chew's three Rebel guns. A number of projectiles flew over the Confederate position and slammed into Culpeper, wounding civilians and damaging homes and buildings.[20]

Davies' brigade, which had led Kilpatrick's division since crossing the Rappahannock River that morning, was called upon to pry Stuart's men away from the high ground. Forming the 2nd New York Cavalry into columns of fours, Davies sent them north of the railroad tracks. Dashing across Mountain Run, they surprised Chew's gunners and captured two pieces (No. 2). "My troopers," Davies wrote proudly in his report, "made a charge that has never been surpassed in the records of the cavalry service, across a deep ravine and a creek, up a steep hill, the road rough and stony, and through a heavy fire of shells, right up to the muzzles of the guns, two of which they captured . . . together with the officer in command of the battery and 20 of his men, using nothing but the saber."[21]

Seeing his opportunity, Custer ordered the 1st Vermont Cavalry to also move northward and gallop into the town (No. 3). Just as the troopers arrived, however, the last fully loaded train began backing out of the station. The Federal horsemen did not see that Chew's last gun had been repositioned, and the Confederate gunners fired into them at point-blank range. Despite the initial confusion, the veterans kept their heads, made a dash for the cannon, and captured it while the gunners were in the act of reloading. Federal cavalry fired at the departing train and galloped after the cars in an effort to catch them, to no avail. It is unclear what was in the train. One recent author believed its cars contained "contraband" (slaves), but a Confederate soldier reported that the train carried "plunder of our people." According to him, the train left behind "four or five boxes of saddles, eight boxes of ammunition, and forty sacks of corn."[22]

With Stuart shoved out of the way, Judson Kilpatrick's Federal cavalry was now in control of Culpeper.

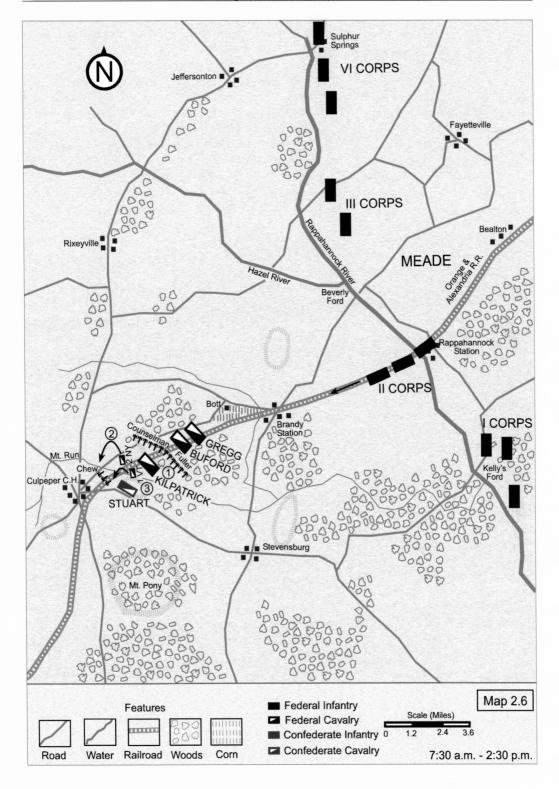

Sulphur
Springs

VI CORPS

Jeffersonton

Fayetteville

III CORPS

Rixeyville

Bealton

Rappahannock River

MEADE

Hazel River

Orange &
Alexandria R.R.

Beverly
Ford

Rappahannock
Station

II CORPS

I CORPS

Bott

Brandy
Station

Counselman

Fuller

GREGG

BUFORD

Kelly's
Ford

Mt. Run

Chew

Culpeper C.H.

KILPATRICK

STUART

Stevensburg

Mt. Pony

Features

■ Federal Infantry
◪ Federal Cavalry
■ Confederate Infantry
◪ Confederate Cavalry

Road   Water   Railroad   Woods   Corn

Scale (Miles)

0   1.2   2.4   3.6

Map 2.6

7:30 a.m. - 2:30 p.m.

Map 2.7: The Fight at Culpeper Ends
(September 13: 2:30 - 5:00 p.m.)

With the train successfully rolling south along the Orange & Alexandria Railroad, Stuart fell back in the same direction. He halted about a mile south of Culpeper on high ground called Greenwood Hill. It was about 1:00 p.m. (No. 1). This good defensive position improved with the arrival of Moorman's horse battery. The exact deployment of Stuart's command remains unclear.

It was now 3:00 p.m. and both Stuart's and Kilpatrick's men were feeling the exhaustion of hard and significant fighting since dawn. The 5th New York Cavalry advanced in column of fours. It was a mismatch from the start. Stuart's defensive line blasted the New Yorkers and forced them to retreat. According to Union brigade commander Col. Henry Davies in his report, his men "charged most bravely, but the ground being bad, were much broken, and on gaining the crest of the hill were attacked by a much larger body of cavalry and driven back." Stuart ordered a counterattack into the reorganizing enemy line and drove the Federals back toward Culpeper.

Kilpatrick arrived on the field about this time and put his own plan into action. He dismounted the 5th New York and put it and the 2nd New York toward Greenwood Hill from the north. When the 1st Vermont and 7th Michigan arrived soon thereafter, they too were ordered to dismount and sent forward. The 1st West Virginia also arrived and was thrown into the spreading combat (No. 2). This immense display of firepower was enough to finally force Stuart's men off the high ground.[23]

Bloodied and beaten yet again, Stuart's troopers fell back southeast of Culpeper toward Pony Mountain, where they prepared anew to take on another Federal onslaught. It was now about 4:00 p.m. When he saw the condition of Kilpatrick's men—who had carried the brunt of the fighting since early that morning—Gen. Pleasonton, the commander of the Army of the Potomac's cavalry arm, ordered up John Buford's and David Gregg's divisions. Both of these commands were waiting in the rear in reserve. Pleasonton deployed the divisions next to Kilpatrick's men (No. 3). For the first time in this young campaign, all three mounted divisions of the Federal Cavalry Corps would fight as one. The large body of troopers made for an impressive sight. The three small and exhausted Confederate brigades were no match for three full Federal divisions, and Stuart knew it. He broke off contact and retired.[24]

During the afternoon, Maj. Gen. Gouverneur Warren led his II Corps across the Rappahannock River in support of Pleasonton's Federal cavalry (No. 4). He halted the column at Brandy Station to avoid announcing his presence to the Confederate signal station atop Pony Mountain. When he learned the heights had been taken, Warren sent Brig. Gen. Alexander Webb's brigade of infantry to occupy it.[25]

The blood expended on September 13 was shed for little gain. Pleasonton's losses amounted to three killed and 40 wounded, compared with about 150 casualties in total for Stuart's command. The losses on both sides could have been significantly higher given all the hard fighting, for the three undersized Southern brigades had valiantly stood in the way of superior numbers for most of the day. Lee knew Stuart could not hold Culpeper without infantry support, and absolved his cavalry leader of any wrongdoing when the town fell into enemy hands.[26]

Maj. Gen. John Newton complained that his I Corps (which had performed poorly in support of the cavalry during the Second Battle of Brandy Station on August 1), and not Warren's II Corps, should have been given the assignment of supporting the large-scale cavalry thrust toward Culpeper. The perceived snub, grumbled Newton, "disappointed and mortified" his men. Gen. Meade tempered his reply to Newton by explaining that to have done so would have broken the "continuity" of the existing line. His explanation seemed to put an end to the matter.[27]

Jeb Stuart was also upset. The loss of some of his famed horse artillery convinced him to issue General Order No. 3, which stated: "Officers . . . will be held to strict accountability for the safety of artillery with their commands. They will see that a sufficient support of cavalry sharpshooters . . . [will provide] support and protection at all hazards."[28]

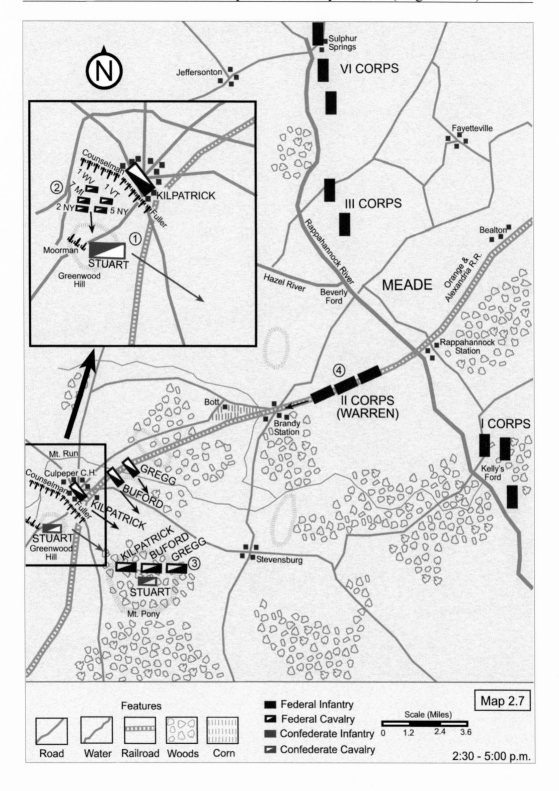

Features

Road   Water   Railroad   Woods   Corn

■ Federal Infantry
◨ Federal Cavalry
▨ Confederate Infantry
◨ Confederate Cavalry

Scale (Miles)
0   1.2   2.4   3.6

Map 2.7

2:30 - 5:00 p.m.

Map 2.8: Meade Crosses the
Rappahannock River (September 14 - 17)

Meade's reconnaissance-in-force toward the Rapidan River continued on September 14. Gregg's cavalry division approached Rapidan Station, about five miles northeast of Orange Courthouse whil Kilpatrick's division rode to Somerville's Ford and Buford pushed ahead for Raccoon Ford about two miles farther east. The strong Confederate defenses on the Rapidan's southern shore prevented the Federal troopers from crossing. Confederate artillery fire precipitated an artillery duel that inflicted light losses on each side. The Southern cavalry was also active, aggressively attacking enemy reconnaissance parties trying to ascertain the positions and strength of Lee's infantry. The exposed Federal cavalry could potentially rely upon Warren's II Corps, which had marched through Brandy Station to Culpeper before moving south of the town to support the mounted arm near the Rapidan River.[29]

The probing of the Rapidan line continued on September 15 as the Federal horsemen searched for a suitable crossing. Gregg's division exchanged gunfire with Kirkland's and Mahone's infantry brigades (A. P. Hill's Third Corps) across the river at the railroad bridge on the Orange & Alexandria line. The same situation transpired at Somerville's Ford about three miles farther north and east, where Kilpatrick's division tried unsuccessfully to force a passage across the river. When some Federal II Corps infantry units arrived to relieve Kilpatrick's men, the Confederates across the Rapidan yelled out, "Lay down, Yanks, we are going to fire on the cavalry as they are relieved!" Horse artillery brought up to the banks of the fords proved no match for the larger Confederate guns. The Southerners also resorted to ploys to deceive the enemy about their strength. For example, trains arriving behind the Southern lines were greeted with cheering and even band music to suggest the arrival of reinforcements. From the Union perspective, it appeared as though Southern morale was once again on the rise. When Pleasonton told Meade that he was worried the Confederates might attack his cavalry, Meade inquired, "What reason have you for supposing

the enemy will attempt to drive you back with infantry?"[30]

Communications between Meade and Washington flew back and forth at a fevered pace. Both Lincoln and Halleck rejected Meade's suggestion for a change of base to Fredericksburg. Lincoln wrote that Meade should "move upon Lee at once in a manner of general attack, leaving to developments whether he will make it a real attack." Lincoln was rapidly growing weary at what he perceived to be the ineffective use of Federal cavalry. "I think this [a general attack] would develop Lee's real condition and purposes better than the cavalry alone can do," he concluded. Halleck supported Lincoln's opinion, but the cautious general warned Meade against making any "rash movements." Halleck hoped that an aggressive approach could "weaken him [Lee] or force him still farther back." A forward movement would have another advantage: "all the country this side of the Rapidan can be stripped of supplies . . . all provisions and forage not required for the immediate support of non-combatants should be taken."[31]

The morning of September 16 found the Army of the Potomac on the move as it changed its base from north of the Rappahannock River to north of the Rapidan River. John Sedgwick's VI Corps crossed the Rappahannock at Fauquier White Sulphur Springs, marched through Culpeper, and halted about four miles northwest of Stone House Mountain. French's III Corps crossed at Fox's Mill Ford about two miles south of Fauquier White Sulpur Springs and halted behind VI Corps. Slocum's XII Corps passed over the river at Kelly's Ford and bivouacked at Stevensburg. Sykes's V Corps crossed at Beverly Ford and camped east of Culpeper, and Newton's I Corps crossed the river at Rappahannock Station and stopped between Culpeper and Stevensburg. Howard's XI Corps remained north of the river guarding the Orange & Alexandria Railroad.

Gen. Lee also rearranged his depleted army, moving Richard Ewell's Second Corps south to occupy Longstreet's former position on the right side of A. P. Hill's Third Corps. Jeb Stuart's cavalry, meanwhile, continued to patrol the approaches to the Rapidan River.[32]

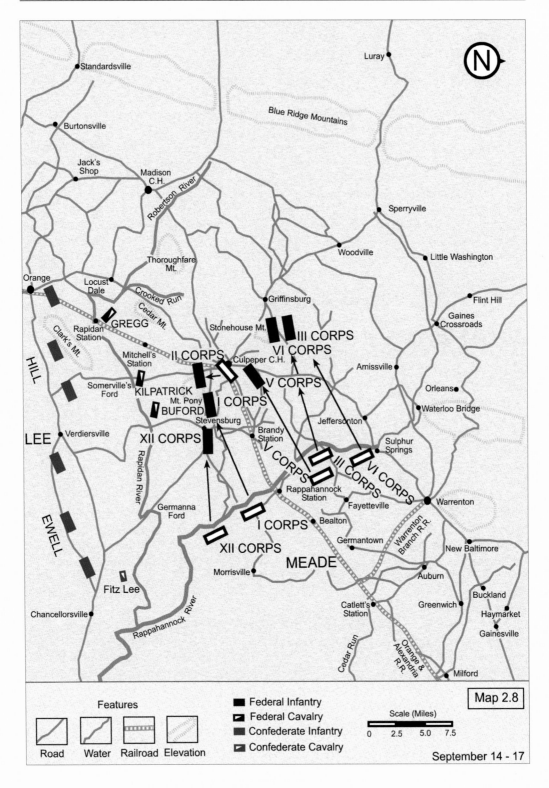

Luray

Blue Ridge Mountains

Standardsville

Burtonsville

Jack's
Shop

Madison
C.H.

Sperryville

Robertson River

Thoroughfare
Mt.

Woodville

Little Washington

Orange

Locust
Dale

Crooked Run

Griffinsburg

Flint Hill

Gaines
Crossroads

Cedar Mt.

GREGG

Rapidan
Station

Clark's Mt.

Stonehouse Mt.

III CORPS

VI CORPS

Amissville

Orleans

Mitchell's
Station

II CORPS

Culpeper C.H.

V CORPS

Waterloo Bridge

HILL

Somerville's
Ford

KILPATRICK

Mt. Pony

BUFORD

I CORPS

Stevensburg

Jeffersonton

Sulphur
Springs

LEE

Verdiersville

XII CORPS

Brandy
Station

V CORPS

III
CORPS

VI
CORPS

Rapidan River

Germanna
Ford

Rappahannock
Station

Fayetteville

Warrenton

EWELL

I CORPS

Bealton

Germantown

Warrenton Branch R.R.

New Baltimore

XII CORPS

MEADE

Auburn

Buckland

Fitz Lee

Morrisville

Greenwich

Haymarket

Chancellorsville

Rappahannock River

Catlett's
Station

Gainesville

Cedar Run

Orange &
Alexandria
R.R.

Milford

Features

Federal Infantry

Federal Cavalry

Confederate Infantry

Confederate Cavalry

Scale (Miles)

0   2.5   5.0   7.5

Road   Water   Railroad   Elevation

Map 2.8

September 14 - 17

Map 2.9: Meade Advances to the Rapidan River (September 17 - 19)

In mid-September, Gen. Lee finished reorganizing his cavalry division into a corps structure to better deal with and match the Union mounted arm. Jeb Stuart's command was now a corps, with two cavalry divisions.

One division was given to Brig. Gen. Wade Hampton. Arguably the wealthiest man in South Carolina, Hampton had organized a "legion" at the start of the war composed of all three arms (infantry, artillery, and cavalry). When the unit was broken up, Hampton led an infantry brigade through the Seven Days before switching to cavalry. Although Hampton had no formal military training, he excelled at the science of war and proved himself a fine combat leader. He and his brigade performed well through 1862 and 1863. A severe head wound at Gettysburg on July 3 on East Cavalry Field, however, kept him off the field during this portion of the war. His command was led by Laurence Baker and then Pierce Young. Hampton's three brigades were led by William "Grumble" Jones (Col. Oliver R. Funsten), Laurence Baker, and Matthew C. Butler. The latter two officers were recuperating from their wounds, so Baker's Brigade was led by Col. Dennis Ferebee and Butler's by Col. Pierce Young. The new division patrolled the left flank of the army in Madison County near the Rapidan River. Stuart's other division was awarded to William Henry Fitzhugh "Fitz" Lee, Robert E. Lee's second son. A large man, Lee had served in the Regular Army prior to the war and distinguished himself on many fields. His new division consisted of brigades led by John Chambliss, Lunsford Lomax, and Thomas H. Owen. Lee's division patrolled the army's right flank near Verdiersville and Fredericksburg.[33]

While Meade crossed the Rappahannock River and deployed in front of the Rapidan, Lee's men were busy building earthworks. The Union troops worried because the works opposite the fords were strong. Meade sent his chief engineer, Maj. James Duane, to examine the Rapidan from Raccoon to Germanna fords for crossing points. Some fords were better defended than others. Although he had easily thrown his army across the Rappahannock, Meade was less than enthusiastic about crossing the Rapidan.[34]

Concerned about the Army of Northern Virginia's strong position on the south side of the Rapidan, Meade wrote to Gen. Halleck on September 18 to again request permission to shift his army to Fredericksburg and there await reinforcements. Halleck replied the following day: "[Y]our objective point, in my opinion, is Lee's army," Halleck reminded the army commander, "and the object to be attained is to do as much harm as possible with as little injury as possible to yourself." If the enemy were too strong for an all-out assault, then "his outposts and detachments can be attacked, his communication threatened by raids, or the supplies of the adjacent country collected for the support of our army." After reading Meade's dispatch, Lincoln posed a question to Halleck: "If the enemy's 60,000 are sufficient to keep our 90,000 away from Richmond, why, by the same rule, may not 40,000 of ours keep their 60,000 away from Washington, leaving us 50,000 to put to some other use." From this legitimate query was born the idea of transferring some of Meade's units to the Western Theater to reinforce Rosecrans's Army of the Cumberland. Lincoln's question was raised during the first day of the battle of Chickamauga (September 19-20). When Rosecrans was driven from the field into the Chattanooga defenses, Lincoln and Halleck accelerated the discussion to send reinforcements away from Meade's army.[35]

Meade, meanwhile, began bringing some of his infantry up to the front line during this period. Slocum's XII Corps on the left advanced to relieve Buford's troopers at Morton and Raccoon fords, while Warren's II Corps relieved both Kilpatrick's and Gregg's troopers. With his headquarters at Mitchell's Station, Warren dispatched Brig. Gen. Alexander Hays's Third Division to the right, from Rapidan Station to where the Robertson River met Crooked Run, Webb's Second Division held the left near Somerville's Ford, and Brig. Gen. John Caldwell's First Division was in the center at Rapidan Station. VI Corps under Sedgwick moved forward to occupy II Corps' former camps just south of Culpeper. I, II, and V Corps in the center of the Federal line could move in either direction to provide support to the right or left flank, as needed. Meade initially pulled his cavalry back to Stevensburg, but later sent Kilpatrick to patrol along the army's right flank.[36]

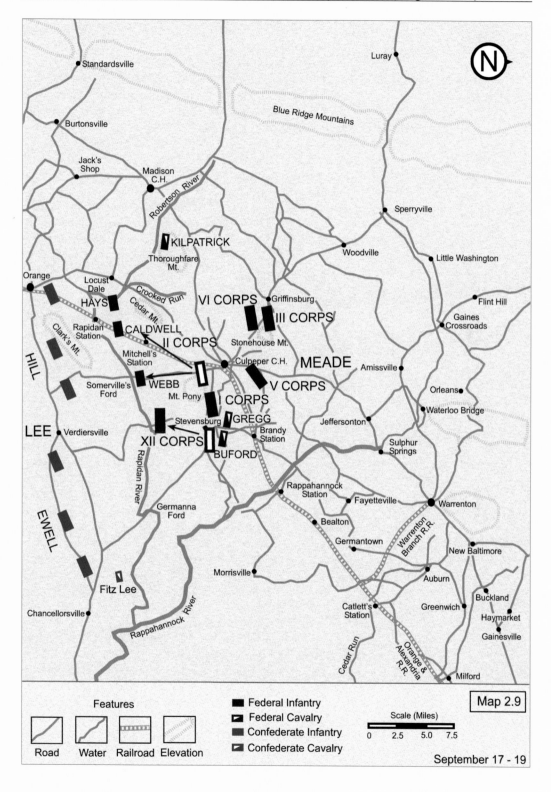

Map 2.9

September 17 - 19

Map 2.10: Pleasonton's Aggressive Reconnaissance (September 20 - 22)

On September 18, Meade ordered Maj. Gen. Henry Slocum to examine Rebel defenses along the Rapidan River from Raccoon to Stringfellow's fords. Slocum reported two days later that crossing at Raccoon Ford could only be effected with "great loss of life." Other points offered slim opportunities balanced against significant disadvantages. Crossing on the army's left was problematic, at best. After receiving Slocum's report, Meade asked Warren of II Corps to perform the same task on the army's right: "Will you have the Rapidan above the fork of Robertsons River examined . . . to ascertain to what degree they are more favorable generally for crossing . . .?" Only enemy cavalry seemed to occupy this area.[37]

Was there an opportunity to turn Lee's left flank? Meade ordered Gen. Pleasonton at 9:30 that night to send two of his cavalry divisions to examine the area around the Robertson River for the possibility of an infantry crossing, and then to continue riding around Madison County to test enemy dispositions and resistance. Pleasonton selected Buford's and Kilpatrick's divisions, with about 7,000 troopers. The cavalry mounted and set spurs between 7:00 and 8:00 a.m. on September 21, crossed the river at Russell's Ford, and took the road to Madison Court House. Kilpatrick's division occupied the town while Buford's brigades camped between the town and Robertson River (No. 1). Buford divided his command the next morning (No. 2), sending Tom Devin's brigade east to Burnett's Ford on the Rapidan, only four miles northwest of Orange Court House. Devin, in turn, spun off the 6th New York Cavalry to scout toward Locust Dale. Buford rode with George Chapman's brigade almost due south toward Jack's Shop and Liberty Mills. Kilpatrick, meanwhile, continued riding south from Madison Court House toward Burtonsville (No. 3). His plan was to reunite near Barnett's Ford. The Union cavalry was now approaching the Confederate positions from three directions.[38]

When Gen. Lee learned from a deserter that enemy cavalry, supported by a corps of infantry, was moving toward his left flank, he notified Jeb Stuart on the evening of September 21: "the

cavalry have disappeared. . . . Be on your guard and ascertain their movements." Fitz Lee's cavalry division was near Verdiersville watching the fords while Wade Hampton's Division was camped near Orange Court House performing the same duty. Stuart received Gen. Lee's message about 1:00 a.m. on September 22. With Hampton still absent, Stuart took personal command of his division and issued orders for the men to be in their saddles by dawn. He led the three brigades north at daybreak. The cavalier wrote his wife Flora that he would "put after him [the enemy] to attack and frustrate his purpose." As Stuart passed through Jack's Shop from the south, a patrol from the 3rd Indiana Cavalry of Chapman's brigade approached the cluster of two or three homes from the north. Both sides opened fire when a company of the 1st North Carolina Cavalry met the Hoosiers. The rest of the Tar Heel troopers arrived and a light but wider stalemated combat broke out. Stuart formed Baker's Brigade and part of Young's command into a line of battle and ordered a saber charge (No. 4). The initial shock forced Chapman's line back. He halted and dismounted his cavalry, who opened a brisk fire with their breech-loading repeating carbines. The steady fusillade emptied many saddles and broke apart Stuart's charge. According to the historian of Young's Brigade, "Stuart [hurled] regiment after regiment upon the strong columns of the enemy without making much impression." When he realized the futility of further mounted attacks, Stuart ordered his men to fall back, dismount, and press forward again. One of his aides noted the results: "a subsequent effort with dismounted men was equally unsuccessful."[39]

Realizing the seriousness of the situation, Buford sent a courier to find Kilpatrick. The rider asked Kilpatrick to break off his reconnaissance and bring his division to aid Buford. The aggressive Kilpatrick complied. Davies' brigade was in the van and it quickly gained a considerable lead over Custer's brigade (under Col. Peter Stagg, since Custer had been wounded at Culpeper a few days before). Col. Davies grew concerned when he realized his regiments were also traveling at different rates. The crack 2nd New York Cavalry was in the lead and pulling ahead of the rest of the brigade. His route over an improved road would bring him into Stuart's rear.[40]

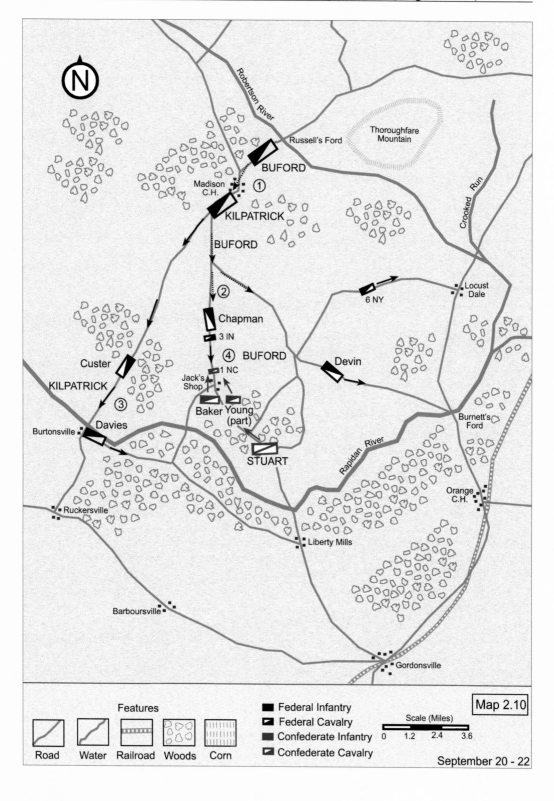

Map 2.10

September 20 - 22

Map 2.11: The Fight at Jack's Shop Continues (September 22)

Jeb Stuart was unaware of the danger posed by Kilpatrick's division approaching his left and rear. His warning arrived in "a rush of riders in hot haste," recorded the historian of the Laurel Brigade. These riders "inform[ed] Stuart of his danger, and the sound of small arms in their rear, soon made the Rebels understand the gravity of the situation. Between the two Federal divisions Stuart was now hemmed." When further word arrived of the 2nd New York Cavalry's arrival in his rear, Stuart sent Col. Funsten's Brigade and part of Young's command to meet this threat southwest of Jack's Shop (No. 1).[41]

Buford knew Kilpatrick had arrived on the scene when he heard firing to the southwest. Stuart was in a trap, and there was a good chance that he might lose a significant portion of his command. Buford ordered his men to redouble their efforts to break through Stuart's line north of Jack's Shop (No. 2). What he did not realize was that only one of Kilpatrick's regiments (the 2nd New York Cavalry) had arrived. Acting on Stuart's orders, Col. Funsten attacked the New Yorkers and within 20 minutes had them mostly surrounded. Col. Davies, however, arrived with more men (No. 3), formed into a line of battle, and aggressively moved forward to relieve the New Yorkers. The tide of battle began shifting in favor of the Federals.

Less than a mile north, meanwhile, Buford's men were pushing Baker's and part of Young's brigades back toward Jack's Shop. Now it was Stuart and most of his command that was nearly surrounded. According to one source, a trooper heard Stuart shout, "Boys, it's a fight to captivity, death, or victory!" A trooper yelled back, "We'll get out of here if there isn't but one of us left!" Luckily for Stuart and his men, McGregor's six-gun battery was on hand to help them. In one of the most unusual tactical situations of the war, three of McGregor's guns faced north and the other three faced south. Realizing he had little choice but to cut his way through Davies' brigade (which had closed the route to Gordonsville), Stuart boldly ordered those of his men facing Buford's thrust to the north to turn around, ride hard south, and assist Funsten's embattled troopers in their fight against Davies.[42]

Stuart's plan was to head for Liberty Mills with his troopers. As they passed through woods south of Jack's Shop, gunfire erupted from the trees lining both sides of the road. Davies had dismounted troopers and positioned them to take aim at the Rebel riders through this half-mile gauntlet of fire (No. 4). Funsten's men attacked these dismounted troopers and eliminated the threat. Stuart's nimble tactics and outstanding leadership skills were on full display. Only his fast action saved his three brigades and all of his artillery from what could have been a serious and perhaps catastrophic defeat. His cavalry fell back to Liberty Mills on the Rapidan River, about five miles from Jack's Shop. The Federal cavalry pursued the fleeing Southern horsemen, but were unable to catch them.

Undeterred by this turn of events, Buford pushed his men across the river and continued on. His determined troopers found themselves face-to-face with Maj. Gen. Cadmus Wilcox's infantry division, which had hustled north from Gordonsville to confront the Union threat. Stuart's other cavalry division under Fitz Lee also arrived about this time after an 18-mile ride from Verdiersville. Buford pulled his men back across the Rapidan River as nightfall approached.[43]

Stuart turned and followed the withdrawing enemy horsemen. He unlimbered his artillery from time to time to fire into them and unleashed mounted charges that were largely ineffective. Buford did not turn to fight, and by that evening was safely behind the Robertson River. Although he did not destroy Stuart's cavalry, Buford had the satisfaction of knowing that he had successfully completed his mission. "The reconnaissance," he boasted to Meade, "has been a triumph."[44]

Even though Stuart had been temporarily caught in a dangerous vise, the losses on both sides were not as one-sided as they might have been. The Federals lost 120 men from all causes, while Stuart lost between 160-180. "Had a successful cavalry fight yesterday—all well," Stuart wired his pregnant wife. Lee also viewed the engagement favorably, writing his cavalry commander, "Congratulations on defeating his [the enemy's] plans and arresting his advance." Not everyone was as complimentary. Col. Thomas Rosser, who would later command Grumble Jones' Brigade and was not one of Stuart's fans, wrote that the cavalry leader "as usual, was whipped."[45]

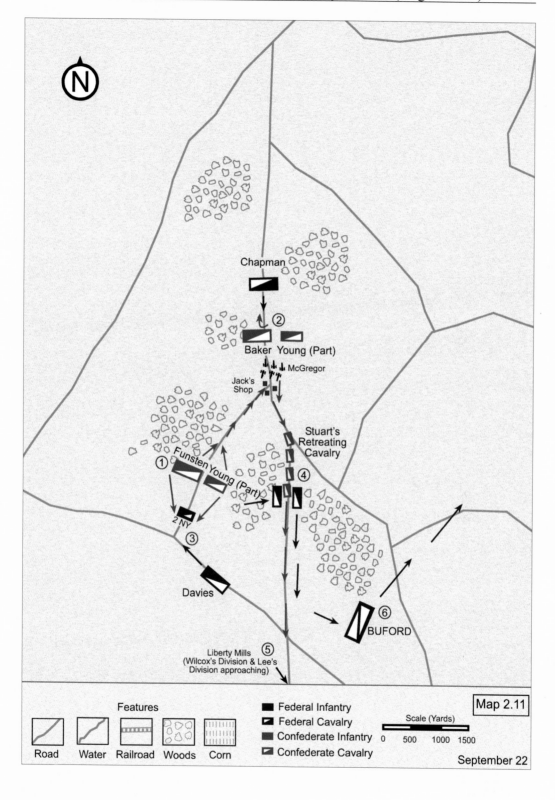

Chapman

② Baker Young (Part)

McGregor

Jack's Shop

Stuart's Retreating Cavalry

① Funsten Young (Part)

2 NY

③

④

Davies

⑥ BUFORD

Liberty Mills ⑤
(Wilcox's Division & Lee's Division approaching)

Features

Road Water Railroad Woods Corn

■ Federal Infantry
◪ Federal Cavalry
■ Confederate Infantry
◪ Confederate Cavalry

Scale (Yards)
0   500   1000 1500

Map 2.11

September 22

Map 2.12: Meade Loses Part of His Army (September 24)

Gen. Rosecrans's defeat at Chickamauga on September 19 and 20 had a profound impact on President Lincoln and his cabinet members. Two days later they had all but decided to pull troops from the Army of the Potomac and send them west. Only Meade's offensive against Lee could shelve these plans, so Halleck ordered the army commander to Washington for a conference.

Meade met with Lincoln and his advisors on September 23. Plans for sending troops to East Tennessee, as well as Meade's failure to heavily engage the Army of Northern Virginia, were openly discussed. Meade offered to resign (this was not on the agenda and was not sought); Lincoln refused. Meade left the meeting thinking he had blunted the effort to reduce the size of his army. Lincoln called some of his advisors back into conference during the early morning hours of September 24 to discuss the question anew, and they decided reinforcements had to be sent to the Western Theater. Left undecided was the number of troops who would make the journey. After additional debate, the decision was made to send the 23,000 men comprising XI Corps and XII Corps to reinforce the embattled Rosecrans. This amounted to about 16 percent of Meade's army.

Halleck remained behind when the others drifted away to catch a few hours of sleep and sent a telegram to Meade at 2:30 a.m.: "Please answer if you have positively determined to make any immediate movement. If not, prepare the Eleventh and Twelfth Corps to be sent to Washington as soon as the cars can be sent to you." By 3:00 a.m., a telegraph worker was keying Meade's response: "I contemplate no immediate movement." Later that morning Halleck replied, "Your telegram of this morning has been shown to the President. He directs that the Eleventh and Twelfth Corps be immediately prepared to be sent to Washington, as conditionally ordered before." Meade obeyed, and by that afternoon the troops were in full preparation for their new combat assignment in the Western Theater.[46]

The sudden turn of events frustrated Meade, who believed that Lee's army now outnumbered his own. In fact, Meade still had some 76,000 men in the field, compared with Lee's 54,000. The departure of two of his seven corps necessarily triggered a reshuffling of the Union front lines. I Corps replaced XII Corps at the Raccoon Ford and Morton's Ford sector. While two divisions of VI Corps remained near Stone House Mountain, Horatio Wright's division accompanied Gregg's cavalry division in guarding the Orange and Alexandria Railroad between the Rappahannock River and Alexandria. III Corps remained behind VI Corps' two divisions in a reserve capacity, and V Corps camped near Culpeper, also in reserve. Meade sent Buford's cavalry division along the north bank of the Rapidan River from the left of I Corps near Morton's Ford to Fredericksburg to guard the army's left flank. Kilpatrick's cavalry division performed the same task on the army's right flank along the Robertson River north of Madison Courthouse. The Army of the Potomac's front was now shorter, with a deeper reserve.[47]

Lee, meanwhile, remained vigilant. "General Meade has been actively engaged collecting his forces and is now up to the Rapidan," he wrote his absent corps leader James Longstreet on September 25. "His cavalry and engineers are constantly reconnoitering." Lee first learned about the Federal troop transfer on September 27, but the information was contradictory. It was not until October 1 that he could confidently wire Jefferson Davis that the Federal XI Corps and XII Corps had inded departed. Lee climbed Clark's Mountain on October 3 to get a better look at the Federal army; his two remaining corps commanders, A. P. Hill and Richard Ewell, and division commander Jubal Early joined him. Snippets of overheard conversation convinced observers that Lee was planning another offensive. One of Lee's aides, Walter Taylor, understood his leader's state of mind, writing, "it was part of a true defensive policy to take the aggressive when good opportunity offered; and by delivering an effective blow to the enemy, not only to inflict upon him serious loss, but . . . to thwart his designs of invasion, derange the plan of campaign contemplated by him, and thus prolong the conflict."[48]

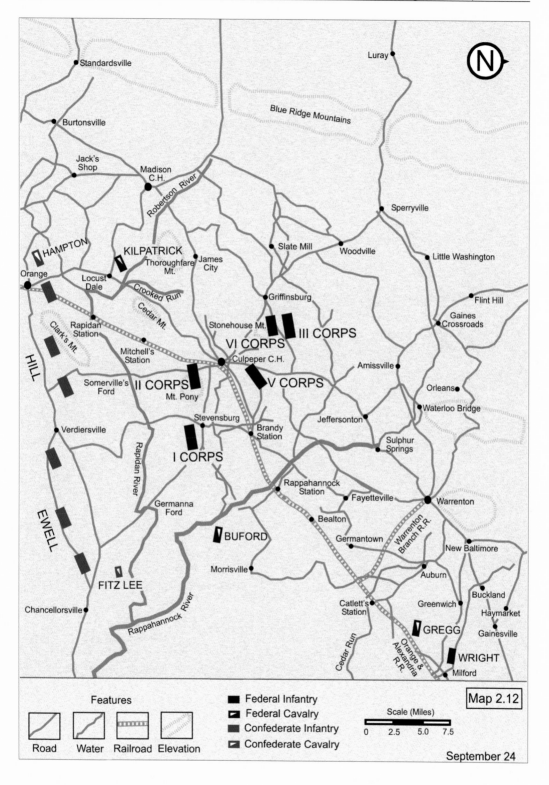

Luray

Blue Ridge Mountains

Standardsville

Burtonsville

Jack's
Shop

Madison
C.H.

Robertson River

Sperryville

HAMPTON

KILPATRICK

Thoroughfare
Mt.

James
City

Slate Mill

Woodville

Little Washington

Orange

Locust
Dale

Crooked Run

Griffinsburg

Flint Hill

Gaines
Crossroads

Cedar Mt.

Rapidan
Station

Stonehouse Mt.

III CORPS

Clark's Mt.

Mitchell's
Station

VI CORPS

Culpeper C.H.

Amissville

HILL

Somerville's
Ford

II CORPS

Mt. Pony

V CORPS

Orleans

Waterloo Bridge

Verdiersville

Stevensburg

Brandy
Station

Jeffersonton

Sulphur
Springs

Rapidan River

I CORPS

Germanna
Ford

Rappahannock
Station

Fayetteville

Warrenton

EWELL

Bealton

Warrenton Branch R.R.

New Baltimore

BUFORD

Germantown

Morrisville

Auburn

Buckland

FITZ LEE

Chancellorsville

Rappahannock River

Catlett's
Station

Greenwich

Haymarket

Gainesville

Cedar Run

Orange & Alexandria R.R.

GREGG

WRIGHT

Milford

Features

| Road | Water | Railroad | Elevation |

Federal Infantry
Federal Cavalry
Confederate Infantry
Confederate Cavalry

Scale (Miles)

0   2.5   5.0   7.5

Map 2.12

September 24

Map Set 3: Approach to Bristoe Station (October 6 - October 14, 1863)

Map 3.1: Lee Decides on an Offensive
(October 6 - 9)

Always looking for ways to seize the initiative, Gen. Robert E. Lee decided the time was right to assume the offensive. He was encouraged by the growing morale of his men, and keenly aware that this was probably the last time he could strike before winter put an end to active operations. Operational success would drive Maj. Gen. George Meade's army back toward Washington and likely prevent any additional troops from going west to reinforce the Army of the Cumberland. A decisive battlefield victory was always possible. Any aggressive action, however, would have to be performed without his senior and most dependable lieutenant, James Longstreet, and most of his veteran First Corps. The remaining men were just as dependable, but their commanders, Lt. Gens. A. P. Hill and Richard Ewell, were not. The quality and quantity of horses remained a considerable concern. Lee's own health was also a factor. The Lee of late 1863 was not the Lee of 1861, and he was now suffering from increasingly frequent bouts of angina pectoris (a form of heart attack). Despite these issues Lee decided to launch an offensive, convinced that the positives outweighed the negatives.

The plan Lee decided upon resembled the Second Manassas Campaign of August 1862. Long considered one of Lee's most successful campaigns, he had used Longstreet's wing (his army did not corps at that time) to divert John Pope's attention while Stonewall Jackson marched his command around Pope's right flank and into his rear. The audacious plan brought both wings of his army together in a set piece battle that swept Pope from the field and opened the door to Lee's first invasion north of the Potomac River. Both Longstreet and Jackson, however, were gone—the former in Tennessee and the latter in his grave. Neither Hill nor Ewell could match either in ability or initiative.[1]

Because his army numbered fewer than 50,000, Lee had to make some adjustments in his new plan. Instead of diverting Meade's attention

with a full corps, he left behind the three brigades of Fitz Lee's cavalry division and two infantry brigades under Robert D. Johnston (Robert Rodes' Division) and Henry Walker's (Harry Heth's Division), fewer than 10,000 men. "Quaker" guns mounted in several locations offered the illusion that the Southern positions were still well defended. The rest of Lee's troops would march around Meade's right in a wide sweep, with Ewell's command taking an inner arc as Hill's swung on the outer edge. Their ultimate goal was the Federal troop concentration near Culpeper Court House. Lee likely realized that, unlike with Jackson's foray, he would need to remain close to his marching infantry corps. Jeb Stuart, still at the head of wounded Wade Hampton's 2,500-man cavalry division, would lead the excursions to scout enemy positions, shield the two infantry corps, and engage the enemy cavalry, when necessary.

Rumors coursed through the army on October 6 as Rebels loaded excess items into wagons and prepared rations for their haversacks. Surmising that a major movement was at hand, and with a tad of disdain for the corps leadership, one soldier in Jubal Early's Division (Ewell's Corps) wrote home, "I think if we had the old man Jackson that we would have been across the river before this."[2]

Hill's men were camped between Barnett's Ford and Rapidan Station and moved first at 7:00 a.m. on October 8; Richard Anderson's Division headed west and then north. The column passed through Orange Court House later that day and during the early morning hours of October 9. Hill crossed the Rapidan at Liberty Mills and at Cave Ford, about four miles west of Orange. Both columns headed for Madison Court House. Ewell's command had been camped near Raccoon and Morton's fords, and so had farther to go to reach Madison Court House. His men also began their march early on October 8. Most camped for the night near Pisgah Church, about seven miles east of Orange Court House. Passing through the hamlet the next day, Early's and Rodes' divisions waded the Rapidan at Barnett's Ford while Edward Johnson's Division crossed at Peyton's Ford two miles north. Another bout of angina forced Lee off his horse and into an ambulance on October 9. By the end of that day Hill was camped just south of Madison Court House with Ewell to the southeast. "Our progress was necessarily slow," Lee reported, "as the march was by circuitous and concealed roads, in order to avoid the observation of the enemy."[3]

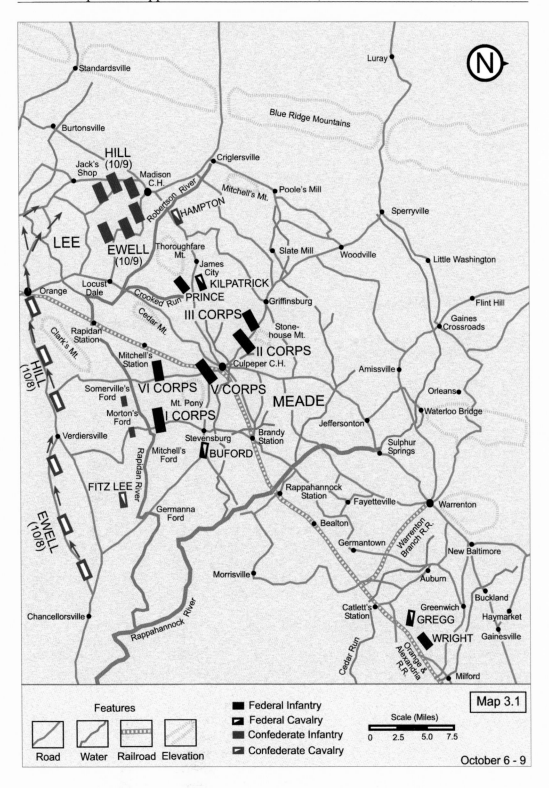

Luray

N

Standardsville

Blue Ridge Mountains

Burtonsville

HILL
(10/9)
Jack's
Shop
Madison
C.H.
Criglersville
Poole's Mill
Sperryville

Robertson River
Mitchell's Mt.
HAMPTON

LEE
EWELL
(10/9)
Thoroughfare
Mt.
Slate Mill
Woodville
Little Washington

James
City
KILPATRICK
Crooked Run
PRINCE
Cedar Mt.
III CORPS
Griffinsburg
Flint Hill

Locust
Dale
Orange
Stone-
house Mt.
Gaines
Crossroads

Rapidan
Station
II CORPS

Mitchell's
Station
Culpeper C.H.
Amissville

Clark's Mt.
HILL
(10/8)
Somerville's
Ford
VI CORPS V CORPS
MEADE
Orleans

Mt. Pony
I CORPS
Jeffersonton
Waterloo Bridge

Morton's
Ford
Stevensburg
Brandy
Station
Sulphur
Springs

Verdiersville
Mitchell's
Ford
BUFORD

FITZ LEE
Rappahannock
Station
Fayetteville
Warrenton

Germanna
Ford
Bealton

EWELL
(10/8)
Germantown
Warrenton
Branch R.R.
New Baltimore

Morrisville
Auburn
Buckland

Chancellorsville
Catlett's
Station
Greenwich
GREGG
Haymarket

Rappahannock River
WRIGHT
Gainesville

Cedar Run
Orange &
Alexandria
R.R.
Milford

Rapidan River

Features

Federal Infantry
Federal Cavalry
Confederate Infantry
Confederate Cavalry

Scale (Miles)
0   2.5   5.0   7.5

Road   Water   Railroad   Elevation

Map 3.1

October 6 - 9

Map 3.2: Meade Ponders Lee's Movements (October 10: 3:00 - 5:00 a.m.)

The morning of October 10 found Lee's army near Madison Court House, on the right flank of Meade's army (No. 1). Lee knew stealth was vitally important to the success of the campaign. One young soldier noted in his diary, "We are ordered to have very little fire, to make no noise, and to keep close in the woods, so that the enemy can't see us."

Earlier in the war, such a movement would likely not have been detected until Lee's attack fell against a Union flank, but Meade was not George McClellan, John Pope, or Joe Hooker. The Old Army Regular leading the Army of the Potomac had developed a new level of sophistication in collecting and interpreting information. The process began with a well-developed network of spies who continually reported on Lee's activities and movements. This information was sent to intelligence agents adept at interpreting seemingly disparate pieces of news rapidly and with a fair degree of accuracy. Unbeknownst to Lee, the Yankees were watching his movement from stations atop both Pony Mountain and Thoroughfare Mountain. Both observation posts reported on the Confederate march and intercepted Confederate signals, whose codes the Federals had essentially broken. As a result, Meade probably knew Lee was moving large segments of his army as early as October 7. The Union leader climbed Cedar Mountain three days later on October 9 and, with powerful telescopes, watched Lee and his men cross the Rapidan River.[4]

After showing an English visitor around the area, Lt. Col. Theodore Lyman of Meade's staff wrote in his diary on October 10: "Took him to Pony Mt. where learned that the enemy, in heavy force, were passing round by our right flank. . . . Behold the Rebs are in motion sure enough! Nobody knows whither and tomorrow, before light, we break up camp! All night the trains were in motion towards the Rappahannock, 3,500 wagons! No joke—."

The massive Confederate movement could mean one of two things, reported Meade: either Lee was "falling back from the Rapidan or making a flank movement against me by way of Madison Court House." Meade leaned toward the former because of the recent predictions of his cavalry commander, Maj. Gen. Alfred Pleasonton. Believing that the south side of the Rapidan was but thinly manned, Meade ordered Maj. Gen. John Newton at Stevensburg to drive across at Morton's Ford with his I Corps and test the theory. At the same time, Brig. Gen. John Buford's cavalry division was ordered to cross the river Rapidan at Germanna Ford and sweep northwest to defeat and capture any Rebels in this sector. If successful, this combined force of infantry and cavalry was to move on Orange Court House, where Maj. Gen. George Sykes' V Corps and Maj. Gen. John Sedgwick's VI Corps would join it before following Lee's army as it fell back from its Rapidan River line. Just in case Lee was indeed attempting to swing around and envelop his right flank, however, Judson Kilpatrick's cavalry division, with support from Henry Prince's III Corps division (about 8,000 men) had orders to delay the enemy's advance until reinforcements arrived. Kilpatrick and Prince were stationed along the Robertson River.[5]

Buford's men were up and in the saddle before dawn on October 10 and reached Germanna Ford at 1:00 p.m. (No. 2). His troopers swept the light Confederate resistance away rather easily and captured scores of enemy cavalrymen. Buford's column turned west and headed for Orange Court House.[6]

More important events were occurring to the northwest, where some of Jeb Stuart's cavalry attacked George Custer's picket line about three miles east of Russell's Ford at 3:00 a.m. (No. 3). George Gordon's Confederate cavalry brigade struck the 5th New York Cavalry of Henry Davies' brigade at dawn, forcing it back to Bethesda Church three miles northeast on the road to James City. The 120th New York (Brewster's brigade, III Corps) was sent to the cavalry's aid. While Gordon's Confederate cavalry formed into a line of battle in front of them, Young's Confederate brigade approached the woods to the west and the two units joined in an attack that almost surrounded the two New York regiments. After some sharp fighting the New Yorkers cut their way through the Southern line.

These actions forced the Union signalmen working on Thoroughfare Mountain to vacate their vital post.[7]

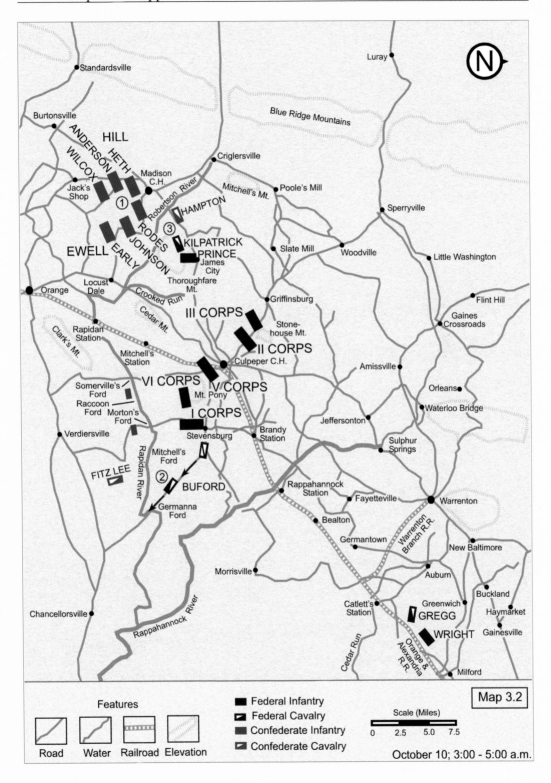

Standardsville

Luray

Blue Ridge Mountains

Burtonsville

HILL

ANDERSON
HETH
WILCOX

Jack's
Shop

Madison
C.H.

Criglersville

Robertson River

Mitchell's Mt.

Poole's Mill

Sperryville

①

HAMPTON

③

RODES
JOHNSON
EARLY
EWELL

KILPATRICK
PRINCE
James
City

Slate Mill

Woodville

Little Washington

Thoroughfare
Mt.

Locust
Dale

Crooked Run

Cedar Mt.

Griffinsburg

Flint Hill

Gaines
Crossroads

Orange

III CORPS

Stone-
house Mt.

Clark's Mt.

Rapidan
Station

Mitchell's
Station

Culpeper C.H.

II CORPS

Amissville

Orleans

Somerville's
Ford
Raccoon
Ford Morton's
Ford

VI CORPS

V CORPS

Mt. Pony

Jeffersonton

Waterloo Bridge

Verdiersville

I CORPS

Stevensburg

Brandy
Station

Sulphur
Springs

Rapidan River

Mitchell's
Ford

FITZ LEE

②

BUFORD

Germanna
Ford

Rappahannock
Station

Fayetteville

Warrenton

Bealton

Warrenton Branch R.R.

New Baltimore

Germantown

Chancellorsville

Rappahannock River

Morrisville

Auburn

Buckland

Catlett's
Station

Greenwich

GREGG

Haymarket

WRIGHT

Gainesville

Cedar Run

Orange & Alexandria R.R.

Milford

Features

Road   Water   Railroad Elevation

Federal Infantry
Federal Cavalry
Confederate Infantry
Confederate Cavalry

Scale (Miles)

0   2.5   5.0   7.5

Map 3.2

October 10; 3:00 - 5:00 a.m.

Map 3.3: Meade Prepares to Meet Lee's Advance (October 10: 5:00 a.m. - 5:00 p.m.)

Although Jeb Stuart's cavalry units were exceptionally aggressive during this period, Judson Kilpatrick was able to collect a considerable amount of information about Lee's movements when his troopers fanned out toward Madison Court House. There was much to learn because Lee's infantry was active on October 10.

The Rebel foot soldiers got up early, broke camp, and set off on a march that would carry them to the flank and rear of Meade's army. A. P. Hill's men were in the lead. They began their march about 5:00 a.m. heading northwest. Once past Madison Court House they struck out toward Criglersville, which they reached about 8:00 a.m. Cadmus Wilcox's Division was in the van, followed by Richard Anderson's and Harry Heth's. The hilly countryside, numerous small streams, and recent rain made the roads sticky and difficult to traverse. Hill's long column split in two to pass around Mitchell's Mountain, probably to avoid being detected by the enemy. The men were pleased when they realized, explained one soldier, that "the pioneer corps was now more energetic and useful than ever before. Nearly every stream was bridged."

Richard Ewell had to wait until Hill's men cleared the road ahead before ordering his Second Corps to follow. Robert Rodes' Division led the corps, followed by the divisions of Edward Johnson and Jubal Early. A few miles beyond Madison Court House, the column turned right and headed for the Robertson River. Crossing at Crigler's Mill, Ewell's wing headed for Griffinsburg. It was not an easy march. As one young Marylander explained, "we avoid frequented roads, hills and open fields, as our object is to flank the enemy."

Marching on the outer loop with a greater distance to traverse, Hill's men finally went into camp at Woodville and Slate Mill on either side of the Hazel River. The exhausting 17-mile march put them within a short distance of the Union rear. Ewell's men camped south of Griffinsburg with Rodes about one mile northwest of the town, Anderson about three miles north of James City, and Early about two miles behind Anderson.[8]

Food remained one of the most basic motivations for Lee's men. According to a soldier in Johnson's Division, "we think now a great deal more of Yankee haversacks and their luscious contents. Visions of sutlers' stores, and abundant delicacies . . . float before our mind's eyes . . . these expectations sustain us in our endless tramp, tramp, tramp after the retreating enemy."[9]

By the morning of October 10, Meade had enough information to conclude that Lee was heading directly for his right flank and rear from Madison Court House. The Union army commander had no choice but to realign his army, for he had broken the basic military maxim of never dividing one's command in the face of the enemy. A slew of orders cascaded out of Meade's headquarters to his lieutenants at 9:00 a.m. He needed to halt the advance of I, V, and VI Corps, which were near the Rapidan River and ready to cross it on their way to Orange Court House. "The enemy is moving from Madison Court-House upon our right," he informed his corps commanders. "I have not yet ascertained whether this is a movement of their whole army upon our flank. Should it prove to be so, the whole army will be concentrated around Culpeper Court-House. You will therefore, hold yourself in readiness to move at a moment's notice back to Culpeper." II Corps was ordered to immediately march to Stone House Mountain to reinforce the right flank, forming on the right of the Culpeper and Sperryville Turnpike. III Corps formed on its right. Gregg's Second Cavalry division was ordered to ride west to support Kilpatrick, who was engaging Wade Hampton's Confederate cavalry division.[10]

Meade also tried to recall John Buford's troopers, but was unsuccessful. Buford continued riding toward Morton's Ford, where his men would spend the night before their planned attack the next morning in tandem with Newton's I Corps. The assault, however, would never come.[11]

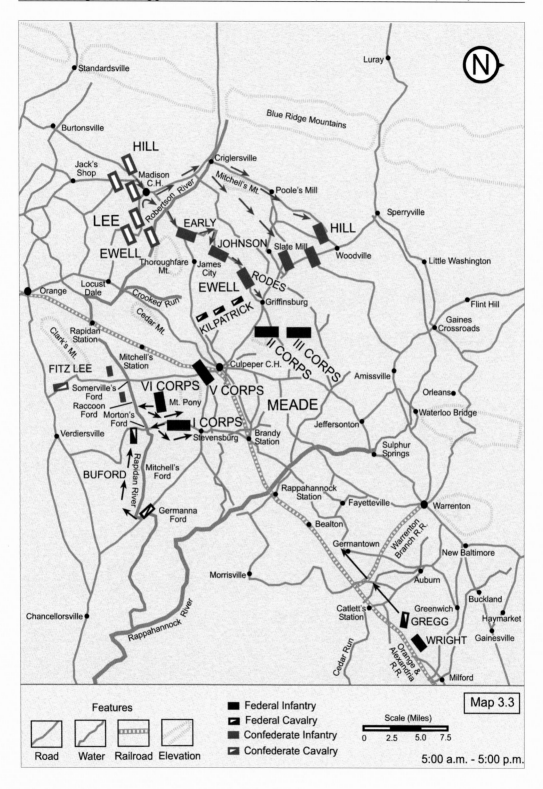

Standardsville

Luray

Blue Ridge Mountains

Burtonsville

HILL

Jack's
Shop

Criglersville

Madison
C.H.

Mitchell's Mt.

Poole's Mill

Robertson River

Sperryville

LEE

EARLY

HILL

EWELL

JOHNSON

Slate Mill

Woodville

Little Washington

Thoroughfare
Mt.

James
City

RODES

Locust
Dale

EWELL

Griffinsburg

Flint Hill

Orange

Crooked Run

Gaines
Crossroads

Cedar Mt.

KILPATRICK

Rapidan
Station

Clark's Mt.

Mitchell's
Station

II CORPS

III CORPS

Amissville

FITZ LEE

Culpeper C.H.

Somerville's
Ford

VI CORPS

V CORPS

Orleans

Raccoon
Ford   Morton's
Ford

Mt. Pony

MEADE

Waterloo Bridge

Verdiersville

I CORPS

Stevensburg

Brandy
Station

Jeffersonton

Sulphur
Springs

BUFORD

Mitchell's
Ford

Rapidan River

Rappahannock
Station

Fayetteville

Warrenton

Germanna
Ford

Bealton

Warrenton
Branch R.R.

Germantown

New Baltimore

Morrisville

Auburn

Buckland

Chancellorsville

Rappahannock River

Catlett's
Station

Greenwich

Haymarket

GREGG

WRIGHT

Gainesville

Cedar Run

Orange &
Alexandria
R.R.

Milford

Features

| Road | Water | Railroad | Elevation |

Federal Infantry
Federal Cavalry
Confederate Infantry
Confederate Cavalry

Scale (Miles)

0   2.5   5.0   7.5

Map 3.3

5:00 a.m. - 5:00 p.m.

Map 3.4: Meade Pulls Back Behind the Rappahannock River
(Evening of October 10 - October 11)

The telegraph wires between Culpeper and Washington buzzed throughout the afternoon of October 10. The "enemy's cavalry in force have crossed Robertson's River . . . and are now engaged with my cavalry . . . are supported by a large force of infantry," wrote Meade to Gen. Halleck about noon. Five hours later, Meade added, "The enemy have succeeded with their cavalry in forcing back my cavalry and infantry support . . . seizing Thoroughfare Mountain . . . enabling them to cover their flank movement. From a deserter and prisoners I learn that A. P. Hill's whole corps and part of Ewell's are turning my right flank . . . My belief now is that his movements are offensive."[12]

Meade learned late that afternoon that the bulk of Lee's army was almost certainly turning his right flank. Rather than stand and fight, he decided to fall back behind the Rappahannock River, even though he must have known that a strategic withdrawal would invoke criticism in Washington. Meade's cavalry was already deployed: Buford's First Division was across the Rapidan River, Gregg's Second Division was near Jeffersonton on the army's right flank, and Kilpatrick's Third Division was in the center engaged with Wade Hampton's cavalry.

Newton's I Corps received orders at 8:00 p.m. to begin moving to Kelly's Ford on the Rappahannock and was in motion an hour later. Sedgwick's VI Corps, also along the Rapidan River, was ordered to move toward Culpeper Court House at the same time, halting on the south side of the Orange and Alexandria Railroad. Sedgwick received subsequent orders to head instead for the Rappahannock, where his corps would deploy just south of Rappahannock Station. I Corps would be on Sedgwick's left, anchoring the left flank of Meade's new defensive line. The rest of the Federal army would also trudge northward, cross the Rappahannock, and eventually form on Sedgwick's right. Sykes's V Corps was ordered to deploy between Rappahannock Station on the left and Beverly Ford on the right; Warren's II Corps would cross just above Rappahannock Station and march north to form on V Corps' left

flank; French's III Corps would cross the Rappahannock River at Freeman's Ford, about eight miles below Fauquier White Sulphur Springs and march north to the latter town. These depositions were completed by the end of October 11.[13]

The Confederate infantry was also on the move on October 11 in what was considered a "cautious" march, the troops trudging along "in no hurry." Hill's men, who had farther to travel to Culpeper Court House, were on the road by 6:00 a.m., but Ewell's troops did not begin moving until two hours later. The slow march was hampered by hungry men breaking ranks to forage for food. Rodes' Division was in the van of Ewell's column, followed by Johnson's and then Early's divisions. Anderson's Division led A. P. Hill's Corps, followed by Wilcox's and Heth's divisions. Perhaps because they realized that Meade had slipped out of the trap, Ewell and Hill marched their men only six to ten miles that day before going into camp for the night. Morale skyrocketed when wagons carrying three days' rations arrived. Ewell's men camped near the Salem Meeting House, about six miles northwest of Culpeper Court House, while Hill's Corps bivouacked to the west (left) of them.[14]

Lee spent much of his time riding in an ambulance during this period because his "rheumatism" had once again flared up. By October 11 he was back in the saddle, although still feeling unwell. He was also frustrated by the media. "I regretted to hear that it was announced in one of the Richmond papers that this army was in motion and had crossed the Rapidan," he wrote President Jefferson Davis.[15]

Although the Rebels now occupied the area near the former Yankee camps, they were disappointed that the enemy had "destroyed along their line of flight all commissary and other stores, which they could not carry away with them" during their move to the Rappahannock River. The men found some useful supplies, but nothing like what they had hoped would be left behind. The days of the Second Manassas Campaign would not be repeated.[16]

October 11 was uneventful for the infantry but a fateful day for Buford's cavalry division, which crossed the Rapidan River in its attempt to reach the Federal army. (See Map Set 3.5.)

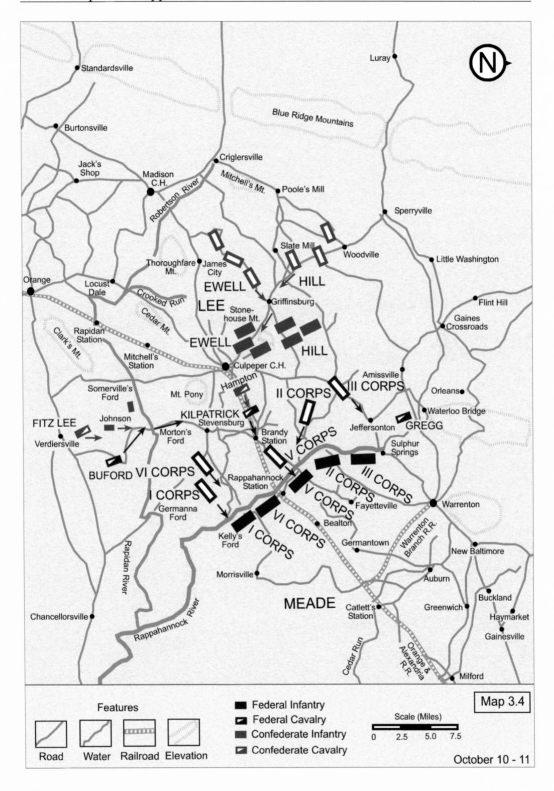

Map 3.4

October 10 - 11

Map 3.5: Buford Makes His Escape
(October 11)

October 11 was an eventful day for John Buford and his cavalry division. It began early when the Federal troopers rose near the Confederate defenses on the southern shore of Morton's Ford, where they had scattered enemy pickets the day before. The men anticipated a busy day because the plan called for as many as three Federal infantry corps to cross the Rapidan River and head for Orange Court House, with Buford's men providing support. At 7:00 a.m., however, Buford learned that Lee was on the offensive and that his own mission had been aborted; the thousands of expected infantry would not cross to his side of the river after all. Worse news reached Buford in a string of communications suggesting that a strong mass of enemy cavalry (Fitz Lee's Division) was approaching with infantry support (Johnston's Brigade of Rodes' Division).

Buford knew time was of the essence. He ordered his men to prepare to cross at Morton's Ford rather than turn east and try to cross at Germanna Ford, the way they had come. Standing between the ford and his men were a couple of infantry regiments from Johnston's Brigade (20th North Carolina and half of the 12th North Carolina), along with the 5th Virginia Cavalry. Buford's division of almost 4,000 troopers was more than a match for the 1,800 Rebels, and he later reported that the Confederates were pushed away from the ford "with ease."[17]

Once in control of the ford, Buford turned his full attention to getting his men across the Rapidan River to safety. He soon discovered that the road leading to the ford was in such poor condition that it could not handle his artillery. He could have turned to his right and headed for Germanna Ford, but decided instead to put his men to work grading and corduroying the road. This decision gave the Confederates time to rush reinforcements into the area. Three cavalry brigades from Fitz Lee's Division appeared along with the remainder of Johnston's infantry. Fitz Lee divided his command, sending brigades under Lomax and Chambliss in a frontal attack with some of Johnston's foot soldiers, while Col. Thomas Owen, commanding Wickham's cavalry

brigade, with another infantry detachment from Johnston's command, crossed the river at Raccoon Ford and headed for Buford's rear.

Buford's repairs were completed about 9:30 a.m. and George Chapman's brigade splashed across, deploying on the north bank to support the crossing of Buford's two batteries and Tom Devin's brigade (No. 1). The latter was under attack by the growing host of enemy soldiers. At one point, Fitz Lee ordered Owens' Virginians to make a mad dash at Buford's artillery on the northern bank of the river, not realizing that three of Chapman's regiments were within easy supporting distance. The 3rd Indiana Cavalry, 8th Illinois Cavalry, and 12th Illinois Cavalry opened a blistering fire and the artillery belched canister, emptying many saddles. Once his entire division was safely across the river, Buford ordered his men to ride to Stevensburg. Sensing the Federals were still in a tough spot, the Confederates continued attacking Buford's rearguard (Chapman's brigade) until it was finally ordered to follow the rest of the division to the small town.

When he reached Stevensburg, however, Buford discovered that his supply wagons had not cleared the town. Another stand against a determined enemy would have to be made. Buford posted his men on high ground south of Stevensburg and awaited the enemy's advance. He did not have long to wait before Johnston's infantry approached while Fitz Lee deployed his three cavalry brigades. The fight that followed was sharp but short (No. 2). When the last of his trains were safely away, Buford began pulling his troopers out of line and pushing them toward Rappahannock Station. First, however, he had to cross Mountain Run, a stream he described as "nasty." This phase of the retreat occurred "without a great deal of molestation from the enemy, although closely followed by him," reported the cavalry general.

Buford encountered V Corps' rearguard during his approach to Brandy Station and learned that Kilpatrick's Third Division would soon arrive. "Arrangements were immediately made to make a stand," he noted in his report.[18]

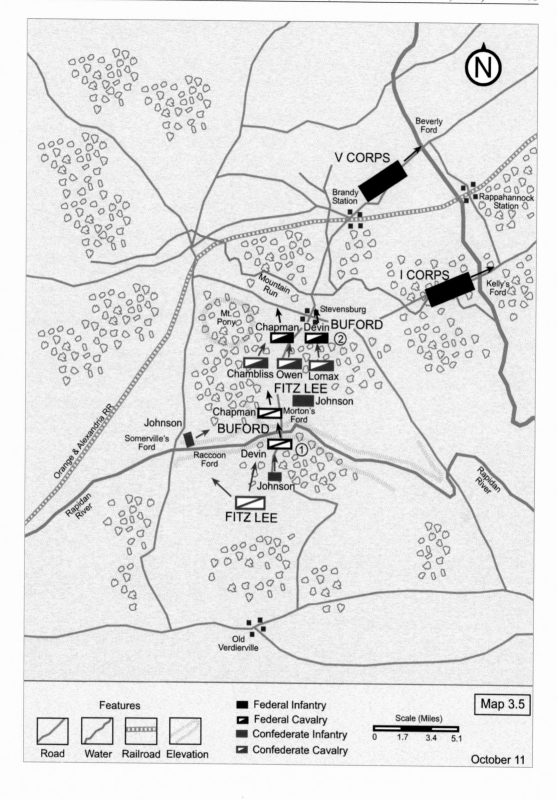

Map 3.5

October 11

Map 3.6: The Cavalry Fight at Brandy Station, Again (October 11)

Jeb Stuart, leading Wade Hampton's Division because its leader was still recovering from his Gettysburg wounds, was greeted on the morning of October 11 with news that Judson Kilpatrick's cavalry and their infantry support were gone. Leaving Young's Brigade behind at James City to guard the army's rear, Stuart rode north with his remaining two brigades. Trotting from Griffinsburg toward Culpeper, they encountered the 1st West Virginia Cavalry near Stone House Mountain and immediately engaged it, but not before Union couriers galloped back to Culpeper with a call for help. Before long the 5th New York Cavalry arrived and formed beside the West Virginians, just about the time Stuart struck. He threw Funsten's Brigade forward in a frontal attack while Gordon's Brigade circled around to attack the Yankee left flank and rear. The aggressive move forced the Federal cavalry regiments to retire, but scores of men from Joseph Carr's infantry division (III Corps) were not so lucky and Stuart's troopers gobbled them up.[19]

Help was on the way in the form of Custer's brigade, which trotted through Culpeper to form into line of battle about a mile from the town near the Wallach house, which had been Meade's headquarters. Davies' brigade soon followed. Stuart had intended to launch one of his preferred flanking assaults, but there were too many blue horsemen occupying the high ground (No. 1). Stuart pulled back instead, after which Kilpatrick ordered his men to continue their retreat toward Brandy Station, guided by the Orange and Alexandria Railroad tracks. Stuart reappeared when Kilpatrick's men passed the Bott plantation, but his 1,500 Rebels were no match for Kilpatrick's 3,000 men, who were vigilant and more than ready for a fight (No. 2). Looking southward, Stuart was happy to see Fitz Lee's Division approaching in rapid pursuit of Buford's troopers from the south (No. 3), but the odds were now even less favorable—about 7,000 Yankee horsemen against his own 3,300.

In an effort to slow Kilpatrick's retreat, Stuart threw two regiments toward Custer's brigade, which was riding to the northeast along the Orange and Alexandria Railroad tracks.

Although ultimately repulsed, the Southern horsemen achieved their goal. As this was occurring, the 2nd New York Cavalry of Davies' brigade galloped toward the Bott Mansion, where the Union troopers encountered the 4th and 5th North Carolina cavalry regiments waiting to be sent into battle. The New Yorkers drove them to the rear in confusion. One North Carolinian admitted that the Federal troops "fell on us like a tornado. We broke and ran." The 8th Pennsylvania Cavalry had similar success against another Southern regiment. Stuart sent in the 7th Virginia Cavalry to strike Kilpatrick's rear, but it encountered the 1st West Virginia Cavalry which quickly broke the charge with their repeating carbines. These actions allowed Kilpatrick to continue his retreat.

Fitz Lee's Division approached through Stevensburg from the south. Kilpatrick realigned his two brigades to face them and ordered a charge. While the blue horsemen attacked toward their front, the 2nd New York drove into Fitz Lee's rear. Buford's men were also approaching and they, too, fired into Fitz Lee's rear. Stuart, meanwhile, smashed into Kilpatrick's flank and rear. The fighting was one swirling tumultuous mass of confusion until Buford and Kilpatrick finally took up defensive positions atop Fleetwood Hill.

Stuart scanned the strong Federal position on Fleetwood Hill and understood that renewed attacks would be folly. Breaking off the fight, he ordered his men toward St. James' Episcopal Church, which stood in the path of the Union cavalry's retreat. When he detected Stuart's move, Gen. Pleasonton ordered his men to continue their retreat to the Rappahannock River, which they crossed by 8:00 p.m. The crossing ended the Fourth Battle of Brandy Station. A member of the 6th Michigan Cavalry probably offered the best summation of the swirling action when he wrote that it was "a brilliant passage at arms in which neither side obtained a decisive advantage."[20]

Two of Meade's cavalry divisions came under heavy attack on October 11 by their Confederate counterparts, and both were able to skillfully retire by employing a running fight during their retreat.[21]

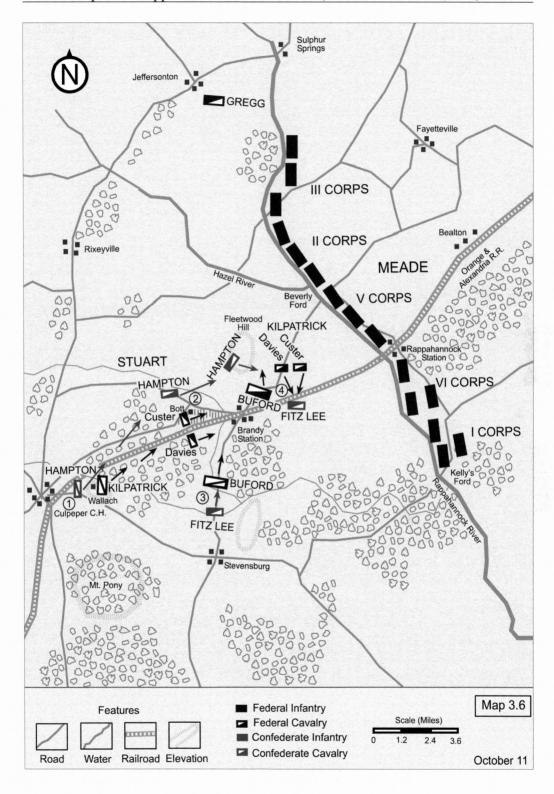

Features

Road   Water   Railroad   Elevation

■ Federal Infantry
◣ Federal Cavalry
■ Confederate Infantry
◤ Confederate Cavalry

Scale (Miles)

0   1.2   2.4   3.6

Map 3.6

October 11

Map 3.7: Lee Pushes Toward Meade's Right Flank and Rear (October 12)

With Meade's army safely across the Rappahannock River, Lee pondered three options: (1) End the campaign and skip below the Rapidan River; (2) End the campaign and remain between the Rapidan and Rappahannock rivers; (3) Continue the offensive. Lee chose the latter and ordered his infantry to rise early on October 12 and head for the enemy's right flank.

The infantry was still marching along parallel tracks and would join up at Warrenton. Ewell (on the inner track) had camped for the night northwest of Culpeper. Today, his foot soldiers would enter the town and head north on the Culpeper-Warrenton Turnpike. Edward Johnson's Division, at the head of Ewell's Corps, was roused at 2:00 a.m. to begin marching, but did not receive orders to move until close to dawn. As they approached Culpeper, the Rebels left the main road and circled around the town to enter the turnpike heading toward Jeffersonton. Fighting between Hampton's and Gregg's cavalry forced the column to halt until the road was clear (see below). Ewell's Corps finally camped just short of Jeffersonton that night.

A. P. Hill's Corps (on the outer or longer route) was closer to Griffinsburg than Culpeper Court House when the sun rose on October 12. Hill's men waited for rations before beginning their march over miserable back roads. They halted for the night at Amissville after tramping a dozen miles. They were just seven miles from Meade's right flank.[22]

Meade continued sifting through conflicting reports about the size and whereabouts of Lee's army. His senior officers debated whether Hill's Corps had followed Longstreet to Tennessee, and whether Lee's movement was a bluff to cover up the fact that two-thirds of his army was no longer in Virginia. Because of the effective screen laid down by Stuart's cavalry, few prisoners were coming in and there were even fewer direct sightings of Lee's infantry. Had Lee tricked him into pulling back behind the Rappahannock River too quickly? Meade finally decided to throw out a strong reconnaissance force to determine what was transpiring across the river. Orders went out at 10:30 a.m. tasking John Sedgwick to command the enterprise. He would have his own VI Corps and Sykes' V Corps for the job, with Buford's cavalry division providing support. Sedgwick's reconnaissance would move toward Culpeper but halt at Brandy Station while the cavalry continued toward the former town. If needed, Warren's II Corps could cross the river to provide support. As Buford's division rode toward Culpeper, its path was blocked by Young's Rebel brigade (Hampton's Division), which denied Buford the information on Lee's army that Meade so desperately wanted.[23]

Gregg's Federal troopers deployed on the right of Meade's main battle line, however, met Stuart's cavalry screen. Behind it, the blue cavalry spotted dense masses of Rebel infantry making their way toward Amissville and Jeffersonton. Fighting broke out between Funsten's Brigade (Hampton's Division) and Irvin Gregg's brigade (Gregg's division) at Jeffersonton. Stuart did not have enough troops, and it was not until late in the afternoon that the last of the Federal cavalry were forced back from Jeffersonton. The action shifted to White Sulphur Springs, where Gregg's men worked frantically to remove the planks from the bridge spanning the Rappahannock River. Four dismounted Federal cavalry regiments supported this effort, along with an artillery battery.[24]

It was about 5:00 p.m. when Lee and Ewell took up position to watch their men prepare to take the vital Sulphur Springs bridge spanning the Rappahannock. Carter's battalion of artillery deployed one-half mile from the river and opened fire, forcing the Federal cavalry to take cover and the lone battery to withdraw. Four Rebel cavalry regiments splashed across the shallows on either side of the bridge and routed the Union defenders, allowing George Doles' Brigade (Rodes' Division) to cross about 6:00 p.m. Gregg moved his division east to Fayetteville, exposing the right flank of French's III Corps. Stuart, meanwhile, pushed his division all the way to Warrenton. Fitz Lee's division was operating farther south. After pushing some of Gregg's cavalry aside, Lee camped for the night on both sides of Fox's Ford on the Rappahannock. Most of Robert. E. Lee's cavalry was now on Meade's right flank or behind his right-rear.

Although the route across the Rappahannock River and around Meade's right flank was now apparently open, Lee decided to rest his infantry rather than push them forward in the dark.[25]

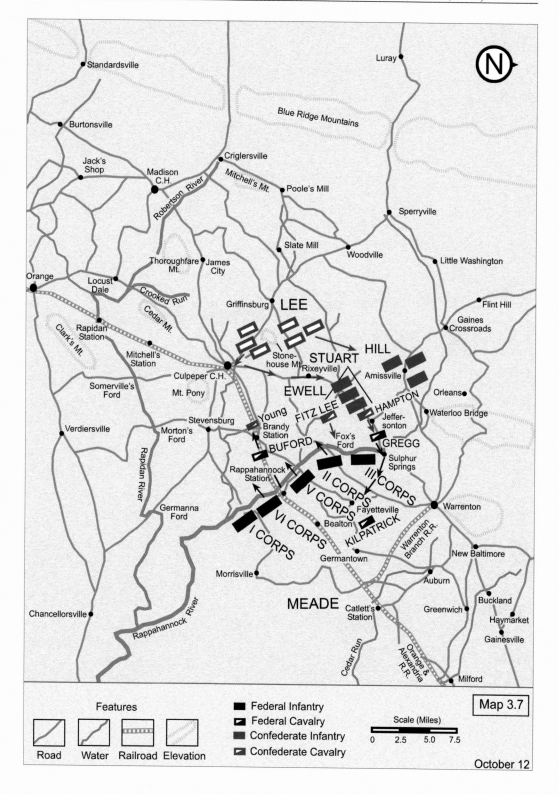

Luray

Blue Ridge Mountains

Standardsville

Burtonsville

Jack's
Shop

Criglersville

Madison
C.H.

Mitchell's Mt.

Poole's Mill

Robertson River

Sperryville

Slate Mill

Woodville

Little Washington

Thoroughfare
Mt.

James
City

Orange

Locust
Dale

Crooked Run

Griffinsburg

LEE

Flint Hill

Gaines
Crossroads

Cedar Mt.

Clark's Mt.

Rapidan
Station

Stone-
house Mt.

STUART

HILL

Mitchell's
Station

Rixeyville

Amissville

Culpeper C.H.

EWELL

Orleans

Somerville's
Ford

Mt. Pony

FITZ LEE

HAMPTON

Waterloo Bridge

Verdiersville

Stevensburg

Young

Brandy
Station

Jeffer-
sonton

Morton's
Ford

BUFORD

Fox's
Ford

GREGG

Rapidan River

Rappahannock
Station

Sulphur
Springs

II CORPS

III CORPS

Germanna
Ford

V CORPS

Warrenton

I CORPS

VI CORPS

Fayetteville

Bealton

KILPATRICK

Warrenton
Branch R.R.

New Baltimore

Germantown

Morrisville

Auburn

MEADE

Catlett's
Station

Greenwich

Buckland

Haymarket

Chancellorsville

Rappahannock River

Cedar Run

Gainesville

Orange &
Alexandria
R.R.

Milford

Features

Road   Water   Railroad   Elevation

■ Federal Infantry
◨ Federal Cavalry
■ Confederate Infantry
◨ Confederate Cavalry

Scale (Miles)

0   2.5   5.0   7.5

Map 3.7

October 12

Map 3.8: Meade in Full Retreat
(October 12 - 13)

It was not until 9:00 p.m. on October 12 that Meade finally learned with certainty from Gen. Gregg that masses of Lee's army were indeed at the Rappahannock River on the army's right flank.

Meade's own army remained divided by the Rappahannock River. Lee had stolen a march on him and was now poised to pounce on his vulnerable flank composed of French's worn-out III Corps, which had been decimated at Gettysburg. A stream of orders flew from army headquarters. All trains and supplies along the Orange and Alexandria Railroad were to be moved quickly to the rear. Of primary concern were the three infantry corps still on the far side of the Rappahannock River near Brandy Station. If Meade had pushed them forward to Culpeper, would Lee have continued moving around his army's right flank? Was there still time to do so? He could not risk the loss of III Corps to find out, so he ordered all three corps (II, V, and VI) back across the river to rejoin the rest of the army. Sedgwick, who was in charge of this reconnaissance, began falling back at 10:00 p.m. that night. II and VI Corps crossed the river at Rappahannock Station, while V Corps did so at Beverly Ford. Buford's cavalry division also joined the retreat, crossing the river after midnight.

Warren's II Corps was ultimately ordered to continue marching to Fayetteville. When he reached the town, Warren received additional orders to form his troops into a line of battle facing Warrenton. The most vulnerable unit, French's III Corps, was pulled back from along the river between Fox's and Beverly fords and realigned to face north toward the growing enemy threat. Newton's I Corps was ordered to march to Warrenton Junction.[26]

When reports placed Hill's Corps at Amissville and Ewell's Corps between White Sulphur Springs and Warrenton, Meade spotted an opportunity and reconsidered his strategy. He could fall upon Ewell's left flank and defeat the advanced corps in detail. Hill's Corps, however, worried Meade. Did Lee intend to push Hill through Salem on a march through the Thoroughfare Gap in the Bull Run Mountains to

fall upon the Union rear at Manassas Junction? Stonewall Jackson used that same route in August of 1862, and Meade thought it was a good bet that Hill was following in his venerable chieftain's footsteps. Never the gambler, Meade decided that withdrawal was more prudent, and so ordered the entire army to march northeast away from Lee's infantry. Meade voided his previous orders to his commanders to approach Fayetteville and Three Mile Station on the Warrenton Branch Railroad, and instead issued marching orders for the heights surrounding Centreville. "I have positive information that Lee's army is moving on my right, Ewell by Warrenton pike, and Hill probably by Salem," Meade telegraphed Gen. Halleck in Washington.[27]

Meade divided his army into two columns on the afternoon of October 13. II and III Corps, supported by Gregg's and Kilpatrick's cavalry divisions, marched from Three Mile Station to Auburn. Lunsford Lomax's Southern cavalry brigade (Fitz Lee's Division) was near Auburn and skirmished with III Corps during its approach. Because III Corps was making such slow progress, Warren ordered his officers to find an alternate road to Auburn. They quickly found one, and the corps halted at Auburn at dusk while III Corps continued its slow trudge. I, V, and VI Corps, escorted by Buford's cavalry division, marched along the Orange and Alexandria Railroad.[28]

Ewell's Corps left White Sulphur Springs at dawn on October 13 and headed toward Warrenton. The entire corps reached this hamlet by 2:00 p.m., covering just one mile per marching hour. To expedite his progress, A. P. Hill, whose men broke camp at 5:30 a.m., divided his corps into two parts: one crossed at Waterloo Bridge and the other at White Sulphur Springs. The head of Hill's column finally reunited with Ewell's at Warrenton at 6:00 p.m. Orders arrived to prepare two days' rations.

Active despite his trooper's worn-down horses, Stuart led Hampton's three cavalry brigades north to scout the enemy's positions in what one modern historian has called "the most harrowing and dangerous expeditions of the war." Skirmishes erupted with the van of III Corps on its way to Greenwich. By nightfall, Stuart was in a vulnerable and dangerous position near Auburn.[29]

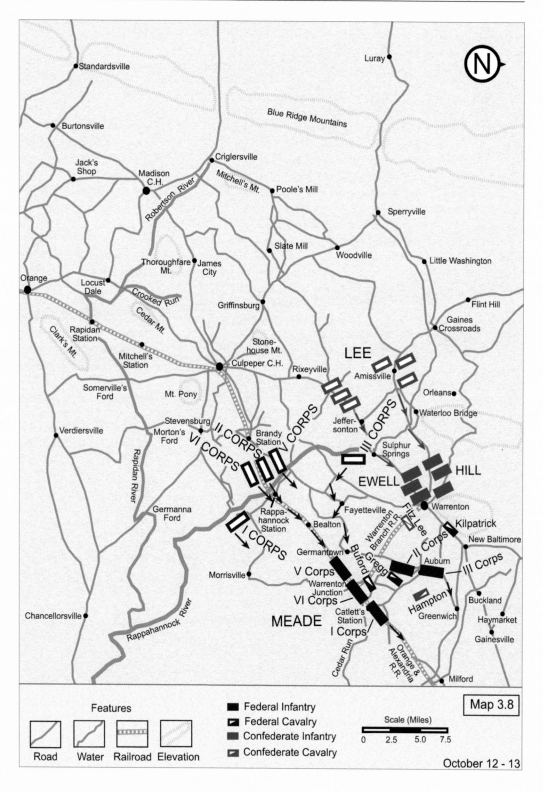

Features

Road   Water   Railroad   Elevation

■ Federal Infantry
◪ Federal Cavalry
■ Confederate Infantry
◪ Confederate Cavalry

Scale (Miles)

0   2.5   5.0   7.5

Map 3.8

October 12 - 13

Map 3.9: The Battle of Auburn: Ewell Approaches Warren's II Corps
(October 14: 5:00 - 6:30 a.m.)

While scouting the Yankee positions and sending back streams of valuable intelligence to Lee, Jeb Stuart rode himself into a potentially fatal situation on the evening of October 13. Meade's change of plans surprised the cavalier, who found himself and his two brigades of cavalry essentially surrounded at Auburn. "In this predicament I was not long in deciding to conceal my whereabouts, if possible, from the enemy," Stuart later reported, "communicate, if possible, to the commanding general the movement of the enemy . . . and patiently await the dawn of morning" (No. 1). It was tedious work, recalled one of his troopers, who asked rhetorically, "did you ever try standing all night holding a mule by the halter, trying to keep him from braying, and trying to keep your sabre and spurs from rattling?" Fortunately for the Confederates, a light drizzle reduced visibility that night.

Stuart dressed six men in enemy uniforms and sent them through the opposing lines to Lee with a suggestion that the infantry make a diversionary attack to help facilitate his escape. That night (October 13-14), Lee dispatched messengers to Ewell with orders to move on Auburn at first light. Ewell put his men on the road between 4:00 and 5:00 a.m. on October 14. Rodes was in the van with his division, followed by divisions under Early and Johnson. Fitz Lee's cavalry screened the moving infantry. Lee may have accompanied Ewell as he rode to Stuart's aid. A. P. Hill's men were also up early, marching through Warrenton as they headed north toward New Baltimore.[30]

While French's III Corps camped at Greenwich during the night of October 13-14, Warren's II Corps rested about five miles southwest at Auburn. Gregg's cavalry division was within supporting distance. Warren did not sleep much that night because new marching orders from Meade arrived at 2:00 a.m. Rather than follow French to Greenwich, Warren was to move from Auburn to Catlett's Station and then along the railroad to Centreville. "My position now was one that caused me anxiety," admitted the corps commander in his report. Warren had

to cross Cedar Run to continue his journey, but the only place to do so was at Auburn. The new route "led me toward the enemy, who had nothing to prevent his concentrating the evening before at Warrenton," explained Warren, who concluded that "the cavalry encountered by the Third Corps, it might almost be considered as certain, had informed General Lee of our position." Warren and his men were vulnerable and he knew it.[31]

Warren had his infantry up between 3:00 and 4:00 a.m. on October 14 to prepare for an early march. The corps' 225 wagons, guarded by Col. Samuel Carroll's brigade (Hays' division), were soon bogged down in the quagmire caused by the recent rains, but Warren managed to get his infantry moving. John Caldwell's division crossed Cedar Run at Auburn in a dense fog before 6:00 a.m. and continued along the Dumfries Road. When he reached the summit of an elevation overlooking the stream (later called Coffee Hill), Caldwell deployed his division facing Warrenton, the presumed direction of any Confederate attack (No. 2). Col. John Brooke's brigade was on the left with Col. Nelson Miles' brigade on its right. The disposition of Caldwell's other two brigades on the right of the line is unclear. The men were permitted to prepare breakfast while waiting for the remainder of the corps to cross. Alexander Hays' division splashed across next about 6:30 a.m. While Caldwell's men watched for a Confederate attack from the direction of Warrenton, Hays' and Alexander Webb's divisions (with the corps' wagons between them) continued marching toward the safety of Catlett's Station (No. 3).

Out on Double Poplar Road, about a mile and a half from Auburn, two companies of the 10th New York Cavalry of Irvin Gregg's brigade watched for any enemy infantry approaching from Warrenton (No. 4). The rest of Gregg's division was deeper in the rear to be better able to support the advanced New Yorkers and protect the wagon train. Although none of the Federals could see them, Rodes' infantry division, spearheading the front of Ewell's Corps, was approaching in the dense fog (No. 5).[32]

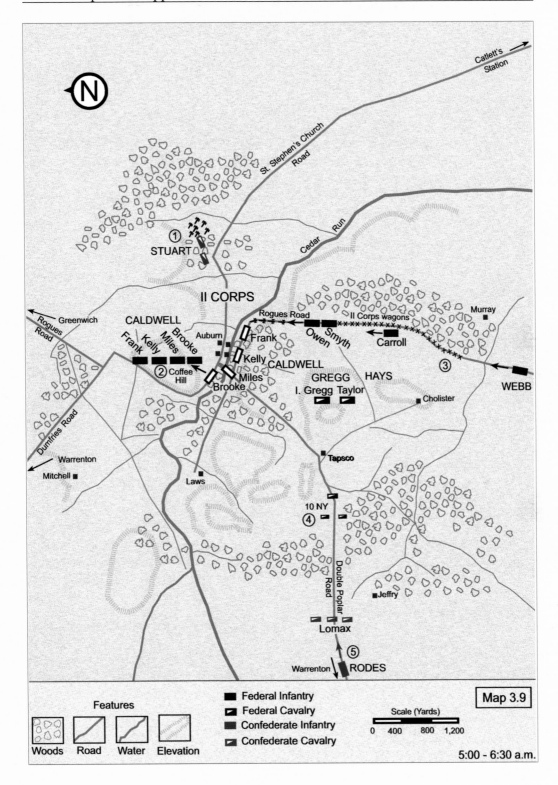

Map 3.9

5:00 - 6:30 a.m.

Map 3.10: The Battle of Auburn:
The Fighting Begins
(October 14: 6:30 - 7:00 a.m.)

Squinting into the morning fog, videttes from the two companies of the 10th New York Cavalry watched as infantry emerged along the Double Popular Road. The gray figures represented the head of Rodes' veteran division, whose mission was to relieve Stuart's two cavalry brigades hiding in a wooded area near St. Stephen's Church Road just east of Auburn. The commander of the cavalry vedettes, Capt. George Vanderbilt, ordered his men to open fire and fall back to a hastily constructed barricade along Double Poplar Road. Although he was told to hold his position until the rest of the regiment came up, Vanderbilt decided to launch a bold charge (No. 1). While there were not nearly enough men to repel the growing number of Rebel infantry stepping out of the mist, Vanderbilt hoped the sudden attack would buy time for reinforcements to arrive.[33]

Jeb Stuart and his 2,000 cavalry had remained hidden in the woods for twelve long hours less than half a mile from the Cedar Run bridge over which Warren's II Corps was crossing (No. 2). Although the last of French's III Corps had passed his hiding spot about midnight, Stuart stayed put. He knew Lee was sending infantry to help him, and he wanted to be in a position to assist. Besides, it was too risky to ride toward Warrenton on a dark and moonless night across a landscape filled with Yankees. Between 6:00 and 6:30 a.m., Stuart could make out Caldwell's men making breakfast on Coffee Hill and the patter of small arms fire was plainly audible from the direction of Lee's arrival. The cavalryman ordered Maj. R. F. Beckham to quietly move his seven artillery pieces onto a ridge about 800 yards east of Caldwell's position (No. 2).

Stuart had mistaken the smattering of small arms fire between Rodes' skirmishers and those of the 10th New York Cavalry for a much larger operation, and believed (incorrectly) that Rebel infantry was up in numbers and ready for a serious fight. Under that mistaken assumption, Stuart ordered Beckham to pull the lanyards of his guns. The artillery fire was accurate and deadly, with one shell killing and wounding seven

men of the 52nd New York (Frank's brigade). The rounds spread pandemonium through the Federal ranks. No one expected a barrage, let alone one from behind their left flank and rear. "[Q]uick as gunpowder, the rebels opened on us in our rear with a battery, and they planted their shells right among us," wrote a soldier in the 53rd Pennsylvania (Brooke's brigade). "The fact of the matter is, it was decidedly bad." The brigade commanders pulled their men from the summit of the hill and repositioned them along its side, providing a large measure of relief from the dropping rounds (No. 3). The troops, reported Col. Nelson Miles, "changed front to the rear covering the command under the slope of the other side of the crest in front of our previous position." Col. Paul Frank ordered the 57th New York forward to silence the guns, but Owen's brigade was just crossing Cedar Run and took up the task because it was closer to Stuart's guns (No. 4). Twelve Federal pieces also opened fire from Coffee Hill. Stuart's predicament had gone from bad to worse.[34]

Warren, who was riding in the rear, worried when the sudden sounds of battle reached his ears. A short time later an aide arrived with news that the road to Catlett's Station was blocked by enemy (Stuart's) cavalry. He also learned that other enemy infantry columns were descending on Caldwell's division from the direction of Warrenton. This message referred to Rodes' command on Double Poplar Road (with Early's and Johnson's divisions behind it). Warren did not have accurate maps to guide him, but he knew he needed to act quickly. His corps was in a vise and in danger of being destroyed. It was, he admitted, a "trying situation."

II Corps' wagons continued rolling toward Auburn Bridge, but their escorts moved toward the sounds of battle. Carroll's brigade was ordered west to help support Gregg's cavalry division, which was attempting to stem the approach of Lomax's cavalry brigade (Fitz Lee's Division) along Double Poplar Road. Webb's division was also ordered into action, but as it passed the wagons it moved to support Hays' division, which was attempting to clear Stuart's horsemen from St. Stephen's Road to open the way to Catlett's Station. Col. Patrick Kelly's Irish Brigade, part of Caldwell's division, was also sent to Double Poplar Road to attempt to hold Ewell's infantry in check (No. 5).[35]

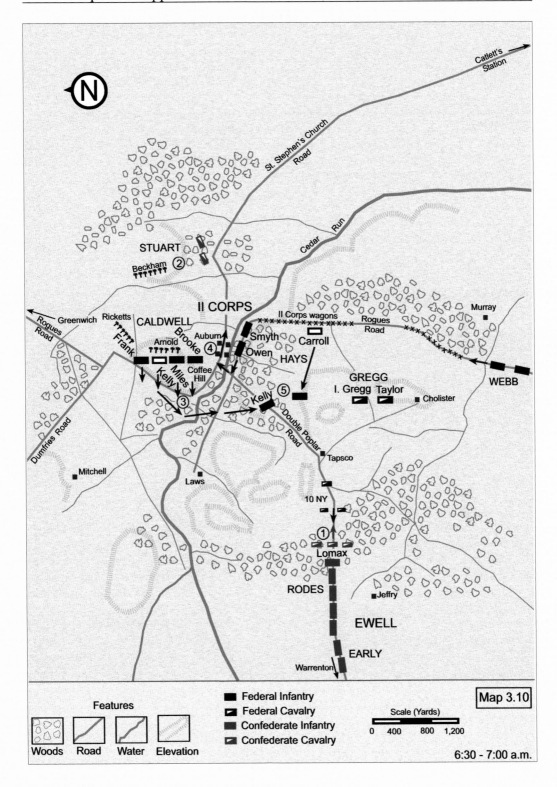

Features

Woods   Road   Water   Elevation

■ Federal Infantry
▰ Federal Cavalry
■ Confederate Infantry
▱ Confederate Cavalry

Scale (Yards)

0   400   800   1,200

Map 3.10

6:30 - 7:00 a.m.

Map 3.11: The Battle of Auburn:
The Federals in Trouble
(October 14: 7:00 - 8:30 a.m.)

Jeb Stuart's situation was now perilous. Beckham's seven guns, which had opened with deadly accuracy on Caldwell's shocked infantry on Coffee Hill, were being pounded by twelve Federal pieces deployed on Coffee Hill (Ricketts' and Arnold's batteries), and a skirmish line from Owen's brigade was heading in their direction. Stuart knew the time had come to order Beckham's withdrawal (No. 1).

Gen. Owen also shook out five companies of the 125th New York and sent them up the St. Stephen's Road toward Stuart, wth three companies on the left of the road and two on the right. A portion of James Gordon's cavalry brigade charged down the road, driving the New Yorkers back. Owen brought up the rest of his brigade, deploying the 126th New York as a skirmish line on the right of the road next to the 125th New York, with his remaining two regiments behind them (No. 2). According to the 126th New York's historian, Col. James Bull "instantly led his men on the double-quick, under sharp fire, toward the wood covered knoll in the front where a battery seemed to be posted. The meadow was covered with strong, tall grass and on the right was a high fence." Col. Thomas Smyth's brigade advanced to support Owen.[36]

The speed of the Union advance surprised a Rebel horseman, who recalled that "the fields were darkened with them and they were fast gaining the rear of our artillery and our only route of retreat." Stuart realized retreat was his only option, but he could not escape with the enemy bearing down on him so quickly. To gain time and distract the enemy, he ordered the 1st North Carolina Cavalry under Col. Thomas Ruffin to charge the approaching Federals. The Tar Heels crashed into the Yankees, their sabers clanking against bayonets and the butts of rifles. The short but deadly encounter gave Stuart just enough time to limber his guns and gallop away with the rest of his men. The close-quarter fight mortally wounded Col. Ruffin and 50 more of his men were killed, wounded, or captured (No. 2).[37]

Like Stuart, II Corps was also in a tough situation. Warren described his predicament this way: "Attacked thus on every side, with my command separated by a considerable stream, encumbered with a wagon train in the vicinity of the whole force of the enemy, and whom the sound of actual conflict had already assured of my position, to halt was to await annihilation, and to move as prescribed carried me along routes in a valley commanded by the heights on each side."[38]

The rest of Caldwell's division was deployed behind Coffee Hill (No. 3). With the approach of Rodes, the gunners of Ricketts' and Arnold's batteries heard their commanders yell, "Fire to the rear!" The gunners picked up the trail of each piece and swung it 180 degrees to face west toward the new threat. The initial salvos convinced Rodes' men to dash for cover. To counter this concentration of Union guns, Brig. Gen. Armistead Long, Ewell's artillery chief, sought suitable platforms for his artillery. He knew he had to work quickly, for "his [the enemy's] batteries were so placed as to command all the direct approaches."

The Confederate infantry deployment was slow and methodical. Rodes' first brigade under Brig. Gen. Junius Daniel deployed at 8:00 a.m. (No. 4), and the rest of the division formed into a line facing east toward the II Corps. Early, marching behind Rodes, left Double Poplar Road and headed north to find the Federal right flank (No. 5). With any luck he could turn it—or better still, slip into Warren's rear. The last of Ewell's divisions under Edward Johnson marched to the left to take up the center of the Confederate line.

With Rodes deployed, Long placed Col. Thomas Carter's artillery battalion on the north side of Cedar Run to support the infantry. Lt. Col. Hilary Jones' and Lt. Col. Snowden Andrews' battalions were still in transit. Carter ordered his artillery to open fire on the Federal infantry visible along the road. The Irish Brigade was on the receiving end of the barrage. "[W]hile resting there," recalled its colonel, Patrick Kelly, "fire was suddenly opened upon us by a battery, with no casualties on our part." As it turned out, Carter's guns were in greater danger than the Federal infantry, for Ames' and Arnold's guns on Coffee Hill found their range and began pounding Carter's position. "The whole ground was exposed to a crossfire from these batteries and would have been untenable," noted Carter. With his commander's permission, he shifted his battalion to the right of side of Rodes' position (No. 6).[39]

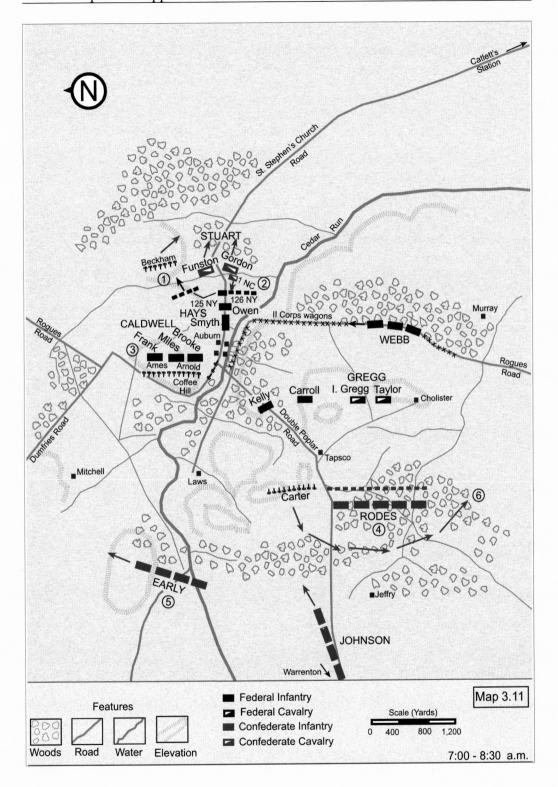

Map 3.11

7:00 - 8:30 a.m.

Features

Woods   Road   Water   Elevation

Federal Infantry
Federal Cavalry
Confederate Infantry
Confederate Cavalry

Scale (Yards)
0   400   800   1,200

Map 3.12: The Battle of Auburn:
II Corps Retreats
(October 14: 10:00 - 11:00 a.m.)

Most of Carter's artillery was in place by 10:00 a.m., when it opened an hour-long artillery barrage against the Federals. Warren had not waited for the Confederate cannon to open before issuing orders for his troops to withdraw. As he noted in his report, "The actual condition of things at the moment was not so bad as reported, for our movement had begun too early for the enemy's preparations to be completed." With Stuart gone, the St. Stephen's Road was now open to Catlett's Station. Wanting no part of a full-scale fight with an enemy of unknown size arriving from two directions, Warren wisely ordered Hays' division, minus Carroll's brigade, to continue marching to Catlett's Station (No. 1). Hays was followed by II Corps' wagons and Alexander Webb's division. Warren also needed to extract his other men, but this would be more difficult because they directly faced the enemy. Fortunately, the Confederate attack was slow in developing. Caldwell put Col. Miles' and Col. Frank's brigades on the St. Steven's Church Road behind Webb's division shortly before 11:00 a.m.[40]

Shortly after 11:00 a.m., Carroll's brigade, followed by Kelly's, pulled back and headed for Auburn and their retreat to Catlett's Station (No. 2). Because of the intense Confederate artillery fire directed against the bridge at Auburn, they were forced to splash across Cedar Run at other locations. The Federal artillery limbered up and departed, leaving only Brooke's and Taylor's brigades as a rearguard. Capt. William Arnold left a section of his battery behind to support Brooke's men. None of these men were to remain long, for Brooke was supposed to pull back, followed by Taylor's cavalry bringing up the rear. Because of the approach of Jubal Early's Division, the section had to be pulled back by prolonge. "The gunners loading the pieces while the horses walked along, stopping long enough to fire then walk on again." Many of the Taylor's cavalrymen were unhappy with this task and simply took off, leaving Brooke's men to primarily shoulder this important responsibility. According to Alford Chapman of the 57th New York, "I received orders to withdraw my men, as

soon as relieved by the cavalry, who proceeded to deploy a line about 100 yards in my rear. I recalled the skirmishers as rapidly as was possible . . . but found that the cavalry had commenced to retire before I had reached the line on which they had deployed and that I was covering their retreat instead of they mine." Early's men closely followed in a desperate effort to cut off Brooke's men and capture the bunch of them. They succeeded in driving a wedge between the 57th New York and the rest of the brigade. Col. Chapman kept his calm, moving his men off the road on a wide detour and later rejoined the brigade.[41]

So ended the small battle of Auburn. The engagement was another lost opportunity for the Confederates, because a concentrated attack from two directions against Warren's II Corps astride Cedar Run could have been disastrous for the Federals. "Strange to say, the fire of our infantry ceased as soon as I opened [with Beckham's guns]," wrote a frustrated Stuart in his report. "A vigorous attack with our main body at the time . . . would have insured the annihilation of that army corps." Stuart seems never to have realized that the Southern infantry was not fully up and ready to fight when he ordered the guns to fire. More importantly, however, was that the Auburn combat delayed half of Lee's army for many hours, which would ultimately contribute to the disastrous events about to unfold at Bristoe Station later that same day.[42]

II Corps division commander Brig. Gen. John Caldwell was pleased about the turn of events. "The conduct of my men . . . was all that could be expected of the best soldiers and most enduring men," he wrote in his campaign report. "The loads carried by the men were very heavy, and the marching severe. . . . The conscripts generally behaved very well, and under the very trying circumstances of the morning at Auburn, their conduct is worthy of admiration."[43]

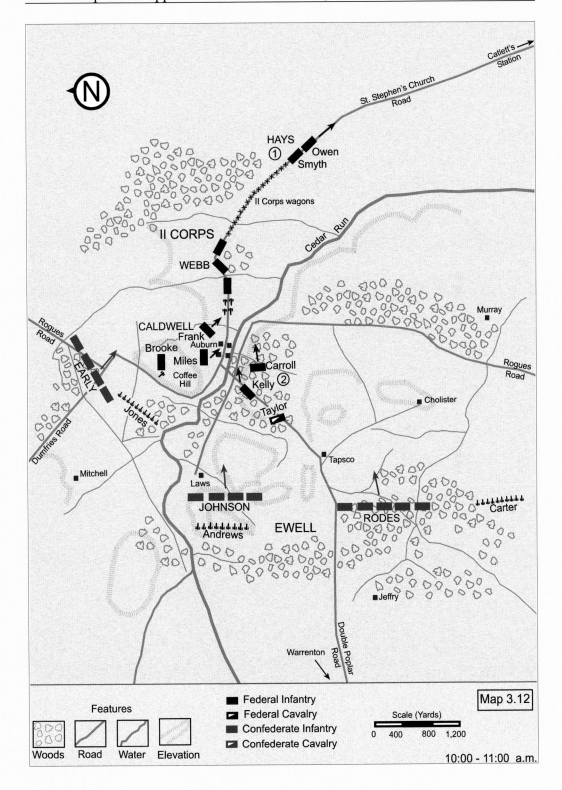

Catlett's
Station

St. Stephen's Church
Road

HAYS
①
Owen
Smyth

II Corps wagons

II CORPS

WEBB

Rogues
Road

CALDWELL
Frank
Brooke   Auburn
Miles
Coffee
Hill

Carroll
②
Kelly
Taylor

Cedar Run

Murray

Rogues
Road

EARLY
Jones

Cholister

Mitchell

Laws

JOHNSON

Andrews

EWELL

Tapsco

RODES

Carter

Jeffry

Double Poplar Road

Warrenton Road

Features

Woods   Road   Water   Elevation

■ Federal Infantry
◁ Federal Cavalry
■ Confederate Infantry
◁ Confederate Cavalry

Scale (Yards)
0   400   800   1,200

Map 3.12

10:00 - 11:00 a.m.

Map Set 4: The Battle of Bristoe Station (October 14, 1863)

Map 4.1: A. P. Hill Pursues Warren's II Corps (October 14: noon - 1:00 p.m.)

Although Gen. Robert E. Lee was unable to force an engagement at Auburn that could have isolated and destroyed a portion of the Federal II Corps, he was not about to give up. After their encounter with Maj. Gen. Gouverneur Warren's men at Auburn, Lt. Gen. Richard Ewell's Second Corps infantry continued marching northeast along Double Poplars Road. They met up with Lt. Gen. A. P. Hill's Third Corps around Greenwich, which became something of a bottleneck. Hill's men were pursuing Maj. Gen. William French's III Corps.

Hill's men broke camp at 5:00 a.m. that morning. According to one of Hill's foot soldiers, the march was to have begun at midnight, but the orders were countermanded. "This change of start time would have a critical impact on the course of events for the day," explained a recent historian of the campaign, "where minutes would become important in deciding events." When they reached Warrenton, Hill's men stopped because Ewell's troops clogged the road to Auburn. With the route clear at about 8:30 a.m., they tromped on through New Baltimore and reached Greenwich between 9:30 a.m. and 10:00 a.m. When Ewell's men reached Greenwich after the skirmish with II Corps at Auburn, it was their turn to wait until the last of Hill's men cleared the road. Maj. Gen. Richard Anderson's Division led the corps, followed by divisions under Maj. Gens. Henry Heth and Cadmus Wilcox.[1]

When Hill received a report that the enemy was moving away from Greenwich on the Warrenton and Alexandria Pike, he dispatched Anderson's Division to intercept the column, probably near Buckland. Hill was confident of the veracity of the report because "the rumbling of wagons . . . could be distinctly heard." The reports were incorrect. There were no wagons, only Federal cavalry. Maj. Gen. Fitz Lee's cavalry division arrived to engage the Yankees, permitting Anderson to rejoin the corps.

Hill's men were not far behind French's III Corps. Its last brigade left Greenwich about 8:00 a.m.; debris along the road indicated a retreat in some haste. During the late morning, the vanguard of Heth's Division encountered French's rearguard, composed of Col. J. Warren Keifer's brigade of Brig. Gen. Joseph Carr's division. When he spotted the approaching grayclad infantry, Keifer calmly halted his men and formed a line of battle across the road. This, in turn, stopped Heth's men in their tracks. Before they could organize into line and probe the Federal line, Keifer reformed his men and continued his march without further incident.[2]

Despite the combat at Auburn and III Corps' rearguard action with Hill's troops, Maj. Gen. George Meade was confident he could extract his army from harm's way with minimal losses. About noon, he wired Maj. Gen. Henry Halleck, "My movement thus far is successful . . . the enemy are advancing from Warrenton, but will hardly be able to arrest my movements." Most of his corps had reached their final destination or were close to it. III and V Corps (under Maj. Gen. George Sykes) were close to Broad Run, Maj. Gen. John Newton's I Corps was approaching Centreville, and Maj. Gen. John Sedgwick's VI Corps was near Manassas. The cavalry were also falling back. Brig. Gen. David Gregg's division had left Auburn and was heading to Catlett's Station, Brig. Gen. John Buford's division was at Catlett's Station, and Brig. Gen. Judson Kilpatrick's was near Warrenton Station, heading toward Catlett's with Fitz Lee's Division nipping at its heals.[3]

Meade's only real cause for concern was the fate of Warren's II Corps. Its 8,000 infantry, 26 artillery pieces, 100 wagons, and 150 ambulances stretched three long miles. "The enemy's infantry are moving on Warrenton Pike," Meade warned Warren. "Move forward as rapidly as you can." Meade concluded by telling Warren that V Corps was within supporting distance, and was in turn supported by III Corps. Any serious encounters with the enemy could bring two corps to his rescue. Warren was rapidly moving along the Orange and Alexandria Railroad. Brig. Gen. Alexander Webb's division, with two batteries, marched on the right-of-way left of the tracks, with Brig. Gen. Alexander Hays' division on the opposite side. Brig. Gen. John Caldwell's division followed behind them on both sides of the tracks. Col. John Taylor's brigade of Gregg's cavalry division was on Webb's left; Col. Irvin Gregg's cavalry brigade brought up the rear.[4]

The II Corps was in potentially serious trouble, and a well-executed Confederate thrust could slice it away from the army and destroy it.

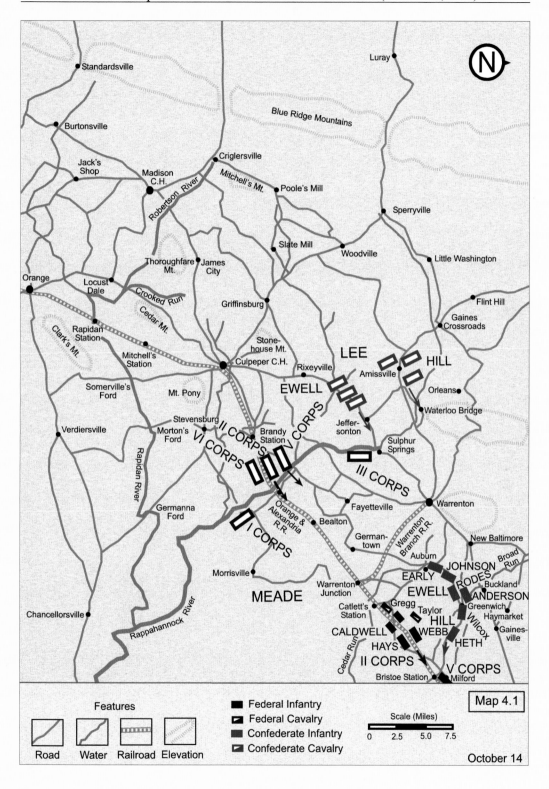

Map 4.1

October 14

Map 4.2: The Confederates
Approach Bristoe Station
(October 14: 1:00 - 2:00 p.m.)

A series of events between 1:30 p.m. and 2:00 p.m. made a fight at Bristoe Station largely inevitable. V Corps leader George Sykes had orders to remain near Bristoe Station at Milford until he could see Warren's corps approaching. Only then could Sykes cross Broad Run and continue to Centreville. Sykes became more agitated as the morning hours passed and Warren's corps failed to make an appearance, especially because French's III Corps had continued to put distance between itself and Sykes' own stationary command. Sykes had no way of knowing II Corps had been delayed by combat at Auburn, and apparently Warren did not notify him of his delay. An erroneous report of a sighting of the front of II Corps along the Orange and Alexandria spurred the agitated Sykes into action. Rather than check the report's veracity, however, the V Corps leader ordered his men across Broad Run. It was 1:00 p.m.

A. P. Hill's Corps approached Broad Run between 1:30 and 2:00 p.m. with Heth's Division leading the way. Hill rode ahead to reconnoiter, using the hills south of Broad Run as an observation platform. He watched Federal troops on the opposite side of the run stand, grab their equipment, and continue marching. This excited the combative Hill, who believed he had finally caught the tail of French's III Corps. "I determined that no time must be lost," he wrote in his battle report, "and hurried up Heth's division, forming it in line of battle along the crest of the hills." Less than three months earlier at Gettysburg, Hill committed Heth's lone division against what he believed was nothing more than militia early on July 1. No one had reconnoitered the enemy's position or strength, no cavalry was on hand to help, and the rest of Hill's Third Corps was strung out behind him and this unable to provide Heth with prompt support. If Hill had taken the time to reconnoiter the area, he would have learned that the enemy he spotted was not III Corps but the rear of Sykes's V Corps—just as at Gettysburg it was not militia, but John Buford's cavalry. Scouts would have also told Hill that Warren's II Corps was advancing just a little more than one mile

away on his right flank, parallel to his line of march. Hill knew none of this. Heth's tired men were told that the enemy was beating a hasty retreat and many were probably anxious to earn back what had been lost at Gettysburg.[5]

With the enemy in sight and apparently vulnerable, Hill sent riders to his other division leaders with orders to march to Heth's aid. Hill also informed Gen. Lee of the situation. "[F]lushed with excitement," wrote his biographer, Hill ordered Capt. Archibald Graham's Battery from Maj. William Poague's battalion to deploy on a hill overlooking Broad Run. The guns dropped trail and opened on the departing V Corps infantry. "A few shots . . . threw them into much confusion, and all that were in sight retreated in disorder across Broad Run," reported Heth after the battle.[6]

Emboldened by the quickened pace of retreat brought about by light artillery fire, Hill ordered Heth to deploy three of his brigades. Brig. Gen. John Cooke's Brigade, which led Heth's column, was thrown out to the right of Greenwich Road while the second brigade under Brig. Gen. William Kirkland formed left of the road. Cooke's command had missed Gettysburg and its losses, and was large with some 2,500 men. Kirkland led James J. Pettigrew's former brigade, which numbered about 1,500 because of its horrendous losses at Gettysburg. Brig. Gen. Henry H. Walker's small 700-man brigade was ordered to move up and form on Kirkland's left, and Brig. Gen. Joseph Davis' Brigade remained in reserve. Nearly 5,000 men were in place to assault what Hill believed was III Corps (but was really the tail of V Corps) if he could quickly cross Broad Run. In another Gettysburg parallel, neither Kirkland nor Walker had ever led a brigade in battle. Pettigrew had opened the combat at Gettysburg, and he too had not led a brigade in combat.[7]

Warren's II Corps on Heth's right was making good progress toward Bristoe Station, but it would not arrive until about 1:30 p.m. Because he feared a Confederate attack, Warren wisely formed his column into line of battle and marched it by the flank toward Broad Run. To avoid the congestion near Bristoe Station, division leader Webb shifted his command from the right-of-way north of the tracks to an unimproved wagon road running parallel to the railroad on the opposite side. His division was approaching the station when the men spotted troops marching about a mile to their left.[8]

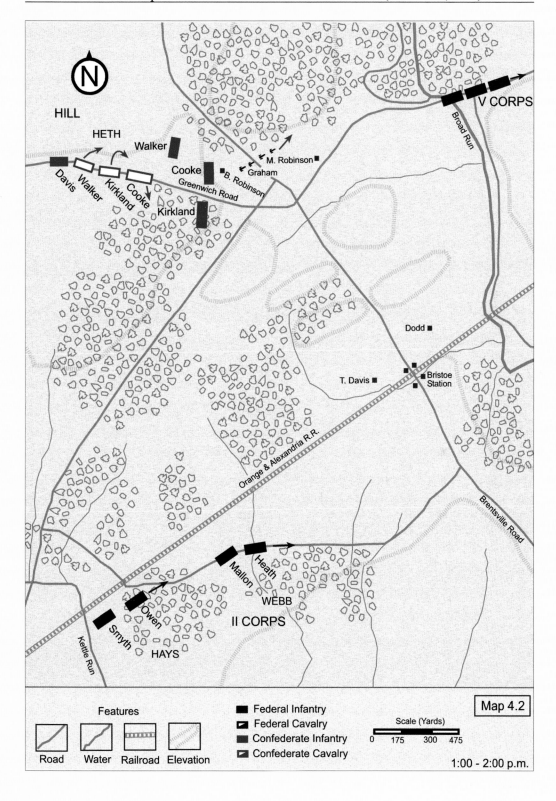

N

HILL

HETH

Walker

Cooke

Davis   Walker   Kirkland   Cooke

Greenwich Road

Kirkland

M. Robinson

B. Robinson   Graham

V CORPS

Broad Run

Dodd

T. Davis   Bristoe Station

Orange & Alexandria R.R.

Brentsville Road

Mallon   Heath

WEBB

Owen

Smyth   II CORPS

Kettle Run   HAYS

Features

Road   Water   Railroad   Elevation

■ Federal Infantry
◢ Federal Cavalry
■ Confederate Infantry
◣ Confederate Cavalry

Scale (Yards)

0   175   300   475

Map 4.2

1:00 - 2:00 p.m.

Map 4.3: The Battle Opens
(October 14: 2:00 - 2:15 p.m.)

About 2:00 p.m., Hill ordered Heth to advance, cross Broad Run, and attack V Corps on the opposite side. The movement to the jumping-off position was not without confusion. "Kirkland had not quite completed the formation of his line," wrote Heth in his battle report, "when orders were received from General Hill to push on with the two brigades then in line [Cooke and Kirkland]." Walker's Brigade had not yet formed on Kirkland's left when Hill's order arrived. Because he had not finished deploying his men and had orders to advance immediately, only Cooke and Kirkland formed the first line.[9]

Shortly after ordering the advance, Heth received a message from Cooke that a large Federal force was on his right flank. Perhaps Heth recalled what had happened on the first morning at Gettysburg when he had ignored Pettigrew's warnings and blundered into Buford's cavalry division. This time Heth prudently halted his men and sent a messenger to Hill with the news. Hill, however, did not seem to have learned from his Gettysburg experience. Rather than advise Heth to determine the veracity of the intelligence as quickly as possible, Hill ordered his subordinate to continue advancing and promised to send help from Anderson's Division now approaching the field. Hill had no idea that the unknown troops were part of Warren's II Corps. Once again Maj. Gen. Jeb Stuart had not properly screened Lee's infantry, and once again Hill compounded the problem by recklessly throwing his men into the unknown.[10]

A surgeon riding at the head of Warren's II Corps with Gen. Webb wrote home that as he approached Bristoe Station, "through the lifting mist, we dimly saw another column marching parallel to ours . . . we supposed it to be one from our own corps. Both columns stopped and stared in amazement at each other." Webb seems to have known about this threat to his left; Lt. Col. Charles Morgan, the II Corps' chief of staff, had been scouting ahead because Gregg's cavalry was well behind the infantry. Morgan galloped up to Webb with a report of Rebels in large numbers just to his left. Wanting to confirm the report, Webb ordered the first regiment in line, the venerable 1st Minnesota of Col. Francis Heath's brigade, to head north to see reconnoiter the area. Webb ordered the remainder of his regiments to "By the left flank, double quick to the railroad cut, march!"[11]

Deployed in a skirmish line, the 1st Minnesota slowly moved northeast with its right flank initially on the railroad. Within minutes, the Minnesotans came upon the right and rear of Col. Edward Hall's 46th North Carolina marching on the right flank of Cooke's Brigade. The appearance of the Federal infantry stunned Hall, who later reported that "the enemy was in heavy force on my right and busily engaged in getting in position . . . soon after the enemy skirmishers commenced firing on my right flank." What he saw next probably remained with him for the rest of his life: "I discovered the [enemy] line of battle behind the railroad, extending as far on my right as I could see."[12]

Heth finally received orders from Hill to continue his advance. Hill reasoned that Anderson's two approaching brigades would soon be up to provide close support. Heth lost about ten minutes waiting for Hill's response. When one of Hill's aides approached Cooke with orders to move forward as previously ordered, Cooke shook his head and replied, "Well, I will advance, and if they flank me, I will face my men about and cut my way out." Cooke ordered the advance renewed. Despite the serious and immediate threat to their right flank, Heth's three brigades continued to march toward Broad Run and the retreating V Corps.[13]

Webb called upon Lt. T. Fred Brown's Rhode Island battery to provide support for his infantry. The four guns, which had seen so much action at Gettysburg, tore through Brig. Gen. Joshua Owen's column in its haste to reach the high ground east of the railroad bed. Brown soon realized that he could not open fire on Heth's men because the 82nd New York stood in the way, so Webb moved the New Yorkers to the right of the 15th Massachusetts, leaving a space through which Brown's guns could fire.[14]

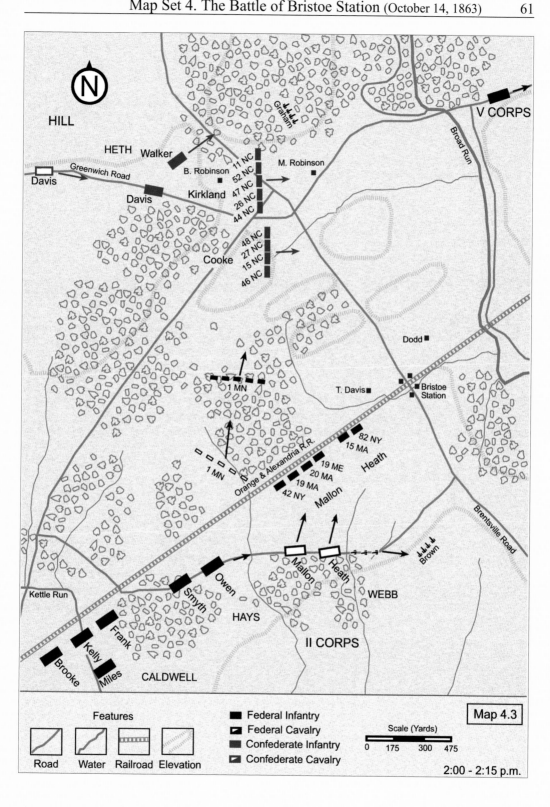

HILL

HETH   Walker

Greenwich Road

Davis

Davis

B. Robinson

Kirkland

11 NC
52 NC
47 NC
26 NC
44 NC

M. Robinson

Cooke

48 NC
27 NC
15 NC
46 NC

V CORPS

Broad Run

Graham

Dodd

1 MN

T. Davis

Bristoe
Station

1 MN

Orange & Alexandria R.R.

82 NY
15 MA
19 ME   Heath
20 MA
19 MA
42 NY   Mallon

Kettle Run

Smyth   Owen

Frank

Kelly

Brooke   Miles

CALDWELL

HAYS

Mallon   Heath

Brown

WEBB

Brentsville Road

II CORPS

Features

Road   Water   Railroad   Elevation

■ Federal Infantry
◨ Federal Cavalry
■ Confederate Infantry
◨ Confederate Cavalry

Scale (Yards)

0   175   300   475

Map 4.3

2:00 - 2:15 p.m.

Map 4.4: Heth Begins His Wheeling Movement (October 14: 2:15 - 2:45 p.m.)

Lt. Brown's four Federal guns, now in a good position with a clear view of two enemy brigades under Gens. Cooke and Kirkland, opened fire with spherical case shot with dramatic effects (No. 1). Cooke, who was driving his men toward Broad Run, realized the peril when the shells tore through his ranks. The threat could no longer be ignored. He ordered his men to make a right wheel to face the railroad tracks due south. When Kirkland spotted Cooke's move, he ordered his regimental commanders to follow suit. Within a few minutes some 4,000 Confederate foot soldiers were undertaking a complex right wheel to front the threat posed from by Webb's division (No. 2). The Confederate regimental deployment remained unchanged. Kirkland's men were deployed from left to right as follows: 11th North Carolina - 52nd North Carolina - 47th North Carolina - 44th North Carolina - 26th North Carolina. Cooke's regiments continued the line to the right, left to right as follows: 48th North Carolina - 27th North Carolina - 15th North Carolina - 46th North Carolina.[15]

The vast majority of Webb's infantry did not see the giant Confederate wheeling movement because most of them were also in motion. The V Corps, Webb later reported, "whose rear guard was just disappearing beyond Broad Run" felt compelled to take immediate action, for his own command could be isolated and subject to attack. Webb decided to "move to the right with the object of connecting with the Fifth Army Corps." He ordered Heath's brigade, holding his right flank, to "move by the right flank." Webb also noted in his report that about one-half of Heath's brigade (probably all of the 82nd New York and part of the 15th Massachusetts) had reached the east side of Broad Run when Warren arrived and ordered him back across the water (No. 3). V Corps was probably too far away to effect a linkage, so Warren ordered his men back on the double-quick. Within a short time Webb's line was reestablished on the west side of Broad Run with its right about 150 yards from it. Col. James Mallon's brigade formed on Heath's left. The 59th New York, which had been thrown out on the skirmish line, screened these movements

and eventually linked up with the 1st Minnesota north of the tracks.[16]

Brown's battery also limbered up and crossed Broad Run about 400 yards south of the bridge. Because enemy batteries commanded this structure spanning the stream, Lt. Brown remained on the north side of the run, where he found a good firing platform for his four Napoleons about 200 yards east of the bridge. Once unlimbered, Brown's pieces opened fire on the approaching North Carolina infantry (No. 4). Other Federal batteries were galloping to the scene of the action west of the waterway. Following Owen's brigade (Hays' division), Capt. William Arnold's battery (Battery A, First Rhode Island Light Artillery) was ordered into position. The battery's elevation allowed its half-dozen three- inch Ordnance Rifles to fire over the heads of Owen's men. Under continuous Confederate artillery fire, Capt. R. Bruce Ricketts' battery (Batteries F and G, First Pennsylvania Light Artillery) also approached its assigned position to the right of Arnold, a couple hundred yards from Broad Run.[17]

Maj. Henry Abbott, the commander of the 20th Massachusetts (Mallon's brigade), watched the Confederate right-wheel and steady approach from behind the safety of the deep railroad bed. "The enemy were soon seen in full," reported Abbott, "advancing in an oblique line to our position from the right, their left toward us, and their right considerably refused."

Walker's small brigade was not part of this movement. Although his men were originally slated to form on Kirkland's left, they were still considerably behind the North Carolinians because of the quick advance (No. 5). Dense woods and the rolling terrain likely shielded these wheeling movements from his vision. Walker therefore still believed his men trailed Kirkland and Cooke, and so he continued marching east toward Broad Run. Anderson's Confederate division of foot soldiers was approaching the battlefield about 2:30 p.m., but were not yet visible to any of the combatants.

The extent of A. P. Hill's miscalculation was about to become evident.[18]

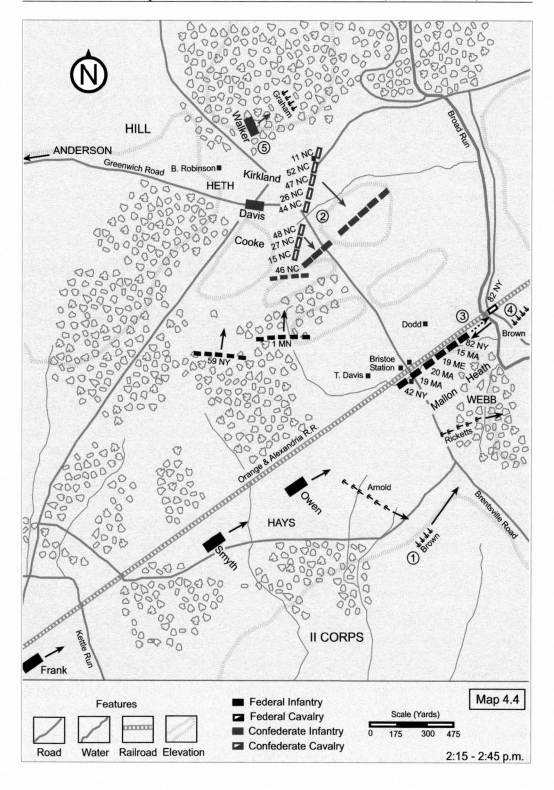

Map 4.4

2:15 - 2:45 p.m.

Map 4.5: Final Preparations Before
the Cooke-Kirkland Attack
(October 14: 2:45 - 3:00 p.m.)

Cooke's and Kirkland's 4,000 North Carolinians completed their wheel without incident and now faced the threat once on their right. It was about 2:45 p.m. (No. 1). No one knew they were facing three Federal brigades (Heath, Mallon, and Owen) totaling about 3,000 troops in a good defensive position (No. 2). Other Federals (Col. Thomas Smyth's brigade of Hays' division and John Caldwell's division) were also approaching the new line of battle, but would not begin to arrive for at least another thirty minutes.

Owen's arrival added to the Federal line, which was deployed from right to left as follows: 82nd New York - 15th Massachusetts - 19th Maine (Heath's brigade); 20th Massachusetts - 19th Massachusetts - 42nd New York (Mallon's brigade); 125th New York - 39th New York - 111th New York - 126th New York (Owen's brigade). The line was more than half a mile long (No. 3). The 1st Minnesota (Heath's brigade) and the 59th New York and 7th Michigan (Mallon's brigade) were on the skirmish line, but they moved back when the wall of North Carolinians turned in their direction.

As it always does, the terrain played an important role in the Bristoe Station combat. The Rebel attack would have to cover about 600 yards of rolling and mostly open fields. A range of low hills extending 200 to 500 feet north of the railroad offered them some protection. Cooke on the right had to march across higher and more uneven ground than Kirkland on their left. Once past this undulating terrain the ground was fairly flat and devoid of any trees and brush—perfect for maintaining a well-ordered battle line. This feature, however, also served the defenders by exposing the Tar Heels to direct rifle and artillery fire. Some of the Union troops (all of Heath's brigade and the right side of Mallon's) enjoyed the protection of the five- to ten-foot deep railroad bed. The position, wrote Gen. Heth, "was as strong, or stronger, naturally and artificially, than military art could have made it by many hours work." Not all of the Federal troops enjoyed the rail bed protection. The center of Mallon's brigade at Bristoe Station had no cover

whatsoever. It was here that Mallon established his headquarters. Owen's brigade arrived on Mallon's left, where his men occupied "the deep cut on the railroad."[19]

The last time Kirkland's infantry dressed their lines and stepped off to attack the enemy, Pettigrew was their official commander and the July 3 attack at Gettysburg was a much larger affair known as Pickett's Charge. Pettigrew, however, directed the division that afternoon because of Heth's earlier wound, leaving his brigade in the hands of Col. James K. Marshall (who was killed). Many of the same Federals they would soon fight had also opposed them on July 3. As the Tar Heels moved forward, sixteen Federal artillery pieces fired into them. One shell from Brown's battery exploded in the middle of Kirkland's line, killing and wounding 15 from the 47th North Carolina.[20]

If Kirkland's North Carolinians looked about for support on their exposed left flank, they did so in vain. Walker's Brigade, which was supposed to be there, was no where to be seen. During the earlier confusion Walker seems not to have known that Cooke and Kirkland had wheeled to the right. He thought he was behind Kirkland and continued west across Broad Run. "While crossing this in line of battle," Walker later wrote, "Kirkland became hotly engaged." Walker ordered his men back to the west side of the stream and "double-quicked my brigade to try and catch up with Kirkland's left" (No. 4). Circumstances beyond Walker's control had conspired against him this day. He could not come up fast enough to provide support, and his brigade was not a reliable organization. At Gettysburg under Col. John Brockenbrough (an officer of limited ability), ill-luck placed the brigade on the far left of the line on July 3. The fitful advance was delivered without much enthusiasm, the position exposed and the men vulnerable. The outfit crumbled in the face of heavy Union artillery fire, exposing their comrades on their right.[21]

Maj. David McIntosh's artillery battalion and a pair of brigades under Brig. Gens. Carnot Posey and Edward Perry (Anderson's Division) were now on the battlefield and heading for their assigned positions (No. 5).[22]

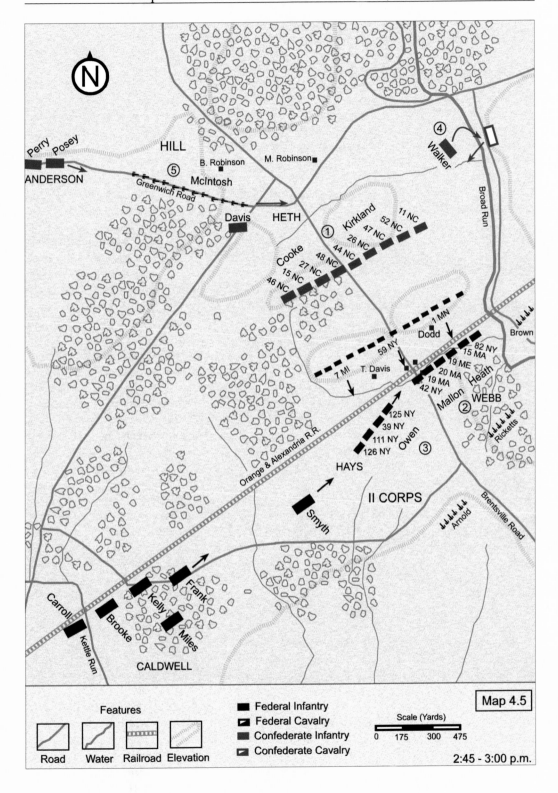

N

Perry Posey
ANDERSON
HILL
⑤ McIntosh
Greenwich Road
B. Robinson
M. Robinson

Davis   HETH

Kirkland 52 NC 11 NC
①   47 NC
         26 NC
   48 NC
Cooke 27 NC
15 NC 44 NC
46 NC

Walker ④

Broad Run

1 MN
Dodd
59 NY   82 NY
             15 MA
7 MI T. Davis 19 ME
             20 MA Heath
           19 MA
           42 NY Mallon WEBB ②

Brown

Ricketts

125 NY
39 NY
111 NY Owen ③
126 NY

HAYS

Orange & Alexandria R.R.

II CORPS

Arnold

Brentsville Road

Smyth

Carroll
Brooke
Kelly
Frank
Miles
Kettle Run

CALDWELL

Features

Road Water Railroad Elevation

■ Federal Infantry
◪ Federal Cavalry
■ Confederate Infantry
◪ Confederate Cavalry

Scale (Yards)
0   175   300   475

Map 4.5

2:45 - 3:00 p.m.

Map 4.6: Cooke and Kirkland Attack
(October 14: 3:00 - 3:15 p.m.)

Richard Anderson's III Corps division arrived on the field to support Heth's efforts, with Maj. David McIntosh's artillery battalion fronting the reinforcements. A. P. Hill instructed where he wanted McIntosh to deploy his guns (No. 1). Although the experienced battalion commander believed the location was too exposed and too close to the Federal infantry lining the railroad embankment, he followed orders and deployed five guns (three rifled pieces from the 2nd Rockbridge (Virginia Artillery) and two others from Capt. William Hurt's Battery) only about 500 yards from the Federal line. He also sent orders for a section of Capt. Robert Rice's Battery to join these pieces. Enemy artillery shells rained down within minutes after the guns were unlimbered, killing and maiming cannoneers and horses alike.[23]

Federal guns continued to inflict terrible losses on Cooke's and Kirkland's brigades as they dressed their lines several hundred yards from the tracks in preparation for the final advance on the Federal line (No. 2). The shellfire, recalled a Union soldier in the 126th New York, "literally blew them to pieces as they stood." Cooke and his men may have assumed the Federals were aligned on the hills south of the railroad. According to artillery officer John Haskell, "our men, seeing only the skirmish line on the hill above them, rushed down to catch it before it could be moved off." A bullet smashed into Cooke's shin around this time and the 46th's Col. Hall assumed command. "The musketry fire from the line of railroad was very heavy," Hall wrote in his report. "I soon saw that a rapid advance must be made or a withdrawal. I chose the former." A Tar Heel in the 44th fighting on the right side of Kirkland's line recalled: "There dashed a [Federal] battery. Another appeared and still others . . . a bugle sounded . . . and a mad race began for the knolls beyond the railroad embankment. We raced, men swore and yelled . . . now see and hear the shriek and crack of the shells and the thud of the shot as they crash into our ranks."

Meanwhile, McIntosh's guns continued its fruitless effort to knock out the opposing Federal artillery. A member of Ricketts' Federal battery dismissed the effort: "We paid no attention to their artillery, though their shells were making wild music in our midst."[24]

Lt. Col. William Saunders of the 46th North Carolina marveled that his men could stand up to the storm of metal ripping through their lines: "the enemy had opened a terrible fire from his infantry, but the men, although fatigued by six successive days' marching, continued to advance steadily and in beautiful line with loud cheers and finest spirits. I saw not a man falter or attempt to shrink."[25] Gen. Warren, watching the battle unfold from the opposite side of the field, agreed: "[A] more inspiring scene could not be imagined. The enemy's line of battle boldly moving forward, one part of our own steadily awaiting it [Webb's division] and another moving against it at the double quick [Owen's brigade] while the artillery was taking up position at a gallop and going into action."[26]

As the Southern infantry closed the distance, Cooke's Brigade on the west side of the Brentsville Road approached Owen's brigade and the left side of Mallon's brigade, while Kirkland's command on the east side of the road headed for Heath's brigade and the center and right side of Mallon's. Although Union regimental leaders cautioned their men to hold their fire until the enemy stepped into easy killing distance (and to lie down as much as possible and only to rise when it was time to fire), many disregarded the advice. Small arms fire killed and wounded Tar Heels at every step. Some of the large Federal regiments along the railroad bed were stacked several ranks deep. When Cooke's men approached the railroad, orders rang out for the Federal infantry to stand and fire. "Suddenly, the order 'Fire' rang along our lines," recalled a Federal surgeon. The devastation was indescribable. "Hundreds of Confederates dropped. Others bewildered rushed back, some forward, while our fellows, with a wild cheer, fired volley after volley into them. Not a man seemed to be left standing," noted the surgeon. The 27th North Carolina on the left-center of Cooke's line got within 75 five yards of the Federal line before being forced back. The same bloody greeting slammed into Kirkland's men, who were now under the 44th North Carolina's Col. Thomas Singeltary after a bullet broke Kirkland's left arm. Handfuls of brave Rebels ran and mounted the railroad bank, but were quickly killed or wounded.[27]

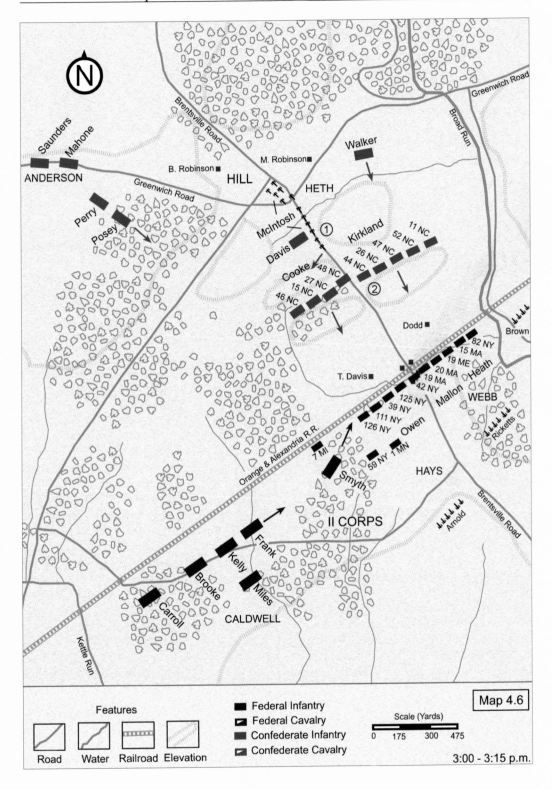

Saunders
Mahone
ANDERSON
Brentsville Road
Greenwich Road
B. Robinson
HILL
M. Robinson
Walker
HETH
Broad Run
Greenwich Road
Perry
Posey
McIntosh
Davis
(1)
Kirkland
47 NC
26 NC
44 NC
52 NC
11 NC
Cooke
48 NC
27 NC
15 NC
46 NC
(2)
Dodd
Brown
82 NY
15 MA
19 ME
20 MA
19 MA
42 NY
Heath
Mallon
WEBB
Ricketts
T. Davis
125 NY
39 NY
111 NY
126 NY
Owen
59 NY 1 MN
HAYS
7 MI
Smyth
Arnold
Brentsville Road
Orange & Alexandria R.R.
II CORPS
Frank
Kelly
Brooke
Miles
Carroll
CALDWELL
Kettle Run

Features

Road   Water   Railroad   Elevation

■ Federal Infantry
◤ Federal Cavalry
■ Confederate Infantry
◤ Confederate Cavalry

Scale (Yards)
0   175   300   475

Map 4.6

3:00 - 3:15 p.m.

Map 4.7: Cooke and Kirkland are Repulsed (October 14: 3:15 - 3:30 p.m.)

Federal casualties paled in comparison to Confederate losses. The 42nd New York had the misfortune of being stationed where the railroad tracks crossed Brentsville Road, and was thus unprotected by the embankment. The steady approach of a wall of enemy infantry was more than some could stand, and they began breaking for the rear (No. 1). Col. Mallon, with sword in hand, rallied his former regiment and brought the men back into line. The recently married officer was pierced soon thereafter by a Rebel bullet and died a short time later. Three other members of his staff were also struck down while rallying the regiment. Command of Mallon's brigade fell to Lt. Col. Ansel Wass of the 19th Massachusetts. Owen's brigade had also taken some losses during its final approach to the railroad, when it was the most exposed to heavy small arms and artillery fire.[28] As the Rebels approached, several general officers made themselves visible to encourage the men. One infantryman wrote after the affair, "Warren, Webb, and Hays, with their staffs . . . gallop up and down along the track, encouraging the men with cheers mingled with imprecations."[29]

The only place along the entire front that offered the Confederates any hope of success was on the far left, where the 11th North Carolina, part of the 52nd North Carolina, and skirmishers from the 47th North Carolina overlapped the right flank of the 82nd New York (Heath's brigade). Despite the heavy oblique fire put down by the New Yorkers, many of the Tar Heels reached the railroad (No. 2). Because of the hot fire thrown at them from the right of Heath's line and the shells pounding them from Brown's battery east of Broad Run, the North Carolinians were unable to roll up the Federal line and were driven back with heavy losses.[30]

While Cooke's men were struggling to close the final yards to the embankment, trouble in the form of an enemy brigade arrived on their right flank. Division leader Brig. Gen. Alexander Hays escorted Col. Thomas Smyth's brigade into position on the left of Owen's brigade along the railroad tracks. Smyth deployed his brigade, from left to right as follows: 108th New York - 12th New Jersey - 14th Connecticut - 1st Delaware (No. 3). The Cooke-Kirkland attack was all but broken by this time, and Hays ordered Smyth's men to cross the railroad and head for Cooke's exposed right flank. When the Tar Heels saw the move, Hall's 46th North Carolina refused its right to face the new threat. The 7th Michigan of Mallon's brigade had been fighting on the skirmish line. When the Confederates attacked, the Wolverines could not find a suitable position in the brigade's main line. Anxious to fight, they slipped west and joined Smyth's brigade, forming between the 108th New York and 12th New Jersey.[31]

By the time Smyth's brigade stepped beyond the tracks, Cooke's and Kirkland's brigades had been decimated. "[A]n order from someone in authority had been given to fall back and our Brigade retired suddenly," recalled a soldier in the 47th North Carolina (No. 4). The problem for the Rebels was how to escape to safety without being shot in the back. Some units moved off in good order. Col. William MacRae of the 15th North Carolina grabbed his regiment's banner and ordered his men into two ranks. Half of the regiment was to fire at the Federal line while the other half fell back a short distance, after which the two parts would reverse roles. This quick-thinking tactical plan saved many lives. MacRae's "firing and withdraw [plan] . . . stayed the enemy and greatly protected the line," wrote one of the grateful survivors. Many other Southern units and men, however, fell apart and fled or surrendered. Chaplain Ezra Simons of the 125th New York watched as the Confederates in front of him were "cut down in great gaps." Many decided it was too dangerous to retreat and threw down their rifles and surrendered. Those who managed to reach the rear and safety would have spotted idle brigades under Joe Davis and Henry Walker (No. 5), neither of which did anything to support the hopeless effort.[32]

All the while Maj. McIntosh had watched the action unfold as the seven or so guns from his battalion did their best to assist the attack. He didn't care for his assigned location, which was exposed and too close to the enemy. When he complained to one of A. P. Hill's aides, the staffer promised to convey the information. Now, with the infantry breaking, McIntosh did his best to support the retreat, without success. All he could do was await further orders.[33]

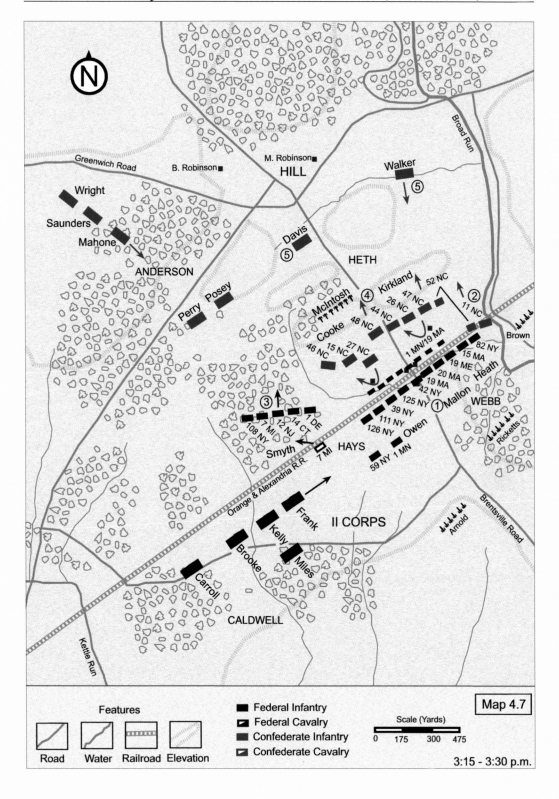

Features

Road | Water | Railroad | Elevation

Federal Infantry
Federal Cavalry
Confederate Infantry
Confederate Cavalry

Scale (Yards)
0   175   300   475

Map 4.7

3:15 - 3:30 p.m.

Map 4.8: Reinforcements Arrive
(October 14: 3:30 - 4:00 p.m.)

The two North Carolina Confederate brigades that made the charge at Bristoe Station suffered heavily. Kirkland lost about 600 men, or 40 percent of his strength; about half (277) were captured. Cooke's losses were even greater at 700 (with 183 captured). Because his brigade was larger, its losses were 27 percent of those engaged. The 27th North Carolina (Cooke) suffered the heaviest, losing 290 of the 416 it carried into battle (nearly 70 percent). The North Carolinians also lost two flags (probably the 26th North Carolina's and either the 47th or 52nd North Carolina's). Walker's Brigade, which was to have supported the attack in general, and Kirkland's left flank in particular, missed almost all the action and lost a dozen men.[34]

Protected by the railroad embankment and fighting on the defensive, Union losses were light. Heath's brigade on the right lost 72 men to all causes, while Mallon's brigade lost 59. Owen's brigade suffered the most with 125 losses, nearly all of whom were lost during its exposed and thus difficult approach to the railroad bed.[35]

Although the main Confederate attack was over, the fighting was not. Now that Cooke's line of battle had disintegrated, McIntosh's seven guns were in serious trouble (No. 1). Already weakened by losses in men and horses as a result of the effective counter-artillery barrage, McIntosh grew alarmed when Cooke's men were "falling back through the guns," reported the artillerist. "My officers joined me in endeavoring to rally and stop them upon the slope in rear of the guns, but without avail." McIntosh fired a few rounds of canister at the approaching enemy infantry and tried to silence their artillery, but a converging fire pounded his position. "I dispatched a messenger hastily to General Hill to say that I was badly enfiladed from the right and regarded the position untenable, which message the general has since informed me he did not receive," reported the major. After riding away briefly to see to the placement of another battery, McIntosh returned to find his seven guns had ceased firing. The pounding Federal shells had killed, wounded, or driven away so many gunners that there were "not enough men left to work the guns." With enemy infantry now bearing down

on his position, "I at once ordered the guns to be dragged down the hill by hand. . . . but at that instant a body of the enemy, apparently skirmishers, appeared stealing over the crest of the hill and in a moment more were among the guns. I saw it was too late to remove them," continued McIntosh, "and directed the limbers and caissons to be drawn off in the edge of the woods, and the men to retire without noise." McIntosh sought help to recapture his pieces, but by the time reinforcements from Walker's command arrived, the Yankees from the 19th Massachusetts and 1st Minnesota had rolled the five undamaged guns safely away. In about one hour of fighting, McIntosh's Battalion lost three men killed, 39 wounded, and 44 horses.[36]

With his brigade aligned, Smyth moved forward into the woods (No. 2). According to the brigade commander, his mission was to "prevent the enemy in our front from moving to the rescue of the enemy's batteries [McIntosh's]." He had advanced about 200 yards when, according to Smyth, "A rebel line then made its appearance about 400 yards from my line, their line of battle moving a little diagonally to mine." Smyth halted and ordered his men to open fire (No. 3). The two Rebel brigades—veteran infantry from Richard Anderson's newly arrived division intended as support for Cooke's right—stopped and returned fire. One was Brig. Gen. Edward Perry's Floridians, and the other a Mississippi command under Brig. Gen. Carnot Posey.[37]

The two sides exchanged fire for only a few minutes. According to a Floridian's account, the 2nd and 8th Florida wheeled to form at right angles to the 5th Florida, presumably to take on Smyth's front and flank. Finding himself in a vulnerable position, Smyth wisely ordered his men to fall back to the Union line at the railroad.[38]

Losses during this phase of the battle were relatively light. According to official tallies, Smyth lost 68 men, Perry lost 24 (three killed, one wounded, and 20 captured), and Posey only lost seven (one killed, two wounded, and four captured). One of the wounded, however, was Gen. Posey, who had been hit in the left thigh by a ball from a spherical case shot. Although his wound was initially believed to be minor, infection set in and Posey died a month later.[39]

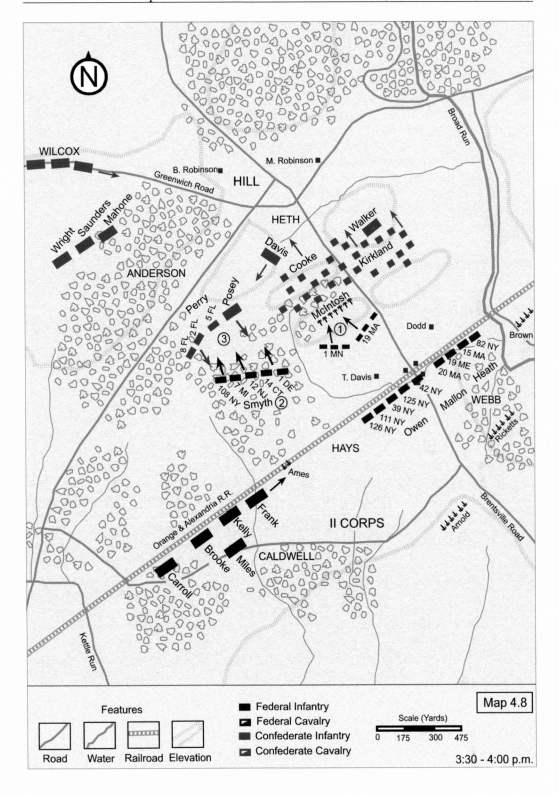

WILCOX

B. Robinson

Greenwich Road

M. Robinson

HILL

HETH

Wright
Saunders
Mahone

Davis

Walker

Cooke

Kirkland

ANDERSON

Perry
5 FL
Posey

McIntosh

8 FL
2 FL
③

①

19 MA

Dodd

Brown

1 MN

82 NY
15 MA
19 ME
20 MA

108 NY
7 MI
12 NJ
14 CT
1 DE

Smyth ②

T. Davis

42 NY

Heath

Mallon

WEBB

125 NY
39 NY
111 NY
126 NY

Owen

Ricketts

HAYS

Orange & Alexandria R.R.

Ames

Frank

II CORPS

Arnold

Brentsville Road

Kelly

Brooke
Miles

CALDWELL

Carroll

Kettle Run

Features

Road   Water   Railroad   Elevation

■ Federal Infantry
◪ Federal Cavalry
■ Confederate Infantry
◪ Confederate Cavalry

Scale (Yards)

0   175   300   475

Map 4.8

3:30 - 4:00 p.m.

Map 4.9: The Confederates Regroup
(October 14: 4:00 - 6:00 p.m.)

Once Perry and Posey were rebuffed and Smyth fell back, both sides spent the hour between 4:00 and 5:00 p.m. realigning their troops and reinforcing their fronts. No one knew whether the fighting was over.

While Smyth was advancing north of the railroad, Caldwell's Federal division arrived and took position on the left of Warren's original line. A brigade under Col. Nelson Miles was not put in line, but was instead split up and portions sent to protect the Federal artillery. Col. Samuel Carroll's brigade (Hays' division) brought up the rear and was positioned facing southwest (No. 1). Two guns from Capt. Nelson Ames' six-gun battery dropped trail along the railroad between Frank and Kelly, while the other four pieces occupied the high ground behind them. Gen. Warren repositioned the batteries already on the field and brought up others to reinforce the line. Brown's battery moved west of Broad Run and deployed next to Arnold. These guns were soon joined by Lt. Frank French's battery. Two other batteries under Capt. Joseph Martin and Lt. Horatio Reed arrived and deployed next to Ames' four guns on the ridge behind the railroad (No. 2) facing northwest toward the Confederate right flank. Two brigades from Gregg's cavalry division arrived after 5:00 p.m. Col. John Taylor's troopers arrived first and deployed across from the bridge over Kettle Run, and Irvin Gregg's cavalry brigade formed on Taylor's left.[40]

Most of the movements and repositioning, however, took place on the Confederate side of the line. The Yankees were still pinned west of Broad Run, and Gen. Lee still had a chance to destroy them. Additional artillery arrived. Capt. William Tanner's Battery galloped into position opposite Ames' two guns near the railroad, where it was joined by a surviving section from McIntosh's Battalion. A. P. Hill reformed his line west of Brentsville Road with Heth's battered division next to the road and Anderson's brigades on Heth's right. Cadmus Wilcox's Division also arrived and took up a position east of Brentsville Road. Twelve out of A. P. Hill's fourteen brigades (Cooke and Kirkland excepted) were fresh and ready for action (No. 3).[41]

The other half of Lee's army, Lt. Gen. Richard Ewell's Second Corps, was approaching Kettle Run from the southwest, squarely on Gen. Warren's left flank. With Broad Run to its right, Hill in its front, and now Ewell coming up on its left, Warren's II Corps was in grave danger of being trapped and destroyed. That level of success, however, would require rapid and coordinated movements on the part of both Confederate corps. After the lack of such a performance at Gettysburg, Lee may well have been anxious about the outcome.[42]

Ewell spurred his horse toward the battlefield with his staff and watched some of the action with Gen. Lee, who rode on to meet with A. P. Hill. The latter suggested that Ewell deploy his corps perpendicular to the railroad and "sweep down on the enemy's flank." Ewell agreed with the plan. Maj. Gen. Jubal Early's Division was the first to arrive on the banks of Kettle Run. Early ordered Brig. Gen. John B. Gordon to deploy his brigade while he brought up the rest of the division. Gordon was in the act of complying when he spotted Federal cavalry and wagons on the far side of Kettle Run. He ordered his men across—without orders and without informing his division commander (No. 4). When he arrived with the rest of his division, Early searched in vain for Gordon. Gordon's command, observed Early after the war, "was more than one-third of my division, and with the other brigades I was not strong enough to advance against the enemy position, especially as there was a very dense thicket of young pines intervening between my position and that of the enemy, which rendered an advance in line almost impossible." The lack of enemy aggression confused Federal Gen. Caldwell, who later observed, "Late in the afternoon a very heavy column moved to my left and partly crossed the track, but for some unexplained reason did not attack with their infantry."[43]

With daylight rapidly fading, Early led the rest of his division across Kettle Run and halted on the right side of Anderson's Division (No. 5). Two divisions under Maj. Gens. Edward Johnson's and Robert Rodes' also approached. Some 40,000 Confederates were arrayed within striking distance of Warren's 11,000 Federals. All Lee's men needed was what they did not have: time.[44]

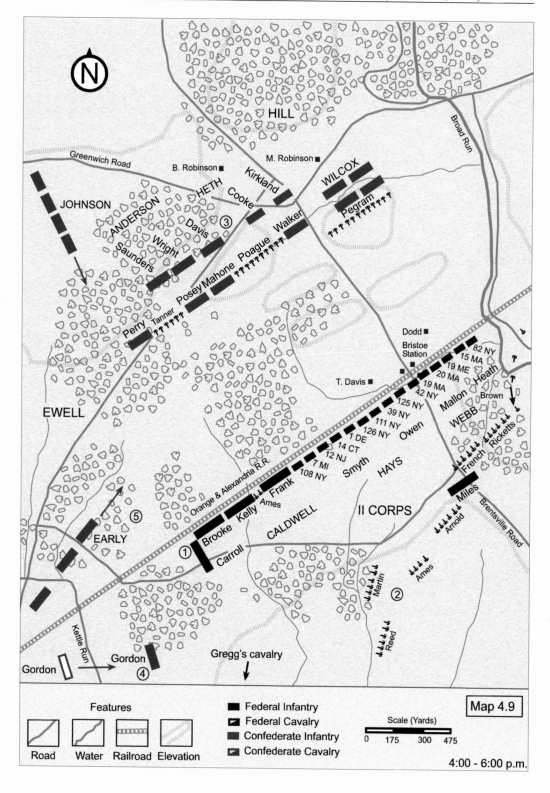

N

HILL

Greenwich Road

B. Robinson ■
M. Robinson ■

JOHNSON

HETH
Kirkland
Cooke

ANDERSON
Davis
③
Wright
Saunders

WILCOX
Pegram

Posey Mahone Poague Walker

Perry Tanner

EWELL

Dodd ■
Bristoe Station
82 NY
15 MA
19 ME
20 MA
19 MA
42 NY
Mallon
Heath
Brown

T. Davis ■
125 NY
39 NY
111 NY
126 NY
Owen
WEBB
French
Ricketts
1 DE
14 CT
12 NJ
7 MI
108 NY
Smyth
HAYS
Miles
Brentsville Road
Brooke Kelly Frank
Ames
①
Carroll
CALDWELL
II CORPS
Arnold
Martin
Ames
②
Reed
⑤
EARLY

Orange & Alexandria R.R.

Kettle Run

Gordon
④
Gordon

Gregg's cavalry

Features

Road   Water   Railroad   Elevation

■ Federal Infantry
◢ Federal Cavalry
■ Confederate Infantry
◢ Confederate Cavalry

Scale (Yards)
0   175   300   475

Map 4.9

4:00 - 6:00 p.m.

Map 4.10: Warren's II Corps Escapes
(October 14: 6:00 - 10:00 p.m.)

John Gordon's untimely and ill-advised advance temporarily cut off the 1st New Jersey Cavalry, but this amounted to nothing. When the rest of the Confederate army facing II Corps stayed put, Gen. Warren ordered his men to shift to their right and begin crossing Broad Run. It was about 9:00 p.m. The dark night aided the withdrawal, as did the officers' commands for the men to keep their remarks to a whisper and their accouterments from clanking as they slipped away. As a young Connecticut soldier recalled it, "in ghostly silence the army was to steal away." During the move, the Federals could clearly hear enemy soldiers talking and the groans of the wounded lying in the fields to their left. By midnight the rearguard had crossed and the Federals were out of harm's way. Warren's exhausted troops marched through the night, and the last of his command crossed Bull Run at Blackburn's Ford about 4:00 a.m. on October 15 and went into bivouac.[45]

Although Warren had occupied an exceptionally strong line along the railroad embankment with ample artillery support, his left flank remained vulnerable throughout the affair. Jubal Early's approaching division was in a perfect position to strike the Federal flank, but neither he nor Ewell was able to take advantage of the rare opportunity. The longer the fight dragged on, however, the more likely it was that Warren would be reinforced, for Sykes' V Corps had reversed its march and was approaching to provide help if needed.[46]

The repercussions of the failed battle began almost as soon as the guns fell silent. A bitterly disappointed (and if angry, justifiably so) Robert E. Lee met with A. P. Hill about 6:30 p.m., just after the shooting died down. Jed Hotchkiss, the distinguished Second Corps cartographer, was present at this meeting. The army commander, he related, exhibited "a great deal of bitter feelings in what he said to Gen. Hill." Uncharacteristically, Lee reprimanded Hill "in the most bitter terms." A private in Early's Division watched as Hill rode away from the meeting "seemingly very much worried."[47]

Hill rode the battlefield with Lee again the next day on October 15. It was a dreary and rainy morning. Lee was still upset by the failure of his lieutenant—despite Hill's effort to put the best spin possible on the battle. According to Brig. Gen. A. L. Long, Lee ended the conversation by telling Hill, "Well general, bury these poor men and let us say no more about it." Others present recalled that Lee continued to speak with some anger to Hill. One claimed Lee told Hill to get his pioneer corps moving and bury these "unfortunate dead." Hill replied that it was all his fault. "Yes, it is your fault," snapped back Lee. "You committed a great blunder yesterday. Your line of battle was too short, too thin and your reserves were too far behind." The Richmond newspapers were even more blunt, calling Hill a woeful blunderer who was guilty of "unpardonable mismanagement." Hill concluded his campaign report by admitting, "I am convinced that I made the attack too hastily"—but then tried to have it both ways when he added that if he had delayed half an hour, "there would have been no enemy to attack. In that event I believe I should equally have blamed myself for not attacking at once."[48]

Some also blamed Gen. Ewell for not vigorously falling upon Warren's flank and destroying II Corps. Young Sandie Pendleton, who had served with Stonewall Jackson and was now on Ewell's staff, wrote ominously home to his mother, "there has been a want of promptness & decisive action, which will surely occur again."[49]

Lee's adjutant, Col. Walter Taylor, criticized Ewell and Hill soon after the battle when he wrote, "we ought to have punished them severely but matters were not managed properly . . . [and] our people were not put in battle correctly." Ironically, Lee is rarely if ever chastised for his own mishandling of the battle. His management of the battle was reminiscent of Gettysburg, a distinctly "hands off" approach in coordinating his two corps, even though both were led by men of questionable ability at that command level.[50]

The reaction from within the ranks centered on more basic concerns. A member of the 16th Mississippi (Posey's Brigade) summed up the enlisted man's view of fighting when he wrote, "we are disappointed at not having an opportunity to capture blankets, &c. which we could use."[51]

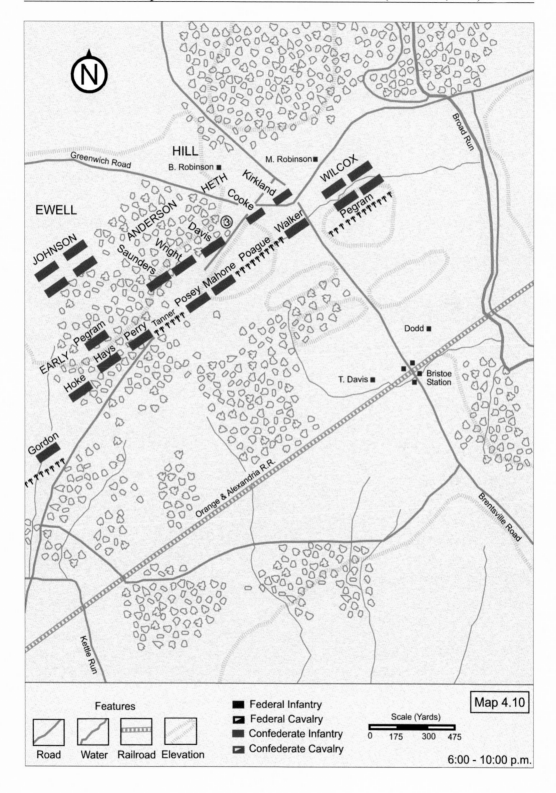

Map 4.10

6:00 - 10:00 p.m.

Map Set 5: General Lee Gives Up the Offensive
(October 15 - 19, 1863)

Map 5.1: The Army of Northern Virginia Retreats (October 15 - 17)

At noon on October 15, Maj. Gen. George Meade wired Maj. Gen. Henry Halleck that the Army of the Potomac "is now at Union Mills, Centreville, Chantilly, and Fairfax County, awaiting the movements of the enemy." Meade placed VI Corps on the right, perpendicular to the Little River Turnpike at Chantilly. On his left was I Corps on the Warrenton Turnpike east of Centreville. II Corps was at Blackburn's and Mitchell's fords on the left of I Corps, and III Corps made up the army's left flank at McLean's Ford and Union Mills on the left of II Corps. V Corps was in reserve near Germantown.

When he was informed that Meade was entrenching behind Bull Run, and that any attempt to continue his movement against the enemy would likely cause Meade to pull back into the strong defenses around Washington, Gen. Robert E. Lee decided to end what would prove to be his last offensive campaign against the Army of the Potomac. Growing shortages of men, a lack of competent corps officers, and dwindling supplies of all kinds mitigated against what was second nature to Lee. Instead of designing another flanking maneuver, he put his men to work destroying the Orange and Alexandria Railroad from Manassas to the Rappahannock River. When this task was finished, the Virginia army began to march south during the afternoon of October 17.[1]

To allow time to complete the destruction of the railroad, Lee dispatched his cavalry to harass Meade's army. Maj. Gen. Jeb Stuart rode from Bristoe Station to Manassas Junction with his entire cavalry corps on the morning of October 15. This was the first time both mounted Confederate divisions had ridden together since the cavalry was reorganized a few months earlier. The aggressive Stuart drove in III Corps pickets on the west side of Bull Run, forcing them to cross the stream and join the main body (No. 1). Stuart was wise enough to know that his cavalry command was no match for III Corps infantry, so he did not institute an aggressive pursuit.[2]

While Stuart (still personally leading Wade Hampton's Division during Hampton's recovery period because of wounds) remained at Manassas, Maj. Gen. Fitz Lee's Division headed to McLean's Ford (No. 2). When scouts spied a large Union Quartermaster wagon train on the west side of Bull Run heading for the safety of Yates's Ford, Stuart sent Brig. Gen. James B. Gordon's Brigade thundering toward the wagons. Instead of wagons, however, the gray cavalrymen encountered veteran troopers from Brig. Gen. John Buford's division guarding the train. A lively skirmish ensued and both sides called up horse artillery. When a guide assured Stuart he knew of a route that would take him to the river and around Buford's left flank, Stuart ordered Gordon to continue fighting while he rode with Col. Oliver Funsten's Brigade to get between the wagon train and the ford. The route proved longer than Stuart had hoped, however, and he did not arrive until nearly dark (No. 3). Once Buford retired across the river, Stuart was dismayed to see the last of the wagons rolling away on the east side of the creek. Prior to taking the "short-cut," Stuart had ordered Fitz Lee to move to Gordon's assistance, and at least a portion of Brig. Gen. Lunsford Lomax's Brigade had engaged the enemy. The Southern cavalry camped near Manassas that night.[3]

The next morning, October 16, Stuart left Fitz Lee's Division at Manassas and rode with Hampton's three brigades toward Groveton. His goal was to cross Bull Run above Sudley Ford and get into the Federal rear north of Centreville. A heavy rain and the muddy roads hindered Stuart's movements (No. 4). The troopers exchanged fire with a VI Corps skirmish line near Groveton and crossed Bull Run at Sudley Ford, bivouacking nearby. Stuart continued his ride the following day, October 17, moving to the Little River Turnpike and then to Gum Springs and on to Frying Pan. There, the lead elements of Col. Pierce Young's Brigade engaged VI Corps infantry. Stuart deployed his troopers to ascertain the position of the Federal army. When a messenger arrived with orders to report to Gen. Lee's army headquarters, Stuart broke off the reconnaissance and rode again on the Little River Turnpike. When he arrived on the evening of October 18, Stuart learned that Lee was pulling the Army of Northern Virginia back toward the Rappahannock River at Rappahannock Station, and that the cavalry was to protect its rear. Any movement promised to be slow because of the recent rains and muddy roads.[4]

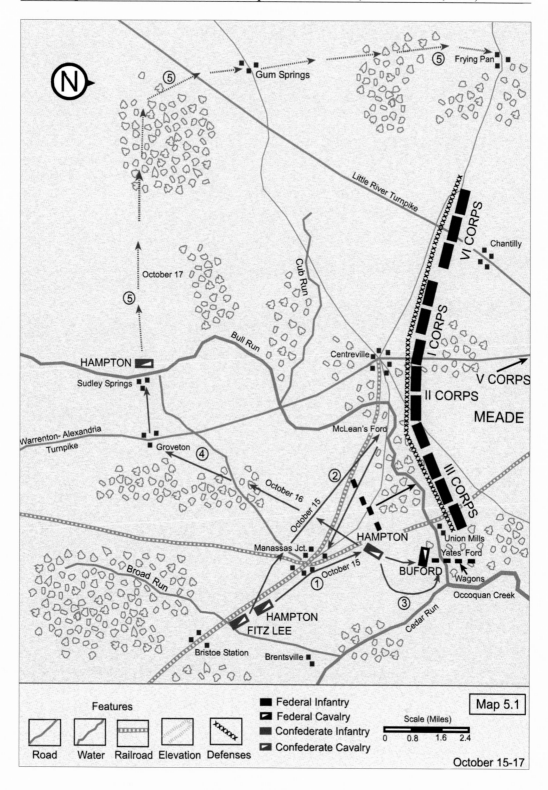

Features

Road   Water   Railroad   Elevation   Defenses

■ Federal Infantry
◹ Federal Cavalry
■ Confederate Infantry
◿ Confederate Cavalry

Scale (Miles)
0   0.8   1.6   2.4

Map 5.1

October 15-17

Map 5.2: The Buckland Races Begin
(October 15 - 19)

Meade's skillful westward withdrawal of his army and the rebuff of A. P. Hill's assault at Bristoe Station pleased newspaper editors, but not President Abraham Lincoln or the members of his cabinet. Halleck and Lincoln struggled with the idea that Meade was much like George B. McClellan, erroneously swelling Lee's army and thinking that he was about to attacked by superior numbers. Both misperceptions were evident in a wire Meade sent to Halleck on October 15 in which Meade estimated Lee's strength at 80,000, who "are advancing on me, their plan being to secure the Bull Run field in advance of me." He openly worried he would be forced away from the east side of Bull Run and back toward the Washington defenses. A quick and thinly veiled chastisement reached Meade: "Reports from Richmond make Lee's present force only 55,000 [in fact, closer to 45,000]. Is he not trying to bully you, while the mass of the rebel armies are concentrating against Rosecrans? I cannot see it in any other light." The telegram concluded, "Instead of retreating, I think you ought to give him battle. From all the information I can get, his force is very much inferior to yours." Although signed by Halleck, it was actually penned by Lincoln.[5]

Unhappy with Meade's continued defensiveness, Lincoln wrote a letter to Halleck, who in turn forwarded it to Meade on October 16. The president reasoned that the Army of the Potomac outnumbered Lee's command by at least 35,000 men, and that Lee was operating too far from his base of supplies. This was indeed the time to attack, urged the president. Lincoln generously wrote that "the honor will be his [Meade's] if he succeeds, and the blame may be mine [Lincoln's] if he fails." Meade replied that he had not aggressively engaged Lee because he had not found a "field no more than equal for us." Perhaps Meade was looking for another Gettysburg-type of battlefield, where he could take up a powerful position and let Lee throw his men against his bayonets. After the fiasco in Pennsylvania, it was doubtful Lee was going to accommodate Meade. Members of Lincoln's cabinet were also beginning to question Halleck's competence because of his inability to get more

out of the many past commanders of the Eastern army.[6]

When Meade learned of Lee's withdrawal after destroying many miles of railroad tracks on the Orange and Alexandria Railroad, he worried that the move signaled Lee's intention to transfer more troops to the Western Theater. That, in turn, would drain more men from his own army. Meade decided to act quickly and decisively. Quickness meant cavalry, and on October 18, Brig. Gen. Judson Kilpatrick's division was sent riding west on the Warrenton-Alexandria Turnpike to find Stuart's troopers. Kilpatrick found Stuart with Hampton's Division near Groveton. With his superior numbers on high quality mounts, Kilpatrick drove the Rebel troopers toward Gainesville. Kilpatrick spun off part of Brig. Gen. Henry Davies' brigade and ordered it toward Haymarket, where it collided with Col. Pierce Young's Brigade in the afternoon. The two sides fought until darkness ended the hostilities. Meanwhile, Kilpatrick with Brig. Gen. George Custer's brigade and the rest of Davies' brigade faced Brig. Gen. Thomas Rosser's and Gordon's brigades east of Gainesville. The incessant rains had turned the roads into muddy thoroughfares, hindering fighting and movements.[7]

Lee's men crossed the Rappahannock River on a pontoon bridge near the destroyed Orange and Alexandria Railroad bridge on October 19. Walter Taylor, one of Lee's staff members, noted that "after destroying the railroad as far as practical, General Lee retired by easy stages to his former position on the Rappahannock, where his army could be more easily supplied." The marches were anything but "easy" given their length (some as much as thirty miles with few rests) and the condition of the roads.

By comparison, Meade's movements on this day were modest. His men crossed Bull Run and marched two or three miles beyond it. I Corps was to march along the Warrenton Turnpike to Haymarket, followed by VI Corps, which was to halt for the night at Gainesville. To the south, III Corps had orders to march along the Orange and Alexandria Railroad to Broad Run, near Bristoe Station, while II Corps made passage for the Milford along the same waterway. Meade's reserve corps, the V, was to march to Groveton. Buford's and Brig. Gen. David Gregg's divisions guarded the flanks of the Federal army.[8]

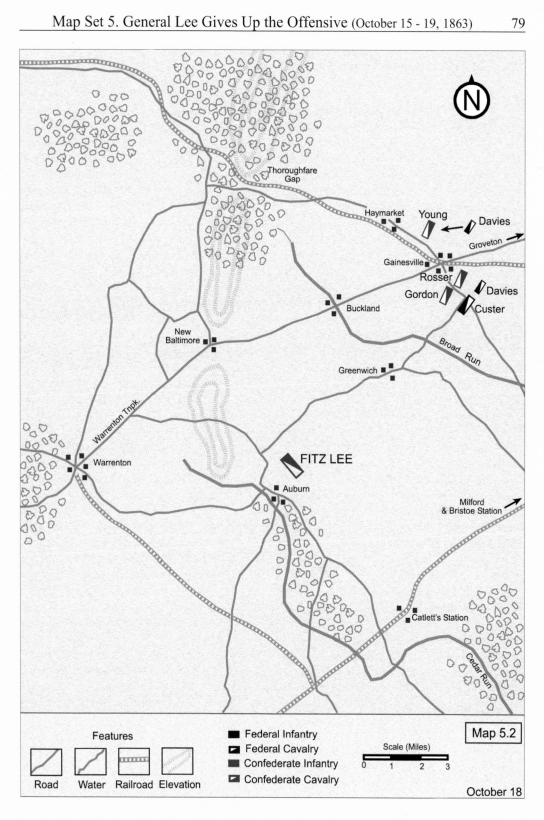

Thoroughfare
Gap

Haymarket   Young   Davies

Groveton

Gainesville

Rosser   Davies

Gordon   Custer

Buckland

New
Baltimore

Broad Run

Greenwich

Warrenton Tnpk.

FITZ LEE

Warrenton

Auburn

Milford
& Bristoe Station

Catlett's Station

Cedar Run

Features

■ Federal Infantry
▰ Federal Cavalry
■ Confederate Infantry
▰ Confederate Cavalry

Scale (Miles)

0   1   2   3

Road Water Railroad Elevation

Map 5.2

October 18

Map 5.3: The Buckland Races Continue
(October 19)

Jeb Stuart crossed a swollen Broad Run with his command during the evening of October 18. He believed the west bank of the high-flowing river held promise in repelling Kilpatrick's cavalry division. The cavalier deployed his sharpshooters along the bank and carefully arranged his artillery. He also sent orders to Fitz Lee to come up from Auburn and protect his right flank.

Custer's Union brigade, meanwhile, approached Broad Run on the morning of October 19 and encountered Confederate skirmishers from Young's Brigade lining the east bank. After deploying three of his regiments, Custer pushed the enemy troopers across the river and ordered a frontal assault against the dismounted Confederates from Gordon's Brigade on the western shore. It was about 10:00 a.m. Kilpatrick called Gordon's defensive effort a "determined stand," and Custer admitted in his report that these initial attempts proved "fruitless" in driving the enemy away (No. 1). Kilpatrick and Custer abandoned this tactic in favor of crossing at a bridge and a ford farther up and down river, respectively. Before long the Michiganders were on both of Gordon's flanks, forcing the brigadier to withdraw his command toward New Baltimore (No. 2).[9]

The Federals almost experienced a significant setback at this time. Custer, together with his staff, had dismounted by the stone bridge over Broad Run to reconnoiter and talk to his men. Rebel gunners spotted the buzz of activity and planted a shell in the midst of the group of officers. The round failed to explode and no one was killed or wounded. Had the round detonated, there is a good change it would have seriously injured or killed the Boy General and many others.[10]

While Gordon's men were falling back, Stuart received word that Fitz Lee's Division had arrived and was riding toward his right flank. Fitz introduced a new idea to his superior. Stuart, he suggested, should continue retreating and lure Kilpatrick's men after him. Lee's command would then strike Kilpatrick's left flank and rear, "inflicting upon him severe injury." The plan was

a good one and Stuart readily agreed. There was no time to spare.[11]

Kilpatrick halted his own advance for about an hour while awaiting word from scouting parties reconnoitering toward Thoroughfare Gap and Auburn. The scouts returned with the encouraging news that no enemy troops had been detected in either direction. Kilpatrick ordered Col. Davies' brigade to head toward New Baltimore. Davies, who had been in reserve behind Custer, took the lead about noon while Custer remained in Buckland. Custer's orders were to follow Davies, but he would have none of it. His men had fought all through the morning, and had finally driven the enemy through the town and out toward New Baltimore. His men were exhausted, and Custer wanted them and their mounts to eat a leisurely meal before moving out for another round of hard riding and fighting. Kilpatrick was not aware of this development as he rode ahead with Davies.[12]

Davies' men encountered Stuart's troopers about a mile west of Buckland and began pushing them toward New Baltimore (No. 3). After the encounter, some of the Federals recalled believing at the time that the enemy troopers were retreating too easily. Riding into New Baltimore, Kilpatrick ordered Davies to leave a detachment in the town and to continue pushing after Stuart. The latter appears to have halted his men behind a low line of hills (Chestnut Hill) about two and one-half miles east of Warrenton. It was now 3:30 p.m. Davies' men were approaching Chestnut Hill when they heard cannonading in their rear—Fitz Lee's troops had arrived from Auburn (No. 4). Kilpatrick initially hoped the noise indicated that his third brigade under Brig. Gen. Wesley Merritt had come up. The division leader sent a detail to make sure, but learned within a short time that Rebels were approaching his rear. Kilpatrick likely believed Custer was behind him, but Custer and his troopers were still around Buckland at this time.[13]

While waiting for Davies' approach, Stuart deployed his cavalry with Gordon's Brigade perpendicular to the Warrenton Turnpike and Rosser's and Young's troopers on each flank. When the sound of firing was heard (Fitz Lee's arrival from Auburn), Stuart ordered his command forward (No. 5).[14]

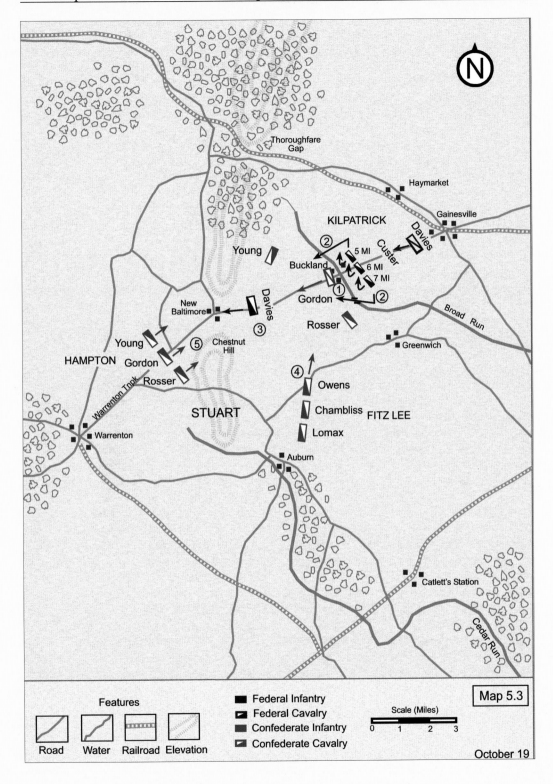

Thoroughfare
Gap

Haymarket

Gainesville

KILPATRICK

Davies

Young

5 MI

Custer

Buckland

6 MI

7 MI

Gordon

New
Baltimore

Davies

Rosser

Broad Run

③

Greenwich

Young

Chestnut
Hill

HAMPTON   Gordon

④

Owens

Rosser

Chambliss   FITZ LEE

STUART

Lomax

Warrenton Tnpk.

Warrenton

Auburn

Catlett's Station

Cedar Run

Features

| Road | Water | Railroad | Elevation |

Federal Infantry
Federal Cavalry
Confederate Infantry
Confederate Cavalry

Scale (Miles)

0   1   2   3

Map 5.3

October 19

Map 5.4: Buckland Races: The Federals Fall Back (October 19: 3:30 - 6:30 p.m.)

Now began a fast-moving cavalry battle involving "confusing attacks and multiple engagements . . . all of which were made possible by the nexus of roads in and around Buckland." The accounts of this fighting submitted by both sides dramatically differ, which make it even more difficult than usual to comprehend the fluid combat.[15]

Knowing that he couldn't remain for long in Buckland when his commanding officer had ordered him to follow Davies' brigade, Custer put his men back on their horses. He sent the 7th Michigan riding south to reconnoiter as far as Greenwich (No. 1) and protect the left flank, while the 1st West Virginia was sent north toward Haymarket to protect the right flank (No. 2). The 6th Michigan held the important stone bridge over Broad Run. With his remaining regiments and guns—the 1st and 5th Michigan and the 1st Vermont, along with the six guns of Lt. Alexander Pennington's battery—Custer moved off to rejoin Kilpatrick and Davies. Danger lurked behind them as the column trotted down the Warrenton Turnpike. Troopers of the 6th Michigan guarding the bridge noticed mounted men approaching. Any doubt as to their identity ended when they fired at the Wolverines, who dismounted, formed a line of battle behind a fence, and returned fire with their Spencer repeating carbines. The Wolverines were battling Col. Thomas Owen's Brigade of Fitz Lee's Division (No. 3). The encounter was a bitter disappointment for Fitz Lee, who had expected to slam into the exposed Yankee left flank and rear instead of a strong line of battle.[16]

The rest of Custer's brigade had not ridden far when the fight at Buckland began, so Custer rushed his troopers back to the town and deployed his brigade into a strong defensive line. The 1st Vermont formed on the left, and the 5th Michigan and 7th Michigan (back from its scouting) formed the brigade's right flank. The 6th Michigan was thrown out on the skirmish line and the 1st Michigan was kept in reserve (No. 4). Pennington's battery dropped trail and opened fire. Custer and his men were dismayed to see that the powerful Confederate line in front of them extended for more than a mile. The general noted in his report that his men "poured a destructive fire upon the enemy as he advanced but failed to force him back." Believing that he was facing a large infantry force, and having expended much of his ammunition during the morning fight to get across Broad Run, Custer had little choice but to re-cross the bridge to safety with the 1st Michigan acting as the rearguard. Custer's men attempted to hold the bridge in case Davies' men also tried to use it. With their carbine ammunition expended, the men resorted to their Colt revolvers. A short time later, Custer abandoned the bridge and rode with his exhausted men to Gainesville.[17]

While Fitz Lee was forcing Custer to retreat, a more serious situation developed farther west where Stuart was preparing to charge Davies' brigade. When Gordon approached Maj. Rufus Barringer of the 1st North Carolina with orders to "Charge that Yankee line and break it," Barringer ordered his men to unsheath their sabers and, with a mighty Rebel Yell, they galloped toward the shocked Northern cavalrymen. Within the span of only minutes, the pursuers had become the prey. The rest of the brigade followed the 1st North Carolinians (No. 5). The Yankees emptied their carbines into the Tar Heels before fleeing.

When Davies learned that Custer's men had been forced across Broad Run and that a large Rebel force was between him and the stream, he ordered his men to ride north while the 2nd New York and 1st West Virginia remained behind as a rearguard. Believing that continued defense was fruitless, Davies ordered "every man for himself." The men took the road heading for Thoroughfare Gap and veered east to head for Haymarket and the Federal I Corps infantry gathering there (No. 6). As one North Carolinian recalled, "we chased them for miles galloping our horses as fast as they could go." According to Federal I Corps commander John Newton, he sent out an infantry brigade that "succeeded in preserving one brigade (I think Custer's) . . . Kilpatrick's main body came in . . . in great confusion." The fluid affair, known as the "Bucktown Races," resulted in the capture of scores of men, though Kilpatrick was able to extract most of his division.[18]

The fluid combat cost Kilpatick about 200 men, and Stuart probably fewer than 50.[19]

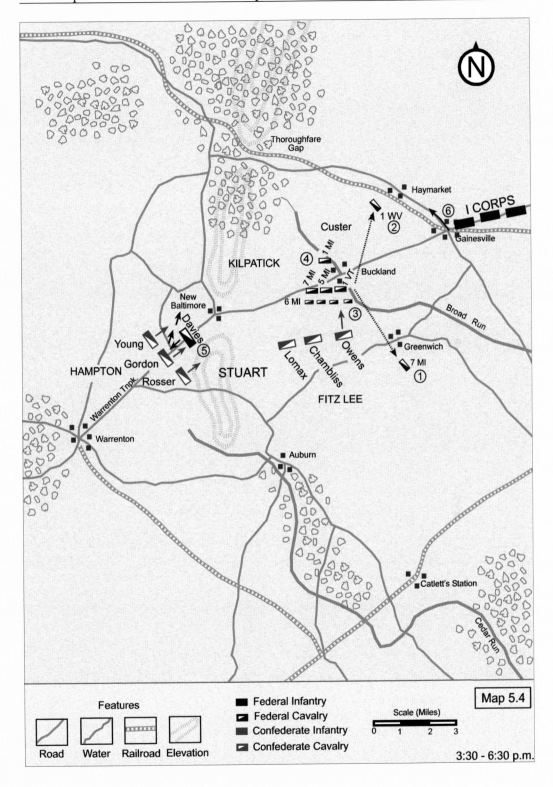

Map 5.4

3:30 - 6:30 p.m.

Map Set 6: Prelude to Mine Run (October 18 - November 7)

Map 6.1: Meade is Ordered to Move on Lee (October 20 - 23)

Maj. Gen. George Meade's Army of the Potomac, which began moving from behind Bull Run to probe Gen. Robert E. Lee's positions on October 18, continued marching the following day. A steady stream of reinforcements swelled the Northern ranks. Despite the loss of XI and XII corps to the Western Theater, returns for the month showed a strength of 95,455. By October 23, the army was deployed on a line running from around Warrenton to Catlett's Station in the following manner and strength: I Corps (13,819) at Georgetown; II Corps (12,556) deployed where the Warrenton Branch Railroad crossed Turkey Run; III Corps (18,659) at Catlett's Station, with one brigade at Bristoe; V Corps (13,185) at New Baltimore; and VI Corps (17,734) near Warrenton. In addition to the infantry, Meade counted 13,687 in his cavalry corps, 2,974 in his artillery reserve, 1,527 engineering troops, and 1,364 assigned to headquarters.[1]

With an army of this size, President Abraham Lincoln and Maj. Gen. Henry Halleck expected Meade to resume the offensive against Lee's Army of Northern Virginia. Neither man was happy with the telegram they received during the evening of October 20. In it, Meade informed them that Lee's army was safely behind the Rappahannock River and had left a destroyed railroad in his wake. After explaining the several problems he would entail moving his troops toward a confrontation with Lee, Meade concluded, "I am afraid the time it will take to repair the [rail]road and the difficulty of advance without the railroad, will preclude my preventing the sending of troops to the southwest by the enemy." Meade continued this theme the next day, writing, "the Orange and Culpeper Railroad has been destroyed from Bristoe Station to Culpeper Court-House. To repair and put in working order . . . will require the use of a considerable part of this army for guards and working parties. . . . It seems to me, therefore, that the campaign is virtually over for the present season, and that it would be better to withdraw the army to some position in front of Washington." Halleck's ominous response arrived that night: "If you can conveniently leave your army, the President wishes to see you tomorrow." Provost Marshall Marsena Patrick lamented, "Meade's head is tolerably clear, generally, but when he gets 'Lee on the Brain' he errs thro' timidity."[2]

Meade rode to Gainesville from his headquarters at Warrenton on the morning of October 22. Entering the station, he changed into new clothing suitable for a meeting with the president. A private car awaited the army commander and by that afternoon Meade was in Washington and heading for Halleck's office. After the meeting, the two officers proceeded to the White House. "[T]he President was, as he always is, very considerate and kind," Meade wrote to his wife after their meeting. "He found no fault with my operations, although it was very evident he was disappointed that I had not got a battle out of Lee." Meade later maintained that during the meeting Lincoln agreed that "there was not much to be gained by a farther advance." Because it was late, Meade and his staff spent the night in the capital before returning to the army the next morning.[3]

Given his perception of the meeting, Meade must have been surprised when he received the following message from Halleck on October 24: "The President desires that you will prepare to attack Lee's army." There was no arguing the point, so Meade set to work devising a plan of action. His efforts were aided by Col. Daniel McCallum, Superintendent of Military Railroads, who was able to repair the Orange and Alexandria Railroad as far south as Warrenton Junction by November 1.[4]

Lee's Army of Northern Virginia had also been reinforced during the autumn of 1863, but its numbers paled in comparison to the Army of the Potomac. According to the October 31 report, Lt. Gen Richard Ewell's Second Corps contained 21,782 men, and Lt. Gen. A. P. Hill's Third Corps sported 20,826. The addition of nearly 10,000 cavalry and another 4,863 in the artillery gave Lee 57,251 men. His soldiers settled into camps on the south side of the Rappahannock River, many fairly confident—or at least hopeful—that the active campaigning season for 1863 had come to an end.[5]

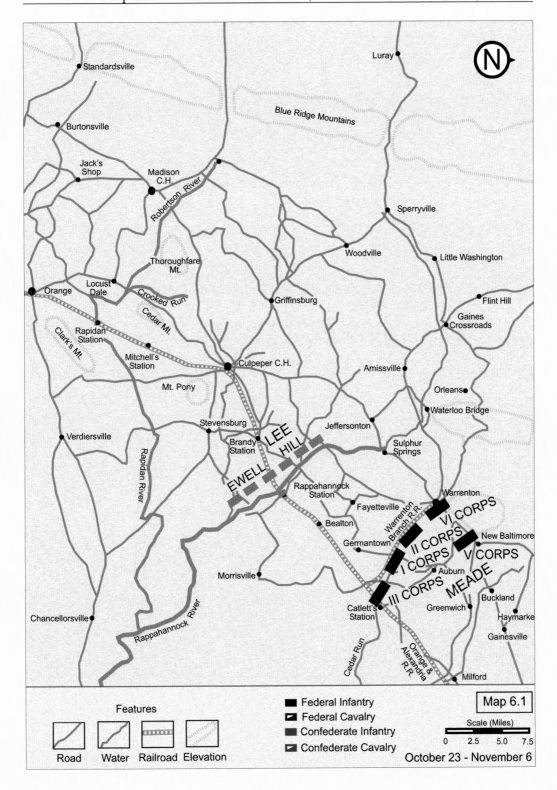

Luray

N

Standardsville

Blue Ridge Mountains

Burtonsville

Jack's
Shop

Madison
C.H.

Sperryville

Robertson River

Thoroughfare
Mt.

Woodville

Little Washington

Griffinsburg

Orange

Locust
Dale

Crooked Run

Cedar Mt.

Flint Hill

Gaines
Crossroads

Clark's Mt.

Rapidan
Station

Mitchell's
Station

Culpeper C.H.

Amissville

Orleans

Mt. Pony

Waterloo Bridge

Stevensburg

Jeffersonton

Verdiersville

Brandy
Station

LEE
HILL

EWELL

Rapidan River

Sulphur
Springs

Rappahannock
Station

Warrenton

Fayetteville

Warrenton
Branch R.R.

VI CORPS

Bealton

II CORPS

Germantown

I CORPS

New Baltimore

Morrisville

Auburn

V CORPS

III CORPS

MEADE

Buckland

Greenwich

Haymarke

Chancellorsville

Rappahannock River

Catlett's
Station

Gainesville

Cedar Run

Orange &
Alexandria
R.R.

Milford

Features

Features legend:
- Road
- Water
- Railroad
- Elevation

■ Federal Infantry
▨ Federal Cavalry
■ Confederate Infantry
▨ Confederate Cavalry

Map 6.1

Scale (Miles)

0   2.5   5.0   7.5

October 23 - November 6

Map 6.2: Meade Ponders His Options
(October 23 - November 6)

After nearly constant campaigning, Union and Confederate troopers especially welcomed the reprieve offered by the two-week period encompassing the end of October and beginning of November. Both sides used this time to rest men and horses and refit equipment after suffering moderate losses during the October 9-22 fighting. Maj. Gen. Alfred Pleasonton reported 1,251 killed, wounded, and missing, while Maj. Gen. Jeb Stuart reported 435 from all causes. The hard actions had also taken a toll on horseflesh. Brig. Gen. John Buford noted that of his 2,000 men and horses present for duty, only half of his animals were capable of enduring a sustained campaign. Southern mounts were in even worse overall condition.[6]

Safely behind the Rappahannock, most of the Rebels believed the fighting was over until the spring. Many were disappointed they had not been able to secure the blankets and clothing needed to weather another winter. Gen. Lee was unsure whether Meade would venture south again before the cold winds of winter descended upon northern Virginia. "If I could only get some shoes and clothes for the men," wrote Lee, "I would save him [Meade] the trouble."

Lee's position along the river was fairly strong, with Ewell's Corps extending from Kelly's Ford east to just above the railroad bridge at Rappahannock Station. Hill's Corps continued the line west and guarded a number of fords. Stuart's cavalry patrolled both flanks. Two points remained especially vulnerable: Kelly's Ford and Rappahannock Station. The wooded bluff on the northern bank at Kelly's Ford (part of Ewell's sector) commanded the southern bank. Lee knew he would have a problem successfully repelling a determined attack there even if he brought up reinforcements. Instead of fighting along the river at that point, he established a stronger position behind it. Farther west, Lee deployed a tete-de-pont on the north side of the river at Rappahannock Station. This bridgehead was designed to force Meade to split his army, thereby reducing the number of troops moving against Kelly's Ford and hopefully delay a Federal advance until reinforcements could be rushed to the area.[7]

Meade used this quiet period to plan his next move. Never known for his sunny personality, Meade had been especially difficult during the fall campaign. Periodically his anger and frustration boiled over, and woe to the officers or men near him at the time. His staff called him "Great Peppery" during this time. It was only in hindsight that Meade realized he had spent too much time worrying about his supply lines. On reflection, Meade observed that "Lee was slow and ought to have been farther ahead as I supposed he was at the time." He felt unjustly criticized by Lincoln and Halleck and was frustrated by their routine rejection of his plans. Meade had offered his resignation several times since winning the battle of Gettysburg, but each time Lincoln and Halleck reassured him of their support and backed away from pressing him into hasty action. Both realized the political consequences of allowing the resignation of the first general to beat Robert E. Lee on the battlefield.[8]

Meade was also losing the confidence of his men. A junior officer noted the army did little but "useless marching and countermarching," adding that "everyone in the army from the highest to the lowest, have lost all confidence in Gen. Meade as a fighting man." A Pennsylvania officer wrote, "we will never do much until some determined man gets command & then catching us by the neck, so to speak, holds us up and forces the fighting." He would get his wish the following spring.[9]

While President Jefferson Davis in Richmond and his own soldiers continued to support him with unwavering trust, Gen. Lee wrestled with his own demons, including his ill-fated invasion of Pennsylvania, which had been successful through the first day of fighting at Gettysburg. Other more tangible challenges included his ongoing concern about the well-being of his men due to a lack of adequate supplies, and by his own lingering health problems. His "violent back pains" were probably the result of the chronic heart problems that would kill him in 1870.[10]

Except for a few forays by elements of both armies, it was a fairly quiet time. Lee expected an end of hostilities for the winter and invited his daughter-in-law, Charlotte Rooney, to visit his camp. His tent, wrote the general, was "in a nice pine thicket and Perry [his manservant] is today engaged in constructing a chimney in front, which will make it warm & comfortable."[11]

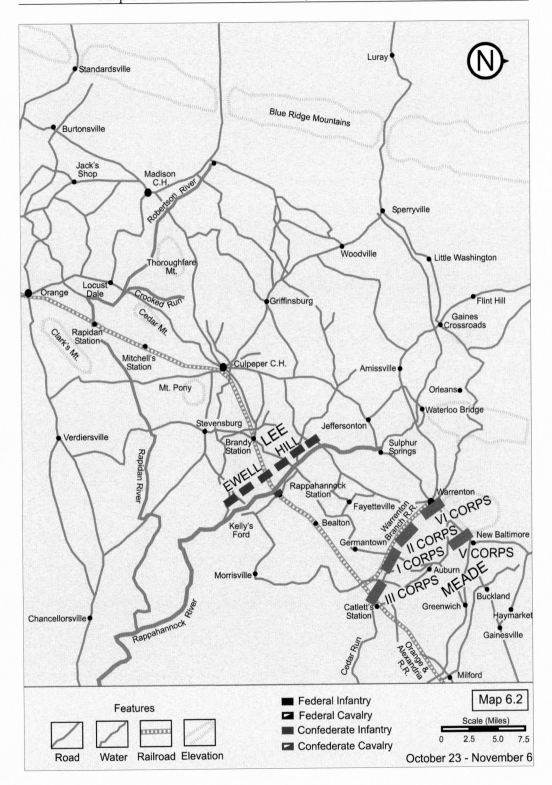

Map 6.3: Meade Boldly Strikes
(November 7)

Like his opponent, Meade was also influenced by a number of factors as he planned his advance against Lee's army ensconced behind the Rappahannock River. Writing to his wife during the latter part of October, Meade admitted that Lee had outgeneraled him during the Bristoe Campaign: "[T]his was a deep game, and I am free to admit that in the playing of it he has got the advantage of me." While he had not suffered any major setbacks, the campaign did indeed bruise his ego. The burden of command responsibility weighed heavily on him. Friends noted with some surprise when they saw him in Washington on October 22, that his "hair and beard were growing prematurely gray and that he was looking a little worn."[12]

Meade never liked the Orange and Alexandria Railroad as the major line of communication, and was unable to discern any weaknesses in Lee's lines. In a telegram sent on November 2, Meade suggested swinging around Lee's right flank, throwing the "whole army rapidly and secretly across the Rappahannock at Banks's Ford and Fredericksburg, and [take] position on the heights [Marye's] beyond the town." Such a move, believed Meade, would force Lee to abandon the Rappahannock line and assume the offensive against a strong position of Meade's choosing. This new position would also permit his army to be easily resupplied by railroad or waterway. Halleck disagreed and wired back the next day, "an entire change of base under existing circumstances, I can neither advise nor approve." According to one interpretation, the "rejection of Meade's proposal can be viewed as a subtle evaluation of their [Lincoln's and Halleck's] concerns about Meade's offensive spirit, a logical view considering his retreat before Lee's numerically inferior army during the Bristoe campaign."[13]

Meade, explained one of his aides, had three objectives as he planned what would become known as the Mine Run Campaign: (1) Catch Lee in a corner and fight a decisive defensive battle; (2) Prevent Lee from catching the Army of the Potomac in a corner; and (3) Cover Washington and Maryland.[14]

When his November 2 proposal was rejected, Meade set to work on a new set of plans, which he completed on November 5. He would split the army into two wings. Maj. Gen. John Sedgwick would command the right wing, composed of his own VI Corps and V Corps. This wing would begin its 17-mile march from Warrenton to its destination at Rappahannock Station. Maj. Gen. William French would lead the other wing, taking his own III Corps, together with I Corps and II Corps, and head from the vicinity of Warrenton Junction to Kelly's Ford. The movements were scheduled to begin at daybreak on November 7. Buford's cavalry division had orders to screen the right side of the army, while Judson Kilpatrick's division performed the same duty on the left; David Gregg's division would remain in reserve guarding the supply trains and the lines of communication.[15]

Given the superior terrain of the north bank, Meade believed that French's wing would have the greatest chance of success at Kelly's Ford. Once across the river, the three corps were to swing west to assist Sedgwick's troops in forcing their way across the Rappahannock River at Rappahannock Station. The two columns would then move quickly on Brandy Station where they would attempt to intercept Lee's army, which by that time should be retreating toward the Rapidan River. Should the fortifications at Rappahannock Station prove too formidable, Sedgwick would have the discretion to move east and cross at Kelly's Ford. A modern military officer called Meade's plans, "remarkable for their clarity and completeness . . . [the] overall operational concept was simple and direct."[16]

The Federal troops marched rapidly toward their destinations. Their trek was made easier because they left much of their equipment and wagons behind. Without the wagons, the men were supplied with eight days of rations—hardtack and pork—which hindered their progress. V Corps headed to Rappahannock Station and arrived there about 11:00 a.m. to await the arrival of VI Corps about an hour later. The van of French's left wing halted at noon at Mount Holly Church, about one mile northeast of Kelly Ford.[17]

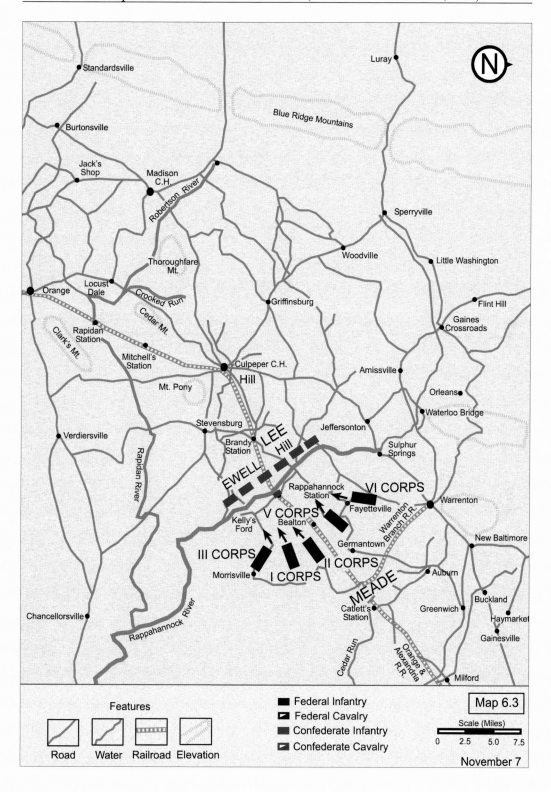

Standardsville

Luray

Blue Ridge Mountains

Burtonsville

Jack's
Shop

Madison
C.H.

Robertson River

Sperryville

Thoroughfare
Mt.

Woodville

Little Washington

Orange

Locust
Dale

Crooked Run

Cedar Mt.

Griffinsburg

Flint Hill

Gaines
Crossroads

Clark's Mt.

Rapidan
Station

Mitchell's
Station

Culpeper C.H.

Hill

Amissville

Orleans

Waterloo Bridge

Mt. Pony

Stevensburg

Jeffersonton

Sulphur
Springs

Verdiersville

Rapidan River

Brandy
Station

LEE
Hill

EWELL

Rappahannock
Station

VI CORPS

Warrenton

V CORPS

Fayetteville

Warrenton Branch R.R.

New Baltimore

Kelly's
Ford

Bealton

III CORPS

Germantown

II CORPS

Auburn

Buckland

Morrisville

I CORPS

MEADE

Greenwich

Haymarket

Chancellorsville

Rappahannock River

Catlett's
Station

Gainesville

Cedar Run

Orange & Alexandria R.R.

Milford

Features

Road   Water   Railroad   Elevation

■ Federal Infantry
◨ Federal Cavalry
■ Confederate Infantry
◨ Confederate Cavalry

Map 6.3

Scale (Miles)
0   2.5   5.0   7.5

November 7

Map Set 7: The Affair at Rappahannock Station
(November 7, 1863)

Map 7.1: Lee's Position at Rappahannock Station
(November 7: 6:00 - 11:00 a.m.)

Gen. Robert E. Lee's decision to place troops in a fortification on the north side of the Rappahannock River is a curious one. Southern troops built what was originally a pair of forts earlier in the war to prevent an enemy incursion toward the river. However, after capturing the area, Union engineers worked from September 3 through September 22, 1863, to modify the works to repulse an attack from the south. Lee's engineers did their best to return the fortification to its original orientation.

There were other problems with this position. A dam upriver had raised the level of the Rappahannock River, which was now deep and unfordable at this point. The Orange and Alexandria Railroad bridge spanning the river had been destroyed by the Yankees when they abandoned the area in October. In an effort to compensate for its loss, Lee threw a pontoon bridge across the river about 800 yards north of the destroyed bridge. This solution, however, offered limited access to and from the north bank. Moving large numbers of troops quickly in either direction was virtually impossible. The upshot was that any troops stationed above the Rappahannock in the fort had their backs to an inhospitable river with little hope of speedy reinforcement.

Two forts constituted the heart of these earthworks. The smaller of the two was about 100 feet from the railroad, while the larger fort was 400 feet farther west. A mile-long infantry trench on a low ridge connected the two works and extended beyond each one to the river. Both flanks were vulnerable. On the right, the enemy could use the railroad embankment for cover and, when within as close as 100 feet, launch an attack against the smaller fort. The left side of the trench was poorly positioned, for it allowed an enemy to approach without being seen until they were almost upon the Confederate works. The ground behind the small fort dropped sharply to the swollen river, while the area behind the larger fort was more gradually sloped.

The labor Lee's engineers performed did little to improve any of the defenses. One oversight was their failure to construct a ditch in front of the Confederate line, which would have hampered a Federal advance. They also failed to erect abatis. Firepower alone would have to repulse any assault, and that possibility left much to be desired. The four pieces of artillery deployed in the forts were poorly positioned because of the layout of the works, which made it impossible to sweep large areas to their front with cannon fire. The infantry trench was similarly ineffective because it was dug on the southern slope (facing the river). In order to see over the top of the ridge in the direction from which the Federals would approach, a soldier had to stand up and look over, which increased his vulnerability to enemy fire. In an effort to compensate for the especially vulnerable right flank of this line, the Confederates built infantry and artillery works on the far (south) side of the river, which also covered the approaches to the pontoon bridge.[1]

One strength of this position was that a veteran brigade of Louisiana infantry under Brig. Gen. Harry Hays (Early's Division, Ewell's Second Corps) occupied the fortifications on November 7. These experienced troops boasted an outstanding record of service in some of the hottest fighting the war had yet witnessed. These men from the Deep South, however, had to deal with the poorly situated forts as well as the absence of their commander, who was serving on a Court of Inquiry. Col D. B. Penn, a 27-year-old from the 7th Louisiana, was in charge of the brigade during Hays' absence. Only the 9th Louisiana was deployed in the works and behind and between the forts. The 6th, 7th, and 8th Louisiana regiments were deployed about a quarter of a mile in front of the line. The brigade's remaining regiment, the 5th Louisiana, was fortunate enough to find itself on the south bank of the river. These men had replaced James Walker's Stonewall Brigade the day before. Two pieces of the Louisiana Guard Artillery under Lt. Robert Moore were unlimbered in each fort.[2]

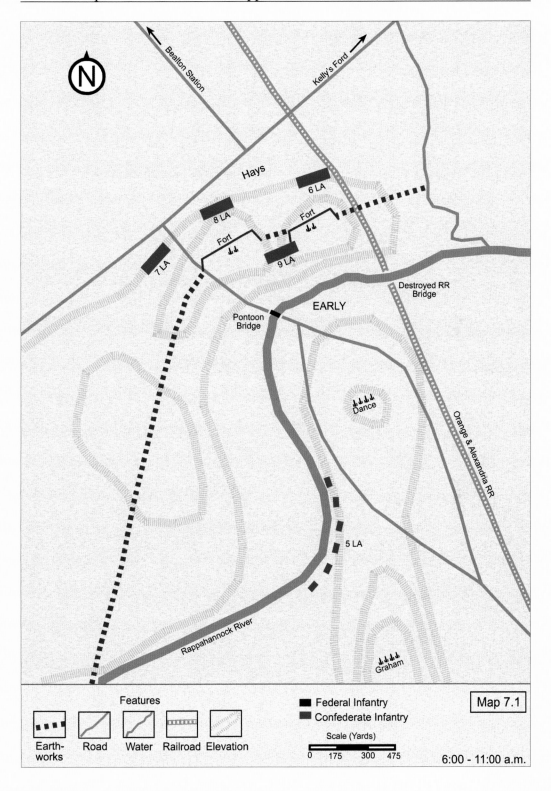

Bealton Station

Kelly's Ford

Hays

6 LA

8 LA

Fort

Fort

7 LA

9 LA

Destroyed RR Bridge

EARLY

Pontoon Bridge

Dance

Orange & Alexandria RR

5 LA

Rappahannock River

Graham

Features

Earth-works   Road   Water   Railroad   Elevation

Federal Infantry

Confederate Infantry

Map 7.1

Scale (Yards)

0   175   300   475

6:00 - 11:00 a.m.

Map 7.2: The Approach of
V Corps and VI Corps
(November 7: 11:00 a.m. - 4:00 p.m.)

Questions about whether Rappahannock Station was defensible plagued the Confederate high command. Both Lt. Gen. Richard Ewell and Gen. Lee realized there were several vulnerable areas in the line, but believed the works were "adequate to accomplish the object for which they were intended." Lee was under the impression that a brigade or two could hold out against almost any assault because the infantry trench was anchored on either side by the river and his artillery could rake the enemy as they advanced.

Not everyone subscribed to this view. Division commanders Jubal Early and Edward Johnson, who were charged with shuttling infantry brigades across the river to defend the position, were very concerned. "The works on the north side of the river, were, in my judgment, very inadequate, and not judiciously laid out or constructed," wrote Early in his report. He also added that the works provided "no obstacle in themselves to an attacking enemy, and only furnished a temporary protection to our troops." The enemy soon reached the same conclusion.[3]

Confederate cavalry scouts reported Yankee infantry approaching Rappahannock Station at 11:00 a.m. The Louisianans watched as the enemy formed into line of battle in front of the vulnerable Confederate works. Inexperienced in brigade command, Col. Penn ventured forward to Warrenton Road to see the movements himself. Satisfied the enemy was moving against his position in force, Penn sent a communication to Early. It was now about 11:45 a.m.

The troops Penn spotted belonged to the First Division of VI Corps. The division, normally under Brig. Gen. Horatio Wright, was commanded by Brig. Gen. David Russell. The change was due to John Sedgwick's elevation from VI Corps commander to wing commander, which in turn bumped Wright to corps command. Russell left his Third Brigade to take over First Division, leaving his former unit under Col. Peter Ellmaker of the 119th Pennsylvania. Col. Emory Upton led Brig. Gen. Joseph Bartlett's brigade because that officer was leading the First Division of V Corps.

The remainder of VI Corps was also deployed and ready for action: Brig. Gen. Albion Howe's division deployed to the right of Russell's, and Brig. Gen. Henry Terry's division was behind Howe in reserve. V Corps infantry deployed on the opposite (left or east) side of the railroad. Bartlett's division formed across the railroad tracks from VI Corps. Brig. Gen. Kenner Garrard threw out a 900-man skirmish line composed of men from various regiments of V Corps. This strong line covered the fronts of both V Corps and VI Corps. Garrard's skirmishers moved forward about 2:30 p.m. "Rappahannock Station is a vile place to approach for attack," concluded one Federal officer as he looked over the open ground in front of him.[4]

On the other side of the line, Col. Penn continued to watch the enemy in his front. A second dispatch from Penn to Early at 1:15 p.m. told of enemy skirmishers advancing on the east side of the railroad. Early apparently did not receive the first dispatch until shortly before 2:00 p.m. When he did, he moved into action by ordering the three other three brigades of his division to prepare to move forward. Because they were preparing their winter huts, "it required some time to them together," he noted. Early also fired off dispatches to Gens. Lee and Ewell about an imminent enemy attack. Early rode forward to examine the situation while his men prepared to march to the front. Along the way he received Penn's second dispatch, which likely hastened his pace. Early met Lee along the way and the two officers rode to the river about 3:00 p.m. When they reached the high ground along the southern bank they spotted: "a heavy force . . . something like a mile or more in front . . . preceded by a heavy line of skirmishers, was gradually, but slowly and very cautiously, moving up toward our position," reported Early. It was also clear that Penn's Louisiana brigade was "manifestly too small for the length of the works." The inadequacy of the works irked Early, as did the knowledge that his engineers had not thrown a second pontoon bridge across the river as he had asked. It was too late now. All he could do was wait for the enemy attack. A bit of good news reached the defenders when Gen. Hays galloped up at 4:00 p.m. The cheering Louisianans would need their seasoned commander. Hays set about reuniting his regiments within the defensive works. He didn't have much time.[5]

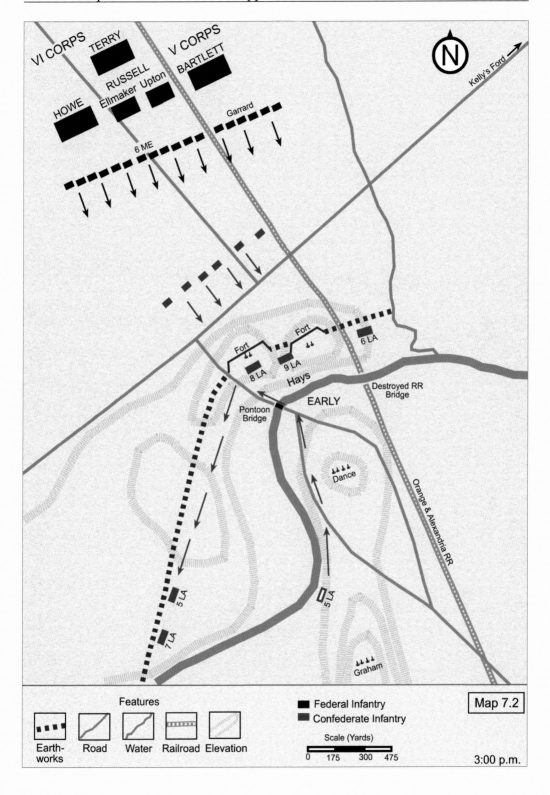

VI CORPS

TERRY

V CORPS

RUSSELL

BARTLETT

HOWE   Ellmaker Upton

Garrard

6 ME

Kelly's Ford

N

Fort

Fort

6 LA

8 LA   9 LA

Hays

Destroyed RR
Bridge

Pontoon
Bridge   EARLY

Dance

Orange & Alexandria RR

5 LA

5 LA

7 LA

Graham

Features

Earth-   Road   Water   Railroad   Elevation
works

■ Federal Infantry
■ Confederate Infantry

Map 7.2

Scale (Yards)

0   175   300   475

3:00 p.m.

Map 7.3: The Federals Plan an Attack
(November 7: 4:30 - 5:00 p.m.)

The Confederates had no idea just how heavily the odds were stacked against them. The roughly 900 men holding the thin line of ill-designed entrenchments faced about 30,000 men belonging to V Corps and VI Corps. As Hays reorganized his front, the North Carolinians of Brig. Gen. Robert Hoke's Brigade completed their seven-mile march at the double-quick and crossed the river on the pontoon bridge to reinforce the position. It was 4:30 p.m. The Tar Heels filed into the trench, filling the gap between the left of the 8th Louisiana and the right of the 5th Louisiana (No. 1). Because Hoke had not yet returned to the army, the 1,100-man brigade was under the command of its senior officer, Col. Archibald Godwin. The new arrivals were in good spirits because they had just received new clothes, equipment, and pay the day before. Early also called up two batteries, Capt. Willis J. Dance's and Capt. Archibald Graham's, and ordered them to unlimber on the near side of the river and provide covering fire.

Gen. Lee was not content to sit and await an attack. Instead, he ordered a gun from Dance's Battery, which occupied a hill on the south side of the Rappahannock, to limber up and reinforce the works on the north side. By this time, however, Federal sharpshooters from V Corps had moved to within a few yards of the river and opened fire on the pontoon bridge, forcing the gun to fall back (No. 2). Three Federal batteries also deployed and opened on the fortifications and the pontoon bridge. Early reported that "the firing from the enemy's guns on the right, left, and center, converging on the point occupied by us, was rapid and vigorous until some time after dusk." The barrage was the first real indication the Rebels received of the immense Federal firepower arrayed against them, which would keep away reinforcements and hamper their own retreat, should one become necessary.[6]

Once he witnessed the ineffectiveness of Graham's and Dance's batteries on the south bank of the river, Lee ordered them to cease fire. He had no way of knowing whether the demonstration in front of Rappahannock Station would turn into a full-scale attack, or whether it was a feint to cover a crossing at Kelly's Ford. As he later wrote in his report, "the increasing darkness induced the belief that nothing would be attempted until morning." Even if the enemy did attack, reasoned Lee, he believed his two brigades (Hays and Godwin) could hold, and if not, could easily retreat over the pontoon bridge.[7]

Gen. Sedgwick had spent considerable time examining the Southern works. While he thought them to be strong, he also identified their many weaknesses. Instead of storming the line with his infantry, he decided to mass his batteries on the heights and blast the enemy into a retreat across the pontoon bridge. Using this fire as cover, the Federal infantry crept closer between 3:00 and 3:30 p.m. as Godwin's Tar Heels were still trotting their way toward the pontoon bridge to reinforce Hays. Kenner Garrard's V Corps skirmish line inched forward, forcing the 6th Louisiana from its defensive trench east of the railroad and into the Confederate main works (No. 3).[8]

If an infantry attack was needed, it would be made by Col. Peter Ellmaker's brigade just west of the railroad and Upton's brigade on its right (No. 4). Ellmaker deployed from left to right as follows: 6th Maine (one-half) - 5th Wisconsin - 49th Pennsylvania - 119th Pennsylvania. The rest of the 6th Maine was on the skirmish line. Upton's men deployed with the 5th Maine on the right and the 121st New York to its left. His other two regiments formed in their rear. The 6th Maine's skirmish line advanced to a sunken road. The bluff with the fortifications loomed before them.[9]

When he spotted Hoke's North Carolinians reinforcing the Louisianans, Gen. Wright ordered the remainder of his VI corps forward. The advanced units were now just 250 yards from the forts. The artillery barrage, however, was not forcing the defenders from their works. "Under most circumstances I should have hesitated in ordering the assault of so strong a position, and believed its success hopeless," he later reported, but his examination of the Rebel positions encouraged Wright. Convinced he had a good chance to flank and collapse line, he ordered Russell to attack. Wright also ordered his gunners to throw a concentrated fire against the fortifications to force the enemy to keep their heads down. The growing darkness, reasoned Wright, "was favorable to the attack."[10]

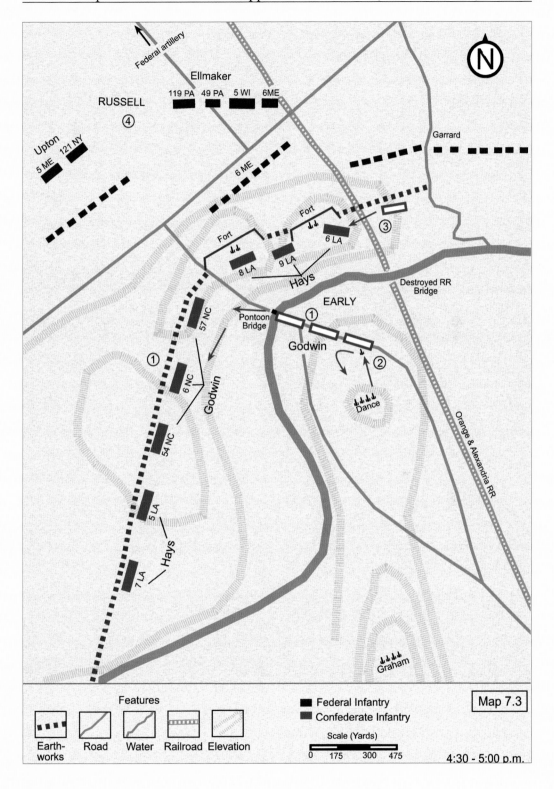

Map 7.3

4:30 - 5:00 p.m.

Map 7.4: The Attack Begins
(November 7: 5:00 - 5:15 p.m.)

Both Federal brigades making the attack were veteran outfits led by colonels (Peter Ellmaker and Emory Upton) with little prior experience commanding large bodies of troops. The combined strength of these two brigades was about 2,120 men, about equal to the number of Confederates (Hays and Hoke/Godwin) manning the works. The attackers, however, would have the benefit of immense artillery firepower, growing darkness, and a concentrated sector over which they would advance.[11]

Given the heavy odds that always favor a defender behind works of nearly any kind, Gen. Russell devised a ruse to improve his odds: he would send forward a force that appeared to be relieving the skirmish line, but when all of the troops were united, they would continue forward to attack the works. Darkness had nearly settled upon northern Virginia when Russell ordered the rest of the 6th Maine forward to the road to reinforce the skirmish line. He also ordered the 5th Wisconsin to move up to support the now-reinforced skirmish line. As soon as the Badgers arrived, the 6th Maine was ordered to rise and attack the Rebel works (No. 1). The strapping lumbermen were told to fix bayonets and remove the caps from their muskets so they would not fire until they were within the enemy's works. After aligning his men for the attack, Maj. George Fuller, the 6th Maine's commander, shouted "Forward, double-quick!"

The 6th Maine's first line of battle was hit by such a sustained fire that it was quickly driven back, but the remainder of the regiment continued on. "The fire grew heavier as the line neared the works, and the men were struck down with fearful rapidity," explained Maj. Fuller, "but unwavering, with wild cheers, the survivors reached the fortifications, and springing over them engaged the enemy in a hand-to-hand conflict." The weight of the sudden attack, coming as it did out of the gloomy darkness preceded by a sustained artillery barrage, shocked the Louisianans. Many fled to their left while others threw down their arms and surrendered. The Federal artillery fire convinced most of the Rebels to keep their heads down, so large segments of the line did not even see the

enemy soldiers dashing forward until they were nearly upon the works. A strong wind blowing that evening may also have played a role in deadening the sound of the approaching Union juggernaut. Despite their surprise, one Louisiana officer claimed that his men "fired vigorously, but with coolness and deliberation."[12]

The left wing of the Federal line entered the smaller redoubt while the right wing hit the larger redoubt and the rifle pits that connected the two forts. The attackers, who engaged the entire 9th Louisiana, the right side of the 8th Louisiana, and the left side of the 6th Louisiana, momentarily stunned the defenders (No. 2), who managed to regroup and, with help from the rest of the 8th Louisiana and 6th Louisiana, counterattack. Maj. Fuller recalled that the Rebel reinforcements "commenced a raking fire down the length of our line, which proved very destructive, and, perceiving the weakness of our force, advanced heavily upon our right." The Maine troops on this part of the line scrambled out of the works, while those in the center and left side of the fort barely held on (No. 3). Just when it seemed that the Maine men were to be killed or captured en masse, the 5th Wisconsin appeared at the top of the fortifications (No. 4). The Badgers had sprinted as fast as their legs could carry them to help support their embattled comrades. These new arrivals hit the larger redoubt and the rifle pits farther to the right (west). The portion of the 6th Maine forced from the right side of the works wheeled and attacked the smaller redoubt. Once again the Louisianans recoiled from the shock of this attack, and once again they stood tall and counterattacked.[13]

This was a confusing time for Gen. Early. He had heard gunfire earlier, but when it stopped for a time both he and Gen. Lee believed the firing was a reconnaissance or feint, "and that it was too late for the enemy to attempt anything serious that night." Lee left the south bank of the river and rode back to his headquarters. Early was not so sure, but when an aide returned with conflicting information, he sent another rider back to the pontoon bridge. This aide returned and accurately assessed the dire situation. Early ordered Brig. Gens. John Pegram and John Gordon to bring up their infantry brigades. By this time some of Hays' men were streaming across the bridge in an attempt to escape.[14]

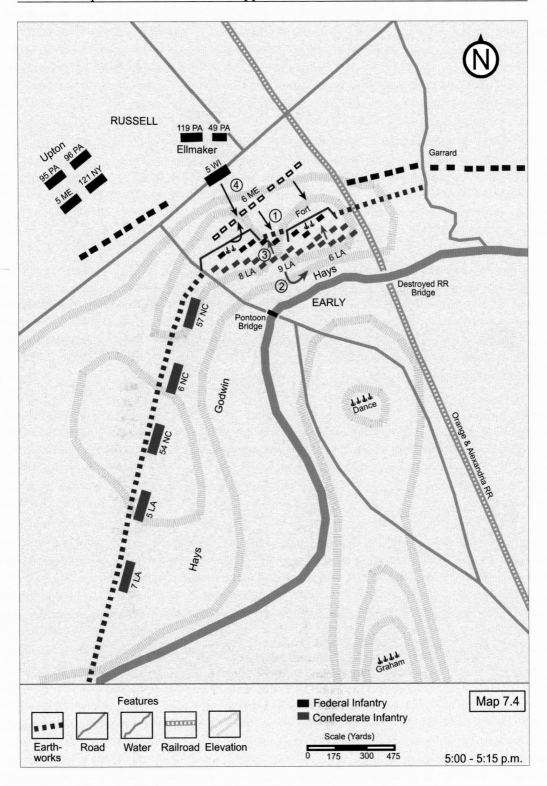

RUSSELL

Upton

95 PA   96 PA

5 ME   121 NY

119 PA   49 PA

Ellmaker

5 WI

④

6 ME

①   Fort

Garrard

8 LA

③

9 LA   6 LA

②   Hays

EARLY

57 NC

Destroyed RR
Bridge

Pontoon
Bridge

6 NC

Godwin

54 NC

Dance

5 LA

Orange & Alexandria RR

Hays

7 LA

Graham

Features

Earth-
works   Road   Water   Railroad   Elevation

■ Federal Infantry
■ Confederate Infantry

Scale (Yards)

0   175   300   475

Map 7.4

5:00 - 5:15 p.m.

Map 7.5: The Confederate Line is Pierced (November 7: 5:15 - 6:30 p.m.)

Gen. Russell watched the fighting from an advanced position. When he realized the artillery barrage and initial infantry attack had not driven the Confederates across the river, he called up the 49th and 119th Pennsylvania, the last two regiments of Ellmaker's brigade. With just four companies in the ranks, the 49th Pennsylvania was severely undermanned.[15]

Advancing against the Rebel works was not easy. As Russell explained in his report, the "ground was of a nature well calculated to check the impetuosity of a charge. . . . The storming column encountered a formidable ditch, 12 or 14 feet wide, some 6 feet deep, and filled with mud and water to an average depth of 3 feet. Crossing this they came to a plain broken with stumps and underbrush . . . [and then] a dry moat or ditch . . . nearly as formidable as the obstacles already passed."[16]

The historian of 49th Pennsylvania recalled that Russell "gave us orders to not double-quick, but to run—that they were driving the Sixth Maine. We see them, and obey his orders." Lt. Col. Thomas Hulings, the 49th Pennsylvania's commanding officer, remembered looking down at his watch. It was 5:15 p.m. Once they covered the intervening terrain, the Pennsylvania troops climbed the muddy parapet and added their weight to swirling close-quarter conflict (No. 1). Hand-to-hand combat was common up and down the line as the two sides battled for supremacy. Ultimately, numbers told as more and more Yankees streamed into the works. Trapped amongst swirling steel and swinging rifle butts, some Louisianans surrendered while others sought to escape across the narrow pontoon bridge.[17]

A Southern officer wrote about the final moments: "The Louisiana Guard battery discharged their pieces when the enemy were upon them and two of their number were bayoneted at the guns. Many of the officers threw away their swords to avoid surrendering them . . . a few others successfully swam across [the river], but many lost their lives in the attempt."[18]

Flushed with victory, the Pennsylvanians rounded up hundreds of prisoners. Without warning, a hail of bullets ripped into the right side of the 119th Pennsylvania. The Confederates, reported the commander of the regiment, Lt. Col. Gideon Clark, "succeeded in gaining a position on our right, and poured rather a disastrous fire into us." The survivors on the right side of the 119th regiment turned and stampeded to the foot of the fortification. One Keystone private recalled how "many cast themselves into the dry ditch at the foot of the slope and added to the horror and confusion of the moment by returning the fire of the rebels regardless of the fact that a line of their own comrades was between the two fires." Officers sorted out the confusion and rallied the men.[19]

The devastating fire was delivered by Hoke's North Carolinians, who until this time had manned their rifle pits awaiting an attack against their front. The Tar Heels could see Upton's Federals in front of their works and were ready to repel them, but the spreading fight farther to the right convinced Col. Archibald Goodwin that the real threat was already inside the walls. He shouted orders for the 6th and 57th North Carolina regiments to wheel to the right and face the Pennsylvania troops who had swept into the forts. The maneuver shifted the Rebels out of their protective trenches and placed them squarely on the vulnerable right flank of the 119th Pennsylvania (No. 2). The Tar Heels delivered a devastating firestorm that cut apart the unsuspecting Federals. While the 6th and 57th regiments executed their pivot, the 54th North Carolina filed to its right to take up the empty earthworks (No. 3). Despite Godwin's outstanding tactical leadership, the Confederate situation was now desperate. The Federal thrust had driven a wedge between Hays' Louisianans and Godwin's North Carolinians; hundreds of grayclad soldiers were heading for the pontoon bridge in their rear as fast as their legs could carry them.[20]

The Federal officers responded to Godwin's deadly pivot in two ways. First, the 119th's Lt. Col. Clark ordered his Pennsylvanians to change front to face the new threat. While Clark's men were turning about, Gen. Russell ordered Col. Upton to advance his brigade, which at this time was about 500 yards away from the Rebel defenses (No. 4).[21]

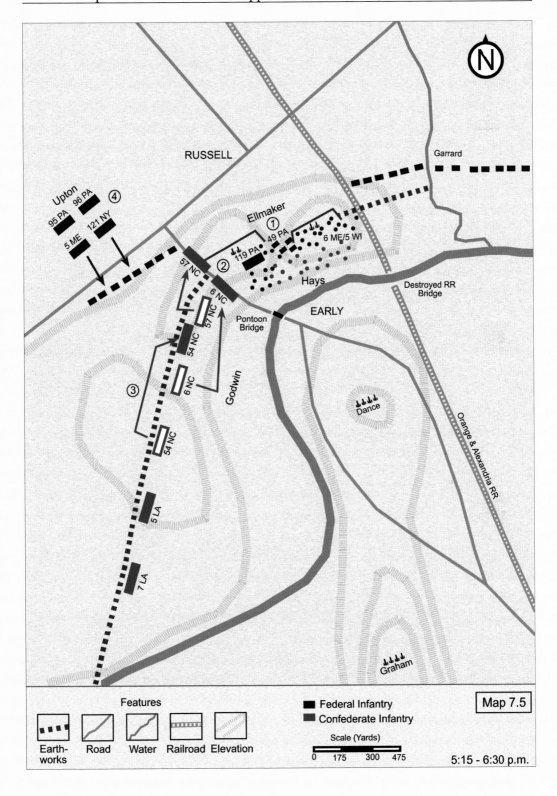

Map 7.5

5:15 - 6:30 p.m.

Map 7.6: Upton's Brigade Joins the Attack (November 7: 6:30 - 7:30 p.m.)

According to Col. Upton, Gen. Russell's orders to advance with two of his regiments reached him after dark, and he immediately complied. His orders were to "hold the redoubts already captured by the Third Brigade." Trotting over to his front line, Upton ordered his two favorite regiments, the 121st New York and the 5th Maine, to move forward. The 5th was on the right and the 121st on the left. There was no time to stop and load, so the colonel ordered his men to do so while they advanced. When the rifles were loaded, he ordered them to double-quick.[22]

During the advance, Russell clarified his orders to Upton: "Dislodge the enemy from a rifle-pit to our right of the redoubt, and from which he [the enemy, probably from the 57th and 6th North Carolina] maintained an enfilading fire." During the advance, Rebel artillery rounds exploded within Upton's ranks, tossing men around like broken rag dolls. The advance finally halted behind a low ridge about 150 yards from the trench of rifle pits. The men did not have long to wait before Upton ordered them to throw off their knapsacks and any other unnecessary impediments and fix bayonets. Upton cautioned them not to open fire, as the element of surprise was of utmost importance. Upton later wrote to his sister that the enemy banners "could be plainly seen outstanding against the sky; while their saucy heads appearing everywhere above the parapets forewarned us how deadly might be our task."[23]

After about ten minutes, the men moved forward at quick-time. When they were within 30 feet of the works, the officers ordered them to charge. Yelling at the top of their lungs, the Federal infantry moved quickly up and over the muddy piled earth (No. 1). The North Carolinians managed to fire a volley that had little or no effect on the assaulting enemy. Darkness, yelling, and gunfire masked the fact that Upton's thrust consisted of more boldness than overwhelming numbers. The Yankees poured up and over the works and smothered the 54th North Carolina. "[S]o sudden and unexpected was our movement upon them that the enemy seemed paralyzed," boasted Col. Clark Edwards of the 5th Maine. Upton proudly wrote after the

battle that "the work was carried at the point of the bayonet, and without firing a shot. The enemy fought stubbornly over their colors, but being overpowered soon surrendered." Isaac Best of the 121st New York explained that there was little firing in the defenses because the sudden attack had stunned North Carolinians, and Upton's men used bayonets and muskets as clubs.

While many Tar Heels were surrendering and others rushing toward the river, the Federal troops turned to their left against the flank and rear of the 6th and 57th North Carolina regiments. The fight that ensued was of short duration for hundreds of North Carolinians who, hit in flank, front, and rear, had little choice but to surrender (No. 2). Buoyed by the victory unfolding all around them, the 121st New York continued forward in an effort to capture the pontoon bridge which, if successful, would close any avenue of escape for the dazed Rebels (No. 3).[24]

Upton's crisp attack drove a firm Federal wedge between Godwin's North Carolinians and the 5th and 7th Louisiana regiments still manning the far left of the Confederate line. When the colonel learned that Rebel troops were on his right, Upton ordered Col. Edwards to gather up as many men from his 5th Maine as he could and move against them (No. 4). Yelling as loudly as he could so both his own men and the Confederates could hear, Upton explained, "When I give the command to charge, move forward. If they fire upon you, I will move six lines of battle over you and bayonet every one of them!" With Albion Howe's Federal division in front and to their left, and now elements of Russell's division about to attack them from their right, many of the Louisiana troops still resisting threw down their arms. As Isaac Best of the 121st New York recalled, "our fellows got around them on the right, and the whole crowd surrendered."[25]

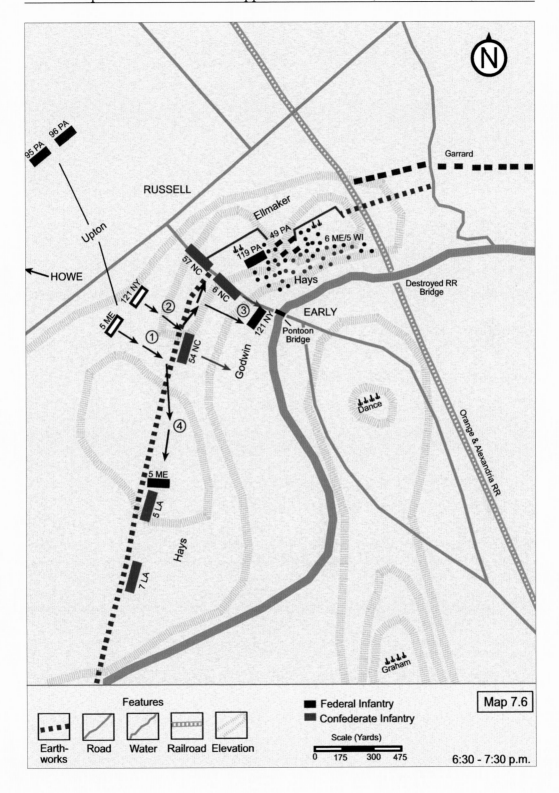

Map 7.6

Features

Earth-works   Road   Water   Railroad   Elevation

Federal Infantry
Confederate Infantry

Scale (Yards)
0   175   300   475

6:30 - 7:30 p.m.

Map 7.7: The Battle Ends
(November 7: 7:30 - 8:30 p.m.)

Not all of the Louisianans on the left of the line were interested in surrendering. Many joined with scores of North Carolinians to fight on. Although heavily outnumbered and with his back to the swollen Rappahannock River, Col. Godwin assumed control of these soldiers and personally led several charges in an effort to break out of the growing enemy encirclement. A Confederate who eventually escaped wrote that Godwin "did not for a moment dream of surrendering." Within a few minutes, enemy bullets and bayonets had cleaved his command down to fewer than 100 men. When someone yelled that Godwin had ordered a surrender, the colonel threatened to blow his brains out, "declaring his purpose to fight to the last moment." According to Gen. Early, "when his men had dwindled to 60 or 70, the rest having been captured, killed, wounded, or lost in the darkness . . . he [Godwin] was literally overpowered by mere force of numbers and was taken with his arms in his hands."[26]

Hundreds of Confederates had surrendered, but hundreds more tried to escape. Those lucky enough to reach the pontoon bridge had to decide whether to swim across the deep cold water or run across a bridge swept by enemy artillery and small arms fire. Those who decided to take to the water were fired upon by Federals lining the bank of the river. Many of these men perished, either from enemy lead or drowning. Two exceptions were the commanders of the 6th and 7th Louisiana regiments.[27]

The most prominent escapee was Brig. Gen. Harry Hays. The Louisiana general had done his best to rally his troops, but was surrounded and captured once the Federals swept over the works. He was trying to return his sword to its scabbard when his horse became startled and bolted away from its captors, racing across the pontoon bridge with Hays holding on for dear life. The commander of the 9th Louisiana also galloped across the bridge to safety.[28]

The brutality of the fighting within the Confederate works matched anything witnessed up to that point in the war. According to one Louisiana Tiger, "our men clubbed their muskets and used them freely over Yankee heads." This was one of the few instances where bayonets were widely utilized. A New Jersey officer walked over the field after the battle and observed, "here the unusual sight of death by bayonet wounds was witnessed." He probably never forgot the sight of "a dozen or more Confederate soldiers showing bayonet wounds, as well as some Union dead."[29]

The collapse of the Rappahannock Station bridgehead was one of the worst experiences of the war for Gen. Early. There was little he could do for his men as he watched the horrendous events unfold from his position on the south side of the river near the pontoon bridge. "I had the mortification to hear the final struggle of these devoted men and to be made painfully aware of their capture, without the possibility of being able to go to their relief," was how he later described it. Early was purportedly ill for two to three days after the fiasco. Once it was clear no one else was escaping over the bridge, he collected volunteers and ordered them to set fire the pontoons so the Federals could not cross.[30]

Losses were especially heavy for the defending brigades. Hays lost 702 killed, wounded, and captured, while Hoke (Godwin) lost 928 to all causes, for a total of 1,630 men. When muster was called for both brigades three days later on November 10, fewer than 500 men answered the call. Hays' command was so decimated there was talk of consolidating it with the other Louisiana brigade in the Army of Northern Virginia (but this did not occur).[31]

Union losses were much lower. Ellmaker's brigade, which carried the brunt of the charge, lost 327 men to all causes and Upton's just 63. Including minor losses to other units, the entire Federal loss stood at 419. As might be expected, the 6th Maine, which initiated the fight and was involved in all phases of the brilliantly led affair, lost 139 men. The 5th Wisconsin, which followed the Maine unit into the action, suffered the second highest regimental loss with 59.[32]

Recriminations flew through the ranks of the Confederate army, which had never suffered such an embarrassment. After the war, a Tar Heel offered one of the true understatements of the entire war: "the wisdom of the generalship by which our two brigades were placed on the north bank of a deep river to meet the advance of a great army is not apparent."[33]

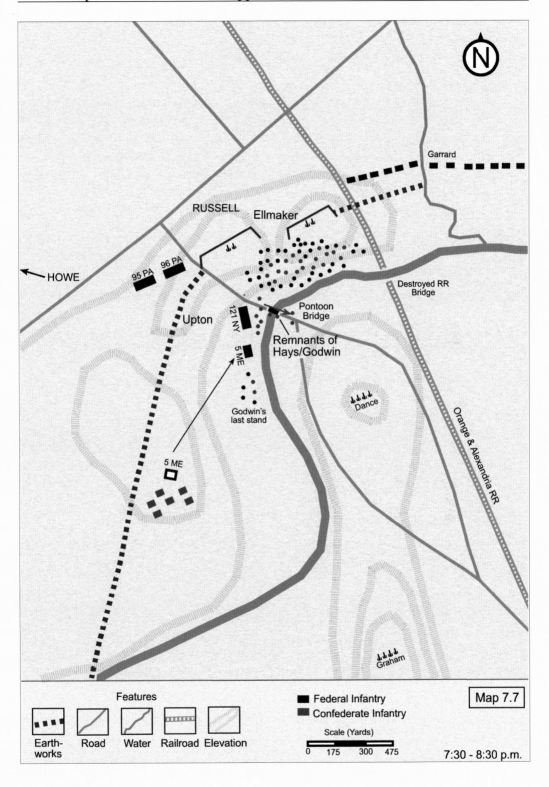

Map 7.7

7:30 - 8:30 p.m.

Map Set 8: Confederate Defeat at Kelly's Ford (November 7, 1863)

Map 8.1: III Corps Arrives at Kelly's Ford (November 7: noon - 1:00 p.m.)

The shocking defeat of the Confederates at Rappahannock Station was the second of two setbacks endured by Gen. Robert E. Lee and his Army of Northern Virginia on November 7. The first was at Kelly's Ford about six miles downstream. Although Southern losses there were smaller, it was another embarrassment.

The important crossing point was defended by Maj. Gen. Robert Rodes' infantry division, part of Lt. Gen. Richard Ewell's Second Corps. Kelly's Ford was difficult to defend because the high ground was on the far (Federal) side of the Rappahannock River. In addition to Kelly's, Rodes was also responsible for Wheatley's, Norman's, and Stevens' fords. Most of his division was camped about a mile and a half back from the river so it could guard all four crossing points and respond accordingly.[1]

A scattered 2nd North Carolina (322 strong) from Brig. Gen. Stephen Ramseur's Brigade picketed the riverbank. Part of the regiment was deployed three-quarters of a mile upriver at Wheatley's Ford while another group watched Stevens' Ford one mile downstream from Kelly's. Three or four companies were stationed in rifle pits behind Kelly's, with the balance in the small town of Kellysville. Because the positions were so widely dispersed explained the regiment's commander Lt. Col. Walter Stallings, "there was no connection between these various posts." Stallings' orders were straightforward: "Hold the ford, if possible." Rodes also placed Capt. John Massie's Battery about three-quarters of a mile behind Kelly's Ford, supported by the 500-man 30th North Carolina regiment.[2]

About noon, Rodes received a message from Col. William Cox, who was temporarily commanding Ramseur's Brigade, that the enemy cavalry picketing in front of Kelly's Ford had been replaced by infantry. Rodes confirmed the information when he rode to the crossing, where he observed five or six enemy regiments and a battery on the far side of the river. Stallings, he noted with approval, had shifted his command so that seven of his Tar Heel companies were near the ford "in the most advantageous positions," and the 30th North Carolina in the rear by Massie's artillery had been alerted to the threat. Rodes issued orders for the rest of his division, stationed well back from the river, to move forward to pre-assigned positions and notified Gen. Lee of the ominous development on the other side of the river. The army commander instructed Rodes not to cross the river and attack the enemy, but to wait for the Federals to give up their elevated position while crossing.[3]

The troops Rodes observed belonged to Maj. Gen. William Henry French's III Corps, which represented the left wing of the Army of the Potomac. Capt. George Randolph deployed the wing's artillery along the heights overlooking the river and Rebel defenses. Three batteries under Capt. Henry Sleeper, Lt. John Bucklyn, and Capt. Franklin Pratt were placed in forward positions, supported by six others. The task of overrunning the Confederate works was assigned to Col. P. Regis de Trobriand's brigade. Two other units, the 20th Indiana and the 2nd U.S. Sharpshooters of Brig. Gen. J. Hobart Ward's brigade had been temporarily added to bulk up the brigade.

As Capt. Pratt arrived, "there was a scattering musketry fire from the ford, and the enemy were throwing forward infantry from the wood into the rifle-pits and buildings on the opposite bank." Division commander Maj. Gen. David Birney's orders were clear: "Open on them as soon as possible." Once unlimbered, the three Federal batteries launched an effective fire against the Tar Heels along the river. Some of the shells disturbed a group of sharpshooters using a brick mill near the ford, which they promptly abandoned. According to Pratt, "my first shot struck the building between the second story windows, passed through it and into the woods beyond. But two other shots were thrown at the building; one exploded at the corner, the other passed through the roof of the one intended." Massie's Confederate battery rolled from the protection of the woods and unlimbered, but was quickly silenced and forced to beat a hasty retreat. With the 2nd North Carolina pinned down, Rodes ordered the 30th North Carolina to leave the woods and approach the ford. Federal cannon fire ended the attempt and the men scampered back into the timber. They advanced two more times with the same result. Many of the men, however, reached the mill and buildings in and around Kellysville.[4]

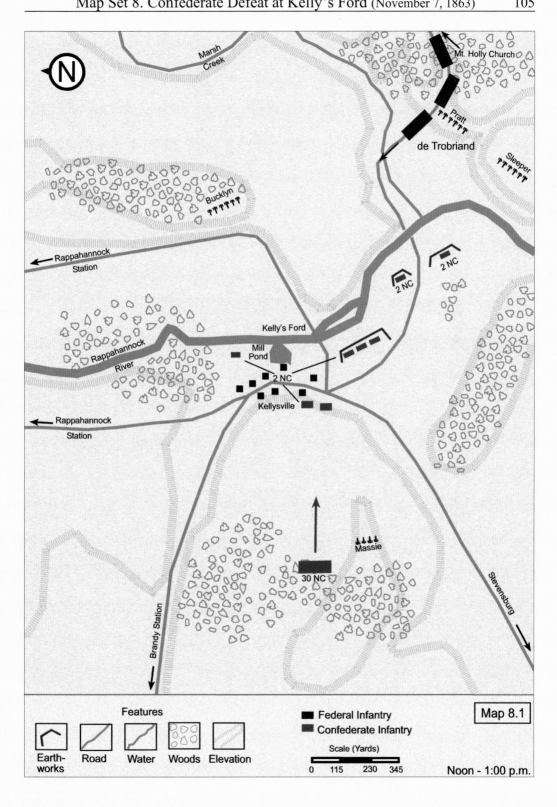

Features

Earth-works | Road | Water | Woods | Elevation

■ Federal Infantry
■ Confederate Infantry

Scale (Yards)

0   115   230   345

Map 8.1

Noon – 1:00 p.m.

Map 8.2: Regis de Trobriand's Troops Cross the River
(November 7: 1:00 - 2:00 p.m.)

The situation was growing more serious by the minute as the heavy Federal cannon fire pinned members of the 2nd and 30th North Carolina in and around the town of Kellysville and nearby Kelly's Ford. While he would later note in his report that the 2nd North Carolina "behaved very handsomely," Gen. Rodes thought otherwise about the 30th North Carolina. That regiment, he explained, was "speedily broken and demoralized under the concentrated artillery fire which swept the ground over which it had to march." The regiment, he continued, "did not sustain its reputation. It arrived at the mills in great confusion and became uncontrollable." Efforts to get the men to withdraw were met with resistance because few wanted to march back across the shell-torn open fields.[5]

The situation was also difficult for the 1st and 2nd U.S. Sharpshooters, who had orders to cross the Rappahannock (No. 1) and take the enemy positions. Both units were under the command of Lt. Col. Casper Trepp, who led them down the bluffs to the right of Pratt's battery, across Marsh Creek, and straight for the swollen river. According to Col. de Trobriand, "it was not until they saw us descending to the river banks that they [the enemy] ran to throw themselves into the entrenchments which defended the ford." Small arms fire from the 2nd North Carolina zipped through the ranks of the Federal sharpshooters as they advanced across the open plain toward the Rappahannock. Trepp's men took cover closer to the river behind anything that could stop a bullet and returned fire.[6]

After a short rest, Trepp ordered the 1st U.S. Sharpshooters across the river. He selected the 1st Sharpshooters for the honor of the initial crossing because the unit was upriver from the Confederate rifle pits. A successful thrust would put them on the flank of the enemy's defenses and almost certainly capture that part of the riverbank. Regardless of why they were selected, many of the veterans hesitated because it looked more likely than not that they would be caught helpless in the middle of the waist-deep water

where they would be easy targets. In an effort to get his men moving, Gen. Birney rode to the bank and used language "not found in military tactics, or the church catechism," recalled an amused artilleryman in Bucklyn's battery. The division commander's invective seems to have worked, and the men advanced down to the river and eased into the cold water. Just because they were upriver, however, did not mean that they could cross unscathed. Scores of men from the 2nd North Carolina still occupied the western bank. One of the sharpshooters vividly remembered the attempt: "A volley, mowing down ten men, received us right upon setting foot in the river. However, we quickly pushed on and succeeded in getting below the line of fire of the Confederates who would now have to rise above the breastworks to aim at us, thereby exposing themselves to our comrades' [2nd U.S. Sharpshooters's] bullets."[7]

Many men slipped on the slimy river bottom and fell into the cold water, ruining their ammunition. Those hit by enemy bullets either made their way back to the eastern shore or drifted downstream. Once they were convinced the determined crossing was for real and could not be stopped, some of the Tar Heels retreated. Once the sharpshooters reached the shore there was little time to reform their ranks. Orders rang out to press on and capture the Rebel rifle pits. Just as planned, they could now catch them in flank (No. 2). One sharpshooter noted that the rugged Michiganders of Companies C and I led the charge. "When within 10 feet of the first pit in their front, the enemy rising up, fired a volley, but, being above, fortunately shot too high and but few were struck. Our men at once charged on them," he continued, "capturing at this place about 80— 'packed in the bottom of the pit like sardines.' . . . It was a lively scrimmage; but more so at the next pit, where through fire and smoke, mid groans and shrieks of wounded men, some bayoneted, others blown through by opposing rifles, the work was carried" (No. 3).

The 2nd North Carolina's Lt. Col. Stallings did his best to explain the swift defeat by noting that the enemy "threw a strong body of troops across the river, cutting off and capturing three companies at the ford."[8]

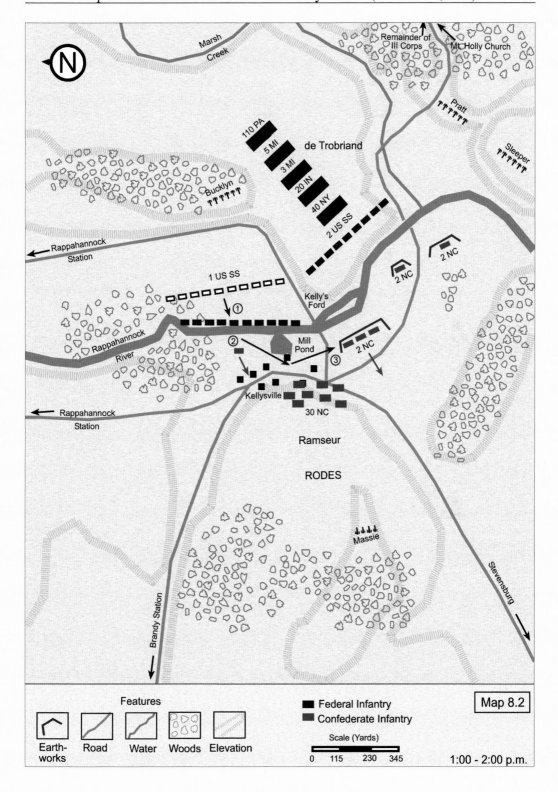

Map 8.2

1:00 - 2:00 p.m.

Map 8.3: The Federals Secure Kelly's Ford (November 7: 2:00 - 2:30 p.m.)

The swift success pleased Col. de Trobriand, who closely watched the crossing and advance of the 1st U.S. Sharpshooters against the left flank of the first enemy entrenchments (No. 1). With victory at hand, he ordered the rest of his brigade forward (No. 2). The 2nd U.S. Sharpshooters was in the first line with the rest of the brigade aligned in column behind it. The column was composed of the 40th New York, 20th Indiana, 3rd Michigan, 5th Michigan, and the 110th Pennsylvania.[9]

Hit in front and flank by the two regiments of sharpshooters, the North Carolinians defending the remaining breastworks either fell back or threw down their arms and surrendered. Lt. Col. Stallings of the 2nd North Carolina explained in his report that the speedy capture of these three companies convinced him to order the rest of his men to "fall back to the hills in the rear, which was effected with the loss of a lieutenant and about twenty men missing."

When he spotted large numbers of enemy soldiers milling around Kellysville (elements of the 30th North Carolina), de Trobriand ordered his column of infantry forward (No. 3). "[W]ithout stopping," recalled the brigade leader, "we advanced on the village on the run. The enemy, who did not expect us there so soon, offered little resistance, and surrendered with a good grace."[10]

The Kelly's Ford victory, though relatively small in the grand scheme of the war, was a complete tactical success. Col. de Trobriand held the sector and his men had killed, wounded, or captured about 330 men of the 2nd and 30th North Carolina regiments—or about 40 percent of the effective Confederate strength. Most of the captured were from the latter regiment. Federal losses from all sources were but 42 men.[11]

According to an embarrassed Gen. Rodes, the large number of captured was the result of malfeasance on the part of the 30th North Carolina, many of whose members "refused utterly to leave the shelter of the houses when he [the regiment's commander] ordered the regiment to fall back. All who refused were of course captured." When he returned from his honeymoon later in the month, Brig. Gen. Stephen Ramseur studied the loss and concluded the affair "was rather badly managed by the [officers] in command." Ramseur believed that the men had developed bad habits, but he was still optimistic that in two or three weeks he would whip them back into shape.[12]

Once the ford was captured the remainder of Birney's division crossed to the Confederate side of the river. By 3:00 p.m., the entire division was assembled on the western shore. A pontoon bridge sped the crossing. Rodes moved to counter Birney's advance by shifting Brig. Gen. Junius Daniels' Brigade from his right to his left. "Every arrangement was made to give the enemy a warm reception," he wrote in his report. Content to remain near the bridgehead and within range of his artillery, Birney refused to cooperate. Rodes considered counterattacking with Daniels' men but dismissed the idea; the enemy was too strong for any reasonable chance of success. Rodes knew that Maj. Gen. Edward Johnson's Division was marching to support him, so he decided to await its arrival. Johnson's brigades arrived just after dark and formed a line of battle on Rodes' right. There would be no counterattack. The fighting was over at Kelly's Ford, but the battle at Rappahannock Station was swelling toward its climax.[13]

November 7, 1863, was a unique day for Robert E. Lee. On the defensive holding ground of his own choosing, his veteran troops sustained not one but two embarrassing losses. Five North Carolina regiments fought in the two encounters, and large numbers of them were lost. That fact, coupled with the capture of a large portion of Harry Hays' Louisiana brigade and two obvious tactical defeats, spread a wave of shock and despair through the army. More than 2,000 men—some of Lee's finest fighters—had been stricken from the rolls. Col. Walter Taylor, one of Lee's staff officers, called the twin defeats "the saddest chapter in the history of this army." A staff officer serving with Gen. Ewell agreed: "it is absolutely sickening, and I feel personally disgraced by the issue of the last campaign, as does every one in the command [Second Corps]. Oh, how every day is proving the value of General Jackson to us!"

The memory of the recent sharp and bloody ambush-style defeat at Bristoe Station had also not been forgotten.[14]

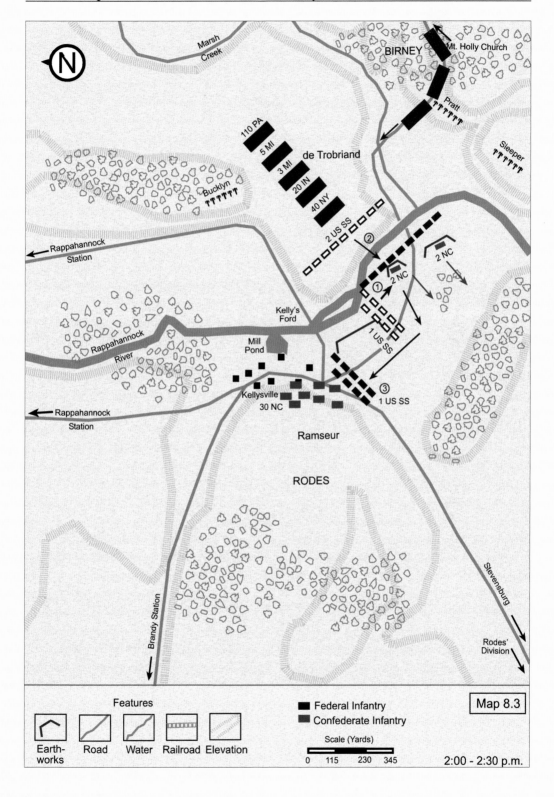

Map 8.3

2:00 - 2:30 p.m.

Features

Earth-works | Road | Water | Railroad | Elevation

■ Federal Infantry
■ Confederate Infantry

Scale (Yards)

0   115   230   345

Map Set 9: Lee Withdraws Below the Rapidan River *(November 8 - 27)*

Map 9.1: Lee's Rapid Retreat (November 7: 11:00 p.m. - 3:00 a.m., November 8)

The twin Federal victories of November 7 gave Maj. Gen. George Meade and the Union Army of the Potomac a much-needed morale boost and shifted the initiative.

Nearly everyone from President Abraham Lincoln down to the lowest foot soldier had questioned Meade's ability to defeat Gen. Robert E. Lee in Virginia. The sharp repulse of Lee's thrust at Bristoe Station the previous month, coupled with the stunning November victories at Rappahannock Station and Kelly's Ford changed that perception. Exuberance coursed through the ranks. The victories, confirmed a staff officer with VI Corps, were "the most, if not the only, decided successes in which I have participated in the War." Even Lincoln, ever so spare in his words of support for Meade, wired his commander, "I wish to say, 'Well done.'" A relieved Meade wrote to his wife, "the army is in fine spirits, and of course I am more popular than ever, having been greeted yesterday as I rode through the ranks with great cheering." A modern army officer described the army's twin successes as "one of the most stunning Union tactical victories of the war. Both columns of the army accomplished their strong attack plans in accordance with Meade's overall concept."[1]

The mood on the opposite bank of the Rappahannock River was not so bright. There were no serious indications that there would be mortal trouble at the bridgehead when Gen. Lee left Rappahannock Station early on the evening of November 7 to ride back to his headquarters at Brandy Station. When a courier galloped into his camp later that evening with the disastrous news, Lee already knew about the loss of Kelly's Ford. That defeat, coupled with the bloody fiasco at Rappahannock Station, made his position immediately behind the Rappahannock River untenable. The last thing Lee wanted to do was cede the area between the Rappahannock and Rapidan rivers to the Federals without a major engagement, but there were few good defensive positions there. If he attempted to fall back to his strong former line below the Rapidan, Meade could fall hard and fast upon his rear with

potentially calamitous results, including the potential loss of his wagon train.

Lee, who knew the region well, decided to fall back several miles west by southwest to a more consolidated position between Brandy Station and Culpeper. He would anchor his right flank on Pony Mountain and stretch his army about five miles northward across the Orange and Alexandria Railroad to cover the approaches to Culpeper. The overall position was good. Lee would have to pay special attention to his left flank, however, which hung dangerously in the air a few miles west of Fleetwood Hill.[2]

The Confederates woke early on November 8 with instructions to collect their belongings and prepare to move to different camps. The news came as a surprise to most of the men. The orders disappointed one soldier in the 16th North Carolina because he and his comrades had nearly completed their winter quarters. "Some of the men had completed nice cabins and expected to move into them the next morning, but such is war," he lamented. The army was to be on the road by 4:00 a.m., but "we found afterward that a force of the enemy had crossed the river at a ford above us and were making an effort to get in our rear. We were on the march before the time ordered."[3]

Officers pointed out the new positions to the troops as they arrived at their assigned locations. According to Capt. Robert Park of Col. Edward O'Neal's Brigade, the men "began to throw up breastworks as a protection against shell . . . using our tin cups, tin plates, and bayonets, in place of spades and picks, of which we had none." A. P. Hill's Third Corps held the left flank, and Richard Ewell's Second Corps the right. The Confederate rearguard was hurrying into position as November 8 was dawning.[4]

Despite his twin victories, the uncertainty of Lee's precise location below the Rappahannock, coupled with the darkness, made Meade uneasy. One of his corps commanders, Maj. Gen. William French, continued to believe that the Rebels would counterattack to retake the lost bridgehead at Kelly's Ford, so Meade ordered Maj. Gen. John Sedgwick at 11:30 p.m. to send the entire V Corps and two brigades of his own VI Corps to reinforce that point. Sedgwick was also ordered to rebuild the pontoon bridge at Rappahannock Station and mount a demonstration at first light on November 8 to distract the enemy from French's exposed bridgehead at Kelly's Ford.[5]

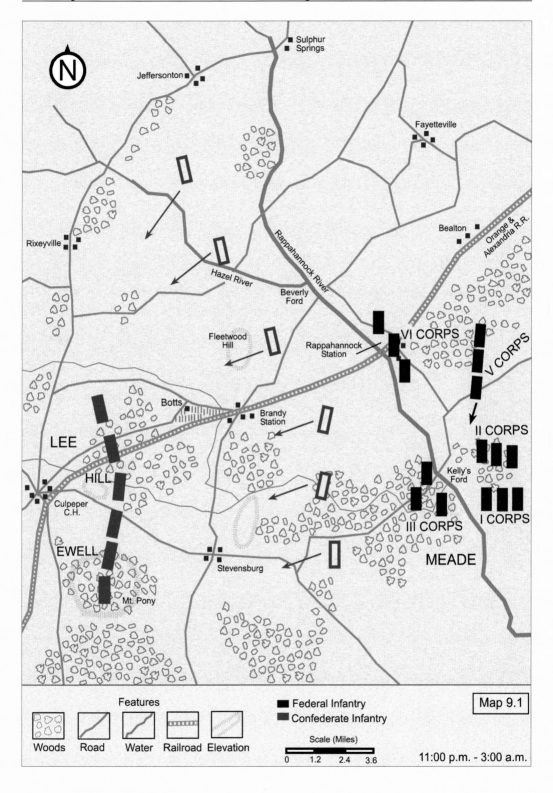

Sulphur
Springs

Jeffersonton

Fayetteville

Rixeyville

Bealton

Orange &
Alexandria R.R.

Hazel River

Rappahannock River

Beverly
Ford

Fleetwood
Hill

Rappahannock
Station

VI CORPS

V CORPS

II CORPS

Botts

Brandy
Station

Kelly's
Ford

LEE

HILL

Culpeper
C.H.

III CORPS

I CORPS

EWELL

Stevensburg

MEADE

Mt. Pony

Features

Federal Infantry

Confederate Infantry

Map 9.1

Woods   Road   Water   Railroad   Elevation

Scale (Miles)

0   1.2   2.4   3.6

11:00 p.m. - 3:00 a.m.

Map 9.2: Meade Moves West
(November 8: 4:00 a.m. - 6:00 p.m.)

Meade would finally learn the location of Lee's army early on November 8. At first light, Brig. Gen. Joseph Carr (III Corps) was ordered to throw out two regiments from his division to determine if any enemy soldiers were near the Rappahannock River. Carr selected the 122nd and 110th Ohio regiments and sent them out under the command of their brigade leader, Col. J. Warren Keifer. When the regiments ventured about a mile and a half below the river without encountering any Confederates, Keifer received orders to reconnoiter westward with his entire brigade. He finally spotted some Rebel cavalry and horse artillery when his men climbed a hill east of Brandy Station. The small enemy force scattered easily and the Federals marched to Brandy Station, where Keifer halted his brigade.[6]

Farther north, Gen. Sedgwick's engineers worked feverishly to throw a pontoon bridge across the river. Smoke and a lingering haze, however, made it difficult to determine whether the enemy was still on the opposite bank in force. In an effort to determine what was in Sedgwick's front, Meade ordered French, whose entire III Corps was on the western shore of the Rappahannock at Kelly's Ford, to slide northward toward Rappahannock Station. To the relief of the men, no enemy were found. Sedgwick's men began crossing once the bridge was finished, and by late afternoon both III Corps and VI Corps were on the Confederate side of the river awaiting further orders.[7]

When Meade's orders arrived, the two corps joined and began marching west, with VI Corps on the right and III Corps on the left. The long front straddled the Orange and Alexandria Railroad. The large-scale movement offered a grand spectacle that was long remembered. "The pursuit began immediately in order of battle. The country was admirably fitted for it," Col. Regis de Trobriand recorded in his memoirs. He continued:

It is almost the only part of Virginia where the open land extends to any distance without obstacles. So that this grand military deployment offered one of the finest spectacles which could be imagined. Let one picture to himself two army corps marching on the centre, in line of battle, in mass, the artillery in the intervals and on the roads, the flanks covered by two divisions in column, the skirmishers in advance, the cavalry on the two wings; the reserves covering the wagons in the rear; and all this mass of humanity in perfect order, rising or falling gradually according to the undulations of the plain, with the noise of the cannon, which did not cease throwing projectiles on the rearguard of the Confederates in retreat. Such was the moving picture which was given us to enjoy during that whole afternoon (No. 1).[8]

Just as Col. de Trobriand recalled, two divisions of Federal cavalry shielded the flanks of the advance: John Buford's division advanced toward Rixeyville on the right (No. 2), and Judson Kilpatrick's troopers made for Stevensburg on the left (No. 3) screening the movements of the I, II, and V corps. Meade and his staff, meanwhile, waited impatiently for news that his men had encountered Lee's army, and finally crossed the Rappahannock at 2:00 p.m. to find out what was happening. The first troops Meade encountered belonged to V Corps, which had just crossed the river at Kelly's Ford. He continued riding west and came upon Maj. Gen. Gouverneur Warren's II Corps, which was on its way to Stevensburg (No. 4). The corps leader appeared crestfallen, recalled one eyewitness. According to a member of Meade's staff, Warren looked "like a man of disappointed hopes, as he gazed round the country and said, 'There's nobody [Confederates] here—nobody!'"[9]

Meade and his staff arrived at Brandy Station late on the afternoon of November 8 in time to observe the bottleneck with III Corps and VI Corps (No. 5). Realizing that it was too late to unravel the mess, Meade ordered the troops to bivouac for the night. He would soon learn that as many as six separate skirmishes had broken out between the two armies on November 8, most involving cavalry.[10]

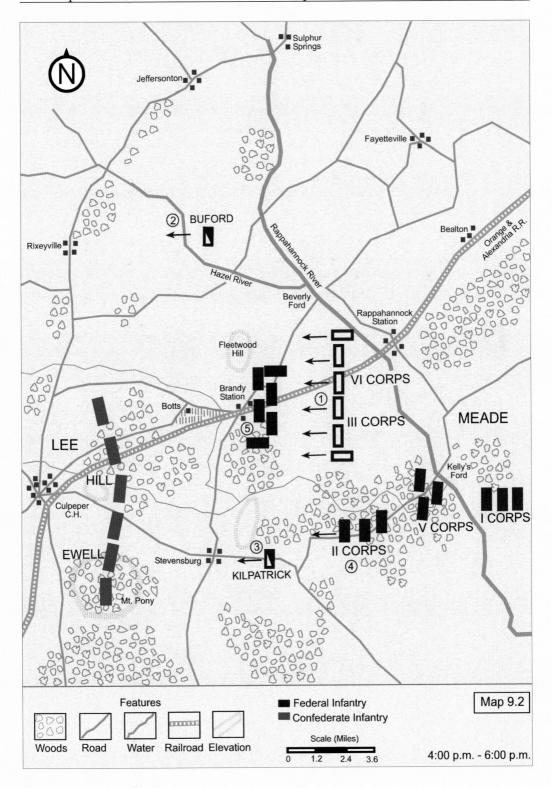

Map 9.2

4:00 p.m. - 6:00 p.m.

Map 9.3: Lee Withdraws Across the Rapidan (November 8 - 9)

None of the soldiers of the Army of the Potomac, including Gen. Meade, realized that they had missed a golden opportunity to inflict a potentially serious defeat while Lee was withdrawing his army across a major river.

After suffering the twin November 7 defeats at Rappahannock Station and Kelly's Ford, Lee weighed his limited options. With both of his flanks in the air, and with Meade's army poised to cross in force against both flanks, Lee's only viable course of action was to fall back, and eventually retreat to the high ground below the Rapidan River. His wagons made the trek toward the Rapidan throughout November 8. With darkness finally setting in, Lee ordered his infantry to withdraw across the Rapidan. The movement was not as easy as it looked on a map.

Although there were numerous fords, the weather on November 8 had turned bitterly cold. Strong winds added to the misery of the men, few of whom were warmly dressed. The march that night, recalled LeRoy Edwards of the 12th Virginia Infantry, was "of no ordinary suffering. Walking was fatiguing and resting was freezing." When they reached the bone-chilling Rapidan River, the men had no choice but to step into the icy water and wade across. John Worsham of the 21st Virginia Infantry recalled the ordeal decades later:

> It was the coldest water I ever forded . . . I can feel it now . . . it was so cold it felt as if a knife had taken one's foot off; and at each step the depth of the water increased . . . the water came to the knee, and one felt as if the leg was off from the knee down. Reaching the shore and halting to put on shoes and let pants down, many of the men were so cold they could not do it.

Once safely below the river, the men returned to the camps they had occupied about one month earlier before stepping off on the Bristoe Campaign. No one at that time knew that the Army of Northern Virginia as a whole would never again have the offensive capacity to reach or cross the Rappahannock River.[11]

Although the recent effort had not been excessively bloody or as extensive as the Maryland or Gettysburg campaigns, Lee's army was simply worn out. "[M]any of us are wearing away in the army," Thomas Taylor, an eternally optimistic soldier in the 6th Alabama Infantry wrote home. "I cannot walk with that elastic step I did before the war broke out. I frequently stumble & fall down now in walking over uneven places in the road or through the woods & over bushes." The youngsters who had entered the army, he observed, were now more like old men. The growing deficiencies in rations added to the misery. Many of Lee's soldiers simply gave up and headed home.[12]

Once established below the river, Lee's new defensive line ran about eighteen miles. His left flank rested at Liberty Mills, about five and one-half miles southwest of Orange Court House. This sector was part of Lt. Gen. Richard Ewell's Second Corps, which held the left half of the army's front. Ewell was absent due to complications with his amputated leg, so Maj. Gen. Jubal Early was in command of his corps. A division under Maj. Gen. Edward Johnson held the right side of Ewell's line between Bartlett's Mill to Mountain Run, with Maj. Gen. Robert Rodes' Division deployed from the latter waterway to Raccoon Ford. Early's Division, now under Brig. Gen. Harry Hays, extended the line from the latter ford to Robertson's Ford.

Lt. Gen. A. P. Hill's Third Corps defended the army's right flank. Hill's line extended from Rapidan Station southeast to Morton's Ford. Lee ordered Hill to refuse the right side of the line so that it rested on Mine Run, a small creek that fed into the Rapidan. Jeb Stuart's cavalry patrolled both of the army's flanks. The strong position occupied bluffs overlooking the Rapidan's north bank. Two good roads, the Orange Turnpike and the Orange Plank Road, ran generally east to west and offered lateral movement capability to shuffle men, guns, and supplies to all parts of Lee's defensive line. Lee maintained his headquarters on the side of Clark's Mountain, roughly in the center of his defensive line.[13]

Many expected a pitched battle on November 9, but it was not to be. When daylight brightened the landscape, Meade learned soon enough that Lee's army had escaped yet again.

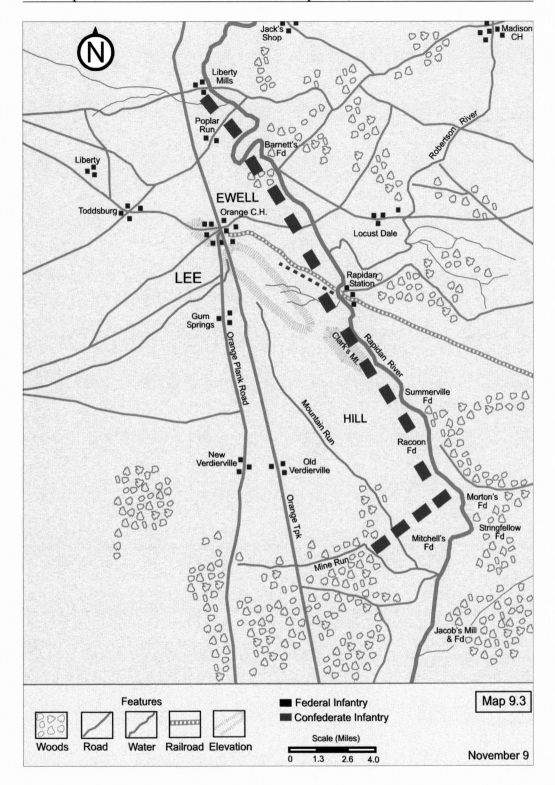

Jack's Shop

Madison CH

Liberty Mills

Poplar Run

Barnett's Fd

Liberty

Robertson River

EWELL

Orange C.H.

Toddsburg

Locust Dale

LEE

Rapidan Station

Gum Springs

Clark's Mt.

Rapidan River

Orange Plank Road

Summerville Fd

Mountain Run

HILL

Racoon Fd

New Verdierville

Old Verdierville

Morton's Fd

Stringfellow Fd

Orange Tpk

Mitchell's Fd

Mine Run

Jacob's Mill & Fd

Features

Woods Road Water Railroad Elevation

■ Federal Infantry
■ Confederate Infantry

Map 9.3

Scale (Miles)

0   1.3   2.6   4.0

November 9

Map 9.4: Lee and Meade Plan
(November 10 - 14)

While Confederate infantry and artillerymen fortified their positions on the south side of the Rapidan River, Lee took up an old refrain: the ongoing shortage of supplies. With winter nearly upon them, the scarcity of food and clothing posed a very real problem.

Lee's men without adequate winter clothing and supplies, and Richmond compounded their problems by sending word to expect even less food in the future. Commissary-General Lucius B. Northrop estimated that he could only supply about 4,000 head of cattle to the army during the forthcoming winter, even though the army had consumed some 40,000 head the previous winter, courtesy of the same Richmond authorities. An alarmed Lee voiced concern to Secretary of War James Seddon in a November 10 dispatch. Lee begged Seddon to use everything within his power to ensure an adequate flow of food and supplies. Two days later he told Seddon that he would be forced to pull his army back to the gates of Richmond unless the railroad was repaired. There was a very real possibility that the Army of Northern Virginia would be asked to survive another winter without minimal levels of sustenance.[14]

Despite a lack of adequate supplies, most of Lee's men continued doing what was asked of them, i.e., remaining with the army and guarding the many Rapidan fords. Not everyone exhibited a high level of commitment, and desertion increased. Lee resorted to firing squads in an effort to discourage desertion. For example, six of Ewell's brigades were called out to witness the execution of three soldiers convicted of desertion. The sight horrified a hardened veteran who freely admitted, "if I live a thousand years, I will never be willing to see another."[15]

When he wasn't lobbying Richmond for more food and supplies, Lee spent his hours reading Northern papers and sifting through intelligence reports to piece together information on Federal movements. Lee believed Meade was preparing another major move and wrote as much to President Davis: "There are indications that this advance will take place on our right by the lower fords, Germanna and Ely's, as if with the intention of striking for the Richmond and Fredericksburg Railroad." Lee used this chance to once again lobby for more provisions. "I will endeavor to follow him and bring him to battle, but I do not see how I can do it without the greatest difficulty. The country through which he will have to pass is barren. We have no forage on hand and very little prospect of getting any from Richmond. I fear that our horses will die in great numbers."[16]

While Lee pondered his adversary's next move, Meade was being chastised for allowing Lee to escape yet again. Any euphoria over the twin November 7 victories in the halls of Washington dissipated when it became known that Meade had not pressed aggressively forward to bring Lee's wounded army to battle. In fairness to Meade, Lee vacated the "Iron Triangle" quickly, and catching him would have been difficult.

With his army now camped between Brandy Station and Culpeper, Meade pondered his options. The biting weather suggested an early winter, and he would have liked nothing more than to go into winter quarters. Knowing the decision was not his to make, Meade wired Gen. Halleck and Secretary of War Edwin Stanton on November 13 to request a conference. The next morning at 6:00 a.m., Meade and his aides left Brandy Station for Bealton to hop a train for Washington. Meade rarely enjoyed his time in the capital and this visit was no different. News arrived that Lee may have left his defensive line behind the Rapidan. Was he was crossing the river to strike his army (now under John Sedgwick)? Meade would not learn until that evening the rumor was false.[17]

Meade said and wrote little about this visit to Washington. He was likely ordered to mount an offensive against Lee while maintaining his current line of communications. Intelligence informed the Union army commander that the lower fords across the Rapidan were undefended, and that the two roads running behind Lee's army (the Orange Turnpike and Orange Plank Road) were unobstructed and in good condition. This news, coupled with orders to remain in the field, helped Meade devise a new operation. He decided to cross the river at three of the lower fords (Jacob's, Culpeper Mine, and Germanna) to gain Lee's flank and rear. A quick march and thrust, hoped Meade, might pin the Confederates against the freezing Rapidan and finish the job he was unable to complete at the end of the Gettysburg Campaign.[18]

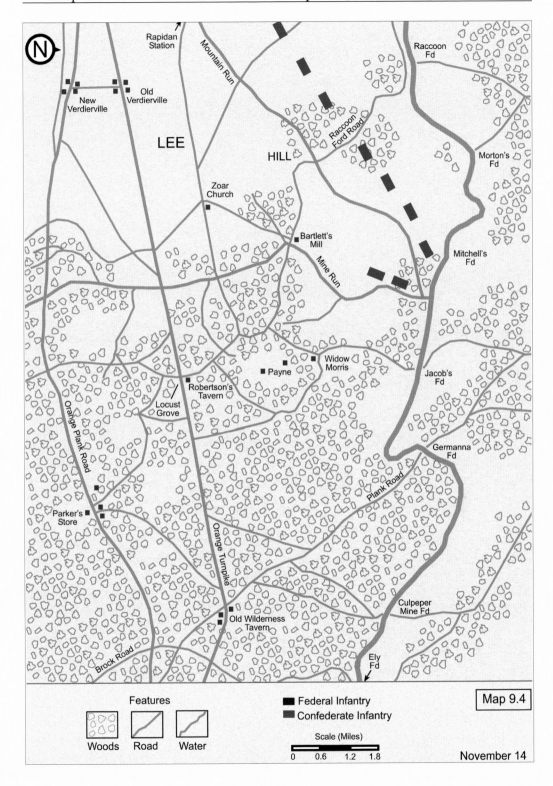

Features

Woods   Road   Water

■ Federal Infantry
■ Confederate Infantry

Scale (Miles)

0   0.6   1.2   1.8

Map 9.4

November 14

Map 9.5: Meade Prepares Another Offensive (November 15 - 26)

In addition to discovering the general location of Lee's army (stretched over a front nearly 20 miles long), Gen. Meade received the welcome news that a railroad bridge had been completed over the wide Rappahannock River. With a siding now ready at Brandy Station on November 19, Meade began stockpiling supplies to continue his planned offensive.[19]

A clear and undefended path across the Rapidan River, good roads, and a dispersed enemy probably boosted Meade's optimism. He would cross at the lower fords and use the Orange Plank Road and the Orange Turnpike to get around Lee's right flank and into his rear. According to a modern army officer, Meade's plan offered a "magnificent opportunity to launch a surprise attack with a high probability of success." Between Lee's right flank and Fredericksburg, however, stretched a thickly wooded region filled with dense underbrush called the "The Wilderness." The two armies had fought there six months earlier at the battle of Chancellorsville. The last thing Meade wanted was to repeat the confusion that operating in that heavy terrain entailed, so after crossing the Rapidan, his corps would quickly traverse the area and head for Lee's flank and rear. As is often the case in combat situations, success would depend upon speed and the element of surprise.[20]

Heavy rains soaked both armies on November 20 and 21 and made the roads impassable, but November 22 dawned with a bright sun. Brig. Gen. Marsena Patrick, the army's provost marshal, scribbled that it was a "glorious day for drying up the roads and hardening them." On November 23, Meade distributed a circular of his plans to his corps leaders and met with them that evening for a briefing and to provide maps of their routes. He emphasized the need for expeditious marches. The corps generals soon came to appreciate the audacity of Meade's plan, which envisioned three columns on the march. Warren's II Corps would cross at Germanna Ford and march for Robertson's Tavern (Locust Grove) on the Orange Turnpike, about four miles southeast of the Confederate right flank. Once there, Warren would rendezvous with William French's III Corps, which would cross the Rapidan at Jacob's Ford, about three and one-half miles upriver from Germanna. French's route to join with the right flank of II Corps was only about seven miles, but it was along small country roads and through large stretches of dense wilderness. Sedgwick's large VI Corps would follow III Corps. Sykes' V Corps, meanwhile, would cross the Rapidan at Culpeper Mine Ford, about four and one-half miles downstream from Germanna Ford and head for Parker's Store and then to New Hope Church on the Orange Plank Road, with Newton's I Corps marching behind it. Once Newton reached Parker's Store, however, he would angle northwest toward Locust Grove to plug the gap between the left of III Corps and the right of V Corps. Gregg's cavalry division was tasked with guarding the army's right flank while the rest of the cavalry watched the various fords and protected the valuable wagon trains. The corps commanders were instructed to provide ten days' rations to the men and cautioned that only the most essential wagons, such as ambulances and those carrying ammunition, could accompany the troops.[21]

Meade's chief of staff, Maj. Gen. Andrew Humphreys, later wrote that "the plan promised brilliant success; to insure it required prompt, vigorous action, and intelligent compliance with the program on the part of corps and other subordinate commanders." Whether it would work remained to be seen. Each corps leader would operate on his own hook because Meade abandoned the wing commander approach he had used successfully at the opening of the campaign.[22]

With the seniors officers briefed, and the men provisioned with food and ammunition, Meade ordered the movement to begin at first light on November 24. Just as the troops were breaking camp, however, a heavy rain made the Rapidan unfordable and turned the roads into ribbons of mud. Meade reset the attack clock for 6:00 a.m. on November 26.

Meade watched with confidence as his troops moved at the appointed time. His plan was to cross the river and reach Robertson's Tavern about noon. The head of II Corps reached Germanna Ford by 9:30 a.m. and V Corps reached Culpeper Mine Ford an hour later. French's III Corps, however, was nowhere to be seen. Meade halted the crossings.[23]

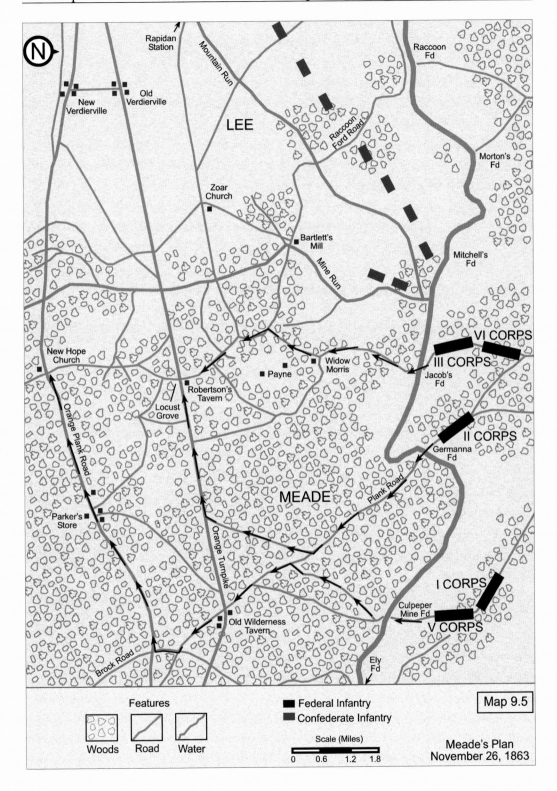

Map 9.5

Features

Woods   Road   Water

■ Federal Infantry
■ Confederate Infantry

Scale (Miles)

0   0.6   1.2   1.8

Meade's Plan
November 26, 1863

Map 9.6: Meade Begins Moving Against Lee (November 26)

John Segwick's VI Corps, which had orders to follow III Corps across the Rapidan River, had his men up and on the road before dawn. When they arrived at III Corps' bivouac sites, however, French's men were still asleep in their tents. French claimed Meade's orders to advance were late in arriving, and Brig. Gen. Henry Prince, the commander of his lead division, was tardy getting his men on the march.

The narrow roads winding down to Jacob's Ford did not help the situation. When Prince finally arrived at the Rapidan, he refused to cross because of concerns that the enemy held the opposite bank. Instead, Prince wasted precious time deploying infantry and artillery, and then sent a detachment of the 11th New Jersey across in boats. Other than Rebel cavalry that quickly scattered, no enemy formations of any strength were discovered. Finally satisfied, Prince ordered a pontoon bridge thrown across. The engineers went to work, but after a time realized they were one boat short. III Corps troops would not set foot on the pontoons until 4:00 p.m. The steep and muddy banks on the southern side of the Rapidan prevented French's wagons from crossing, so Meade ordered them to Germanna Ford about 4:30 p.m.[24]

Warren's II Corps shared a similar problem with French's: he was also one pontoon boat short. His engineers fashioned a trestle to span the rest of the river and the men began crossing. By the end of November 26, Meade had three infantry corps (II, III, and V) across the river, but none had progressed more than three miles inland. I Corps and VI Corps remained on the north bank of the river. The foreboding tangles of the Wilderness, coupled with the possibility of bushwhackers or a surprise major attack, convinced Meade to halt for the night. He spent that anxious and unhappy Thanksgiving evening munching hardtack and salt pork knowing all the while that he was behind schedule and on the cusp of losing the element of surprise. He ordered his men to be on the road early the next day. After reaching Robertson's Tavern they were to head for Old Verdiersville, where the army would reunite. This would put the Army of the Potomac well beyond Lee's line, where

Meade would then have the choice to attack or take up a strong defensive position and hope the Rebels assumed the tactical offensive.[25]

Because of intelligence from his cavalry patrols and his signal station atop Clark's Mountain, Lee already knew that Meade was crossing the Rapidan. The move did not come as a surprise, for he had been expecting it for two weeks. "The country in that vicinity was unfavorable for observation, being almost an unbroken forest," he would later write in his report, "and it could not be discovered whether it was the design of the Federal commander to advance toward Richmond or move up the Rapidan upon our right flank."

Lee decided on his course of action: if Meade headed for Richmond, he would attack his rear and flank; if Lee's army was Meade's objective, Lee would either assume a defensive stance or vigorously attack. Lee drew up plans to put his army in motion, shifting it entirely to his former right flank. Rodes' and Hays' divisions of Ewell's Second Corps (under Maj. Gen. Jubal Early during Ewell's absence), would march along the Orange Turnpike while Maj. Gen. Edward Johnson's Division slipped away from its post along the river by marching along Raccoon Ford Road toward Locust Frove. A. P. Hill's Corps would move east along the Orange Plank Road screened by Wade Hampton's cavalry division. Everything about the operation—from Meade's intent to turn the Rebel right to Lee's planned response—suggested that a major battle was about to be waged.[26]

Meade may have lost the element of surprise, but he still had the advantage of numbers and superior equipment and supplies. Returns for the Army of the Potomac on November 20 put his strength at 95,857 compared with 56,088 for the Army of Northern Virginia. Desertion continued to be a major concern for both armies. During the month of October, 4,391 men left the Union armies without permission and another 3,376 left in November. The number of new recruits and bad weather contributed to the numbers. Confederate numbers are unavailable, but were also high. The campaign unfolding would push the men to their limits. Bitter cold, drenching rains, and the fatigue from constant marching (often on muddy roads) would sap their strength. So would the constant threat of major battle.[27]

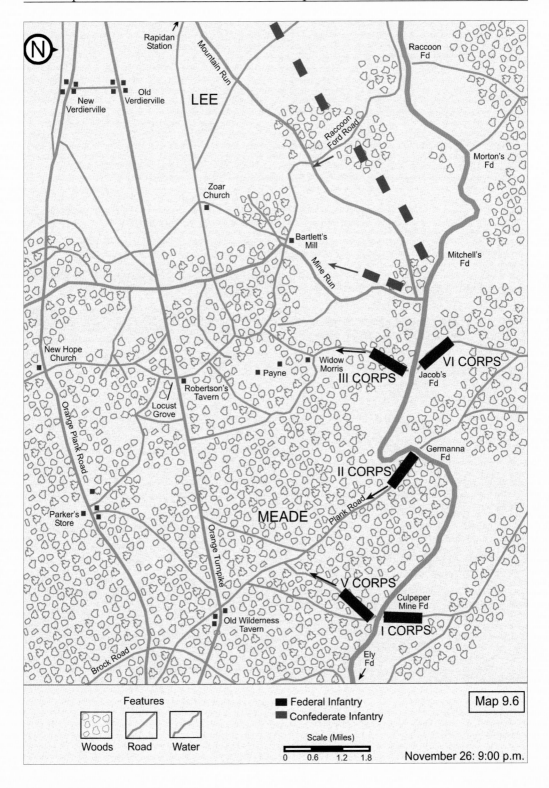

N

Rapidan
Station

Mountain Run

Raccoon
Fd

New
Verdierville

Old
Verdierville

LEE

Raccoon Ford Road

Morton's
Fd

Zoar
Church

Bartlett's
Mill

Mine Run

Mitchell's
Fd

New Hope
Church

Widow
Morris

III CORPS

Jacob's
Fd

VI CORPS

Payne

Robertson's
Tavern

Orange Plank Road

Locust
Grove

II CORPS

Germanna
Fd

Parker's
Store

MEADE

Plank Road

V CORPS

Culpeper
Mine Fd

Orange Turnpike

Old Wilderness
Tavern

I CORPS

Ely
Fd

Brock Road

Features

Woods   Road   Water

■ Federal Infantry
■ Confederate Infantry

Scale (Miles)

0   0.6   1.2   1.8

Map 9.6

November 26: 9:00 p.m.

Map 9.7: Contact
(November 27: 6:00 – 11:00 a.m.)

The Southerners enjoyed strong defenses along the south side of the Rapidan and most believed that active campaigning was over for the year. For the third time in fewer than 45 days, officers ordered their men to draw rations and prepare to march at a moment's notice. The weather was so cold that icicles formed on the men's beards. Few were anxious for another fight, but Lee saw Meade's movement as a chance to get even for Bristoe Station in October and the equally embarrassing losses at Kelly's Ford and Rappahannock Station earlier in the month.[28]

After the sloth-like marches of November 26, Meade notified his corps leaders to be in motion by 7:00 a.m. on the 27th. He did not yet know that Lee was already moving. Warren's II Corps would resume marching south along the Plank Road before cutting over to the Orange Turnpike and heading west to Robertson's Tavern. There, he would link up with French's III Corps moving south on Raccoon Ford Road. Sedgwick's VI Corps would follow French. Sykes' V Corps would continue on back roads to the Plank Road below Warren's cut-off point, turn south, and reach Orange Plank Road to march west about two miles below Warren's II Corps toward New Verdiersville. Newton's I Corps would follow V Corps. The orders were straightforward; the only question was whether the commanders would successfully execute them—and whether Lee would let them.[29]

II Corps broke camp at dawn and marched as described toward Robertson's Tavern (Locust Grove). Brig. Gen. Alexander Hays' division led, followed by Brig. Gen. Alexander Webb and Brig. Gen. John Caldwell (No. 1). The head of II Corps reached Robertson's at 10:00 a.m. Meade told Warren to stay put until III Corps arrived. Warren deployed his corps on the high ground west of the small hamlet with Webb on the right, Hays in the center, and Caldwell on the left.[30]

Neither Meade nor Warren knew that two Rebel divisions were moving east on the same road toward Robertson's. Early's Division under Harry Hays was in front, followed by Maj. Gen. Robert Rodes' Division (No. 2). Hays' skirmishers exchanged fire with Union pickets about 11:00 a.m. just west of Locust Grove. New to division command and unable to ascertain the enemy's strength, Hays waited for Rodes to arrive, deeming "it inexpedient to attack without co-operation." Rodes pushed up his men and deployed on Hays' left. A quick scout told both men that the enemy was present in strength, and they deemed it advisable to wait until Johnson's men arrived before moving against Warren.[31]

Another collision between cavalry was unfolding at the same time farther south on the Orange Plank Road. Hampton's cavalry division under Jeb Stuart and Brig. Gen. David Gregg's cavalry were heading toward one another while screening their respective infantry. Maj. Gen. Henry Heth's Division of Hill's Corps marched behind Stuart (No. 3), and Sykes' infantry behind Gregg (No. 4). Skirmishers from the two cavalry divisions collided about 11:00 a.m. near New Hope Church, two miles south of Locust Grove. Neither opponent was ready to commit to a serious engagement, so a fitful stalemate developed as both sides waited for their infantry to arrive.[32]

A large portion of the Federal army was still missing: French's III Corps, with Sedgwick's large VI Corps behind it, was needed to protect Warren's exposed right flank and plug the hole in the middle of the line, but French was nowhere to be found (No. 5). Without III Corps, Warren was isolated on the army's right flank, which was the direction from which some of Lee's infantry would likely arrive. In addition, a two-mile gap yawned between Warren's left and Sykes' right. Meade sent several messages to French to make haste to support II Corps. At 11:00 a.m., soon after the skirmishing flared up at Locust Grove and New Hope Church, Meade wrote, "General Warren is at Robertson's Tavern. Considerable force of the enemy in his front. Move forward as promptly as possible." The worried Meade fired off another dispatch a few minutes later: "General Warren has met the enemy in strong force (two divisions) at Robertson's Tavern. Communicate this to General Sedgwick, who is to keep close on you. If you cannot unite with General Warren by the route you are on, you must move through to him by the left. It is highly important that you should unite with Warren at once."

Meade had no way of knowing such a simple message would trigger confusion and jeopardize the entire campaign.[33]

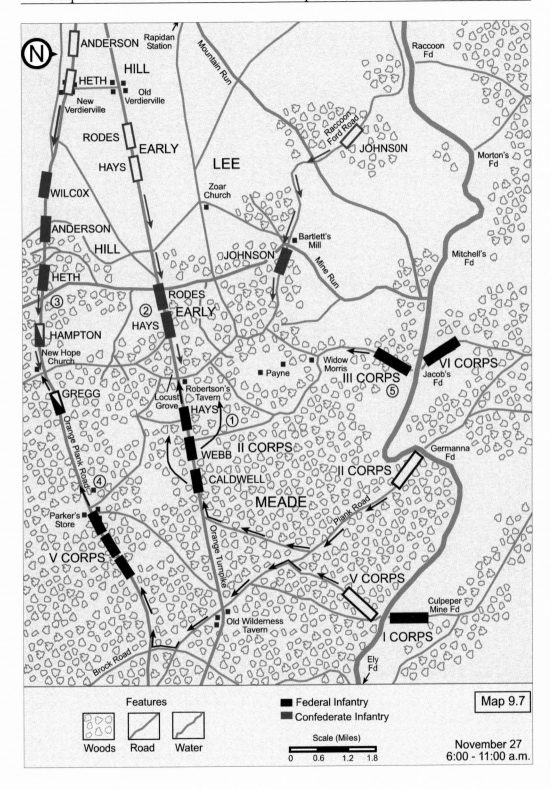

ANDERSON   Rapidan
            Station

HILL

HETH
            Old
New   Verdierville
Verdierville

RODES   EARLY

HAYS

LEE

WILCOX   Zoar
                            Church

ANDERSON

HILL

HETH   JOHNSON

③   RODES
            EARLY
②
HAYS

HAMPTON

New Hope
Church

GREGG   Locust   Robertson's
            Grove   Tavern
                     HAYS ①

WEBB   II CORPS

④   CALDWELL

Parker's   MEADE
Store

V CORPS

Mountain Run

Raccoon
Fd

Raccoon
Ford Road

JOHNSON

Morton's
Fd

Bartlett's
Mill

Mitchell's
Fd

Mine Run

Widow
Morris   Jacob's
III CORPS   Fd
         ⑤
Payne

VI CORPS

Germanna
Fd

II CORPS

Plank Road

V CORPS

Orange Plank Road

Orange Turnpike

Old Wilderness
Tavern

Brock Road

Culpeper
Mine Fd

I CORPS

Ely
Fd

Features

Woods   Road   Water

■ Federal Infantry
■ Confederate Infantry

Scale (Miles)

0   0.6   1.2   1.8

Map 9.7

November 27
6:00 - 11:00 a.m.

Map 9.8: The Armies Assemble
(November 27: 11:00 a.m. - 3:30 p.m.)

Meade finally heard from his errant III Corps leader at 11:30 a.m. French wrote his message more than three hours earlier at 9:20 a.m.: "the head of my column is near the plank road and waiting for General Warren." The stunned army commander sharply questioned the messenger and became more upset: III Corps had marched only three miles from Jacob's Ford! "What are you waiting for?" Meade shot back to to his subordinate. "No orders have been sent to wait for General Warren . . . Robertson's Tavern is the point where he takes precedence and he is there engaged with the enemy, who are in strong force. He is waiting for you . . . move forward as rapidly as possible to Robertson's Tavern where your corps is wanted."[34]

The four remaining miles French still needed to cover were through heavy terrain with limited visibility and restricted routes of movement. Since divisions could not rotate their marching order as they normally did each day, the tardy and inept Henry Prince continued to lead the column. "Being in command of the advance, and having no guide, I conceived it to be my duty to exert my judgment as to the route, and by reconnoitering to clear up the way if I could," Prince later reported. He had his men up and ready to march by daylight, but had only moved about a mile before reaching a fork in the road near the Widow Morris farm (No. 1). Prince was stumped. Which road should he take? According to his map the right fork was the most direct route, but it intersected Raccoon Ford Road about one mile southwest, which would surely be filled with enemy troops. The left fork was safer, but it was also longer and would delay his arrival at Robertson's. Unable to decide, Prince sent some cavalry down the right fork. The troopers returned to report that Rebel infantry was marching on the road. Prince at the head of III Corps did nothing as he wasted more than two hours trying to decide which route to take. French was within 300 yards of Prince's division, but used couriers to communicate instead of riding to the fork and making a decision.[35]

Meade received another dispatch from French at 1:45 p.m. This one, penned two hours earlier, observed, "General Prince reports . . . that the enemy are throwing out a large force of infantry upon my right flank upon the Raccoon Ford Road. I am making dispositions accordingly." Meade shot back: "attack the enemy in your front immediately, throwing your left forward so as to connect with General Warren at Robertson's Tavern. The object of the attack is to form a junction with General Warren, which must be effected immediately." News of enemy infantry marching like an arrow toward Meade's exposed right suggested that Lee was mounting a flanking movement while the rest of his army pressed against Meade's center and left. The need to unite his army was now greater than ever. Warren could be turned or crushed, and French cut off and destroyed with Sedgwick's VI Corps jammed behind him. Meade's anger erupted at 2:00 p.m. According to a staffer, he "became greatly out of temper about it."[36]

Farther south on the Orange Plank Road, Heth's division arrived at New Hope Church about 2:30 p.m. and relieved Stuart's cavalry (No. 2). When Heth's skirmishers were driven back by Gregg's troopers, he rode rearward to find Hill and seek permission to attack. He found Gen. Lee instead, who consented. When it took Heth more time to deploy than anticipated, Lee changed his mind and ordered him to await further orders.[37]

While Heth was preparing to attack, Sykes' V Corps arrived to relieve Gregg's cavalry about 3:00 p.m. (No. 3). It had taken Sykes six hours to march three miles from Parker's Store to New Hope Church. Once he got to the front and examined the terrain, Sykes realized that Hill's infantry occupied the high ground west of the village. Like Lee, Meade ordered Sykes to hold his position. He didn't want to go into battle until French and Sedgwick had rejoined the army. A steady patter of skirmishing spread across the southern front of the line.[38]

The center of the two armies along the Orange Turnpike was also experiencing an increasing level of small arms fire. John Gordon's Brigade of Hays' Division (Ewell's Second Corps) deployed to the front and opened a brisk skirmish with troops from Warren's II Corps, which by this time was fully deployed and ready for action (No. 4). Early's third division under Robert Rodes was also coming up on Hays' left to add weight to the Confederate front.[39]

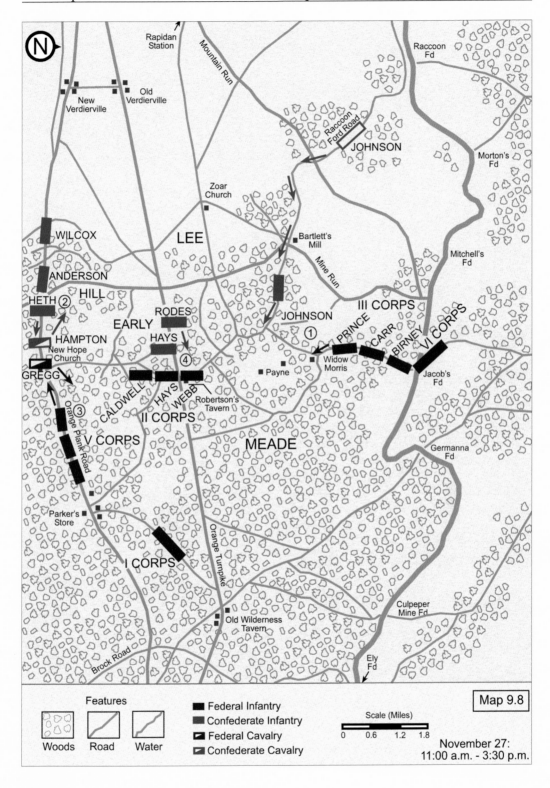

N

Rapidan Station

Mountain Run

Raccoon Fd

New Verdierville

Old Verdierville

Raccoon Ford Road

JOHNSON

Morton's Fd

Zoar Church

WILCOX

LEE

Bartlett's Mill

Mitchell's Fd

ANDERSON

HILL

Mine Run

HETH ②

RODES

JOHNSON

III CORPS

VI CORPS

EARLY

HAYS

①

PRINCE

CARR

BIRNEY

HAMPTON

New Hope Church

④

Widow Morris

Jacob's Fd

GREGG

Payne

Orange Plank Road

CALDWELL

HAYS

WEBB

Robertson's Tavern

③

II CORPS

V CORPS

MEADE

Germanna Fd

Parker's Store

Orange Turnpike

I CORPS

Culpeper Mine Fd

Old Wilderness Tavern

Brock Road

Ely Fd

Features

Woods   Road   Water

■ Federal Infantry
■ Confederate Infantry
◪ Federal Cavalry
◪ Confederate Cavalry

Scale (Miles)

0   0.6   1.2   1.8

Map 9.8

November 27:
11:00 a.m. - 3:30 p.m.

Map Set 10: Encounter at Payne's Farm

Map 10.1: The Combatants Approach
(November 27: 10:00 a.m. - 2:00 p.m.)

As the hours passed on November 27, Maj. Gen. George Meade worried that III Corps commander William French had wasted a second day of what was to have been a speedy march to flank Gen. Robert E. Lee's Army of Northern Virginia. French's lead division under Brig. Gen. Henry Prince remained at the Widow Morris crossroads while Prince vacillated about the best route to reach Meade and the balance of the army. Bottled up behind Prince was the balance of III Corps and the entire VI Corps, the largest in the Army of the Potomac. With any hope of surprise long gone, Meade worried that the tables had turned and that his own army would be the bait, with Lee turning away from the Rapidan River to pounce on his exposed right flank.

While Prince dallied and Meade worried, Maj. Gen. Edward Johnson's Division marched along the Raccoon Ford Road to join the left flank of Maj. Gen. Robert Rodes's Division at Locust Grove. Johnston knew the enemy had crossed Jacob's Ford and were off to his left-front, so each of his brigade leaders threw out skirmishers left of the road. It was a vulnerable march, with four infantry brigades, artillery, and wagons stretched for two miles along a narrow road lined with heavy timber and brush.

A brigade of Virginians under Brig. Gen. John M. Jones led Johnson's column, followed by Leroy Stafford's Louisianians and then more Virginians in James Walker's Stonewall Brigade. Next came the division's wagons and Anderson's artillery battalion. A mixed brigade of Maryland, North Carolina, and Virginia troops under George H. Steuart brought up the rear. It was Steuart's task, wrote Johnson, "to guard against any sudden dash upon the artillery."[1]

The head of Johnson's column reached Rodes's left about 2:00 p.m. Within minutes a rider arrived with an urgent message from Steuart: an enemy skirmish line "supposed to be dismounted cavalry" had filtered through the woods and was attacking the ambulance wagons in front of him. Johnson turned his horse and galloped to the rear. As he would later learn, several of the wagons had turned and disrupted Steuart's infantry. The brigadier sorted out the mess and ordered his men to deploy for action.

By the time Johnson reached Steuart (the narrow road was clogged with his own troops and artillery, and there was precious little space on either side for a clear ride to the rear), "the enemy's infantry was in our front, heavy bodies of them in line of battle having been discovered." Johnson ordered his other three brigades to about-face and close on Steuart.[2]

Fortunately for the Army of Northern Virginia, Edward "Allegheny" Johnson was a seasoned officer leading a solid division. After graduating from West Point in 1838, the native Virginian saw action in the Seminole and Mexican wars, received promotions for his leadership abilities during combat, and saw extensive action on the frontier. His rise in rank and stature in the Confederate army was also impressive. He resigned his U.S. Army commission when the Civil War broke out and began as a colonel of the 12th Georgia in July 1861. After service with Gen. Lee in the Cheat Mountain Campaign he was promoted to brigadier general to date from December 13, 1861—the day he earned him his famous nickname "Allegheny," the result of having led six infantry companies (essentially a brigade tagged with the unofficial moniker "Army of the Northwest") in a skirmish on Allegheny Mountain. During the early days of Stonewall Jackson's Valley Campaign, Johnson was severely wounded in the ankle at McDowell on May 8, 1862. He returned to duty about one year later as a major general leading a division on the march north to Gettysburg. Bad luck placed his command at the foot of the rocky and wooded Culp's Hill, which he resolutely stormed during the evening of July 2 and again on the early morning of July 3. His losses were heavy with nothing of value gained. Johnson had seen much of war, and he knew his craft. This was the general who pulled up his mount to witness the last brigade in his line deploying for battle. The skirmishers were briskly engaged.[3]

Although Johnson did not yet know it, the men who had stumbled into his column belonged to Henry Prince's Federal division. The two officers had a few things in common: both were West Pointers and both had distinguished themselves in the Seminole and Mexican wars. But the similarities ended there. Prince—the leader on a tight schedule who could not decide which road to take, and so took neither for hours—was cautious to a fault. Johnson, as Prince would soon discover, was not.[4]

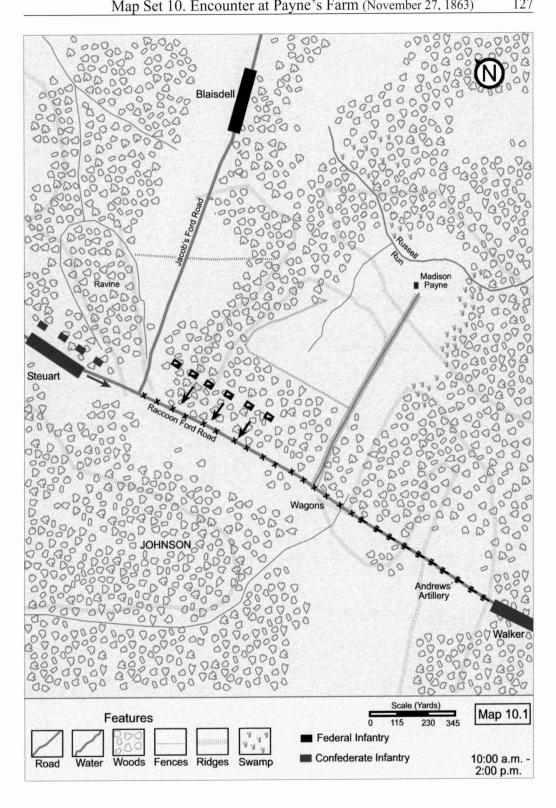

Blaisdell

Jacob's Ford Road

Russell Run

Madison Payne

Ravine

Steuart

Raccoon Ford Road

JOHNSON

Wagons

Andrews' Artillery

Walker

Scale (Yards)

0   115   230   345

Map 10.1

Features

Road   Water   Woods   Fences   Ridges   Swamp

■ Federal Infantry

■ Confederate Infantry

10:00 a.m. - 2:00 p.m.

Map 10.2: Prince's Fitful Advance
(November 27: 3:00 - 3:30 p.m.)

The field on which the battle of Payne's Farm would be fought was far from ideal for combat. Other than the open land around the two Payne farmsteads, the terrain consisted of heavy woods clotted with choking underbrush lining an undulating ravine-laced wilderness, all fed by sluggish swampy streams. The timber and brush was so thick in many places that neither side could be sure of the strength of the other directly to their front.

The accidental meeting took place after French finally ordered Prince to move his division on the right fork. "I shall take the road and having obtained possession of it," replied Prince, "I shall reconnoiter and act according to circumstances." More confusion was about to set in because it was only after ordering Prince to move out that French received the "What are you waiting for?" dispatch from Meade chastising him for not moving aggressively to join Warren at Robertson's Tavern.[5]

Heeding orders, Prince directed his lead brigade under Col. William Blaisdale to deploy along a fringe of timber a short distance south of the Widow Morris house and unlimbered Lt. John Bucklyn's Battery E, 1st Rhode Island Artillery in the Morris clearing. Blaisdale pushed out the 1st and 11th Massachusetts as a strong skirmish line and formed his main line of battle, from left to right, as follows: 16th Massachusetts, 26th Pennsylvania, and 11th New Jersey on the left side of Jacob's Ford Road, and the 84th Pennsylvania on the right side. Col. William Brewster's New York Excelsior Brigade was next in line. Prince sent two of its regiments, the 74th and 120th New York, forward to bolster the right side of Blaisdall's main line. Somehow the former regiment occupied a space between the road and the 84th Pennsylvania within Blaisdell's line of battle. The 120th New York formed on the right of the Pennsylvanians. After five hours of inactivity, Prince and his men were finally showing signs of life.

It was just before 2:00 p.m. and Prince was about to give the order to advance when a messenger arrived from French ordering him to stop because he was on the wrong road. French had sent another dispatch to Meade confirming the presence of enemy troops, which triggered a reply to attack the enemy while "throwing your left forward so as to connect with General Warren at Robertson's Tavern." Prince complied and his men waited, which gave Johnson and his brigadiers additional time to march back into position and deploy. Well aware of French's growing frustration, Prince rode back to headquarters to advise the corps leader about the heavy skirmishing situation to his front. Mindful of his own orders, French told Prince to continue but call upon Brig. Gen, Joseph Carr's division, if needed.[6]

Properly cautious (in this case), Prince sought out Gen. Carr to bring up his Third Division on his left flank so he could continue his advance. "He declined to do so," wrote a frustrated Prince. "I replied, 'But I order it.' He begged me to understand that it was with no personal view toward me that he declined, but that his instructions were to follow." Prince complained in a scribbled message to French, which the corps leader returned with the messenger in the form of a five-word verbal rebuke: "The general says go on."

Given the difficult terrain, Prince told his brigade commanders to advance only to the Raccoon Ford Road, but not cross it. The Union line stepped off again but within a few minutes yet another aide arrived with orders for Prince to halt until Carr's division could form on his left. The relieved Prince gladly obeyed the order, noting, "to my extreme surprise, I succeeded in halting my command in good order." French also issued orders to his First Division commander, Maj. Gen. David Birney, to advance and take a position behind the Second and Third Divisions and prepare to support either unit as needed.[7]

Just a half-mile south of Prince's line were Confederates under Gen. George Steuart, who were taking full advantage of the fitful advances to position his brigade for battle. At the first contact, he had ordered his regiments to face left and told Col. Edward Warren, the commander of the 10th Virginia on his far right, to throw five companies forward to guard the wagons. The 23rd Virginia was next in line to the left, followed by the 1st North Carolina, 3rd North Carolina, and the 37th Virginia. In all, Steuart's command numbered about 1,400 men.[8]

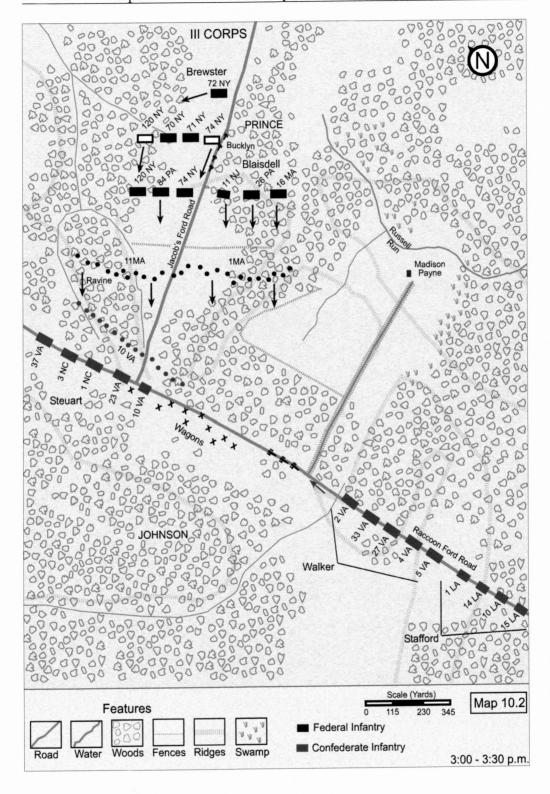

III CORPS

Brewster
72 NY

120 NY 70 NY 71 NY 74 NY

PRINCE

Bucklyn

Blaisdell

120 NY 84 PA 74 NY 11 NJ 26 PA 16 MA

Jacob's Ford Road

11MA 1MA

Madison
Payne

Ravine

Russell
Run

37 VA 3 NC 1 NC 23 VA 10 VA

10 VA

Steuart

Wagons

JOHNSON

Walker

2 VA 33 VA 27 VA 4 VA 5 VA

Raccoon Ford Road

1 LA 14 LA 10 LA 15 LA

Stafford

Features

Road   Water   Woods   Fences   Ridges   Swamp

Scale (Yards)
0   115   230   345

Map 10.2

■ Federal Infantry

■ Confederate Infantry

3:00 - 3:30 p.m.

Map 10.3: Prince Delays;
Johnson Deploys for Battle
(November 27: 3:30 p.m.)

Steuart reported that his skirmishers "had scarcely proceeded 20 paces when they encountered a strong line of infantry skirmishers. These were driven back some distance and the enemy discovered drawn up in line of battle. At this time the enemy also opened upon us with one or two pieces of artillery." These were not dismounted cavalry. Steuart's men had stumbled into Prince's main line of battle.[9]

While waiting for Carr's division to form on his left, Prince directed the balance of Col. William Brewster's New York regiments into position on Blaisdell's right. The 74th New York was already in line just to the right of the Jacob's Ford Road, and the 120th New York angled right during its advance joining the 1st and 11th Massachusetts on the skirmish line and extending the cover for the main line. Brewster's remaining elements, the 72nd, 70th, and 71st New York, marched to the right of the 84th Pennsylvania and extended the line in that order.

As the main line formed behind them, the two Massachusetts regiments on the skirmish line (soon joined by the New Yorkers of the 120th) maintained a noisy rattling fight with their counterparts in Steuart's command. Most of the 1st Massachusetts was on the left side of Jacob's Ford Road, with the 11th Massachusetts fighting on its right, and the 120th New York extending the line farther still. The long thin line of Massachusetts skirmishers overlapped both of Steuart's flanks, an advantage enhanced when the New Yorkers joined the line. "Slowly advancing through the woods into an open field, tearing down a fence, we came upon the enemy's pickets, and proceeded down a small hill, and on arriving at the edge of the woods received a full volley from the enemy's front," reported Col. Porter Tripp of the 11th Massachusetts. The fighting intensified. Rebel skirmishers scraped out shallow rifle pits between rounds.[10]

Holding Steuart's far left was the 37th Virginia, with the 3rd North Carolina extending the line toward the Jacob's Ford Road, which bisected the next regiment in line, the 1st North Carolina. Steuart's last two regiments, the 23rd and 10th Virginia, extended the line on the right

side of the road. A section of guns from Carpenter's Battery unlimbered in the road junction. The situation rapidly worsened for Steuart when Col. Titus Williams, commanding the 37th Virginia, reported the enemy "crossing the road on his left for the evident purpose of flanking the brigade." These Federals were part of the 11th Massachusetts and perhaps the 120th New York.

Gen. Johnson, meanwhile, arrived about this time after threading his way back along the narrow country road clogged with his own troops and artillery to reach Steuart's embattled command. "Steuart's skirmishers," he wrote, were "briskly engaged with those of the enemy, who were endeavoring to turn his left." Johnson ordered Steuart to "throw back his left and form his brigade at right angles to the road," and his other three brigades to about-face and "close up upon General Steuart's right, and throw out skirmishers."[11]

Johnson maneuvered his mount up and down the congested line in an effort to determine the size and location of the enemy. With Steuart's command exposed and vulnerable on both flanks, Johnson was especially anxious to get his entire division onto the firing line. Pursuant to orders, Steuart positioned his right regiment (Warren's 10th Virginia) on the Raccoon Ford Road and maneuvered the remainder of his brigade into the trees and brush south of the road. Satisfied that his left was being refused, Johnson oversaw the deployment of each of his remaining three brigades. After reversing course and marching about a quarter of a mile, Walker's Stonewall Brigade reached Steuart's right flank. Leroy Stafford's Louisiana brigade tramped behind Walker. The tail of Johnson's last brigade under John Jones was just leaving Locus Grove to march back about one mile toward the scene of the fighting. The somewhat chaotic movement took time to accomplish, which the Federals were graciously allowing in spades.[12]

Col. Williams fell back back as instructed and ordered his men to "change front to the rear on my first company," which shifted his line perpendicular to the Raccoon Ford Road. This was not an easy maneuver for the men. Just as he completed it, Williams received orders from Steuart to "advance and attack the enemy in my front." Unfortunately for Williams, he was facing in the wrong direction.[13]

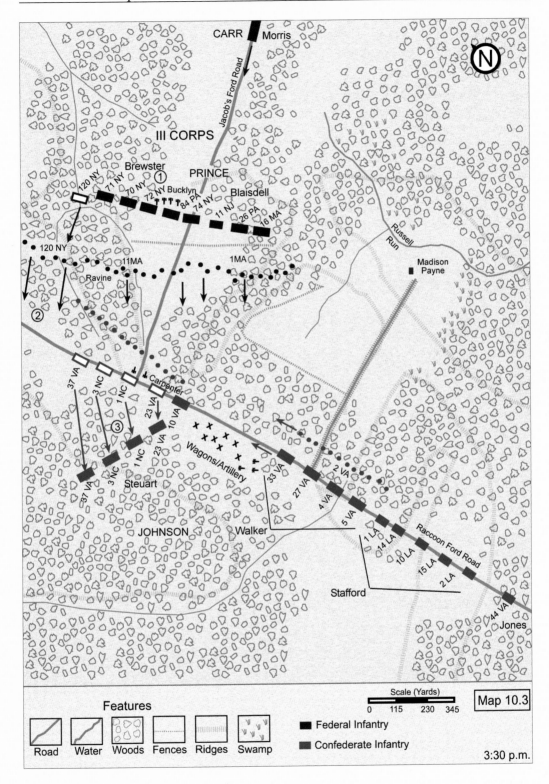

Features

Road   Water   Woods   Fences   Ridges   Swamp

■ Federal Infantry
■ Confederate Infantry

Scale (Yards)

0   115   230   345

Map 10.3

3:30 p.m.

Map 10.4: Johnson Plans for Battle
(November 27: 3:30 - 3:45 p.m.)

As Prince cooled his heels in front of Steuart's Brigade, Carr's division marched along Jacob's Ford Road to support it as requested. When just north of Prince's division, Carr spun off a mixed brigade of New York, Vermont, and New Jersey troops under Brig. Gen. William Morris to the left. Morris's three regiments had to contend with thick vegetation and struggled to assume a position on Blaisdell's flank. Morris' brigade was followed at some length by Col. J. Warren Keifer's brigade. Carr's last brigade under Col. Benjamin Smith brought up the rear. Trailing some distance behind Smith was Maj. Gen. David Birney's division, which was in a good position to support both Prince and Carr.[14]

While French and Prince dithered, Johnson worked at pace to position his division and secure his front. His 5,300 men now faced the enemy along Raccoon Ford Road in an almost solid front, covered by a swarm of skirmishers. One of Jones' men would later recall that the redeployment of Johnson's men was "one of the promptest movements I saw during the war." Steuart and Stafford threw several companies from each regiment out on the line; Walker selected the 2nd Virginia to cover his front and Jones the 25th Virginia for his, supplemented in places with companies from the other regiments. The firing on the skirmish line was heavy. Alexander Baird of the former regiment wrote home after the battle that Gen. Walker threw the regiment out on the skirmish line with orders that we "must hold that ground at all hazards." A soldier from the 3rd North Carolina of Steuart's Brigade later wrote that "it seemed as if the enemy was throwing minie-balls upon us by the bucket-full, when the battle got fairly underway." Johnson expected an attack at any moment, so he ordered the men to throw up light works of fence rails and dirt along the road.[15]

As he rode along his line, Johnson formulated a plan. The enemy fire in his front seemed to be slackening. Was it time to act? He could face his command to the right and follow his original orders by retracing his steps toward Locust Grove where Rodes was waiting with his division. Johnson ruled out this option as it would jeopardize the rest of Lee's army. He also

had to have known that an enemy attack on his division while it was marching on the narrow Raccoon Ford Road would invite panic and potential disaster. He could also remain in place to await an enemy attack. Because he did not know the exact numbers or location of the Federals opposing him, he also ruled this out. Johnson instead settled upon a third option. The ever-aggressive leader decided to attack the stationary enemy in his front. Because most of the firing was coming from the area opposite the right-center of Steuart's Brigade, Johnson concluded that the enemy's right flank ended there and was vulnerable. He also concluded that the Federal left flank ended somewhere opposite Walker's right flank. Not only was he wrong on both counts, but he also did not know that a second Federal division was at that very moment sliding into position (Carr) and a third (Birney) was within supporting distance. If that was not bad enough, the powerful Federal VI Corps under Maj. Gen. John Sedgwick was behind Birney. Johnson's 5,300 Confederates were facing up to as many as 32,000 enemy soldiers in the thickets of the Wilderness.[16]

The Confederate skirmish line was extremely aggressive during this early period. It was not content to merely screen the division behind it, for Johnson ordered it to "feel the enemy" to develop its position. Both sides rotated their units on the skirmish line when they ran low or out of ammunition.[17]

Meanwhile, Col. Williams's 37th Virginia remained in a precarious position on the extreme left flank of the division. The Virginians faced fluid lines of Federal skirmishers who seemed to be attempting to flank their position and possibly get into its rear and turn the line. Williams ordered his men forward and they cleared their front in a short time, taking a number of prisoners in the process. Before the men had time to savor their small victory, however, Williams received a report that a large force, perhaps as large as a brigade, was approaching his left flank and would cause serious trouble if not dealt with. Williams sent this bit of troubling information to Steuart and pondered his next move.[18]

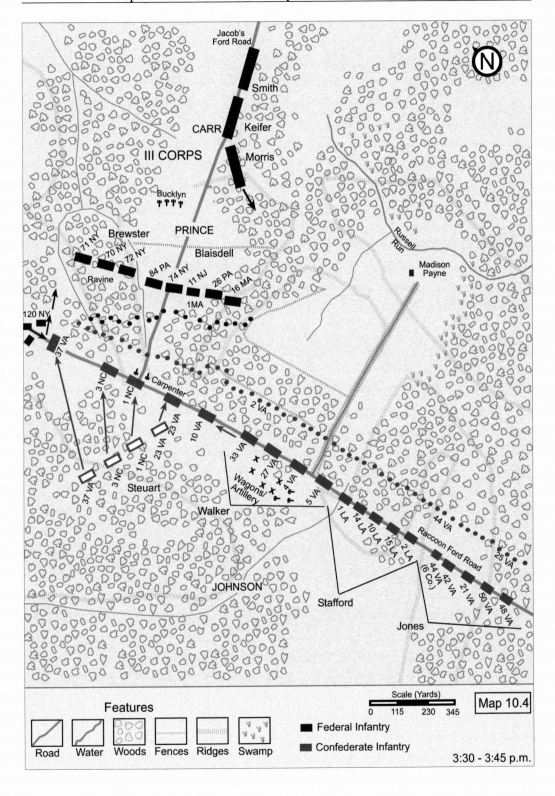

Scale (Yards)

0   115   230   345

Map 10.4

Features

| Road | Water | Woods | Fences | Ridges | Swamp |

■ Federal Infantry

■ Confederate Infantry

3:30 - 3:45 p.m.

Map 10.5: Carr's Division Deploys as Johnson Finalizes his Plans
(November 27: 4:00 - 4:15 p.m.)

As Gen. Johnson put the finishing touches on his plan of attack, the division was ordered to move forward about "50 paces" according to the commander of the 5th Virginia (Walker's Brigade), which is where the men threw up light fortifications of brush and fence rails. No sooner had they begun their work than orders arrived to prepare to advance. Earlier they had been told not to worry because "there was nothing but the enemy's cavalry in our front," scoffed one Virginia officer. By this time the men knew better, although none of them had any real idea of exactly what they would find once they stepped off to attack.[19]

Johnson's skirmish line advanced ahead of the rest of the division, pushing the enemy's skirmishers back toward their main line. The fighting was particularly heavy along some parts of the line, especially in front of Lt. Col. Raleigh Colston's 2nd Virginia of the Stonewall Brigade. Colston's regiment, which had brought up the rear during the march, was trotted forward at the beginning of the engagement to man the skirmish line. They moved by the left flank to link up with Steuart's skirmishers. Because of the rough and heavy terrain, explained Capt. Charles Stewart of the 2nd Virginia, "our line of skirmishers got in advance of General Steuart's line some 200 yards, and overlapped the right of his line some considerable distance." Despite the brisk firing Colston conspicuously rode his mount back and forth along the line, encouraging his men to hold steady. Many of his men pleaded with their commander to stop exposing himself in such a reckless fashion. Colston failed to heed their warnings. Within a few minutes he cried, "Oh my God, I am shot!" and fell off his horse with a shattered leg. As he was carried from the field Colston told Capt. Stewart to assume command of the 2nd Virginia and shift the left of the skirmish line farther right and rearward to better align with Steuart's skirmish line and Leroy Stafford's front line on the right (No. 1). These maneuvers were underway when the Federal skirmish line aggressively advanced and the fighting flared anew. Gen. Walker commended the 2nd Virginia

for "gallantly holding the enemy in check until the brigade advanced to its support."[20]

Johnson's men were preparing to step off for their attack just minutes after Morris' brigade of Carr's division, led by the 151st New York, deployed on the left of Prince's division (No. 2). Col. J. Warren Keifer's brigade was behind Morris and deeper in the woods, where its members struggled through the dense vegetation to find good terrain to hold on Morris's left. "On account of the density of the undergrowth in the woods and the absence of roads," explained Keifer, "it was with some difficulty that I succeeded in reaching the position designated."[21]

While Carr deployed and Blaisdell awaited orders to advance, two regiments from Brewster's Excelsior Brigade (70th and 71st New York) bore down on Steuart's left flank (No. 3). All that stood between them and the Confederate rear was Titus Williams's 37th Virginia, which had recently beaten off the 120th New York deployed on a skirmish line.[22]

By 4:00 p.m., Gen. Johnson was convinced of the merit of his plan of attack and sent orders to each of his brigade commanders accordingly. Despite the thick and almost impassable vegetation, Johnson chose a complicated (and nearly impossible) double envelopment. On the right, Stafford's and Jones's brigades would advance straight ahead for an undisclosed distance and wheel left to find and strike the Federal left and drive into their rear. At the same time, Steuart's Brigade on the far left of the line would wheel to the right to turn and crush what Johnson thought was the Federal right flank. Walker's Stonewall Brigade, meanwhile, would advance straight ahead and act as the foundational element between the two flanking operations.

Johnson hoped to catch the aggressive Federals in a vise and destroy or force a panicked retreat. Jones on the far right had the most ground to traverse, so it would take him much longer to reach the enemy. The division commander seems not to have factored this into his calculations because he launched his entire division at the same time.[23]

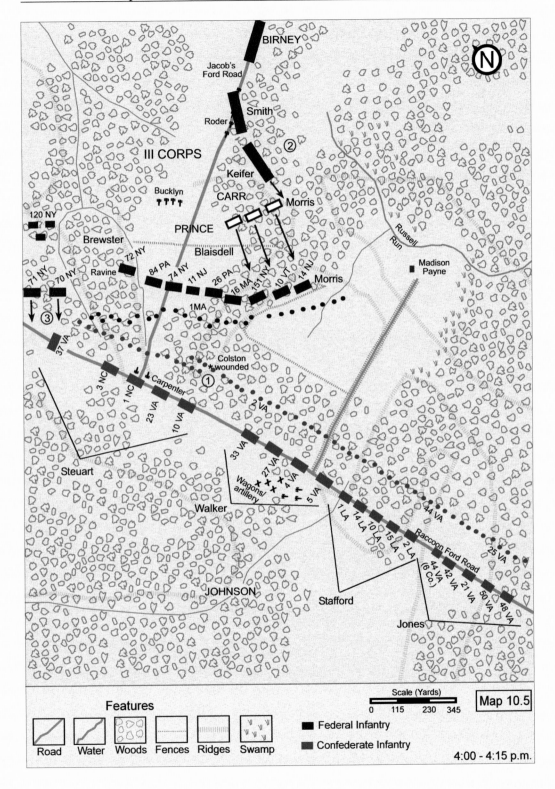

Features

Road   Water   Woods   Fences   Ridges   Swamp

Scale (Yards)
0   115   230   345

■ Federal Infantry

■ Confederate Infantry

Map 10.5

4:00 - 4:15 p.m.

Map 10.6: Johnson Launches his Double Envelopment
(November 27: 4:15 - 4:30 p.m.)

The Federal line was still taking form when Johnson's men stepped off. Prince's division was on the right side, with Brewster's brigade forming the right front and Blaisdell's brigade on its left. Carr's division was jockeying into position through exceptionally difficult terrain, forming right to left as follows: Morris's brigade, Kiefer's brigade, and Smith's brigade coming up behind. David Birney's division was leaving the Jacob's Ford Road or about to do so.

Additional artillery support also arrived for both sides. Lt. John Roder's six guns comprising Battery K, 4th U.S. Artillery, dropped trail between Jacob's Ford Road and Bucklyn's four guns. On the Southern side, Capt. William Dement's four-gun battery (1st Maryland Artillery) was about to be called into action, though at this time it was parked south of the Raccoon Ford Road near the junction with the Madison Payne farm lane in the right-rear of Walker's Brigade.

Steuart/Prince: The left-center of Steuart's Brigade (the left element of Johnson's Division) advanced a short distance and wheeled to the right as ordered. Although the distance the men needed to travel to engage the enemy was much shorter than Stafford's and Jones's, Steuart had the added burden of maintaining a connection with Walker on his right and his own far left regiment, the 37th Virginia. As Steuart noted in his report, "I was subsequently ordered to throw forward and to right oblique my left, so as to occupy a position nearly parallel to that previously held along the road. . . . I was instructed at the same time to keep up the connection on my right, so as to leave no interval between it and the Stonewall Brigade. As a result, the 1st and 3rd North Carolina on the left and center of the brigade made the oblique movement, while the 10th and 23rd Virginia on the right continued moving forward in concert with Walker (No. 1).[24]

Col. Williams' 37th Virginia did not participate in the advance because it had its hands full with other Federals. After driving back the 120th New York from the flank, Williams learned (as noted earlier), that "the enemy, a brigade strong, was turning my left flank." Williams had no choice but to immediately maneuver his men to face this new threat, but New Yorkers from Brewster's brigade were already threatening his flank and rear (No. 2). Williams was about to be surrounded and none of his comrades were visible to his right. A dangerous gap about 200 yards wide was now open in Steuart's line.[25]

Walker/Morris: Morris was assuming his position on Prince's left when enemy skirmishers (Walker's Virginians) were found behind a fence. According to Gen. Carr, "I ordered him [Morris] to charge and drive them from it, which they did, driving the enemy through the fields beyond." Col. A. B. Jewett of the 10th Vermont added detail, writing in his after-battle report that the brigade had "drove the enemy, in much confusion and with great loss, from the crest of the hill."[26] Morris's three regiments took their place behind the fence overlooking the field. He pushed his men across the open field and into the woods beyond, but within minutes his skirmishers tumbled back in the face of a Confederate advance.

Of Johnson's four brigades, Walker's command had by far the easiest task. Rather than a wheeling or pivot movement, his five regiments simply walked straight ahead (No. 3) to the edge of the Payne farm field. Walker noted that "the ground in my front for about 500 [250] yards was thickly wooded and brushy, and beyond was a cleared farm." Abraham Spengler of the 33rd Virginia recalled that during the early stages of the attack, the line moved "at first in quick time and then in double-quick time and with a shout, it appearing that the enemy with a heavy line of battle, was driving our skirmishers back."[27]

Stafford/Jones: Johnson's two brigades on the right (Stafford's Louisianans and Jones's Virginians) had the longest and most difficult route to finding the enemy. (No. 4). Stafford's men had a tighter wheel over easier terrain, and so made better progress (No. 5) than did Jones. As Stafford noted in his report, "an advance of some quarter of a mile freed us from the woods with which our front had been covered. The enemy's skirmishers were immediately driven in."[28]

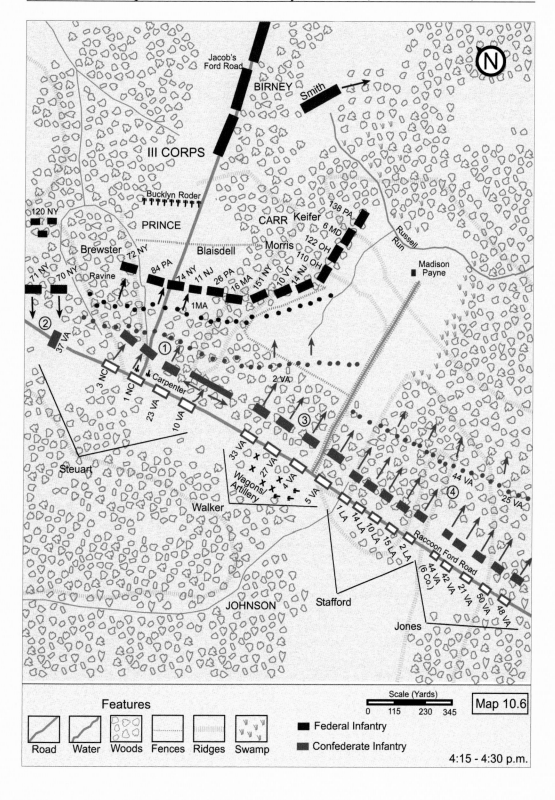

Map 10.6

Scale (Yards)
0   115   230   345

Features

| Road | Water | Woods | Fences | Ridges | Swamp |

■ Federal Infantry

■ Confederate Infantry

4:15 - 4:30 p.m.

Map 10.7: Steuart Finds Prince's Division (November 27: 4:30 - 4:45 p.m.)

Steuart/Prince: With the 70th and 71st New York threatening to surround his 37th Virginia, Col. Williams adopted a novel tactic. Rather than retreating or trying to fight what he thought might be a full enemy brigade, Williams deployed his regiment as one long skirmish line. By extending his front to more than twice its normal length, he hoped to trick the enemy into thinking that his command was just a skirmish line, and that the main Confederate battle line was lying in wait in the thick woods behind him (No. 1). This clever ruse used the thickets to his advantage. Once aligned, Williams ordered his men to fire volleys into the approaching 71st New York, halting its movement. The Virginians could see the 70th New York approaching their right flank, but they held their ground.[29]

Meanwhile, a gap opened between Williams' right and the rest of the brigade. The 3rd North Carolina formed in a ravine that provided protection from the Federal guns raking the trees above them (No. 2). With a shout the men of the 3rd, together with the 1st North Carolina on their right, moved in tandem across the Jacob's Ford Road into the woods beyond on an oblique against Blaisdell's front. Shot and shell greeted the 3rd North Carolina as it emerged from the ravine, followed a short time later by small arms fire. One Tar Heel recalled this was "as warm a contest as this regiment was ever engaged in for the same length of time." He also noted that it seemed "as if the enemy was throwing minie balls upon us by the bucket-full."[30]

The 23rd Virginia advanced on the right of the 1st North Carolina, with Steuart's right-most regiment, Col. E. T. H. Warren's 10th Virginia (No. 3). Half of Warren's regiment had originally been assigned to move forward to protect the wagons after they were attacked. He was never able to fully reform his command, but attempted to advance and keep pace with Walker's left. This proved an impossible task and a gap about 150 yards wide opened, which Warren filled by spreading his line dangerously thin.[31]

Steuart wrote that the advance was difficult, for "the extraordinary density of the thicket prevented the different parts of the line from conforming to the movement with regularity and promptude." What were once well-dressed lines were now squeezed, ragged, unaligned, and in most cased unconnected from one another.[32]

Walker/Morris: Walker's Stonewall Brigade, meanwhile, tramped through the heavy trees and underbrush for a few hundred yards until they found the Federals at the edge of the woods and in the open field beyond. According to Walker, he ordered an attack and the enemy, "gave way in confusion." The Federal skirmishers sprinted backward and to Walker's left into a small ravine and heavy stand of timber (No. 4). In an effort to maintain the initiative and momentum, Walker ordered his men to continue the attack over the fence and into the large open field. Walker's line was also in some disorder. On the far right, Col. John Funk's 5th Virginia found itself struggling through underbrush on the right side of the Madison Payne farm lane. "My regiment was very much scattered owing to the denseness of the undergrowth. I halted and reformed it." Walker did not know that Morris's brigade was deployed in line of battle and waiting for the Confederates to step into killing range.[33]

Stafford/Jones: Johnson's right two brigades under Stafford and Jones continued their advance in an effort to play the role of the attack hammer. The Louisiana troops struggled about a quarter-mile through the woods without meeting any enemy skirmishers until they broke free from the timber. Once in the open they drove back clouds of Federals pickets and, now on higher ground, spotted strong forces of the enemy more than one-half mile away on a strong series of ridges. Walker's men were visible fighting from the edge of the woods on their left (No. 5). According to Capt. E. D. Willett of the 1st Louisiana Infantry on Stafford's left, "After advancing some 300 or 400 yards we came to an open field near Payne's house, when, finding the enemy were not in our immediate front, but firing on our left flank, which necessitated a change of front, after which we became engaged."

On the far right, Jones's Virginians could hear heavy firing to their left and, as Col. William Witcher of the 21st Virginia reported, "as the other brigades moved obliquely to the left, it became necessary for our brigade to wheel rapidly in the same direction. Under the difficulties of so long and rapid a wheel, the troops kept in rank remarkably well."

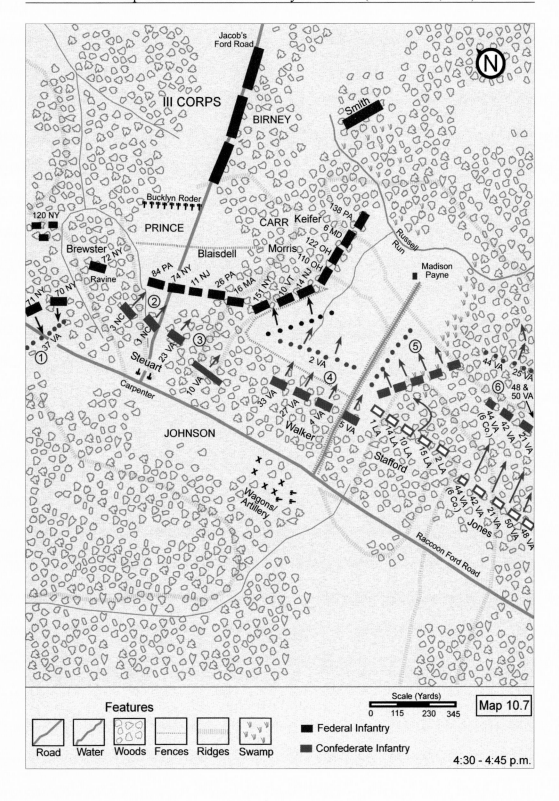

Map 10.7

Scale (Yards)

0   115   230   345

Federal Infantry

Confederate Infantry

4:30 - 4:45 p.m.

Map 10.8: Steuart Collapses Blaisdell's Brigade; Walker is Repulsed
(November 27: 4:45 - 5:00 p.m.)

Steuart/Prince: Col. Titus Williams's 37th Virginia on the left of Steuart's line continued fighting what was likely two regiments from Brewster's brigade pressing in front and trying to get around its left flank (No. 1). The balance of Steuart's regiments headed at an oblique right toward Blaisdell's main line. Williams knew he had no support on either flank, and that it was just a matter of time before the 70th New York crossed Raccoon Ford Road and completely flanked his position. When this finally occurred, Williams knew he had done all he could to prevent the inevitable and ordered his men to fall back. The New Yorkers never fully appreciated the golden opportunity their deep thrust presented: if they had realigned their front and advanced together using the Raccoon Ford Road as a guide, they could have used the heavy terrain to their advantage and completely flanked Steuart's entire brigade.

By the time Williams fell back, the rest of Steuart's regiments were heavily engaged with Blaisdell's men (No. 2). Col. Stephen Thruston's 3rd North Carolina, now effectively Steuart's left regiment, headed for the Federals deployed on both sides of the Jacob's Ford Road (the 84th Pennsylvania and the 74th New York). Thruston noted in his report that "the action was quite sharp for a short time, when the men with a yell charged the position." The Tar Heels' oblique approach in the rapidly fading light (coupled with the 1st North Carolina on its right) unnerved the New Yorkers and Pennsylvanians while striking the right front of Col. Robert McAllister's small 150-man 11th New Jersey.

Lt. Col. Brown's 1st North Carolina, advancing with the 23rd Virginia on its right and 3rd North Carolina on its left, also struck the embattled New Jersey men and part of the 26th Pennsylvania, which quickly broke. The stampeding Pennsylvanians peeled away the left companies of the small New Jersey command, but their officers returned the men to the firing line. The 16th Massachusetts, which formed the left side of Blaisdell's brigade, also joined in the confused retreat.

Lt. Col. Simeon Walton's 23rd Virginia moved forward with the Tar Heels and engaged the enemy, "driving him from the woods to the north across an open field some 200 yards beyond, and charging across this field, which was some 150 yards wide, drove him from the edge of the woods on the north side of the field and continued the pursuit far into the body of the woods."[34]

All along Steuart's front, Blaisdell's command was falling part. The 11th New Jersey was the last regiment to completely collapse. Col. McAllister wrote home that he watched the regiments on each side of him flee to the rear "with astonishment." The small band was able to resist the pressure in front, but with both flanks being overlapped they could not hold for long. McAllister encouraged his men to stand strong as they engaged in hand-to-hand combat with screaming Tar Heels. One New Jersey man was dragged over a fence and captured. "Three minutes more and my regiment and I would have been prisoners," McAllister reported. He ordered a retreat.[35]

Thruston pressed his 3rd North Carolina onward after the fleeing enemy. McAllister somehow managed to reform his thinned ranks in the open field where the two Federal batteries were making the enemy pay for their audacious charge. According to the commander of the 74th New York, the fire from the Union guns caused the North Carolinians "to waver."[36]

Walker/Morris: While Steuart's regiments collapsed Prince's front, Walker's Virginians climbed the fence and charged into the open field beyond (No. 3). As one young Confederate put it, "the line was reformed and with a rebel yell we dashed forward, but were met with such a terrible fire that we were compelled to halt." The deadly rounds were slicing through Walker's front from the left front, where Morris' three regiments were waiting about 250 yards away on a small rise behind a stout fence. Unable to withstand the fighting, the Virginians withdrew into the woods as fast as they could run. Col. Funk's 5th Virginia on the far right missed the attack. Once clear of the woods, he realized the enemy was well to his left and so wheeled his men in that direction, forming them in the Payne farm lane (No. 4) perpendicular to the balance of Walker's Brigade.[37]

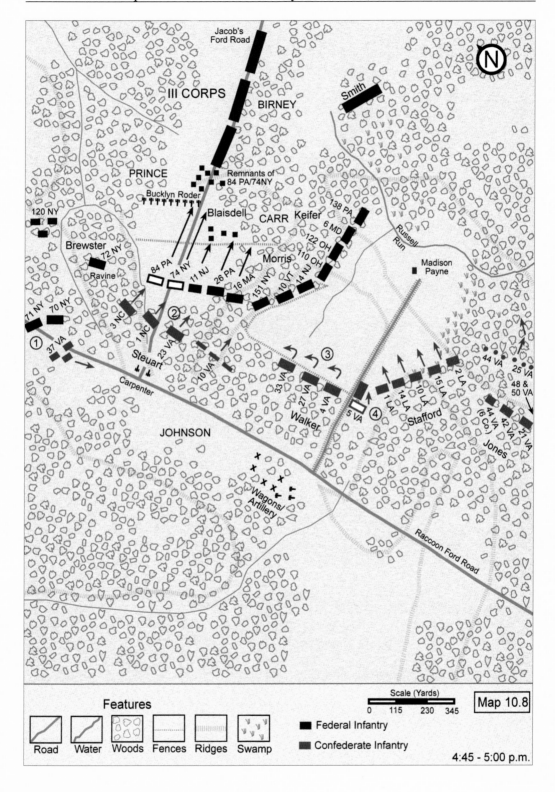

Map 10.8

4:45 - 5:00 p.m.

Features

Road   Water   Woods   Fences   Ridges   Swamp

Scale (Yards)
0   115   230   345

■ Federal Infantry
■ Confederate Infantry

Map 10.9: Stafford Stalls, Jones Comes up; Ward Supports the Union Front
(November 27: 5:00 - 5:15 p.m.)

Stafford/Jones: With the battle raging to his far left, Gen. Stafford wheeled tightly, dipped his line into the low ground, and advanced up to the thin ridge upon which ran the farm lane. There, his left regiment, the 1st Louisiana, joined the right side of Walker's line (No. 5) represented by the 5th Virginia. The stout fences lining the lane temporarily interrupted the movement.

By the time Stafford's regiments arrived, Walker's Virginians were being driven back into the woods by Morris's well-positioned brigade. "The action soon became furious," reported Stafford. "An effort was made to charge the enemy from his position, where he maintained a galling fire of musketry; but as the brigade of Brigadier-General Jones had not yet reached its position on our right, we found it impossible to advance beyond" the farm lane. The Union troops that opened fire on Stafford and drove his first assault back included some of Morris's men, together with most of Col. Warren Keifer's brigade situated on a powerful ridge to Stafford's distant right-front.[38]

Before Stafford's ragged first attack effort and while his men were struggling to knock down the Payne lane fencing, Jones's Brigade stepped out of the woods behind Stafford's right-rear and halted. The Virginians were up on a ridge and enjoyed the best view of the expansive field. From the high ground they could see Walker's men well off to their left-front, Stafford's entire brigade line in the Payne farm lane, and the Yankees strongly positioned in the distance (No. 6) behind a fence (Morris) and on a crescent-shaped ridge (Keifer). According to John Worsham of the 21st Virginia, "we could see the enemy behind a rail fence on the edge of a wood on the far side of this field."

Jones ordered his men to move down the slope and slide into position on Stafford's right. The low land in front was little more than a quagmire, recalled John Worsham of the 21st Virginia. "We soon came to a swamp in a bottom, the most miry place I ever entered. How the men crossed it I don't know. Many left one or both shoes in the mud, the horses could not

cross, the officers were compelled to dismount and take the mud too."[39]

Gen. Jones saw very little of the frustrating fighting soon to follow. According to the brigade's senior colonel, William Witcher of the 21st Virginia, "about the time the wheel was completed, and we had formed upon the line of the division, General Jones, while gallantly exposing himself, was struck down by a shot in the head, and the command thereby devolved upon me as senior colonel."[40]

Maj. Gen. David Birney's division had slogged its way off the Jacob's Ford Road and through the wood and was now in position to provide support to the heavily engaged front line. "I was ordered by Major-General French to form a second line in rear of the center of the first line, composed of the divisions of Generals Prince and Carr, and to grant support to either when necessary during the expected battle," recalled Birney in his report. Birney pushed his brigades up behind Carr's division. Thomas Egan's brigade was in the first line, with Charles Collis's and Hobart Ward's in the second (No. 3).[41]

David Birney was the ideal commander for the situation at hand, a dependable combat leader in stark contrast to corps leader William H. French. "In my belief," wrote the observant Lt. Col. Theodore Lyman of Meade's staff, "we had few officers who could command 10,000 men as well as he. He was a pale, Puritanical figure, with a demeanor of unmovable coldness; only he would smile politely when you spoke to him." Lyman was also impresed with how he handled his immediate circle. Birney, explained Lyman, "took very good care of his Staff and saw they got due promotion." Unfortunately for Birney, he had formed an alliance with Gens. Joe Hooker and Dan Sickles, which did not endear him to many fellow general officers and politicians.[42]

The fighting, meanwhile, continued to escalate. The small-arms exchange was rapid, heavy, and uninterrupted on this part of the field. Keifer's command, in its good position on the expansive ridge, enjoyed the best position from which to pour a devastating fire into both Stafford and Jones, whose own men returned fire as best as they could from their lower and distant position.

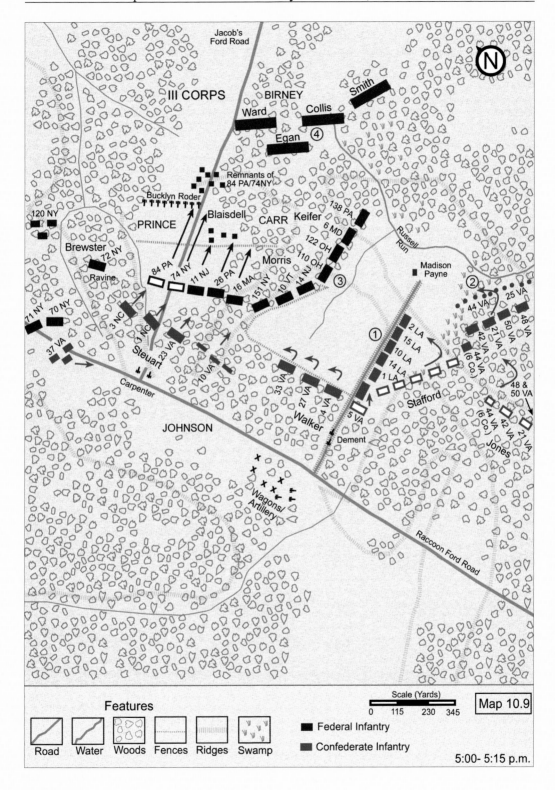

Features

Road Water Woods Fences Ridges Swamp

Scale (Yards)
0   115   230   345

Map 10.9

Federal Infantry

Confederate Infantry

5:00- 5:15 p.m.

Map 10.10: Steuart Fails; Morris and Keifer Beat Back Walker, Stafford, and Jones (November 27: 5:00 - 5:30 p.m.)

Steuart/Prince: Flushed with victory after defeating the 74th New York and 84th Pennsylvania, the 3rd North Carolina headed for Roder's and Bucklyn's batteries deployed in the rear of what had been the right of Blaisdell's brigade (No. 2). The cannoneers shoved double canister into the mouths of their cannon as the Carolinians advanced, and cut wide swaths in the their ranks.

Col. Thruston had long been concerned about his left flank, which hung in the air as he advanced. As the guns pounded his front, he received a report of a large Federal infantry force approaching from that vulnerable direction. The new threat was the 72nd New York (Brewster's brigade), which had taken position on the right of the 84th Pennsylvania. Thruston immediately ordered his regiment to wheel to the left to face the oncoming Federals. The 3rd North Carolina was already shy a company, which had been sent to support the 37th Virginia on the far left. The six companies forming the regiment's left and center obeyed Thruston's order, but the right three companies continued advancing with the 1st North Carolina on their right flank. No one on that side of the line seems to have heard the order. The six companies were outgunned, with the remnants of the 84th Pennsylvania and 74th New York joining in the defensive effort by firing into the North Carolinians' flank. Realizing that he could not hold his position, Thruston ordered his men to fall back. They withdrew across Jacob's Ford Road.[43]

The right side of Steuart's line, composed of the 1st North Carolina and 23rd Virginia (the 10th Virginia was still floundering in the woods just north of the Raccoon Ford Road), closely followed the retreating 11th New Jersey, 26th Pennsylvania, and 16th Massachusetts (No. 3). Like Blaisdell's other regiments, these units reformed in the rear and fired volleys into the approaching foe. Unable to advance farther against this determined resistance, these Confederates fell back behind a fence. While there, Lt. Col. Hamilton Brown of the 1st North Carolina was struck down and forced to relinquish command to Capt. Louis Latham.[44]

Walker/Morris: Hit by a raking crossfire, the Stonewall Brigade fell back to the protection of the woods on the edge of the field and returned the fire. Frustrated by the unwillingness of his men to venture out into the open field a second time, Gen. Walker grabbed the Virginia colors and jumped his horse over the fence and yelled for his men to follow. Walker rode to within eighty yards of Morris's Federal position, with the Yankees firing at him the entire time. None hit home, but only a few men joined him in the effort. The concentrated fire repulsed the feeble effort and the men returned to the shelter of the fence and heavy woods (No. 4).[45]

Dement's Battery, which had been waiting with the balance of Andrews's artillery battalion south of the Raccoon Ford Road, received orders to move a section (two guns) up the farm lane leading to the Madison Payne home to provide some support for the embattled infantry. The section unlimbered and opened fire in the field just to the left of the lane between Funk's 5th Virginia and Edward Willett's 1st Louisiana. These guns, wrote Johnson, "played with telling effect upon the ranks of the enemy." Another eyewitness recalled that the two pieces opened "a most terrible fire" on Carr's troops, who returned it with waves of small arms fire.[46]

Stafford/Jones: With Johnson's last brigade (Jones) now in position in the Madison Payne farm lane, Stafford once again attempted to launch his own brigade on another attack (No. 5). "Again we endeavored, under a murderous fire, to charge the enemy . . . but as no concert of action was manifested by the remainder of the line, the attempt was futile, resulting only in the loss of several gallant soldiers," explained Stafford.[47]

Jones's Virginians arrived after a long wide wheel through the dense vegetation. They could see Kiefer's brigade far in front of them and Morris to their distant left-front. Because Stafford was in trouble, Jones ordered the 44th Virginia to form behind the 2nd Louisiana. Jones also ordered an attack, but like Stafford, only some regiments moved, and those that did were thrown back to the lane (No. 6). The commander of the 42nd Virginia reported that his men were the only ones that he could see advancing against the enemy, and "under a galling fire and entirely exposed (men falling thick and fast), I ordered them to retire."[48]

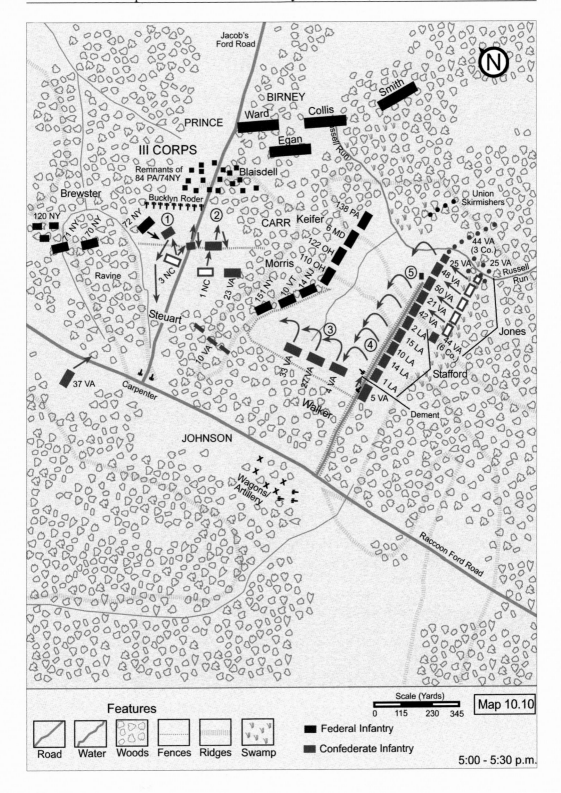

Jacob's
Ford Road

BIRNEY

PRINCE   Ward   Collis   Smith

III CORPS

Remnants of
84 PA/74NY   Blaisdell

Brewster   Bucklyn Roder

120 NY   72 NY   ①   ②   CARR   Keifer   138 PA   6 MD

71 NY   70 NY   3 NC   122 OH   110 OH   Union
Skirmishers

44 VA
(3 Co.)

Morris   1 NC   23 VA   151 NY   10 VT   14 NJ   25 VA   25 VA   Russell
Run

Ravine   48 VA

⑤   50 VA   44 VA
(6 Co.)   Jones

Steuart   21 VA

33 VA   42 VA   2 LA

10 VA   27 VA   ③   15 LA   10 LA   Stafford

4 VA   ④   14 LA

37 VA   Carpenter   1 LA

5 VA   Dement

Walker

JOHNSON

✕
✕   ✕   ✕   ✕
Wagons/
Artillery

Raccoon Ford Road

Features

| Road | Water | Woods | Fences | Ridges | Swamp |

Scale (Yards)

0   115   230   345

Map 10.10

■ Federal Infantry

■ Confederate Infantry

5:00 - 5:30 p.m.

Map 10.11: The Federal Line Stabilizes
(November 27: 5:30 - 6:00 p.m.)

Steuart/Prince: Col. Thruston halted his six 3rd North Carolina companies in the ravine near Carpenter's guns, where he ordered the men to throw up make-shift works of brush, rails, and dirt (No. 1). Gen. Steuart arrived soon thereafter leading Col. Williams's 37th Virginia back into position north of the Raccoon Ford Road on Thruston's left to re-anchor his embattled flank. Light skirmish fire continued along this front, but the heavy fighting was at an end.

Although they remained at the Jacob's Ford and Raccoon Ford Road intersection, Carpenter's guns had a hot afternoon, pounded by the Federal guns. When Federal infantry had earlier flanked the 37th Virginia and reached the Raccoon Road, Carpenter's left piece swiveled to confront them with double canister.[49]

After reorganizing the 1st North Carolina, Capt. Latham ordered another attack (No. 2). The flag bearer of the 11th New Jersey calmly "unfurled the national flag, and waved it in the face of the enemy," noted the 11th's Col. McAllister. Federal guns along the road poured a devastating fire into the Tar Heels. Watching the action from behind the guns, Gen. French screamed, "Now then, double shot 'em! Double shot 'em!" "[We drove] the enemy in disorder before us and inflicted heavy punishment upon his ranks," wrote Latham. "Had not our ammunition . . . given out, the battery stationed in our front would have fallen into our hands." Unable to find more, Latham ordered his men to retreat. He took up a position on the right of the 3rd North Carolina near Carpenter's section.

Lt. Col. Simeon Walton's 23rd Virginia fought along a fence line on the northern edge of a large field. "We held the enemy in check for nearly an hour," explained the 23rd's report, "but were forced again to fall back, the regiment on our left having first given way. It was while posted behind this fence that Lieut. Col. S. T. Walton was killed by a ball passing through his head." The Virginia line fell apart. "I immediately took command of the regiment," wrote Maj. John P. Fitzgerald, "and after retiring across the open field rallied it behind the fence along its southern border and continued to fire upon the enemy, separated from us only by the open field,

until night set in." Steuart's right regiment, Col. Warren's 10th Virginia, remained a non-factor. Thinned earlier by the large detachment of skirmishers, Warren spent the entire battle moving his Virginians ahead a short distance and falling back, trying to keep his right aligned with Walker and his left with the 23rd Virginia (No. 3).[50]

Walker/Morris: The Stonewall Brigade continued fighting at the edge of the woods bordering the Payne field until nightfall (No. 4).

Stafford/Jones: Jones's and Stafford's uncoordinated attacks continued. None made it far into the deadly field. Carr's division, with Col. Warren Keifer's brigade, was well-positioned on a powerful timber-lined ridge and poured thousands of rounds into the gray line crammed into the narrow lane. At no time was Carr's front seriously threatened (No. 5). Given the distances involved and the open space, attacking at all was foolhardy and reckless. Lt. Col. Henry Monier of the 10th Louisiana pushed his men into the field three times. Regimental leaders in both brigades recall their unsupported and uncoordinated assaults.[51]

Capt. John Johnson of the 50th Virginia (Jones's Brigade) performed a valiant act. His narrow front was unprotected by the heavy fence lining the farm lane, and many of his veterans were reluctant to stand in place and be shot down by an enemy so strongly positioned. Johnson, a stout man about 50 years old, walked in front of his line, lay down along the crest, and offered his body as a breastwork. Perhaps to his surprise, several men took up his offer. How long this lasted is unknown, but Johnson emerged unscathed.[52]

Birney's Division: When Morris's brigade began running low on ammunition, Gen. Carr requested help from Gen. Birney's division (No. 6). Birney ordered Brig. Gen. Hobart Ward's brigade up behind Morris's right-rear. Another aide arrived requesting support for Keifer's men, who were rapidly firing off their cartridges beating back Stafford's disjointed attacks. Birney pushed Col. Thomas Egan's brigade up and replaced Keifer's command except for the 138th Pennsylvania, which "enjoyed favorable cover." "The musketry fire was incessant," reported Birney, "and the enemy [Jones] made constant efforts to break through my line. They were driven back, and the ridge was firmly held by us." Birney used Col. Charles Collis's brigade to plug a gap between Egan's left and Smith's right.[53]

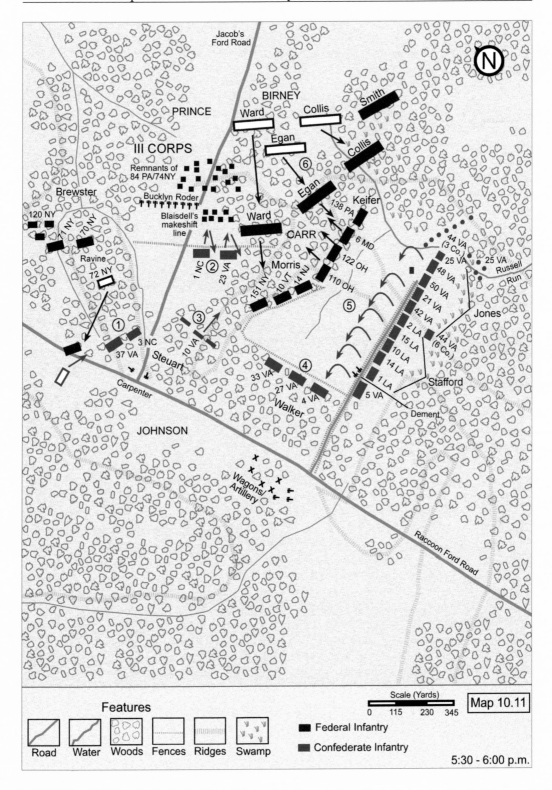

Jacob's
Ford Road

BIRNEY

PRINCE

Ward   Collis   Smith

Egan   Collis

III CORPS

Remnants of
84 PA/74NY

Brewster

Bucklyn Roder

Blaisdell's
makeshift
line

6

Egan

Keifer

138 PA

120 NY

71 NY

70 NY

Ward

CARR

6 MD

44 VA
(3 Co.)

25 VA   25 VA
Russell

Ravine

72 NY

1 NC

2

23 VA

Morris

122 OH

110 OH

48 VA

50 VA

21 VA

42 VA

Run

Jones

5

2 LA

44 VA
(6 Co.)

1

3 NC

3

10 VA

151 NY

10 VT

14 NJ

15 LA

10 LA

Steuart

14 LA

37 VA

Carpenter

33 VA

4

1 LA

Stafford

27 VA

5 VA

4 VA

Walker

Dement

JOHNSON

Wagons/
Artillery

Raccoon Ford Road

Features

Road	Water	Woods	Fences	Ridges	Swamp

Scale (Yards)

0   115   230   345

Map 10.11

■ Federal Infantry

■ Confederate Infantry

5:30 - 6:00 p.m.

Map 10.12: The Battle Ends
(November 27: 6:00 - 7:00 p.m.)

By the time Birney's three brigades moved into position at the front line, dusk was descending upon the battlefield and the temperature plummeted. Neither Gen. Ward nor any of his regimental commanders filed a report for Payne's Farm, but it appears the 17th Maine and 124th New York (and possibly the entire brigade) moved forward to relieve Morris's embattled line (No. 1).

Through the deepening gloom, the men could see scattered flames of rifle fire from the Stonewall Brigade flickering in the woods beyond. Morris's men were more than happy to be relieved (No. 2). Although they had thrown back the Stonewall Brigade, the fighting took a toll as these men were unaccustomed to battle. At least one of Morris's inexperienced regiments, Col. Albert Jewett's 10th Vermont, let the excitement of the moment supersede judgment and orders. "They were only ordered to go to the fence," wrote the regiment's historian, "where the other regiment halted, but the Vermonters went over it. They had to come back the best they could, through a terrible crossfire from the right and left, and many a poor fellow never got back." Jewett agreed: "My loss was heavy, about one-sixth of my command having been killed or wounded, but my regiment has sustained the reputation already established by our brave Green Mountain boys."[54]

Walker's Virginians stood fast in the woods behind the fence and continued to exchange a heavy fire with Morris's regiments, followed by a slowly diminishing fire with Ward's men (No. 3). The fighting had been especially frustrating for Walker's elite veterans, who experienced none of the fruits of victory gained (at least temporarily) by Steuart's men. In their more distant front, Col. Thomas Egan's brigade, which had replaced Keifer's command (No. 4), threw back Jones's and Stafford's piecemeal efforts. A sergeant in the 3rd Michigan (Egan's brigade) noted that "the rebels, we find, are not in very heavy force in our front, but enough to give us all the fighting we want for a cold day."[55]

Col. Charles Collis's Pennsylvania brigade advanced to plug the gap between Smith's and Egan's brigades (No. 5). Although his men were engaged only a short time, Collis watched the fighting from a forward position and later recalled the engagement as "one of the sharpest and best fought affairs of the war. . . .The musketry was the most terrific any of us had ever heard, and the chances of getting off without a decent wound was about as poor as it could possibly have been."[56]

With no support on his left, and darkness having set in fully, Johnson ordered his division to move off by the left. Walker was the first to move, pulling his men back to the slight works they had constructed along the Raccoon Ford Road. Walker noted in his report that his Virginians brought "off all of our wounded and a portion of our dead." According to Stafford, "Soon after dark information was given me that the Stonewall Brigade, on our left, had been ordered to withdraw from the field. My left being thus entirely unsupported and exposed to a flank movement of the enemy, I at once gave orders to retire to the breastworks in front of our original position" (No. 6). Col. William Witcher, commanding Jones's Brigade on the far right of the division, was "informed that the division was moving by the left flank to the former position on the road, which movement I ordered the brigade to follow."[57]

Just after what would prove to be the climax of the fighting that evening, Gen. Johnson had dispatched a rider to Maj. Gen. Robert Rodes with a plea for assistance. "Though night was rapidly falling and the fire gradually slackening on the part of the enemy," reported the division commander, "it was deemed prudent, in view of the exhausted cartridge-boxes of the men, to send to General Rodes, with the request that he should order a brigade to our support." Gen. Robert E. Lee, who was with Rodes at the time, agreed and Rodes dispatched a brigade under Brig. Gen. George Doles. The Georgians moved quickly and took up a position on the left of Johnson's line, relieving Steuart's embattled regiments.

The battle of Payne's Farm was over.

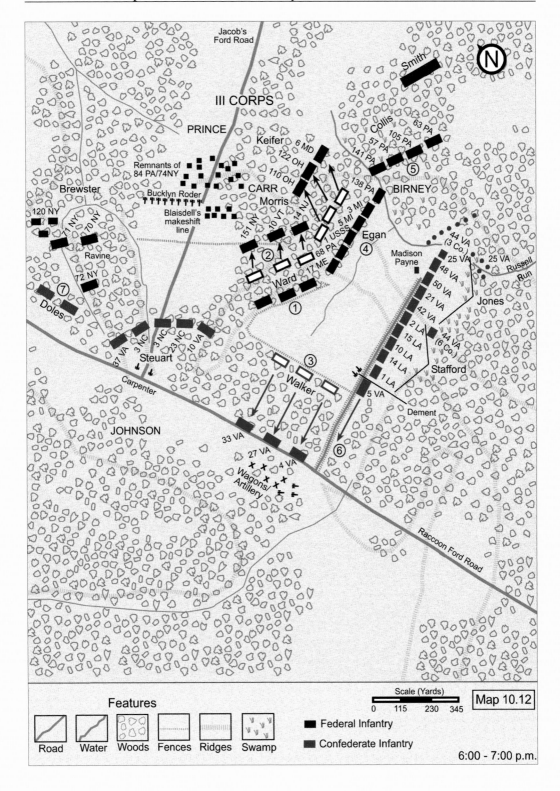

Map 10.12

6:00 - 7:00 p.m.

Map 10.13: Payne's Farm Assessment

Gen. Johnson's ambitious double-wheel attack into the unknown, through the thick tangled vegetation and swampy terrain of the Wilderness, had almost no chance for tactical success. His aggressive attack did stun the enemy, and the terrain hid his own exposed flanks and overall weakness from Gen. French and his subordinates.

On the Confederate left, Steuart's Brigade took advantage of the rough terrain and Prince's haphazardly arranged front to enjoy some initial success, collapse Blaisdell's brigade, and drive back several other regiments. Steuart's own mostly piecemeal effort, however, coupled with his failure to pay close attention to his own left, made it impossible to maintain any momentum. Too little manpower and too little ammunition decided Steuart's day. Walker's Stonewall Brigade had no possibility of achieving anything in the center of the line, and Stafford and Jones were too far away with no reasonable way to reach the powerful Union line and force a decisive decision.

The performance of Henry Prince's division was decidedly subpar, with portions outflanked and forced to the rear. Some regiments from Brewster's Excelsior Brigade, however, completely flanked the left of the Confederate line and penetrated all the way to the Raccoon Ford Road. An opportunity beckoned to roll up Steuart's entire brigade. Once again, the terrain conspired to hide what we know today to have been a rare military opportunity. Morris's and Kiefer's brigades of Carr's division assumed good ground, held their own, threw back several sharp attacks, and had the good sense of not attempting a counterattack of their own. Egan's command, part of Birney's division, moved up to replace Kiefer at the climax of the fighting and continue the killing. Carr's third brigade under Col. Benjamin Smith, however, became lost in the tangled underbrush and barely engaged the enemy (and suffered from long range fire the men found nearly impossible to return). Somehow, Smith was unable to even connect with Kiefer's left, forcing Gen. Birney to send in Collis's brigade to plug the gap. Had the terrain been more favorable, Smith's brigade (and indeed many other Federal commands) were in a

position to turn and crush one or both of Johnson's flanks. Smith tried to spin his miserable performance by writing in his report, "I used every effort to make the best of the circumstances. I did not know the ground, and there was no one to give me information."[58]

Strategically, however, the battle of Payne's Farm was a Confederate success. Johnson's Division faced and halted the march of two Union corps (French's III and Sedgwick's VI) toward Locust Grove and Gen. Lee's exposed left flank. Gen. Meade needed these two powerful corps to solidify his own right under Warren, and either defend against a possible Confederate attack or go over on the offensive.

The losses on both sides were moderate. Johnson lost just under 500 from his 5,300-man division, or just under ten percent. Steuart's Brigade, whose regiments had fought throughout nearly all of the engagement, lost 170 men killed, wounded, captured, and missing. Walker's Stonewall Brigade lost 144, Stafford 104, and Jones 81. The latter brigade arrived last and its losses were commensurate with the length of time it engaged the enemy and its relative position and distance. The same could be said about the other brigades' losses. With 72 casualties, the 3rd North Carolina fighting on the left center of Steuart's wheeling column lost the most men of any regiment in Johnson's command.[59]

At 932, French's III Corps losses were nearly double Johnson's. Carr's division left the most men on the field with 399 (Morris, 183; Keifer, 172; Smith, 44). Birney's division entered the fight as it reached its crescendo and lost 333 men (Egan, 204; Ward, 89; and Collis, 40). Although Prince's division opened the fight, most of its regiments never managed a firm stand or delivered long uninterrupted firing as part of a cohesive front. It lost the fewest men at 187 (Blaidsell, 129; Brewster, 58).[60]

A member of the 151st Pennsylvania of Morris's brigade probably summed up the battle best when he wrote, "The engagement was in the woods and commenced about the middle of the afternoon, and ceased only when it became too dark to see. It was one of the sharpest engagements of the war, and was strongly contested by both sides. Neither could claim a victory."[61]

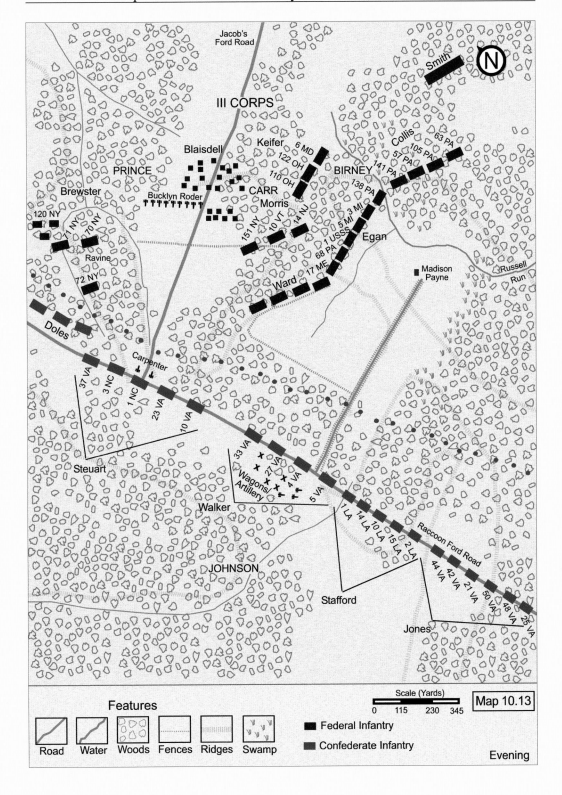

Jacob's
Ford Road

Smith

III CORPS

N

Keifer   6 MD
Blaisdell   122 OH
PRINCE   110 OH
Brewster   Bucklyn Roder   CARR
                            Morris
120 NY   151 NY 10 VT 14 NJ
    71 NY 70 NY
    Ravine
    72 NY

Collis   63 PA
          105 PA
57 PA
141 PA
BIRNEY
138 PA
3 MI
5 MI
1 USSS
68 PA
17 ME
Ward

Egan

Madison
Payne   Russell
                     Run

Doles

Carpenter
37 VA 3 NC
    1 NC
    23 VA
    10 VA
Steuart

33 VA
    27 VA
    4 VA
Wagons/
Artillery   5 VA
Walker

7 LA
14 LA
10 LA
15 LA
2 LA

Raccoon Ford Road

JOHNSON

Stafford

44 VA
42 VA
21 VA
50 VA
48 VA
25 VA

Jones

Features

Road	Water	Woods	Fences	Ridges	Swamp

Scale (Yards)
0   115   230   345

Map 10.13

■ Federal Infantry

▬ Confederate Infantry

Evening

Map Set 11: Confrontation at Mine Run

(November 27 - December 2, 1863)

Map 11.1: The Armies in Motion (November 27)

By the end of November 27 Maj. Gen. George Meade realized he had squandered a good opportunity to defeat Gen. Robert E. Lee. His planned rapid advance into Lee's right-rear fell apart at the outset with sloppy marching and indolent corps-level leadership. What should have been a swift thrust near Robertson's Tavern triggered instead three disjointed fights (New Hope Church on the Orange Plank Road, Robertson's Tavern along Orange Turnpike, and Payne's Farm on Raccoon Ford Road). The tone and substance of his dispatches this day evidence his anxiety. He remained at his headquarters at Robertson's rather than visit his corps leaders.

The Payne's Farm combat was especially frustrating because the Rebels should have been crushed and Lee's left exposed. Meade's chief of staff, Maj. Gen. Andrew Humphreys, summed up the collective disappointment after the war: "[W]ith three times the force of Johnson, and having besides the whole of the Sixth Corps . . . General French remained on the defensive."[1]

Meade intended to use the 28th to finish concentrating his army. While waiting for French and Sedgwick to disengage from Payne's Farm and reach Robertson's (the army's left flank), the army's other corps leaders maintained their fronts and did not press the enemy. I Corps (John Newton) and V Corps (George Sykes) stretched out along Orange Plank Road from Parker's Store back to New Hope Church, respectively. In their front was Lt. Gen. A. P. Hill's Third Corps. Gouverneur Warren's II Corps, holding the center of Meade's front at Robertson's, was harassed by the aggressive Jubal Early, who was in temporary command of Lt. Gen. Richard Ewell's Second Corps. "[T]he enemy showed so much enterprise in extending around my right flank . . . that I was compelled to make a feint of a general attack by advancing my skirmish line," reported Warren. "This brought on a brisk little contest along my front, in which Colonel Carroll's brigade behaved very handsomely, driving the enemy down the turnpike to his main line of battle." Warren also knew he was

in a potentially dangerous position. "Though it was impossible to say how much force was near me, the prisoners from two divisions of Ewell's corps, and the report that the other was near, required caution on my part. General Ewell was probably as ignorant of my real strength as I of that of his corps opposed to me," confessed Warren, "else, by rapid concentration, it was in his power to have overwhelmed me and cut our army in two." An hour before dark, "when I could afford to venture, trusting to nightfall to cover me if I met superior force, I again advanced my skirmish line, strongly supported. The enemy resisted stubbornly and could be driven but a little way." Warren's loss for the day was "about 50 killed and wounded."

That afternoon during Payne's Farm combat, Meade ordered Sedgwick to march VI Corps around III Corps for Robertson's. Sedgwick reached Warren's right that evening. When Payne's Farm ended that night, Meade ordered French to follow.[2] Surprising Lee was no longer possible, but Meade could still defeat the Confederates. I Corps on the left, II Corps in the center, and VI Corps on the right would attack the Confederates at first light while III and V Corps remained in reserve.[3]

Lee left Orange Court House at 3:00 a.m. for Verdiersville, where he set up his new headquarters. The most important news was from Edward Johnson about his heavy fight with III Corps at Payne's Farm. Other critical news arrived from Brig. Gen. Tom Rosser, whose cavalry brigade found I Corps' and V Corps' ordnance trains. Rosser's message was especially insightful because the wagons rapidly rolled toward Orange Court House—a sure sign Meade intended to fight Lee and not capture Richmond. Rosser captured eight wagons, seven ambulances, 230 mules, 95 prisoners, and destroyed nearly 40 wagons.

Lee set a course of action. The current disposition of his divisions was not optimal for defensive purposes. He issued orders for the entire army to fall back to the higher terrain west of Mine Run. There, the men immediately began to throw up breastworks to receive a Federal assault. The night was rainy and cold, but the troops worked diligently to improve their positions. According to Capt. Robert Park of the 12th Alabama (Cullen Battle's Brigade), we were "busily employed throwing up breastworks of poles and earth . . . with tin cups and cups, and bare hands. It is marvelous with what rapidity a fortification sufficiently strong to resist minie balls can be thrown up. A sense of danger quickens a man's energies."[4]

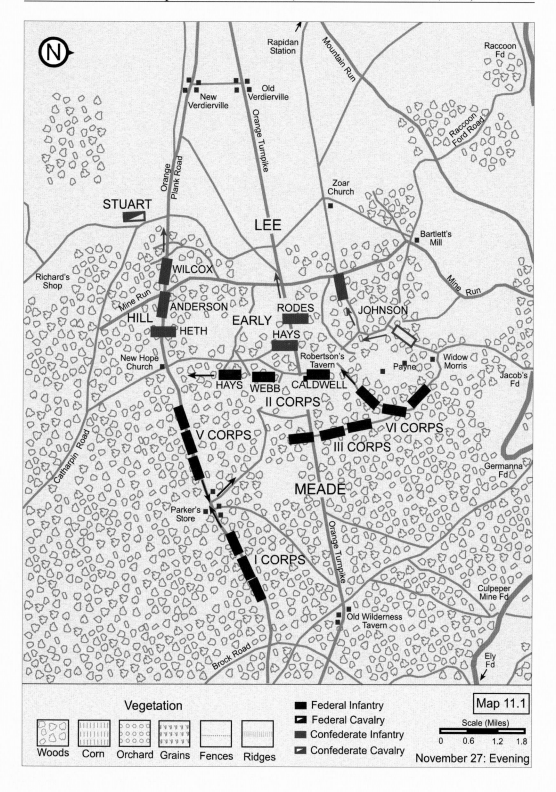

Map 11.1

November 27: Evening

Map 11.2: Lee Waits, Meade Plans
(November 28)

Meade had I, II, and V corps in motion at first light on November 28, fully expecting their advance to trigger a sharp engagement. To his surprise, the giant punch caught nothing but air. Once the enemy pickets were shoved back the Federals discovered the main Confederate trench line was empty. A steady cold rain drenched the men and added to their misery. The weather hindered Meade's ability to determine exactly what Lee was up to, but he had a good idea that the Southerners had simply pulled back due west.[5]

Meade ordered Warren's II Corps to take the road toward Mine Run. Implementing the simple order was no easy task. According to Lt. Col. Theodore Lyman of Meade's staff, "it was a tremendous job, in the narrow wood-roads, deep with mud; and occupied fully the whole day." When the Federal foot soldiers arrived at Mine Run, about two miles from their former position, their already low spirits fell even further: all across their front was an entrenched position stronger than any they had ever seen. Meade described the new Confederate line as "extremely formidable."

It all started with the natural position west the creek, which loomed about 100 feet above the meandering waterway. "The summit, on which was the enemy's line of battle, was already crowned with infantry parapets, abatis, and epaulements for batteries," reported Meade. About 1,000 yards of cleared ground led up to the Army of Northern Virginia's new position. To make matters worse, "the creek itself was a considerable obstacle, in many places swampy and impassable," wrote Meade. Another observer wrote home that he "never saw a more imposing sight—the red battle-flags . . . a long, dark column of men, their bright arms gleaming in the morning sun—the dark and frowning muzzles of eighteen to twenty pieces of artillery." A frontal attack would be nothing short of folly.[6]

Lee was pleased with his strong defensive position. A. P. Hill's Third Corps held the right side of the line, with Ewell's Second Corps under Jubal Early holding the left. Early placed his own division, now under Brig. Gen. Harry Hays, astride the Orange Turnpike with Robert Rodes'

and Edward Johnson's divisions on its left. Hill's corps finished the line farther south, with Richard Anderson's Division on Hays' right, Harry Heth's next in line straddling the Orange Plank Road, and Cadmus Wilcox's anchoring the right flank. Wade Hampton's cavalry division was patrolling off the right flank at Richards Shop to guard against a Federal flanking movement.

The men continued to toil throughout the day to make the position impregnable. Although safely behind their works, the Confederate foot soldiers were nearly as miserable as their counterparts. According to a soldier in the 6th Alabama:

> [T]he weather was extremely cold & cheerless. It rained almost incessantly 2 days & nights and the wind tried to see how hard it could blow & after the rain ceased every thing was frozen. The ground was as hard as a rock. All this time a general engagement was expected. We suffered from fear, from loss of sleep, from cold & hunger, & from smoke. Altogether it was one of the severest times I ever experienced in the army.[7]

When Meade saw Lee's new line he muttered, "we have got another Gettysburg in front of us." Like the Federal position there, it made use of a semi-circular line, which would allow Lee to use shorter interior lines to reinforce various segments of his position. This time, however, Meade was the aggressor holding exterior lines.[8]

Meade's men scanned the enemy works with dread. "To make the charge, we had to pass over this hill, down into a ravine, over a fence, through a marsh, up another hill, and then over their works," wrote Col. Robert McAllister of the 11th New Jersey (Henry Prince's division, III Corps). Even though his corps was in the second line opposite Hill's front, he was experienced enough to have taken the time to scout the front to see what his men might have to deal with should the order to advance come down. "The more we looked at it," he concluded, "the more difficult the task seemed to be—and the more doubtful the result."[9]

An engineer by education and experience, the cautious Meade weighed the risks of a direct assault and decided against it. The position was too strong. Unbeknownst to the army commander, the new plan he needed was about to fall into his lap, courtesy of his least experienced corps leader.

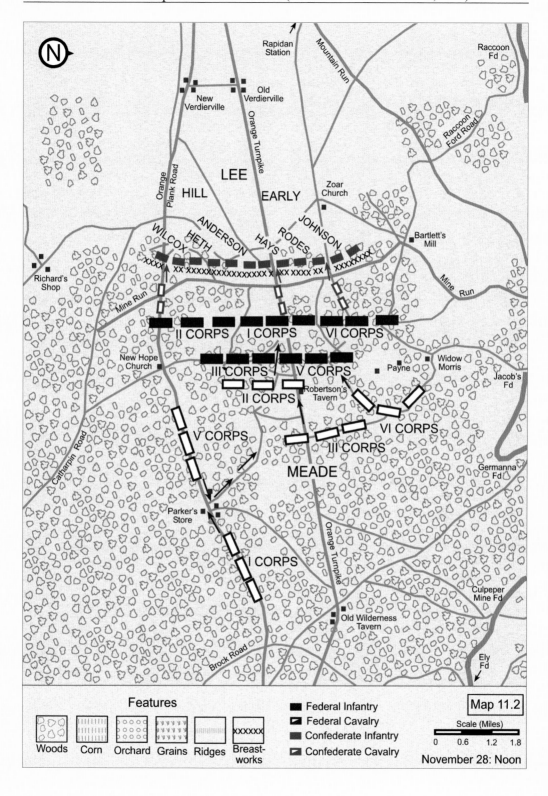

Features

Woods | Corn | Orchard | Grains | Ridges | Breast-works

■ Federal Infantry
▨ Federal Cavalry
■ Confederate Infantry
▨ Confederate Cavalry

Map 11.2

Scale (Miles)

0   0.6   1.2   1.8

November 28: Noon

Map 11.3: Warren Proposes an Attack
(November 28: evening)

Once Meade decided early on the evening of November 28 that Lee's position was too strong for a frontal attack, both armies had nothing much to do except wait in place.

The 11th New Jersey's Col. McAllister, a keen military observer, despaired about the army's probability of success. After carefully describing the forbidding terrain to his wife (see Map 11.2), he added, "we had no artillery to bear on this part of the line, while the enemy had their batteries placed to enfilade, or cross-fire, and rake us in all directions. If we once started, we could not stop, for it would be our destruction. . . What we saw were only the outer works. Timber was felled in every direction in the rear. If we drove them from the first, we would still have to fight them in the last." The heavy defenses—something as of yet uncommon in the Eastern Theater—were bad enough. Almost as disturbing (and even more so for the green recruits) was a particular sound drifting down from the enemy position. According to one soldier, "the effect of the enemy's peculiar, uncanny yelping upon our new men was very demoralizing."[10]

Meade was trying to determine a viable course of action when Gen. Warren rode up that evening with a suggestion. "A personal reconnaissance, during which I lost 20 men and wounded along our front . . . failed to discover to me a promising point of attack," explained the II Corps commander, who requested permission to "take my corps and make a demonstration in the enemy's right, to threaten it, and endeavor to discover a more favorable position to assault . . . if this could not be done, to move on around as if to get in his rear, with the intention of making him abandon his present front."[11]

The idea had merit, and Meade decided to accept his young subordinate's offensive-minded plan. His orders for the following day (November 29) included the following: II Corps would withdraw from its front line during the night and march to the left, so that in the morning it would be in position to "move on the enemy's right flank . . . so as to threaten it, and endeavor to discover a vulnerable point of attack, and if necessary to continue the movement, threatening to turn his right." In addition to his own II Corps, Warren would have Brig. Gen. Henry Terry's 6,000-man division (VI Corps) and 300 cavalrymen to carry out his key assignment—a total of 18,000 men (No. 1). While Warren was maneuvering around Lee's right flank, the rest of Meade's corps commanders would reconnoiter their fronts and, if the possibility of success beckoned, launch an attack across Mine Run.[12]

The new plan required a reshuffling along the line. With Warren's reinforced II Corps shifting south and then west, III Corps, which had been holding the left front of the second line, would move up from its reserve position near Robertson's Tavern to assume Warren's prior position in the middle of the Federal first line. V Corps, holding the right side of the second line, would also advance and take up the right flank of the army. When completed, Meade's front would stretch an impressive eight miles along the east side of Mine Run. His V and VI corps would be on his right flank, and with some luck, might find and turn Lee's left. I and III corps, meanwhile, would hold the center of the long line.[13]

On the other side of the front, meanwhile, Lee sent Jeb Stuart (who was personally leading Hampton's cavalry division) riding toward Parker's Store that evening to determine what the Yankees were up to. Stuart rode down an empty Orange Plank Road until he collided with a Federal cavalry brigade (probably Col. John Taylor's). The Federal troopers fell back after a brief skirmish (No. 2).[14]

The men of both armies, meanwhile, continued to suffer under the miserable weather. Many had thrown away or otherwise lost their overcoats and blankets. "The night [of November 28-29] was bitter cold," recalled a Union colonel. "The north wind and cold frost made us suffer. Those who had no blankets suffered terribly. I tried to sleep with only my overcoat, not having any blanket, but soon awoke almost frozen."[15]

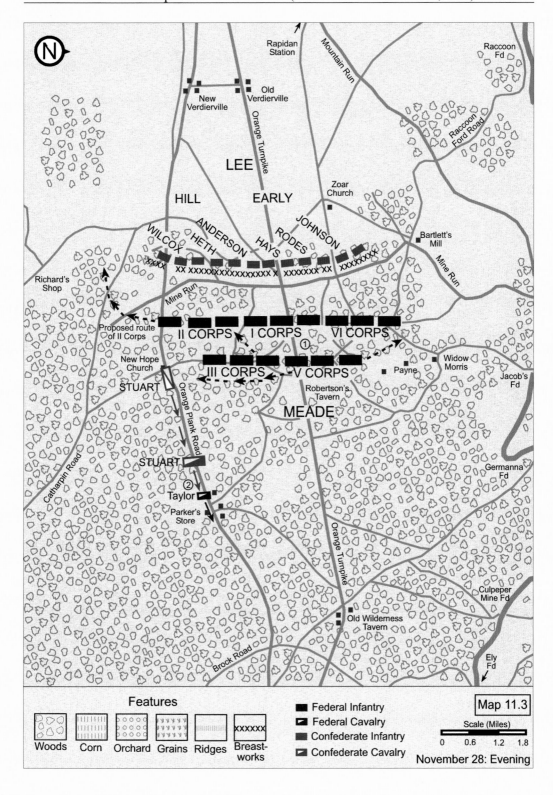

Map 11.3

November 28: Evening

Map 11.4: Warren Moves Into Position
(November 29)

Meade put his offensive plan in motion during the early hours of November 29. His men were probably happy to be moving since it was a means of combating the numbing cold. Gen. Warren, whose II Corps was the trump card of the entire operation, recalled the movement:

No inconsiderable preparations were required to issue rations, dispose of surplus trains, relieve our line, etc., along the enemy's front, and all combined determined me not to start till daybreak. The night was dark and stormy, and our route, after going to the rear as far as Robertson's Tavern, lay through woods along bad roads. . . . Our march on the 29th was rapid and unobstructed until we reached (about 10:30 [a.m.]) the cavalry outposts of General Gregg on the plank road. Our march up to this point was 8 miles.[16]

The move did not go unnoticed. When Jeb Stuart's cavalry videttes observed the build-up of Federals along the Plank Road that morning, a rider galloped to Lee's headquarters to report the activity. The news convinced Lee that Meade was trying to turn his right, so he ordered his men to extend the line south to fend off the effort. His guns opened fire on the head of Warren's men.[17]

By mid-morning Warren's troops were past the Mine Run headwaters. The difficult creek was no longer an obstacle to an offensive action, "and there was no stream or commanding ground between us and their base of supplies, but there was not enough time to advance farther." The long slow march was finally over. Lt. Col. Francis Walker, a staff officer with II Corps, believed success was at hand. The enemy works were "slight and thinly occupied . . . success seemed to be without our grasp, and so it would have been but for one circumstance—the day was nearly spent."[18]

Warren rode to Meade's headquarters about 8:00 p.m. He expressed "such confidence in his ability to carry everything before him as to induce him to give the opinion that he did not believe the enemy would remain over night, so completely did he command him," Meade recalled in his campaign report. "The earnest confidence that General Warren expressed of his

ability to carry everything before him, and the reliance I placed on that officer's judgment . . . induced me to modify my plan so far as to abandon the center attack, and re-enforce Warrens column with two divisions of the Third Corps, which would give him six divisions, nearly half the infantry force under my command." Meade did not verify Warren's claims with his own reconnaissance.[19]

With the new intelligence in hand, Meade decided to attack Lee's left flank with the V and VI corps while Warren turned and crushed Lee's right flank—essentially a double envelopment. Due to Gen. French's continued pessimism about success on his front (and perhaps because of his blundering at Payne's Farm on November 27), Meade snatched two of his divisions and added them to Warren's command, giving the young leader six infantry divisions tallying 28,000 men. Newton's I Corps and the remaining division of French's III Corps would feign an attack against the center of Lee's line to hold it in place. The plan called for Federal artillery to open at 8:00 a.m. on November 30, followed immediately by Warren's infantry attack. Sykes' V Corps and Sedgwick's VI Corps would begin attacking at 9:00 a.m.[20]

Lee and his top generals realized their plight. A. P. Hill, whose corps held the right side of the army's long line, realigned his troops into better defensive positions. Hill's men also redoubled their efforts in constructing fortifications. It was a difficult task because many had no tools at all other than a single axe per company, which forced them to use bayonets, knives, and their bare hands. Somehow they managed to erect a formidable line of works within just a few hours. The Southerners knew that an assault could come at any time, so "[we kept] our things on all the time and one-half of the men up all night, in case of an attack," wrote one of the men.[21]

Early's (Ewell's) Second Corps soldiers (on Hill's left) kept a wary eye on the enemy across Mine Run. They seemed to be preparing to receive an attack of their own. John Worsham, a member of Johnson's Division on the far left flank of the line, recalled, "when we arose the next morning [November 29] we saw that the hills in our front had a line of fortifications from one end to the other of the enemy's line, and more formidable than our own."[22]

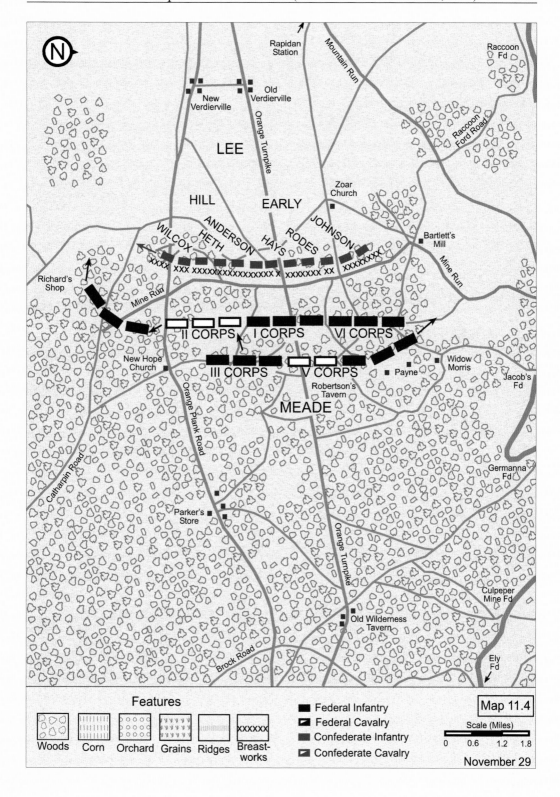

Map 11.4

November 29

Map 11.5: Warren Aborts the Charge
(November 30: morning)

The night of November 29-30 was difficult for the Union men. Both sides suffered through the same bitter wind and cold temperature, but Meade's assault troops were so close to the enemy that no fires were allowed. Few slept, for "each soldier knew that to sleep uncovered in that bitter air would be the sleep of death." Water froze in canteens and pickets were relieved every half hour to prevent them from falling to sleep and perhaps freezing to death. The men greeted the dawn with ambivalence; they welcomed higher temperatures, but heavy fighting and the death and maiming of perhaps many thousands of men surely awaited. "[I]t was terribly uncomfortable lying upon the frozen ground hour after hour waiting for the signal to spring to their feet," wrote Col. Mason Tyler of the 37th Massachusetts. "[T]he men would have almost have welcomed the command, since it would have stirred the blood and warmed the benumbed limbs."[23]

The men were roused at 3:00 a.m. and ordered to prepare for the charge. Word passed through Warren's ranks that the assault would begin at 8:00 a.m., and that they were to carry blankets to wrap around them should they be shot. Anyone returning to the lines without orders would be shot by their own men. The day dawned bright and frigid. "The day was so cold," Col. McAllister wrote his wife, "that that the breath was freezing on the bridle bits of the horses." Waiting to move into battle against a veteran enemy stationed behind breastworks was difficult. "Many went to take a peek at the works that they were to storm," noted McAllister, who claimed that nearly every officer "took a view of them." Perhaps to steady himself so he could effectively lead his men into what appeared would be certain defeat, the colonel rationalized, "I made up my mind that we could take it, but that it would be at a fearful loss of life . . . and if it should fail, it would destroy our army."[24]

The enlisted men were more pessimistic. A chaplain in the 14th Connecticut, part of Col. Thomas Smyth's brigade of Alexander Hays' division, Warren's II Corps, had made the long march the previous evening. The Rebels, he recalled, "had prepared strong and high works of timber and earth, with abatis. . . . It was plain that they could pour upon us a heavy fire in front and an enfilading [fire] from a long distance. . . . So confident were the rebels of success that they stood in crowds upon their works and tauntingly beckoned us to come on."[25]

So sure were the Union men of their pending demise that many pinned their names to their clothing to avoid the eternal indignity of being laid to rest in a mass burial trench. Fond goodbyes were tendered between the men, particularly those who had shared so many campfires during the long war. "Stillness mingled with sadness pervaded our ranks. The men sat and wrote final letters to their loved ones at home and tendered them to their chaplains. Personal belongings were also conveyed for transport to their loved ones back home. Many, no doubt, were the secret prayers that went up to God that day," admitted Col. McAllister.[26]

Warren mounted his horse at first light and rode out to observe the enemy line. Federal artillery opened promptly at 8:00 a.m. The 28,000 men under Warren awaited order to move against the Southern lines. The minutes ticked slowly past, but no order arrived. Anticipation coursed through the tense ranks. What none of the men yet knew was that Warren had canceled the assault. Lee's men had spent the night strengthening their lines. Warren calculated it would take eight minutes to reach the enemy works. During that time, the men would be exposed to "every species of fire." An assault now—regardless of how determined and well led—would be suicidal.[27]

Because he was too far from Meade's headquarters to share his observation and confirm his conclusion, Warren took it upon himself to call off the attack. Stationed behind the center of his long line, Meade heard the artillery open, but the expected heavy rattle of small arms fire never developed. What was happening on his left? One of Warren's aides arrived at 8:50 a.m. with the answer in a scribbled message: "[The enemy] position and strength seem so formidable in my present front that I advise against making the attack here. The full light of the sun shows me that I cannot succeed." One of Meade's aides penciled in his diary, "This was a terrible shock to all." Gen. Sedgwick was scheduled to launch his two-corps assault at 9:00 a.m. "Meade instantly ordered the whole movement to be suspended, sending off his aides as fast as horses could carry them."[28]

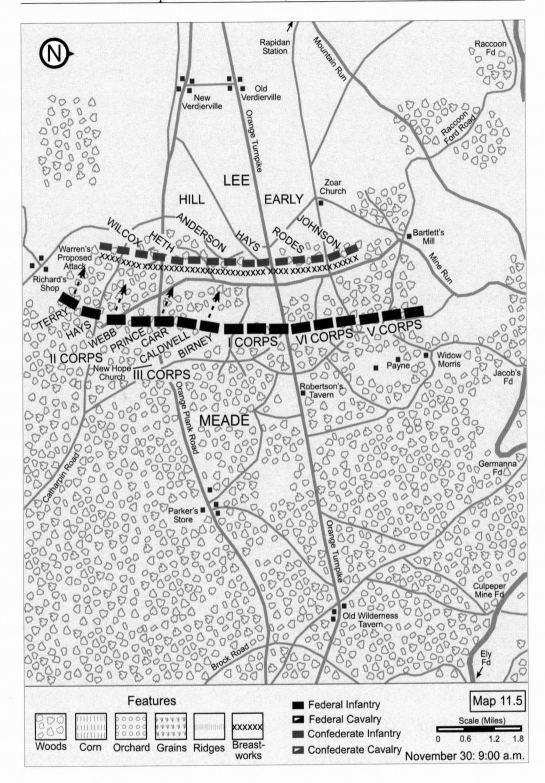

Map 11.6: Meade Ends the Campaign
(November 30 - December 2)

With winter weather settling in across central Virginia, Meade knew this was his last opportunity to gain an advantage and strike Lee with the odds in his favor. He simply had to see for himself whether the attack plans could be salvaged. Between 10:00 and 11:00 a.m., he rode to his left flank to confer with Warren and observe the situation firsthand. Those who saw him knew he was angry. The commanding general, remembered one eyewitness, was "looking as savage as anyone could."[29]

After conferring with Warren and observing the Rebel positions, however, Meade agreed with Warren's decision. Attacking those earthworks under these conditions was akin to begging for a bloody defeat. Meade ordered a council of war that evening to discuss the situation. From Sedgwick he learned that the artillery barrage along the front had tipped off the enemy, who immediately reinforced their works. As Sedgwick would later write, "I do not believe the enemy's works can be carried in my front by an assault without numerous sacrifices. I regard the chances as three to one against the success of such an attack." Meade ordered Carr's and Prince's divisions to return to French's III Corps, as well as the return of Terry's division to Sykes' V Corps.[30]

Thousands of men were disappointed with Meade's decision to cancel the attack, but all of them wore gray uniforms. "I never saw men so anxious for a fight as were ours," noted Leroy Edwards of the 12th Virginia. He added, "they really rejoiced when the Yankee line of battle emerged from the woods . . . and started to advance, and it was with infinite regret that they saw them retire without assaying our position."[31]

December 1 found Meade reviewing his now rapidly dwindling options. First, he could still launch a frontal assault against Lee's lines, but the chances of it succeeding were nil. Second, he could attempt to march around Lee's right flank and head toward Orange Court House. This option required the abandonment of the Orange and Alexandria Railroad, which was his primary line of communications. A third option was to withdraw to Fredericksburg and take up a strong defensive position, but Gen. Halleck had

already dismissed this idea. That left one viable option—re-cross the Rapidan River and go into winter quarters. Meade would later tell Congress that by this time he was already running low on supplies because of the poor roads and horrendous winter weather. After carefully reviewing these possibilities, Meade issued a circular ordering his men across the Rapidan that night.[32]

Newton's I Corps withdrew at 4:00 p.m. on December 1 and headed for Germanna Ford, where it would deploy to protect and hold the crossing open until Sykes' V Corps and Sedgwick's VI Corps crossed. French's III Corps was ordered to pull back at 6:00 p.m. and use the Orange Plank Road to march to Culpeper Ford. Warren's II Corps would follow French.[33]

Gen. Lee, however, was not privy to Meade's plans. All he knew was that his line had not yet been attacked. Lee always preferred to gain the initiative and control the field, and Mine Run was no different. If Meade was not going to attack him, he would assault the Unionists. Lee ordered A. P. Hill to pull Wilcox's and Anderson's divisions from their defenses and march them south around the Federal left flank, which he learned was free of trenches and other defensive entanglements. The movement began at dawn on December 2. All they found was an abandoned Federal line; the enemy was already in the process of crossing the Rapidan into the Iron Triangle between the Rappahannock and Rapidan rivers. Like Meade, Lee's frustration bubbled to the surface when he learned that an opportunity to get at the enemy had yet again slipped from his grasp. "I am too old to command this army," he exclaimed to an aide. "We should never have permitted these people to get away!"[34]

The long and eventful campaigns of the fall of 1863 were finally at an end. Both armies settled into winter quarters.

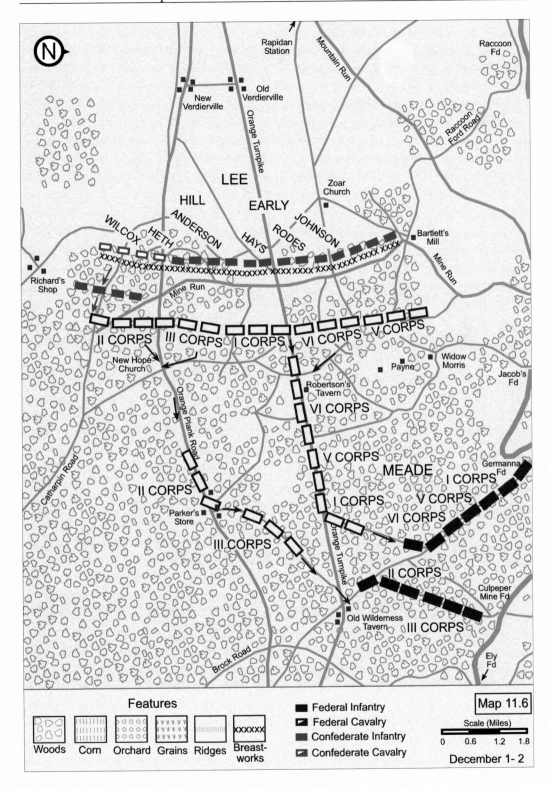

Map 11.6

Scale (Miles)

0   0.6   1.2   1.8

December 1- 2

Features

Woods   Corn   Orchard   Grains   Ridges   Breast-works

■ Federal Infantry
◪ Federal Cavalry
■ Confederate Infantry
◪ Confederate Cavalry

Map Set 12: Winter Interlude, 1863 - 1864
(December 2, 1863 - March, 1864)

Map 12.1: Confederate Winter Quarters

Once it became obvious that Maj. Gen. George G. Meade was not going to attack him behind his powerful Mine Run entrenchments, and after his own attempt to turn and crush Meade's left flank revealed that the Union Army of the Potomac had retreated, Gen. Robert E. Lee ordered a pursuit. Lt. Gen. A. P. Hill's Third Corps moved directly east on the Orange Plank Road while Lt. Gen. Richard Ewell's Second Corps (under Maj. Gen. Jubal Early) moved in the same direction farther north along the Orange Turnpike. After his infantry marched about eight miles, however, Lee realized that Meade had skillfully withdrawn his army and that he would not catch him. The Southern Army of Northern Virginia returned to its former quarters around Orange Court House.[1]

Lee turned his attention to other theaters of the war. "I have considered with some anxiety the condition of affairs in Georgia and Tennessee," he wrote President Jefferson Davis on December 3 before suggesting actions to consider. "I think that every effort should be made to concentrate as large a force as possible, under the best commander, to insure the discomfiture of Grant's army." Lee saw the writing on the wall: The South could not defend everywhere and increasingly aggressive Union actions in various theaters would make it harder to keep his own army reinforced and in the field. It was all a prelude of what was to come in the spring of 1864.[2]

Once his army was in winter quarters (Hill's Corps occupied the area around Orange Court House while Ewell's Corps camped to the northeast, protecting the Rapidan River fords), concerns closer to home weighed heavily on Lee. His army was shrinking. Lt. Gen. James Longstreet's First Corps was still in Tennessee, and after the Mine Campaign ended Lee had only 56,785 men in the ranks. Hill's command numbered 22,202 men and Ewell's 19,969. Maj. Gen. Jeb Stuart's cavalry corps added an additional 9,381, and the artillery 5,233.[3]

The lack of food continued to plague Lee's army. Brig. Gen. Stephen Ramseur wrote home that the daily issue of between 1/8 to 1/4 of a pound of meat and less than two pounds of flour depressed morale. "[T]he army must be fed even if people at home must go without it," Ramseur believed. Sometimes days passed without any meat ration at all. Lee was so concerned that he wrote Davis soon after the new year began, "I fear I shall be unable to retain it [his army] in the field. . . . I do not see how we can operate with our present supplies."[4]

Desertions continued apace. Lee harshly dealt with those captured and returned, and firing squads were fairly common that winter. While some of the troops felt compassion for men who left the ranks without authorization, most understood their duty and that severe punishment was required. "We are soldiers," wrote one North Carolinian, "and we have to stay as long as there is any 'war.'"[5]

The string of defeats and disappointments from Gettysburg through Mine Run, coupled with the lack of supplies, miserable living conditions, and harsh penalties played havoc with morale. A religious revival initiated the previous year swept through the army and played a significant role in stabilizing confidence. Nearly every brigade built a log chapel, and on most nights it was filled with men seeking sustenance from scripture. As many as 15,000 men recommitted to Christianity during the winter months. According to one account, "night after night, the men crowded to hear fervent preachers tell of an everlasting life that robbed the minie of its terror." Other diversions, such as large-scale snowball fights and furloughs, also helped.[6]

Lee was probably ambivalent about Ewell's return to command Second Corps. His constitution during the Bristoe Campaign concerned Lee. When President Davis suggested that Lee travel west to assume command of the troubled Army of the Tennessee, Lee responded that a seasoned hand would be required to lead the army. Ewell was his senior officer, but not up to the task. "General Ewell's condition, I fear, is too feeble to undergo the fatigue and labor incident to the position," was Lee's charitable explanation. Jubal Early had performed credibly in Ewell's absence. Ewell's return to head Second Corps sent Early back to his division. Lee was also concerned about A. P. Hill, whose had yet to effectively perform as a corps commander. James Longstreet, Lee's most trusted and effective lieutenant, was still in Tennessee, but would soon be back with the army.[7]

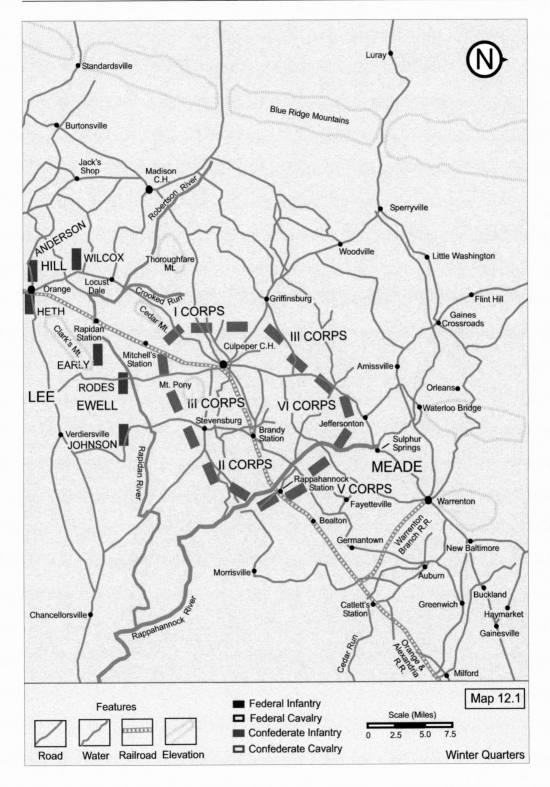

Map 12.1

Map 12.2: Federal Winter Quarters

With his army safely across the Rapidan River, Meade put his men into winter quarters. The Union camps faced Lee's army on the opposite side of the river. His line stretched in a semi-circle from Mitchell's Station and Cedar Mountain (I Corps) on the right to Welford's Ford and Rappahannock Station on the Rappahannock River (V Corps), with the VI Corps anchoring the line and more to the rear around Jeffersonton. Maj. Gen. Alfred Pleasonton's cavalry patrolled the no-man's land between the two armies.[8]

Although it had not been a bloody fall campaign season, it had been a grueling one. The armies had come several times within a whisker of fighting large-scale battles that would have rivaled any that had come before. One soldier wrote in a letter home what was surely on the minds of thousands of others: "Thank heaven that we are back to our old camping ground, and that I still live."[9]

Meade's strength during the cold winter of 1863-1864 was 94,151, almost 70 percent larger than Lee's army. The returns filed at the end of December 1863 offered the following strengths: I Corps (13,443); II Corps (12,382); III Corps (17,474); V Corps (12,914); VI Corps (16,530); Cavalry (16,088); Artillery Reserve (3,015). Rounding out the Union army was the general headquarters staff (947) and engineers (1,358). Meade contracted pneumonia in January 1864 and spent much of that winter away from the army convalescing at home. VI Corps leader Maj. Gen. John Sedgwick commanded the army in his absence. Meade would not return until February 15.[10]

Many of the men thought differently about Meade after the Mine Run Campaign ended. Those who had served under Meade when he led V Corps usually had few complementary things to say about him, even after he was promoted to lead the army in late June of 1863 and defeated Gen. Lee at Gettysburg. The marching and countermarching that comprised the Bristoe Campaign and early stages of the Mine Run effort took its toll. But when Meade refused to throw his men against Lee's strongly entrenched position, their estimate of him as a caring and careful commander grew. "[I]f Meade ever did a

noble act in his life, it was when he concluded not to fight Lee," was how a surgeon in VI Corps put it. Staff officer Theodore Lyman agreed, writing, "I shall always be astonished at the extraordinary moral courage of General Meade." The army commander, concluded Lyman, "had the firmness to say, the blow has simply failed and we shall only add disaster to failure by persisting."[11]

Like their Confederate counterparts, the Union soldiers passed the winter in the relative comfort of their log huts. They used up their time with a host of activities, including reading, writing letters home, games, and theatrical pursuits. Many spent considerable time in prayer. Each brigade erected a chapel and regularly used it. The cold and muddy conditions precluded regular drilling, much to the satisfaction of the men. It was a season filled with thousands of difficult individual decisions. Many three-year enlistments were about to expire and earnest requests to re-enlist pressured the men to remain in the army. Incentives for the men of the First New Jersey Brigade included a $402 Federal bounty, and a 30-day furlough. Anxious to supply the requested number of men, some New Jersey counties offered as much as $300 more.[12]

None of the activities exceeded the importance of what transpired on March 23, 1864, when the War Department reorganized the Army of the Potomac. The XI Corps and XII Corps had been transferred out of the army the previous fall. This time, I Corps and III Corps were the targets. Both veteran organizations were merged into the remaining corps and officially purged from the army's rolls. Meade indicated that these moves were only temporary, but they were not. His rationale for the sweeping structural change was the "reduced strength of nearly all the regiments serving in this army," which had "imperatively demanded" the "temporary reduction of the number of army corps to three." Left unspoken was the desire to rid the army of a pair of under-performing corps commanders: John Newton of I Corps and William French of III Corps. Meade also hoped to facilitate the efficient movement of large bodies of men by having fewer corps to contend with. Although the old veterans of I Corps and III Corps were allowed to retain their distinctive corps badges, no one was happy with the change.[13]

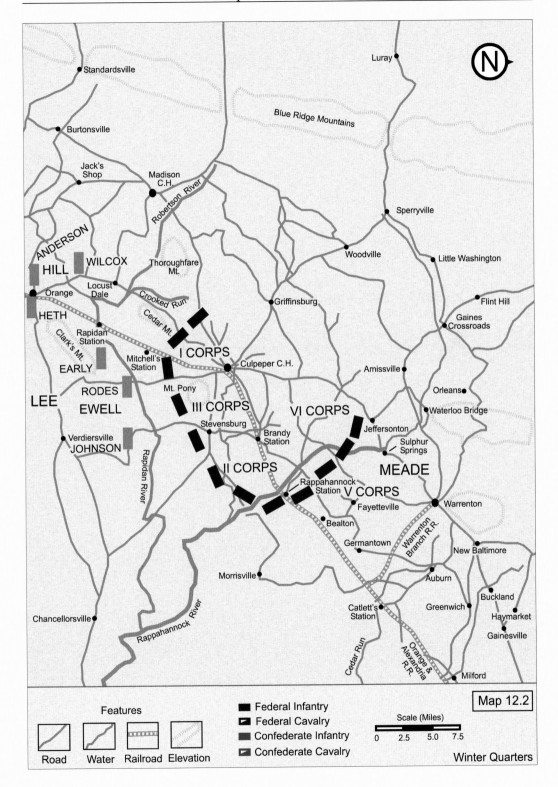

Map 12.2

Winter Quarters

Map Set 13: The Affair at Morton's Ford (February 6-7, 1864)

Map 13.1: Ben Butler Has a Plan to Capture Richmond (February 3-5, 1864)

Fully recuperated from his bout with pneumonia, Maj. Gen. George Meade stepped off a railroad car in Washington, D.C. It was February 12, 1864, and rumors were swirling that Meade was about to be removed from command of the Army of the Potomac.

The whispers that coursed through the ranks were nothing new, but after the failed campaigns of the previous fall, a change in command would not come as a surprise. According to some accounts, Brig. Gen. William (Baldy) Smith was in line for the job, as was the highly successful Maj. Gen. Ulysses S. Grant. Justifiably insecure about his position, Meade called upon Secretary of War Edwin Stanton on February 13 and received assurances that President Lincoln and his cabinet continued to have confidence in his abilities. "The Secretary was, as he always is, very civil and ready to accede to all my suggestions," a relieved Meade wrote to his wife. "He gratified me very much by saying that there was no officer in command who had to so great a degree the implicit confidence of all parties as myself." However, Meade continued, "he said there were several officers in my army that did not have the confidence of the country, and that I was injuring myself by retaining them." The two met the following day to discuss the identity and fate of these officers, who included corps commanders John Newton and William H. French. This meeting led to a major reorganization of the army the following month (as discussed in Map 12.2).[1]

When he returned to his army, Meade received a full briefing on a combat action at Morton's Ford on February 6. The genesis of what was essentially a heavy reconnaissance began with Maj. Gen. Benjamin Butler, the infamous "Beast Butler" of New Orleans who was now in command of the Department of Virginia and North Carolina. Butler came up with a plan to march a small force of 4,000 infantry, 2,200 cavalry, and a pair of batteries up the Virginia peninsula from Fortress Monroe, capture Richmond, and release Federal troops imprisoned there. Because he believed that any such movement toward the capital would force Gen. Robert E. Lee to dispatch troops in his direction, Butler sent a telegraph to Maj. Gen. Henry Halleck on February 3, 1864, requesting that the Army of the Potomac (then under the temporary command of John Sedgwick during Meade's absence) conduct an operation to distract Lee's attention and thus prevent the shifting of troops to defend Richmond. Halleck agreed and the plan was put into motion.[2]

Halleck had second thoughts when intelligence suggested that Lee had sent more than 8,000 men to attack New Bern, North Carolina (the number was less than half that figure). Butler went over Halleck's head to Stanton, who ordered Halleck to continue to support Butler's operation.[3]

Sensing less than enthusiastic support from the Army of the Potomac, Butler wired Halleck that he "could get no co-operation from Sedgwick." Halleck repeated his request on February 5 that Sedgwick cooperate with Butler. Sedgwick was not impressed. A flank movement, he wrote, "is impossible in the present condition of the roads and state of the weather. Demonstrations in our front at the present time may, however, spoil the chances for the future." Knowing that Halleck expected his cooperation, however, Sedgwick issued orders the following day. John Buford's former cavalry division, now under Wesley Merritt, would demonstrate at Barnett's Ford on the Federal right flank while Judson Kilpatrick did the same at Culpeper Mine Ford on the left. I Corps and II Corps were issued three days' rations. The former would head for Raccoon Ford and the latter to Morton's Ford. III Corps and VI Corps, meanwhile, would remain in their camps, ready to join their comrades if needed.[4]

The operation began early on February 6. Because of a minor illness, Maj. Gen. Gouverneur Warren did not accompany his II Corps. Worried that exposure would exacerbate his condition, he turned his corps over to Brig. Gen. John Caldwell. Muddy roads hampered movement, so the infantry did not approach Morton's Ford until after 10:30 a.m. The Rapidan River was 30 to 40 feet wide at this point and about four feet deep. A small island bifurcated the river.

Caldwell's precise orders are unclear. It appears that he was directed to approach the river and, if possible, throw some units across it to attract attention. However, he was not to bring on a general engagement.[5]

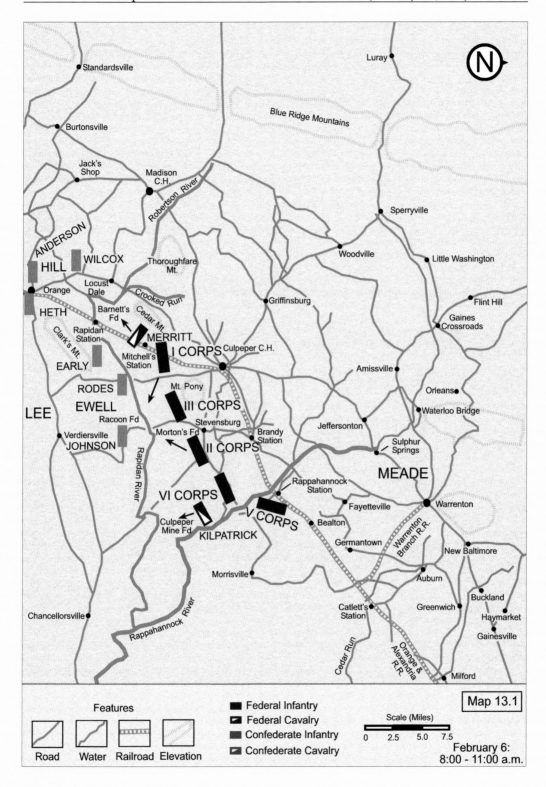

Luray

Blue Ridge Mountains

Standardsville

N

Burtonsville

Jack's Shop

Madison C.H.

Robertson River

Sperryville

ANDERSON

WILCOX

HILL

Thoroughfare Mt.

Woodville

Little Washington

Locust Dale

Orange

Crooked Run

Griffinsburg

Flint Hill

HETH

Barnett's Fd

Cedar Mt.

Gaines Crossroads

Clark's Mt.

Rapidan Station

MERRITT

I CORPS

Culpeper C.H.

Mitchell's Station

Amissville

EARLY

RODES

Mt. Pony

Orleans

LEE

EWELL

Racoon Fd

III CORPS

Waterloo Bridge

Verdiersville

JOHNSON

Morton's Fd

Stevensburg

Brandy Station

Jeffersonton

Sulphur Springs

MEADE

Rapidan River

II CORPS

VI CORPS

Rappahannock Station

Fayetteville

Warrenton

Culpeper Mine Fd

V CORPS

Bealton

KILPATRICK

Germantown

Warrenton Branch R.R.

New Baltimore

Morrisville

Auburn

Buckland

Chancellorsville

Rappahannock River

Catlett's Station

Greenwich

Haymarket

Gainesville

Cedar Run

Orange & Alexandria R.R.

Milford

Features

Federal Infantry

Federal Cavalry

Confederate Infantry

Confederate Cavalry

Map 13.1

Scale (Miles)

0   2.5   5.0   7.5

Road   Water   Railroad   Elevation

February 6: 8:00 - 11:00 a.m.

Map 13.2: Hays' Division Crosses the River (February 6: 11:00 a.m. - 1:00 p.m.)

A heavy mist shrouded the Rapidan and the bank beyond. Caldwell could see rifle pits and unfinished abatis, but had no way of knowing the enemy's strength opposite the ford. Rather than cross indiscriminately and risk a sharp defeat, Caldwell ordered Brig. Gen. Alexander Hays, whose division was in the van of II Corps, "to throw forward as skirmishers 300 of the best veteran troops of his command." The men who made the move were drawn from every regiment in Brig. Gen. Owen's brigade, which led II Corps to the ford. Hays was the brigade's former commander, and he was particularly proud of the New Yorkers. Still, the brigade had a checkered past. It was captured, lock, stock, and barrel during the siege of Harpers Ferry during the Antietam Campaign. Its performance at Gettysburg, however, had gone a long way toward redeeming the unit's reputation.[6]

Removing their shoes, socks, and cartridge belts, the men waded into the icy waist-deep water. All, that is, except for the shortest because the frigid water would have come up to their armpits. The tight ford allowed for a narrow column of only four men abreast. About 80 Confederates manned the works on the opposite side of the river, and they opened fire when they spotted the move. The New Yorkers pushed across as fast as possible, and "with slight loss" climbed the opposite bank (No. 1). One soldier recalled an interesting incident. Apparently the members of the 39th New York selected to cross the river refused because they objected to the difficult crossing conditions. Hays "jumped from his horse, without saying a word, leaving his horse by the side of the river, waded across to the other side, pointing out good footing, and then returned and mounted his horse." The brave demonstration seems to have stirred those particular New Yorkers into action.

Some of the men fell into the icy water because of the slippery riverbed, but they rapidly regained their footing and kept moving. Once across they faced another barrier: an eight-foot clay bank. Hays grabbed an axe from one of the men and used it to help clear a path through the tangled vegetation, yelling "we will cut them down as I do this brush!" Once they reached the top and pushed over, the Union men snatched up about 30 enemy soldiers who had lingered too long; the rest headed for the breastworks behind them (No. 2).

Gen. Owen ordered the rest of his brigade across the river and his regiments forward about three-quarters of a mile to reconnoiter. The New Yorkers halted in a hollow north of the Morton house facing the enemy's line of breastworks (No. 3). Artillery fire opened on them from somewhere beyond the Morton place. Owen communicated the situation back to Hays, who was probably still at the river crossing, and the rest of his division moved to cross. Col. Samuel Carroll's brigade began to cross about 12:30 p.m., with Col. Charles Power's brigade coming up behind Carroll.[7]

The Morton's Ford sector was defended by Lt. Gen. Richard Ewell's Second Corps, with the immediate responsibility belonging to a division of infantry under Maj. Gen. Jubal Early. Early's brigades rotated positions, with one stationed at the crossing until it was relieved by another. Brig. Gen. William "Extra Billy" Smith's Brigade, now under Brig. Gen. John Pegram, was manning the works on February 6. Because no one was expecting anything out of the ordinary, most of the men had fallen back to return to the warmth of their camps. Unfortunately, they did so before Brig. Gen. John Gordon's Brigade arrived to replace them. As a result, when the head of the Federal II Corps crossed the river, only a thin band of skirmishers manned the bank and works inland with several batteries belonging to Henry Cabell's Battalion. The careless mistake offered the Federals a good opportunity to exploit, and nothing stood between them and the vulnerable Confederate artillery.[8]

Cannoneer William Dame recalled the dangers he and his fellow gunners faced that morning: "so it was, that, with one brigade gone; the other not up; the pickets withdrawn, at this moment there was nobody whatsoever on the front . . . and, here was the enemy across the river, moving on us and no supports [sic]."[9]

When he reached the ford, Caldwell conducted his own reconnaissance. According to a recent dispatch from Maj. Gen. Andrew Humphreys, Meade's chief of staff, "if the brigades that have crossed the river are not able to maintain themselves on the other side, he [Sedgwick] desires that they be withdrawn to this side."[10]

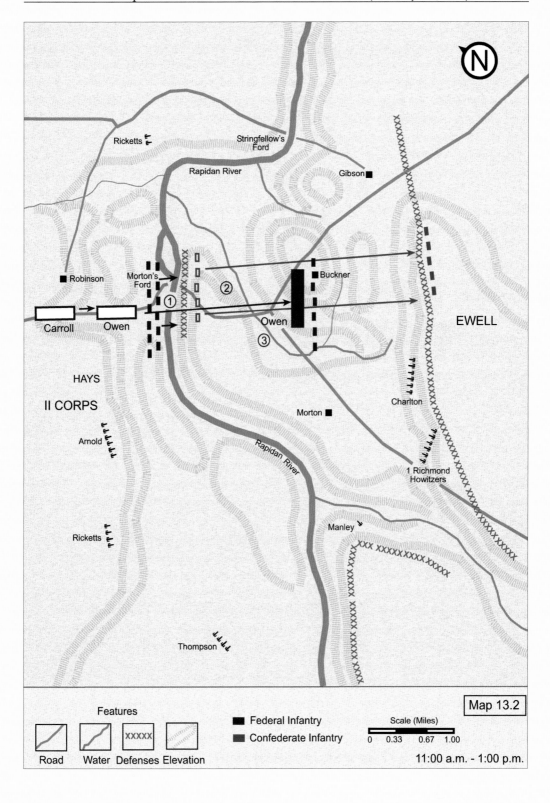

N

Ricketts

Stringfellow's
Ford

Rapidan River

Gibson ■

Robinson ■

Morton's
Ford

Buckner

① ②

Carroll   Owen   Owen   EWELL

③

HAYS

II CORPS

Charlton

Arnold

Morton ■

1 Richmond
Howitzers

Ricketts

Rapidan River

Manley

Thompson

Features

Road   Water   xxxxx   Defenses   Elevation

■ Federal Infantry

■ Confederate Infantry

Scale (Miles)

0   0.33   0.67   1.00

Map 13.2

11:00 a.m. - 1:00 p.m.

Map 13.3: The Opponents Assemble
(February 6: 1:00 - 4:00 p.m.)

Gen. Ewell, commander of Second Corps, had recently returned to the Army of Northern Virginia after recuperating from the exertions of the fall 1863 campaigns and a period of hospitalization in Charlottesville. During the middle of January, his horse had slipped on the ice and snow and rolled over. Fortunately for the chronically unlucky Ewell, he escaped with nothing more than bruises. Ewell's headquarters were less than three miles away from Morton's Ford.

Shortly after the rattle of small arms fire and the thunder of artillery reached his ears that morning, a dispatch rider delivered a message informing him that the enemy was massing at the ford. Ewell climbed atop his horse and headed for the threatened sector. The combative general returned to his former pre-wound self, riding the lines tirelessly in preparation for what looked like a potentially serious engagement.[11]

At the moment, however, there were few troops for Ewell to command. Pegram's men had left and their relief (Gordon's Brigade) had not yet come up. A stunned Ewell galloped to the rear, found Pegram's troops (under Col. John Hoffman), and ordered them to about face and head back to the ford. The men trotted back into the line of works just after Owen's Federals had crossed the river and were slowly approaching the fortifications. The arriving Virginians added their small arms fire to the deep throated thundering artillery (No. 1).[12]

With Pegram's men in place, Ewell called up Gordon, whose brigade was to have relieved Pegram's. As it turns out Gordon was absent and his brigade was under Col. Clement Evans of the 31st Georgia. This may have led to some confusion about relieving Pegram's men at the ford. Evans was in mid-sentence writing a letter to his wife when one of Ewell's aides dashed up and "a most hurried order came for me to bring the brigade without delay to Morton's Ford. Of course I went at it with a vim and was soon on the march," wrote Evans. The men marched at the double-quick. Evans, a good and experienced officer, understood the gravity of the situation. When he reached the front, the Georgia officer marched his men parallel to Pegram's line and formed the brigade to the left of the Virginians (No. 2). The Southern veterans could see Owen's men "drawn up in line beyond Dr. Morton's house, while their skirmishers held the grove around it (No. 3).[13]

Owen's New Yorkers watched the buildup of enemy troops with dismay. Within the space of minutes they found themselves in a precarious position. A member of the 126th New York wrote that the swift-moving river with steep banks "on two sides of us, and the enemy, confident in numbers and position" put the men in harm's way. He continued, "to retreat was destruction; to hold our position our only salvation." Another soldier in the 125th New York recalled that "the cannonballs were cutting through our ranks, the men for a moment appear demoralized. But Col. [Levin] Crandell called them into line, bade them dress on the colors and then, all being in good order, he commanded, 'Lie down.'" Some relief was forthcoming when Carroll's brigade arrived about 1:15 p.m. Powers' brigade reached the area about an hour later. With the new arrivals, Owen shifted his brigade to the left to take advantage of a ridge. Carroll formed on his right, while Powers took up a position to his left. Several batteries also dropped trail on the high ground and opened fire on the Confederate positions.[14]

Perhaps seeking to justify their inability to drive the enemy from their defenses, many of the Union soldiers greatly exaggerated the strength of the Confederates (which was about 2,000 in total). "Confederate troops could be seen moving toward the breastworks from all directions, until it was evident that the enemy had many more troops than the Union," wrote the historian of the 14th Connecticut after the war. In fact, Hays had three large brigades at his disposal, some 6,000 men within striking distance of the Confederate position.

A light rain fell all day. Combined with the cold, the drizzle created a penetrating discomfort that further demoralized the Union men who wanted nothing more than to be left alone in their winter quarters. Several who would survive the Morton's Ford fighting were later struck down by illness.[15]

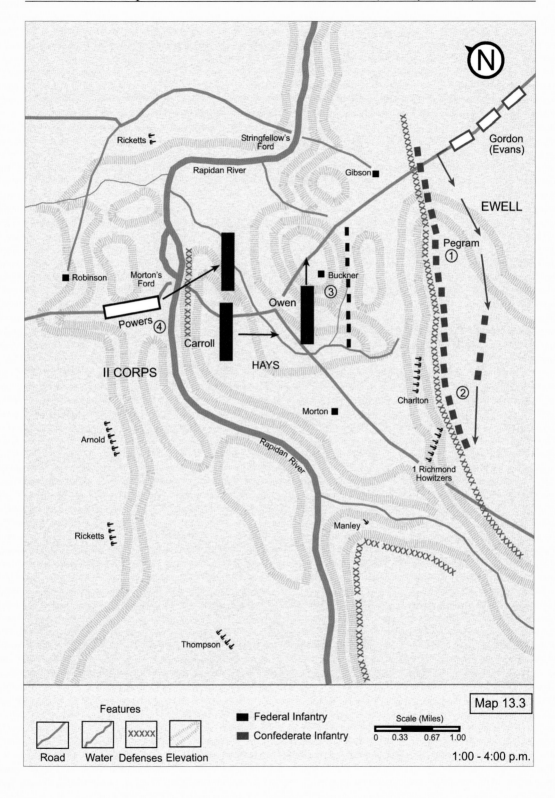

N

Ricketts

Stringfellow's Ford

Rapidan River

Gibson

Gordon (Evans)

EWELL

Robinson

Morton's Ford

Buckner

Pegram
①

Owen

③

Powers ④

Carroll

HAYS

II CORPS

Charlton

②

Arnold

Morton

1 Richmond Howitzers

Ricketts

Manley

Thompson

Features

Road   Water   Defenses   Elevation

XXXXX

■ Federal Infantry

■ Confederate Infantry

Scale (Miles)

0   0.33   0.67   1.00

Map 13.3

1:00 - 4:00 p.m.

Map 13.4: Stalemate
(February 6: 4:00 - 6:30 p.m.)

When he learned that the feint across Morton's Ford was developing into a full-fledged fight, Gen. Warren left his camp and rode to the river. It did not take long for him to conclude that Hays had gotten himself into a tight situation. The enemy, wrote Warren, "had complete control with his fire over the point of land our troops had gained on his side of the stream. Our troops then were in a kind of cul-de-sac—a focus of fire. I soon determined . . . to wait until night before withdrawing my command, as the movement of the troops drew the fire of the enemy's artillery upon them whenever attempted." It was a race against time, and darkness could not come fast enough.[16]

Concerned that enemy skirmishers had occupied the buildings populating the Morton farm, Col. Evans sought a way to extract them. "I observed by reconnoitering the ground, that three companies of infantry could be conducted down a valley under cover of two hills, one protecting them from observation & artillery fire from across the river, and the other from observation of the enemy on this side, until they could approach within seventy-five or one hundred yards of the barn & other outhouses in which these sharpshooters were concealed," wrote Evans after the battle. Before launching his attack, Evans sent a message to Col. Hoffman, commanding Pegram's Brigade, to throw out a skirmish line to distract the enemy. Once all was ready, Evans gave the word and the line advanced, forcing the Union skirmishers to retreat toward their main battle lines (No. 1).[17]

Realizing the need to stabilize his skirmish line, particularly the left side (which was being flanked), Hays ordered the 39th New York of Powers' brigade to move forward. "They were mostly foreigners, and could not understand the language of the order," reported the historian of the 14th Connecticut. "As they came over the crest of the hill and encountered the enemy's fire, these New Yorkers became confused and instead of keeping their line, recoiled in confusion and huddled together in groups, upon which the enemy's shot made sad havoc." Hays ordered the 14th Connecticut to take their place (No. 2).

The Nutmeggers heard their commander yell in a clear voice, "Fall in Fourteenth!" The regiment moved forward as a skirmish line with four or five feet between each man. According to the regimental historian, "the bullets fell thick and fast and the noise was indescribable." Confederate artillery and small arms fire hit them from three sides and the attack ground to a halt.[18]

Combat flared on the Union right. The Yankees, wrote one of Gordon's men, "were never farther than 250 yards, and were sometimes as near as fifteen or twenty yards." Carroll refused his right (No. 3) to counteract Evan's push near the Morton house. Help was on its way when Warren sent Col. DeWitt Baxter's brigade (Brig. Gen. Alexander Webb's division) across the river to stabilize this part of the line (No. 4). Baxter slid into position on Carroll's right about 6:30 p.m., but the fighting was all but over. Carroll's men had blunted Evans' attack, and darkness was draping the field.[19]

Ewell's two brigades had lost 49 men killed and wounded and another 30 captured during the initial Federal crossing. Hays lost many more—252 men killed, wounded, and captured. Almost half of his losses were in the 14th Connecticut, which suffered 115 from all causes. "I regret to forward such a long list of casualties," Hays wrote in his report, "but it is solely attributable to the faltering of two regiments of conscripts or substitutes comprising the Fourteenth Connecticut and Thirty-ninth New York Volunteers. If supported by our whole corps I have not the least doubt that we would have been enabled to capture the whole force of the rebels, including camps and artillery, with less loss than we have suffered." By midnight, all of Warren's II Corps troops were back across the Rapidan River. The entire premise behind the mishandled Morton's Ford feint was to distract from Butler's expedition. The Massachuetts general made good progress until he reached Bottom Bridge on the Chickahominy River just 13 miles from Richmond. When he found the enemy in force there, however, he had little choice but to withdraw and return to Fortress Monroe.[20]

Gen. Lee dismissed the Federal cross-river thrust as "only intended to see where we were and whether they could injure us." The Morton's Ford fighting was the last important combat action during the winter of 1863-1864.[21]

On March 10, 1864, Ulysses S. Grant was promoted to lieutenant general and placed in command of all U.S. armies. The fighting in the Eastern Theater would never be the same.

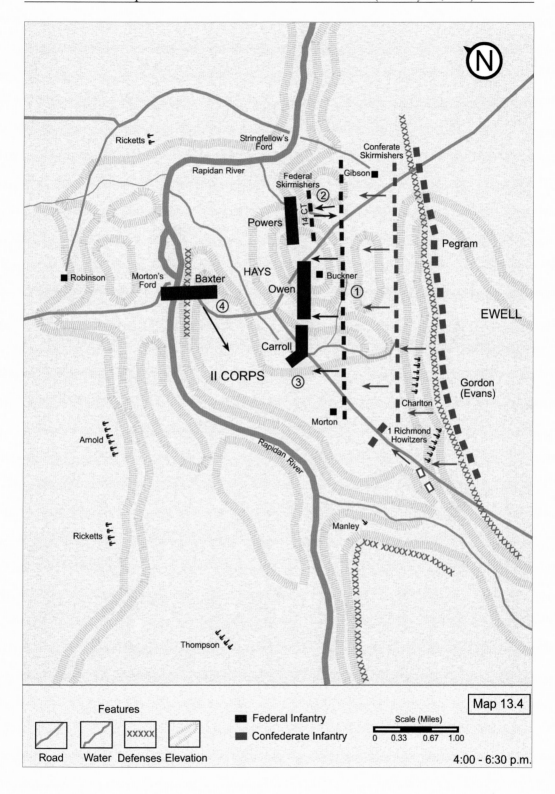

Map 13.4

Features

Road   Water   Defenses   Elevation

■ Federal Infantry
■ Confederate Infantry

Scale (Miles)
0   0.33   0.67   1.00

4:00 - 6:30 p.m.

Summation

Despite the fascinating series of maneuvers, command decisions, engagements, politics, and "what-ifs" that comprise the Bristoe Station and Mine Run campaigns, they remain among the least studied in the Eastern Theater. They are, however, instructive of the state of both armies at what was certainly a critical time of the Civil War.

For Robert E. Lee and his Army of Northern Virginia, both operations offered an opportunity to engage and defeat the Union army in decisive combat with an eye toward redeeming the Gettysburg defeat. The major organizational changes put in place after Thomas J. "Stonewall" Jackson's death at Chancellorsville in May 1863 did not serve the army well in Pennsylvania, where heavy losses in generals and colonels further drained a rapidly diminishing pool of capable officer material. The Bristoe Station and Mine Run operations gave Lee an opportunity to test his subordinates in the field for the first time after the failed summer offensive. The experience did nothing to alleviate his concern about the capabilities of many of his subordinates in general, and about Lt. Gens. Richard Ewell and A. P. Hill in particular. Whether a few more months of maturation and reflection, coupled with the return of Lt. Gen. James Longstreet and First Corps in the spring (which remained in doubt), would suffice to correct the army's ills remained to be seen.

The lack of basic resources, manpower, healthy horses, and other necessities to keep an army in the field also hampered Lee's efforts. The Army of Northern Virginia of late 1863 was a far cry from the army Lee had led to repeated victories.

*   *   *

The fall operations offered George Meade an opportunity to placate President Abraham Lincoln and his cabinet and finally put to rest any lingering concerns about his abilities. Meade had defeated Lee in Pennsylvania, but he had done so on the defensive on Northern soil. Defeating the Confederacy and saving the Union would require an aggressive invasion strategy into Virginia—a much more complex operation that required a very different mindset and ability. Did Meade possess these qualities? Neither Bristoe Station nor Mine Run provided a conclusive answer to that fundamental question.

In reviewing the Federal high command's approach to the war, particularly during the Fall 1863 campaigns, Lt. Col. Kavin Coughenour (Ret.) recently observed:

> After two years of war Lincoln's administration still lacked a single national military strategy that coordinated the efforts of all Federal armies in the field. Between June and November 1863 Meade received substantial guidance from Washington, but its orientations were operational rather than strategic. The aid of the guidance was to coax Meade into attacking and destroying the Army of Northern Virginia.[1]

When the campaign season ended in December 1863 and the armies went into winter quarters, the questions and concerns both sides possessed after Gettysburg remained: Meade maintained his reputation as a cautious but capable army commander, and Lee now led an army that was weaker and less capable than it had once been.

The fighting sure to follow in the spring of 1864 would provide more conclusive answers.

Appendix 1

Orders of Battle

ARMY OF THE POTOMAC
Major General George G. Meade

First Army Corps
Maj. Gen. John Newton

First Division
Brig. Gen. Lysander Cutler

First Brigade (Iron Brigade)
Col. William W. Robinson

19th Indiana, Col. Samuel J. Williams
24th Michigan, Capt. Albert M. Edwards
1st New York Sharpshooters (battalion),
Capt. Joseph S. Arnold
2nd Wisconsin, Lt. Col. John Mansfield
6th Wisconsin, Col. Edward S. Bragg
7th Wisconsin, Maj. Mark Finnicum

Second Brigade
Brig. Gen. James C. Rice

7th Indiana, Col. Ira G. Grover
76th New York, Lt. Col. John E. Cook
84th New York ("14th Brooklyn Militia"),
Col. Edward B. Fowler
95th New York, Maj. Edward Pye
147th New York, Maj. George Harney
56th Pennsylvania, Col. J. William Hofmann

Second Division
Brig. Gen. John C. Robinson

First Brigade
Col. Samuel H. Leonard

16th Maine, Lt. Col. Augustus B. Farnham
13th Massachusetts, Lt. Col. N. Walter Batchelder
39th Massachusetts, Col. Phineas S. Davis
94th New York, Maj. Samuel A. Moffett
104th New York, Col. Gilbert G. Prey
107th Pennsylvania, Col. Thomas F. McCoy

Second Brigade
Brig. Gen. Henry Baxter

12th Massachusetts, Maj. Benjamin F. Cook
83rd New York (9th Militia), Col. Joseph A. Moesch
97th New York, Maj. Charles Northrup
11th Pennsylvania, Col. Richard Coulter
88th Pennsylvania, Capt. John S. Steeple
90th Pennsylvania, Maj. Alfred J. Sellers

Third Division
Brig. Gen. John R. Kenly

First Brigade
Col. Chapman Biddle

121st Pennsylvania, Lt. Col. Alexander Biddle
142nd Pennsylvania, Col. Alfred B. McCalmont

Second Brigade
Col. Langhorne Wister

143rd Pennsylvania, Col. Edmund L. Dana
149th Pennsylvania, Lt. Col. Walton Dwight
150th Pennsylvania, Maj. Thomas Chamberlain

Third Brigade
Col. Nathan T. Dushane

1st Maryland, Lt. Col. John W. Wilson
4th Maryland, Col. Richard N. Bowerman
7th Maryland, Lt. Col. Charles E. Phelps
8th Maryland, Col. Andrew W. Denison

Artillery Brigade
Col. Charles S. Wainwright

5th Maine Light, Capt. Greenleaf T. Stevens
Maryland Light, Battery A, Capt. James H. Rigby
1st New York Light, Battery H,
Capt. Charles E. Mink
1st New York Light, Batteries E & L,
Capt. Gilbert H. Reynolds
1st Pennsylvania Light, Battery B,
Capt. James H. Cooper
4th US, Battery B, Lt. James Stewart

II Corps
Maj. Gen. Gouverneur K. Warren

First Division
Brig. Gen. John C. Caldwell

First Brigade
Col. Nelson A. Miles

26th Michigan, Col. Judson S. Farrar
61st New York, Lt. Col. K. Oscar Broady
81st Pennsylvania, Col. H. Boyd McKeen
140th Pennsylvania, Col. John Fraser

Second Brigade (Irish Brigade)
Col. Patrick Kelly

28th Massachusetts, Col. Richard Byrnes
63rd New York, Capt. Thomas Touhy
69th New York, Capt. Richard Moroney
88th New York, Capt. Denis F. Burke
116th Pennsylvania, Capt. Garrett Nowlen

Third Brigade
Col. James A. Beaver

52nd New York, Lt. Col. Charles G. Freudenberg
57th New York, Lt. Col. Alford B. Chapman
66th New York, Lt. Col. John S. Hammell
148th Pennsylvania, Lt. Col. George A. Fairlamb

Fourth Brigade
Col. John R. Brooke

2nd Delaware, Col. William P. Baily
64th New York, Maj. Leman W. Bradley
53rd Pennsylvania, Capt. Archibald F. Jones
145th Pennsylvania, Col. Hiram L. Brown

Second Division
Brig. Gen. Alexander S. Webb

First Brigade
Col. Francis E. Heath

19th Maine, Lt. Col. Henry W. Cunningham
15th Massachusetts, Lt. Col. George C. Joslin
1st Minnesota, Maj. Mark W. Downie
82nd New York (2nd Militia), Col. Henry W. Hudson
152nd New York, Maj. Timothy O'Brien

Second Brigade (Philadelphia Brigade)
Col. De Witt C. Baxter

69th Pennsylvania, Maj. James Duffie
71st Pennsylvania, Col. Richard Penn Smith
72nd Pennsylvania, Lt. Col. Theodore Hesser
106th Pennsylvania, Lt. Col. William L. Curry

Third Brigade
Col. James E. Mallon

19th Massachusetts, Maj. Edmund Rice
20th Massachusetts, Lt. Col. George N. Macy
7th Michigan, Col. Norman J. Hall
42nd New York, Lt. Col. William A. Lynch
59th New York, Capt. Horace P. Rugg
1st Company (Andrew) Massachusetts Sharpshooters,
Lt. Samuel G. Gilbreth

Third Division
Brig. Gen. Alexander Hays

First Brigade
Col. Samuel S. Carroll

14th Indiana, Col. John Coons
4th Ohio, Maj. Gordon A. Stewart
8th Ohio, Lt. Col. Franklin Sawyer
7th West Virginia (battalion),
Lt. Col. Jonathan H. Lockwood

Second Brigade
Col. Thomas A. Smyth

14th Connecticut, Col. Theodore G. Ellis
1st Delaware, Lt. Col. Daniel Woodall
12th New Jersey, Col. J. Howard Willets
10th New York (battalion), Maj. George F. Hopper
108th New York, Col. Charles J. Powers

Third Brigade
Brig. Gen. Joshua Owen

39th New York, Maj. Hugo Hildebrandt
111th New York, Col. Clinton D. MacDougall
125th New York, Col. Levin Crandell
126th New York, Col. James M. Bull

Artillery Brigade
Capt. John G. Hazard

1st New York Light, Battery G, Capt. Nelson Ames
Pennsylvania Light, Battery C, Capt. James Thompson
Pennsylvania Light, Battery F, Lt. James Stephenson
1st Pennsylvania Light, Batteries F and G,
    Lt. Beldin Spence
1st Rhode Island Light, Battery A,
    Capt. William A. Arnold
1st Rhode Island Light, Battery B,
    Capt. Thomas Frederick Brown
5th US, Battery C, Lt. Richard Metcalf

III Corps
Maj. Gen. William H. French

First Division
Maj. Gen. David B. Birney

First Brigade
Col. Charles H. T. Collis

57th Pennsylvania, Col. Peter Sides
63rd Pennsylvania, Maj. John A. Danks
105th Pennsylvania, Col. Calvin A. Craig
110th Pennsylvania, Maj. Levi B. Duff
114th Pennsylvania ("Collis' Zouaves"),
    Maj. Edward R. Bowen
141st Pennsylvania, Col. Henry J. Madill

Second Brigade
Brig. Gen. John H. H. Ward

3rd Maine, Col. Moses B. Lakeman
4th Maine, Col. Elijah Walker
20th Indiana, Col. William C. L. Taylor
86th New York, Maj. Michael B. Stafford
124th New York, Lt. Col. Francis M. Cummins
99th Pennsylvania, Col. Asher S. Leidy
2nd US Sharpshooters, Lt. Col. Homer R. Stoughton

Third Brigade
Col. P. Régis de Trobriand

17th Maine, Col. George W. West
3rd Michigan, Col. Byron R. Pierce
5th Michigan, Lt. Col. John Pulford
40th New York, Lt. Col. Augustus J. Warner
68th Pennsylvania, Lt. Col. Jacob W. Greenawalt
1st US Sharpshooters, Lt. Col. Casper Trepp

Second Division
Brig. Gen. Henry Prince

First Brigade
Col. William E. Blaisdell

1st Massachusetts, Col. Napoleon B. McLaughlen
11th Massachusetts, Lt. Col. Porter D. Tripp
16th Massachusetts, Lt. Col. Waldo Merriam
11th New Jersey, Col. Robert McAllister
26th Pennsylvania, Lt. Col. Robert L. Bodine
84th Pennsylvania, Lt. Col. Milton Opp

Second Brigade ("Excelsior Brigade")
Col. William R. Brewster

70th New York, Col. J. Egbert Farnum
71st New York, Col. Henry L. Potter
72nd New York, Lt. Col. John Leonard
73rd New York, Lt. Col. Michael W. Burns
74th New York, Maj. Henry M. Alles
120th New York, Maj. John R. Tappen

Third Brigade
Brig. Gen. Gershom Mott

5th New Jersey, Col. William J. Sewell
6th New Jersey, Col. George C. Burling
7th New Jersey, Maj. Frederick Cooper
8th New Jersey, Col. John Ramsey
115th Pennsylvania, Lt. Col. John P. Dunne

Third Division
Brig. Gen. Joseph B. Carr

First Brigade
Brig. Gen. William H. Morris

14th New Jersey, Col. William Snyder Truex
151st New York, Lt. Col. Erwin A. Bowen
10th Vermont, Col. Albert B. Jewett

Second Brigade
Col. Joseph W. Keifer

6th Maryland, Col. John Watt Horn
110th Ohio, Lt. Col. William N. Foster
122nd Ohio, Col. William H. Ball
138th Pennsylvania, Col. Matthew R. McClennan

Third Brigade
Col. Benjamin F. Smith

106th New York, Lt. Col. Charles Townsend
126th Ohio, Maj. Aaron W. Ebright
67th Pennsylvania, Col J. F. Staunton
87th Pennsylvania, Lt. Col. James A. Stahle

Artillery Brigade
Capt. George E. Randolph

4th Battery Maine Light, Capt. O'Neil W. Robinson, Jr.
10th Massachusetts Light Battery,
Capt. J. Henry Slepper
1st Battery New Hampshire Light,
Capt. Frederick M. Edgell
1st New Jersey Light, Battery B, Capt. A. Judson Clark
1st New York Light, Battery D,
Capt. George B. Winslow
12th Battery New York Light, Lt. George K. Dauchy
1st Rhode Island Light, Battery E, Lt. John K. Bucklyn
4th US, Battery K, Lt. John W. Roder

V Corps
Maj. Gen. George Sykes

First Division
Brig. Gen. Joseph J. Bartlett

First Brigade
Col. William S. Tilton

18th Massachusetts, Lt. Col. William B. White
22nd Massachusetts, Lt. Col. Thomas Sherwin, Jr.
1st Michigan, Lt. Col. William A. Throop
118th Pennsylvania, Maj. Henry O'Neill

Second Brigade
Col. Jacob B. Sweitzer

9th Massachusetts, Col. Patrick R. Guiney
32nd Massachusetts, Col. George L. Prescott
4th Michigan, Lt. Col. George W. Lumbard
62nd Pennsylvania, Lt. Col. James C. Hull

Third Brigade
Col. Joseph Hayes

20th Maine, Maj. Ellis Spear
16th Michigan, Capt. George H. Swan

44th New York, Lt. Col. Freeman Conner
83rd Pennsylvania, Maj. William H. Lamont

Second Division
Brig. Gen. Romeyn B. Ayres

First Brigade
Col. Sidney Burbank

2nd US (6 companies), Capt. Samuel A. McKee
3rd US (6 companies), Capt. Richard G. Lay
11th US, Maj. Jonathan W. Gordon
12th US, Maj. Luther B. Bruen
14th US, Capt. Edward Mck. Hudson
17th US, Lt. Col. James D. Greene

Third Brigade
Brig. Gen. Kenner Garrard

140th New York, Col. George Ryan
146th New York (Zouaves), Col. David T. Jenkins
91st Pennsylvania, Col. Edgar M. Gregory
155th Pennsylvania, Lt. Col. Alfred L. Pearson

Third Division
Brig. Gen. Samuel W. Crawford

First Brigade
Col. William McCandless

1st Pennsylvania Reserves, Col. William C. Talley
2nd Pennsylvania Reserves,
Lt. Col. Patrick C. Donough
6th Pennsylvania Reserves, Col. Wellington H. Ent
13th Pennsylvania Reserves,
Maj. William R. Hartshorne

Third Brigade
Col. Martin D. Hardin

5th Pennsylvania Reserves, Lt. Col. George Dare
9th Pennsylvania Reserves, Maj. Charles Barnes
10th Pennsylvania Reserves, Lt. Col. James B. Knox
11th Pennsylvania Reserves, Col. Samuel M. Jackson
12th Pennsylvania Reserves, Lt. Col. Richard Gustin

Artillery Brigade
Capt. Augustus P. Martin

3rd Battery Massachusetts Light, Lt. Aaron F. Walcott

5th Battery Massachusetts Light,
Capt. Charles A. Phillips
1st New York Light, Battery C, Capt. Almont Barnes
1st Ohio Light, Battery L, Capt. Frank C. Gibbs
3rd US, Batteries F and K, Lt. George F. Barstow
5th US, Battery D, Lt. Benjamin F. Rittenhouse

VI Corps
Maj. Gen. John Sedgwick

First Division
Brig. Gen. Horatio G. Wright

First Brigade
Brig. Gen. Alfred T. A. Torbert

1st New Jersey, Lt. Col. William Henry, Jr.
2nd New Jersey, Col. Samuel L. Buck
3rd New Jersey, Col Henry W. Brown
4th New Jersey, Lt. Col. Edward L. Campbell
15th New Jersey Col. William H. Penrose

Second Brigade
Col. Emory Upton

5th Maine, Col. Clark S. Edwards
121st New York, Maj. Andrew E. Mather
95th Pennsylvania, Lt. Col. Edward Carroll
96th Pennsylvania, Capt. James Russell

Third Brigade
Col. Peter C. Ellmaker

6th Maine, Maj. George Fuller
49th Pennsylvania, Lt. Col. Thomas M. Hulings
119th Pennsylvania, Lt. Col. Gideon Clark
5th Wisconsin, Lt. Col. Theodore B. Catlin

Second Division
Brig. Gen. Albion P. Howe

First Brigade
Brig. Gen. Alexander Shaler

65th New York, Col. Joseph E. Hamblin
67th New York, Col. Nelson Cross
122nd New York, Lt. Col. Augustus Wade Dwight
23rd Pennsylvania, Col. John Ely
82nd Pennsylvania, Col. Isaac C. Bassett

Second Brigade
Col. Lewis A. Grant

2nd Vermont, Col. James H. Walbridge
3rd Vermont, Col. Thomas O. Seaver
4th Vermont, Lt. Col. George P. Foster
5th Vermont, Maj. Charles P. Dudley
6th Vermont, Col. Elisha L. Barney

Third Brigade
Brig. Gen. Thomas H. Neill

7th Maine, Col. Edwin C. Mason
43rd New York, Col. Benjamin F. Baker
49th New York, Col. Daniel D. Bidwell
77th New York, Lt. Col. Winsor B. French
61st Pennsylvania, Lt. Col. George F. Smith

Third Division
Brig. Gen. Henry D. Terry

Second Brigade
Brig. Gen. Henry L. Eustis

7th Massachusetts, Col. Thomas D. Johns
10th Massachusetts, Lt. Col. Joseph B. Parsons
37th Massachusetts, Col. Oliver Edwards
2nd Rhode Island, Col. Horatio Rogers, Jr.

Third Brigade
Brig. Gen. Frank Wheaton

62nd New York, Col. David J. Nevin
93rd Pennsylvania, Maj. John I. Nevin
98th Pennsylvania, Col. John F. Ballier
102nd Pennsylvania, Col. John W. Patterson
139th Pennsylvania, Lt. Col. William H. Moody

Artillery Brigade
Col. Charles H. Tompkins

1st Massachusetts Light, Battery A,
Capt. William H. McCartney
1st Battery New York Light, Capt. Andrew Cowan
3rd Battery New York Light, Capt. William A. Harn
1st Rhode Island, Battery C, Capt. Richard Waterman
1st Rhode Island, Battery G, Capt. George W. Adams
4th US, Battery C, Lt. Charles L. Fitzhugh
5th US, Battery F, Lt. Leonard Martin
5th US, Battery M, Capt. James McKnight

Cavalry Corps
Maj. Gen. Alfred Pleasonton

First Division
Brig. Gen. John Buford

First Brigade
Col. George H. Chapman

8th Illinois, Maj. John L. Beveridge
3rd Indiana, Maj. William S. McClure
8th New York, Maj. William H. Benjamin

Second Brigade
Col. Thomas Devin

4th New York, Lt. Col. Augustus Pruyn
6th New York, Maj. William E. Beardsley
9th New York, Lt. Col. George S. Nichols
17th Pennsylvania, Col. Josiah H. Kellogg
3rd West Virginia (Companies A & C),
    Maj. Seymour B. Conger

Reserve Brigade
Brig. Gen. Wesley Merritt

19th New York (1st Dragoons), Maj. Rufus Scott
6th Pennsylvania, Maj. Henry C. Whelam
1st US, Capt. Marcus A. Reno
2nd US, Capt. George A. Gordon
5th US, Capt. Abraham K. Arnold

Second Division
Brig. Gen. David McM. Gregg

First Brigade
Col. John P. Taylor

1st Massachusetts, Col. Horace B. Sargent
1st New Jersey, Col. Percy Wyndham
6th Ohio, Lt. Col. William Stedman
1st Pennsylvania, Lt. Col. David Gardner
3rd Pennsylvania, Col. John B. McIntosh
1st Rhode Island, Lt. Col. John L. Thompson

Second Brigade
Col. J. Irvin Gregg

1st Maine, Col. Charles H. Smith
10th New York, Maj. Theodore H. Weed

2nd Pennsylvania, Lt. Col. Joseph P. Brinton
4th Pennsylvania, Maj. George H. Covode
8th Pennsylvania, Col. Pennock Huey
13th Pennsylvania, Maj. Michael Kerwin
16th Pennsylvania, Maj. Seth T. Kennedy

Third Division
Brig. Gen. Judson Kilpatrick

First Brigade
Brig. Gen. Henry E. Davies, Jr.

2nd New York, Lt. Col. Otto Harhaus
5th New York, Maj. John Hammond
18th Pennsylvania, Col. Timothy M. Bryan Jr.
1st West Virginia, Maj. Harvey Farabee

Second Brigade
Col. Charles H. Town

1st Michigan, Maj. Melvin Brewer
5th Michigan, Capt. Stephen P. Purdy
6th Michigan, Lt. Col. Henry E. Thompson
7th Michigan, Lt. Col. Allyne C. Litchfield
1st Vermont, Col. Edward B. Sawyer

Horse Artillery

First Brigade
Capt. James M. Robertson

6th Battery New York Light, Capt. Joseph W. Martin
2nd US, Batteries B and L, Lt. Edward Heaton
2nd US, Battery D, Lt. Edward B. Williston
2nd US, Battery M,
    Lt. Alexander C. M. Pennington, Jr.
4th US, Battery A, Lt. Rufus King
4th US, Battery E, Lt. Edward Field

Second Brigade
Capt. William M. Graham

1st US, Battery E, Lt. Egbert W. Olcott
1st US Light, Battery I, Capt. Alanson M. Randol
1st US, Battery K, Lt. John Egan
2nd US, Battery A, Lt. Robert Clarke
2nd US, Battery G, Lt. William N. Dennison
3rd US, Battery C, Capt. Dunbar R. Ransom

Artillery Reserve
Brig. Gen. Robert O. Tyler

First Volunteer Brigade

Lt. Col. Freeman McGilvery
6th Maine Light, Capt. Edwin B. Dow
9th Battery Massachusetts Light, Capt. John Bigelow
4th Battery New York Light, Lt. William T. McLean
1st Ohio Light, Battery H, Lt. George W. Norton

Second Volunteer Brigade
Capt. Elijah D. Taft

1st Connecticut Heavy, Battery B,
Capt. Albert F. Brooker
1st Connecticut Heavy, Battery M,
Capt. Franklin A. Pratt
1st New York Light, Battery B, Capt. Albert S. Sheldon
5th Battery New York Light, Capt. Elijah D. Taft
1st West Virginia Light, Battery C, Capt. Wallace Hill

Third Volunteer Brigade
Maj. Robert H. Fitzhugh

1st New Jersey Light, Battery A,
Capt. William Hexamer
1st New York Light, Battery K, Lt. Edward L. Bailey
15th Battery New York Light, Capt. Patrick Hart
1st US, Battery H, Lt. Philip D. Mason

*   *   *

ARMY OF NORTHERN VIRGINIA
General Robert E. Lee

Second Army Corps
Lt. Gen. Richard Ewell

Early's Division
Maj. Gen. Jubal A. Early

Pegram's Brigade
Brig. Gen. John Pegram

13th Virginia, Lt. Col. J. B. Terrill, Maj. John W. Daniel
31st Virginia, Col. J. S. Hoffman
49th Virginia, Lt. Col. J. C. Gibson
52nd Virginia, Lt. Col. J. H. Skinner
58th Virginia, Col. F. H. Board

Gordon's Brigade
Brig. Gen. John B. Gordon

13th Georgia, Col. James M. Smith
26th Georgia, Col. E. N. Atkinson,
31st Georgia, Col. Clement A. Evans
38th Georgia, Col. J. D. Mathews,
Lt. Col. Philip E. Devant
60th Georgia, Col. W. H. Stiles, Maj. Waters B. Jones
61st Georgia, Col. John H. Lamar,
Lt. Col. Charles W. MacArthur

Hays' Brigade
Brig. Gen. Harry T. Hays

5th Louisiana, Col. H. Forno
6th Louisiana, Col. William Monaghan
7th Louisiana, Col. D. B. Penn, Lt. Col. Thomas Terry
8th Louisiana, Col. A. De Blanc, Capt. A. L. Gusman
9th Louisiana, Col. Leroy A. Stafford,
Col. William R. Peck

Hoke's Brigade
Lt. Col. Samuel M. Tate

6th North Carolina, Col. R. F. Webb
21st North Carolina, Lt. Col. W. S. Rankin
54th North Carolina, Col. K. M. Murchison
57th North Carolina, Col. A. C. Godwin,
Lt. Col. Hamilton C. Jones, Jr.
1st Battalion North Carolina Sharpshooters,
Maj. Rufus W. Wharton

Johnson's Division
Maj. Gen. Edward Johnson

Walker's Brigade (Stonewall Brigade)
Brig. Gen. James A. Walker

2nd Virginia, Col. J. Q. A. Nadenbousch,
Lt. Col. Raleigh T. Colston
4th Virginia, Lt. Col. R. D. Gardner,
Maj. William Terry
5th Virginia, Col. John H. S. Funk
27th Virginia, Col. J. K. Edmondson,
Maj. Philip F. Frazer
33rd Virginia, Col. F. W. M. Holliday,
Lt. Col. Abraham Spengler

Steuart's Brigade
Brig. Gen. George H. Steuart

1st North Carolina, Col. J. A. McDowell, Lt. Col.
Hamilton Brown, Capt. L. C. Latham
3rd North Carolina, Col. Stephen D. Thruston,
Col. W. L. De Rosset
10th Virginia, Col. Edward T. H. Warren
23rd Virginia, Col. A. G. Taliaferro, Lt. Col. Simeon T.
Walton, Maj. John P. Fitzgerald
37th Virginia, Col. Titus V. Williams

Jones' Brigade
Brig. Gen. John M. Jones

21st Virginia, Col. William A. Witcher
25th Virginia, Col. John C. Higginbotham
42nd Virginia, Lt. Col. Robert W. Withers
44th Virginia, Col. Norval Cobb,
Lt. Col. Thomas R. Buckner
48th Virginia, Col. R. H. Dungan,
Capt. W. L. McConnell
50th Virginia, Col. Alexander S. Vandeventer,
Lt. Col. Logan H. Salyer

Stafford's Brigade
Brig. Gen. Leroy A. Stafford

1st Louisiana, Col. W. R. Shivers,
Capt. Edward D. Willett
2nd Louisiana, Col. Jesse Williams,
Capt. Martin C. Redwine
10th Louisiana, Col. E. Waggaman,
Lt. Col. Henry D. Monier

14th Louisiana, Col. Zebulon York,
Lt. Col. David Zable
15th Louisiana, Col. Edmund Pendleton,
Capt. J. F. Witherup

Rodes' Division
Maj. Gen. Robert E. Rodes

Daniel's Brigade
Brig. Gen. Junius Daniel

32nd North Carolina, Col. Edmund C. Brabble
43rd North Carolina, Col. T. S. Kenan,
Lt. Col. William G. Lewis
45th North Carolina, Lt. Col. S. H. Boyd,
Maj. T. McGehee Smith
53rd North Carolina, Col. William A. Owens
2nd North Carolina Battalion, Maj. J. M. Hancock,
Capt. Edward Smith

Ramseur's Brigade
Brig. Gen. Stephen D. Ramseur

2nd North Carolina, Col. W. R. Cox,
Lt. Col. Walter Stallings
4th North Carolina, Col. Bryan Grimes
14th North Carolina, Col. R. T. Bennett
30th North Carolina, Lt. Col. William W. Sillers,
Col. F. M. Parker

Doles' Brigade
Brig. Gen. George P. Doles

4th Georgia, Col. P. Cook, Lt. Col. William H. Willis
12th Georgia, Col. Edward S. Willis, Maj. J. T. Carson
21st Georgia, Col. John T. Mercer
44th Georgia, Col. William H. Peebles,
Col. S. P. Lumpkin

Battle's Brigade
Brig. Gen. Cullen Battle

3rd Alabama, Col. Charles Forsyth
5th Alabama, Col. Josephus M. Hall
6th Alabama, Col. J. N. Lightfoot, Maj. Isaac F. Culver
12th Alabama, Col. S. B. Pickens,
Maj. Adolph Proskamer
26th Alabama, Lt. Col. John S. Garvin

Johnston's Brigade
Brig. Gen. Robert D. Johnston

5th North Carolina, Col. T. M. Garrett,
Lt. Col. John W. Lea
12th North Carolina, Col. H. E. Coleman
20th North Carolina, Col. Thomas F. Toon
23rd North Carolina, Col. C. C. Blacknall,
Lt. Col. William S. Davis

Second Corps Artillery
Brig. Gen. Armistead L. Long

Andrews' Battalion
Maj. Carter M. Braxton

1st Maryland Artillery, Capt. W. F. Dement
Chesapeake (Maryland) Artillery, Lt. W. S. Chew
Alleghany (Virginia) Artillery, Capt. J. C. Carpenter
Lee (Virginia) Battery, Capt. Charles I. Raine

Carter's Battalion
Lt. Col. Thomas H. Carter

Jefferson Davis (Alabama) Artillery, Capt. W. J. Reese
King William (Virginia) Artillery, Capt. W. P. Carter
Morris (Virginia) Artillery, Capt. R. C. M. Page
Orange (Virginia) Artillery, Capt. C. W. Fry

Jones' Battalion
Lt. Col. Hilary P. Jones

Louisiana Guard Artillery, Capt. Charles A. Green
Charlottesville (Virginia) Artillery,
Capt. J. McD. Carrington
Courtney (Virginia) Artillery, Capt. W. A. Tanner
Staunton (Virginia) Artillery, Capt. A. W. Garber

Nelson's Battalion
Lt. Col. William Nelson

Milledge's (Georgia) Battery, Capt. John Milledge, Jr.
Amherst (Virginia) Artillery, Capt. T. J. Kirkpatrick
Fluvanna (Virginia) Artillery, Capt. J. L. Massie

First Regiment Virginia Artillery
Col. John T. Brown

2nd Richmond (Virginia) Howitzers,
Capt. David Watson
3rd Richmond (Virginia) Howitzers,
Capt. B. H. Smith, Jr.
Powhatan (Virginia) Artillery, Capt. W. J. Dance
Rockbridge (Virginia) Artillery, Capt. A. Graham
Salem (Virginia) Flying Artillery, Capt. C. B. Griffin

Third Corps
Lt. Gen. Ambrose P. Hill

Anderson's Division
Maj. Gen. Richard H. Anderson

Wilcox's Brigade
Col. John C. C. Sanders

8th Alabama, Col. Y. L. Royston
9th Alabama, Col. J. H. King
10th Alabama, Col. W. H. Forney
11th Alabama, Col. J. C. C. Sanders
14th Alabama, Col. L. Pinckard

Posey's Brigade
Brig. Gen. Carnot Posey, Col. Nathaniel H. Harris

12th Mississippi, Col. W. H. Taylor
16th Mississippi, Col. S. E. Baker
19th Mississippi, Col. N. H. Harris
48th Mississippi, Col. J. M. Jayne

Mahone's Brigade
Brig. Gen. William Mahone

6th Virginia, Col. George T. Rogers
12th Virginia, Col. D. A. Weisinger
16th Virginia, Col. J. H. Ham
41st Virginia, Col. W. A. Parham
61st Virginia, Col. V. D. Groner

Wright's Brigade
Brig. Gen. Ambrose R. Wright

3rd Georgia, Col. E. V. Walker
22nd Georgia, Capt. G. W. Rush
48th Georgia, Col. William Gibson
2nd Georgia Battalion, Capt. C. J. Moffett

Perry's Brigade
Brig. Gen. Edward A. Perry

2nd Florida, Col. L. G. Pyles
5th Florida, Col. T. B. Lamar
8th Florida, Col. David Lang, Lt. Col. William Baya

Heth's Division
Maj. Gen. Henry Heth

Kirkland's Brigade
Brig. Gen. W. W. Kirkland, Col. Thomas C. Singletary

11th North Carolina, Col. C. Leventhorpe
26th North Carolina, Col. J. R. Lane
44th North Carolina, Col. T. C. Singeltary
47th North Carolina, Col. G. H. Fairbault
52nd North Carolina, Col. J. K. Marshall

Cooke's Brigade
Brig. Gen. John R. Cooke, Col. Edward D. Hall

15th North Carolina, Col. W. MacRae
27th North Carolina, Col. J. A. Gilmer, Jr., Lt. Col.
George F. Whitfield, Maj. Joseph C. Webb
46th North Carolina, Col. E. D. Hall
48th North Carolina, Col. R. C. Hill,
Lt. Col. Samuel H. Walkup

Davis' Brigade
Brig. Gen. Joseph R. Davis

2nd Mississippi, Col. J. M. Stone
11th Mississippi, Col. F. M. Green
42nd Mississippi, Col. H. Moseley
55th North Carolina, Col. J. K. Connally

Walker's Brigade
Brig. Gen. Henry H. Walker

40th Virginia, Col. J. M. Brockenbrough
47th Virginia, Lt. Col. J. W. Lyell, Maj. James D. Bruce
55th Virginia, Col. W. S. Christian,
Maj. Charles N. Lawson
22nd Virginia Battalion, Col. E. P. Tayloe
5th Alabama Battalion, Maj. A. S. Van de Graaff
13th Alabama, Col. B. D. Fry
1st Tennessee (Provisional Army), Col. P. Turney
7th Tennessee, Col. J. A. Fite
14th Tennessee, Col. William McComb

Wilcox's Division
Maj. Gen. Cadmus M. Wilcox

Lane's Brigade
James H. Lane

7th North Carolina, Col. Edward G. Haywood
18th North Carolina, Col. John D. Barry
28th North Carolina, Col. Samuel D. Lowe
33rd North Carolina, Col. Clarke M. Avery
37th North Carolina, William M. Barbour

McGowan's Brigade
Brig. Gen. Abner M. Perrin

1st South Carolina (Provisional Army),
Col. D. H. Hamilton
1st South Carolina (Orr's Rifles),
Col. Francis E. Harrison
12th South Carolina, Col. John L. Miller
13th South Carolina, Col. Benjamin T. Brockman
14th South Carolina, Col. Joseph N. Brown

Thomas' Brigade
Edward L. Thomas

14th Georgia, Col. Robert W. Folsom
35th Georgia, Col. Bolling H. Holt
45th Georgia, Col. Thomas J. Simmons
49th Georgia, Col. Samuel T. Player

Scales' Brigade
Brig. Gen. Alfred M. Scales

13th North Carolina, Col. Joseph H. Hyman
16th North Carolina, Col. John S. McElroy
22nd North Carolina, Col. Thomas S. Galloway, Jr.
34th North Carolina, Col. William Lee J. Lowrance
38th North Carolina, Col. William J. Hoke

Artillery
Col. R. Lindsay Walker

Cutts' Battalion
Lt. Col. Allen S. Cutts

Irwin (Georgia) Artillery, Capt. J. T. Wingfield
Patterson's (Georgia) Artillery, Capt. G. M. Patterson
Ross' (Georgia) Artillery, Capt. H. M. Ross

McIntosh's Battalion
Maj. David G. McIntosh

Hardaway (Alabama) Battery, Capt. W. B. Hurt
Danville (Virginia) Artillery, Capt. R. S. Rice
Johnson's (Virginia) Battery, Capt. M. Johnson
2nd Rockbridge (Virginia) Artillery,
Capt. W. K. Donald

Poague's Battalion
Lt. Col. William T. Poague

Madison (Mississippi) Artillery, Capt. George Ward
Graham's (North Carolina) Battery, Capt. J. Graham

Albemarle (Virginia) Artillery, Capt. J. W. Wyatt
Brooke's (Virginia) Battery, Lt. A. W. Utterback

Garnett's Battalion
Lt. Col. John J. Garnett

Donaldsonville (Louisiana) Artillery, Capt. V. Maurin
Huger (Virginia) Artillery, Capt. J. D. Moore
Lewis (Virginia) Artillery, Capt. N. Penick
Norfolk (Virginia) Light Artillery, Capt. C. R. Grandy

Pegram's Battalion
Maj. William R. J. Pegram

Pee Dee (South Carolina) Artillery,
Capt. E. B. Brunson
Crenshaw (Virginia) Battery, Lt. A. B. Johnston
Fredericksburg (Virginia) Artillery, Capt. E. Marye
Letcher (Virginia) Artillery, Capt. T. A. Brander
Purcell (Virginia) Battery, Capt. J. McGraw

Haskell's Battalion
Maj. John C. Haskell

Branch (North Carolina) Artillery, Capt. A. C. Latham
Rowan (North Carolina) Artillery, Capt. J. Reilly
Palmetto (South Carolina) Artillery,
Capt. H. R. Garden

Reserve Artillery
Brig. Gen. William N. Pendleton

Cabell's Battalion
Col. Henry C. Cabell

Callaway's (Georgia) Battery, Capt. J. C. Fraser
Troup (Georgia) Artillery, Capt. H. H. Carlton
Manly's (North Carolina) Battery, Capt. B. C. Manly
1st Richmond (Virginia) Howitzers,
Capt. E. S. McCarthy

Cavalry Division
(Through September 9, 1863)
Maj. Gen. James E. B. Stuart

Hampton's Brigade
Col. Pierce M. Young
1st North Carolina, Col. L. S. Baker
1st South Carolina Cavalry, Col J. L. Black
2nd South Carolina Cavalry, Lt. Col. T. J. Lipscomb

Cobb's (Georgia) Legion, Col. Pierce Young
Phillips (Georgia) Legion, Lt. Col. W. G. Delony
Jeff Davis (Mississippi) Legion,
Lt. Col. Joseph F. Waring

Fitz Lee's Brigade
Brig. Gen. Fitz Lee

1st Maryland Battalion, Maj. Harry Gilmor
1st Virginia, Col. James H. Drake
2nd Virginia, Col. T. T. Munford
3rd Virginia, Col. Thomas H. Owen
4th Virginia, Col. William C. Wickham
5th Virginia, Col. Thomas L. Rosser

Robertson's Brigade
Brig. Gen. Beverly H. Robertson

4th North Carolina, Col. D. D. Ferebee
5th North Carolina, Lt. Col. Stephen B. Evans

Jones' Brigade
Brig. Gen. William E. Jones/Col. L. L. Lomax

6th Virginia, Maj. C. E. Flournoy
7th Virginia, Lt. Col. Thomas Marshall
11th Virginia, Col. L. L. Lomax

William H. F. Lee's Brigade
Col. R. L. T. Beale

9th Virginia, Col. R. L. T. Beale
10th Virginia, Col. J. Lucius Davis
13th Virginia, Col. J. R. Chambliss, Jr.

Horse Artillery

Beckham's Battalion
Maj. Robert F. Beckham

Breathed's (Virginia) Battery, Capt. James Breathed
Chew's (Virginia) Battery, Capt. R. P. Chew
Griffin's (Maryland) Battery, Capt. W. H. Griffin
Hart's (South Carolina) Battery, Capt. J. F. Hart
McGregor's (Virginia) Battery, Capt. W. M. McGregor
Moorman's (Virginia) Battery, Capt. M. N. Moorman

Cavalry Corps
(After September 9, 1863)
Maj. Gen. James E. B. Stuart

Hampton's Division
Maj. Gen. James E. B. Stuart

Gordon's Brigade
Brig. Gen. James B. Gordon

1st North Carolina, Col. Thomas Ruffin
2nd North Carolina, Maj. C. M. Anderson
4th North Carolina, Col. Dennis D. Ferebee
5th North Carolina, Lt. Col. Stephen B. Evans

Young's Brigade
Brig. Gen. Pierce M. B. Young

1st South Carolina Cavalry, Col J. L. Black
2nd South Carolina Cavalry, Lt. Col. T. J. Lipscomb
Cobb's (Georgia) Legion, Col. Pierce Young
Phillips (Georgia) Legion, Lt. Col. W. G. Delony
Jeff Davis (Mississippi) Legion,
Lt. Col. Joseph F. Waring

Rosser's Brigade
Brig. Gen. Thomas L. Rosser

7th Virginia, Lt. Col. R. H. Dulany
11th Virginia, Col. O. R. Funsten
12th Virginia, Col. A. W. Harman
35th Virginia Battalion, Lt. Col. E. V. White

Fitzhugh Lee's Division
Maj. Gen. Fitzhugh Lee

William H. F. Lee's Brigade
Col. John R. Chambliss, Jr.

9th Virginia, Col. R. L. T. Beale
10th Virginia, Col. J. Lucius Davis
13th Virginia, Col. J. R. Chambliss, Jr.

Lomax's Brigade
Brig. Gen. Lunsford L. Lomax

1st Maryland (Battalion), Lt. Col. Ridgely Brown
5th Virginia, Col. T. L. Rosser
6th Virginia, Col. Julian Harrison
15th Virginia, Col. W. B. Ball

Wickham's Brigade
Col. Thomas H. Owen

1st Virginia, Col. R. W. Carter

2nd Virginia, Col. T. T. Munford
3rd Virginia, Col. Thomas H. Owen
4th Virginia, Lt. Col. W. H. Payne

Horse Artillery

Beckham's Battalion
Maj. Robert F. Beckham

Breathed's (Virginia) Battery, Capt. James Breathed
Chew's (Virginia) Battery, Capt. R. P. Chew
Griffin's (Maryland) Battery, Capt. W. H. Griffin
Hart's (South Carolina) Battery, Capt. J. F. Hart
McGregor's (Virginia) Battery, Capt. W. M. McGregor
Moorman's (Virginia) Battery, Capt. M. N. Moorman

ENDNOTES

PART 1: THE BRISTOE STATION CAMPAIGN

Map Set 1: End of July, 1863

1. John W. Busey and David G. Martin, *Regimental Strengths and Losses at Gettysburg* (Hightstown, NJ: Longstreet House, 2005), 125; William D. Henderson, *The Road to Bristoe Station: Campaigning With Lee and Meade August 1-October 20, 1863* (Lynchburg, VA: H. E. Howard, 1987), 1, 4-5; William H. Powell, *Fifth Army Corps* (New York: G. P. Putnam Sons, 1896), 572. For example, the entire First Division of V Corps assembled to see the sentences carried out on five deserters from the 148th Pennsylvania.

2. Henderson, *The Road to Bristoe Station*, 3; David S. Sparks, ed., *Inside Lincoln's Army: The Diary of Marsena Rudolph Patrick, Provost Marshal General, Army of the Potomac* (New York: Thomas Yoseloff, 1964), 286.

3. Roy P. Basler, ed., *The Collected Works of Abraham Lincoln*, 8 vols. (New Brunswick, NJ: Rutgers University Press, 1953), vol. 6, 327-28; George Gordon Meade, *The Life and Letters of George Gordon Meade*, 2 vols. (New York: Charles Scribner's Sons, 1913), vol. 2, 134; Adrian G. Tighe, *The Bristoe Campaign: General Lee's Last Strategic Offensive with the Army of Northern Virginia October 1863* (XLibris, 2011), 35. Meade was 47 years old during the Fall 1863 campaigns. He had performed well in every capacity up to this point in the war. Meade has been described as a "gaunt, grizzled, and stern" man. His personality was aloof, uncongenial, and abrasive. One contemporary called him a "clear-headed" officer who "knows where and how many his men are; where and how many his enemy's men are; and what sort of country he has to go through." T. Harry Williams, *Lincoln and His Generals* (New York: Alfred A. Knopf, 1952), 259; Charles A. Dana, *Recollections of the Civil War* (New York: D. Appleton and Co., 1902), 189; Edwin B. Coddington, *The Gettysburg Campaign: A Study in Command* (New York: Charles Scribner's Sons, 1968), 213.

4. United States War Department, *The War of the Rebellion: A Compilation of the Official Records of the Union and Confederate Armies*, 128 volumes (Washington, DC: U.S. Government Printing Office, 1880-1901), 27, Part 3, 792-93, 858-59, cited hereafter as *OR*. Col. Robert McAllister of the 11th New Jersey wrote home, "The whole country is a barren waste. You cannot imagine the distress of the inhabitants of this part of Virginia, starvation stares them in the face." James I. Robertson, Jr., *The Civil War Letters of General Robert McAllister* (Harrisburg, PA: The Archive Society, 1997), 347.

5. Busey and Martin, *Regimental Strengths and Losses at Gettysburg*, 260; Henderson, *The Road to Bristoe Station*, 1.

6. Joseph T. Glatthaar, *General Lee's Army: From Victory to Collapse* (New York: Free Press, 2008), 408-09; John H. Worsham, *One of Jackson's Foot Cavalry* (New York: Neale Publishing Co., 1912), 181.

7. Clifford Dowdey and Louis H. Manarin, *The Wartime Papers of R. E. Lee* (New York: Bramhall House, 1961), 591, 594; Henderson, *The Road to Bristoe Station*, 6; Douglas Southall Freeman, *R. E. Lee: A Biography*, 4 vols. (New York: Charles Scribner's Sons, 1951), vol. 3, 170-71; James Longstreet, *From Manassas to Appomattox: Memoirs of the Civil War in America* (Bloomington, IN: Indiana University Press, 1960), 432.

8. Douglas Southall Freeman, *Lee's Lieutenants: A Study in Command*, 3 vols. (New York: Scribner, 1944), vol. 3, 220-28; *OR* 29, pt. 1, 146-96, vol. 29, pt. 2, 699, 700-01.

9. Daniel A. Grimsley, *Battles in Culpeper County, Virginia, 1861–1865: And Other Articles (1900)* (Culpeper, VA: Raleigh, Travers, Green, 1900), 14.

10. Sparks, ed., *Inside Lincoln's Army*, 280; Lt. Col. George B. Davis, "The Bristoe and Mine Run Campaigns," in *Campaigns in Virginia, Maryland, and Pennsylvania, 1862-1863* (Boston: Griffith-Stillings Press, 1903), 475.

11. Jay Luvaas and Wilbur S. Nye, "The Campaign that History Forgot," *Civil War Times Illustrated*, vol. 8, (November 1969), 38.

12. Lt. Col. Kavin L. Coughenour, "The Mine Run Campaign—An Operational Analysis of Major General George G. Meade." (Study Project, U.S. Army War College, Carlisle, Pennsylvania, March 1, 1990), 30-31.

13. Davis, "The Bristoe and Mine Run Campaigns," 475; Coughenour, "The Mine Run Campaign," 49.

14. *OR* 29, pt. 2, 28, 709; Emerson G. Taylor, *Gouverneur Kemble Warren: The Life and Letters of an American Soldier, 1830-1882* (Boston: Houghton Mifflin and Co., 1932), 152.

15. Jacob Nathaniel Raymer, *Confederate Correspondent: The Civil War Reports of Jacob Nathaniel Raymer, Fourth North Carolina*, E. B. Munson, ed. (Jefferson, NC: McFarland Publishing, 2009), 88; William D. Lyon to brother, July 18, 1863, Lyon

Papers, Navarro College, Pearce Civil War Collection, Corsicana, TX; Richard W. Waldrop to father, July 18, 1863, Waldrop Papers, Southern Historical Collection, University of North Carolina, Chapel Hill; Jeffry D. Wert, *A Glorious Army: Robert E. Lee's Triumph 1862-1863* (New York: Simon & Schuster, 2011), 280.

Map Set 2: Cavalry Actions (August 1863)

1. *OR* 27, pt. 3, 792-93.

2. Benjamin W. Crowninshield, *A History of the First Regiment of Massachusetts Cavalry Volunteers* (Boston: Houghton Mifflin and Co., 1891), 168-69; Abner Hard, *History of the Eighth Cavalry Regiment, Illinois Volunteers* (Dayton, OH: Morningside Bookshop, 1986), 268; *OR* 27, pt. 3, 819-21.

3. Henderson, *The Road to Bristoe Station*, 19-20; Grimsley, *Battles in Culpeper County, Virginia*, 14.

4. *OR* 27, pt. 3, 819-27; Robert J. Trout, *After Gettysburg: Cavalry Operations in the Eastern Theater, July 14, 1863 to December 31, 1863* (Hamilton, MT: Eagle Editions, Ltd., 2011), 57-58.

5. Henderson, *The Road to Bristoe Station*, 20-23; George M. Neese, *Three Years in the Confederate Horse Artillery* (New York: Neale Publishing Co., 1911), 203-04; *Richmond Enquirer*, August 7, 1863; *Richmond Daily Dispatch*, August 11, 1863.

6. Trout, *After Gettysburg*, 58-59; Henderson, *The Road to Bristoe Station*, 22-24; *OR* 27, pt. 3, 819-27; Richard T. Couture, ed., *Charlie's Letters: The Correspondence of Charles E. Denoon* (n.p., 1982), 181-82; Hard, *Eighth Illinois*, 268.

7. Henderson, *The Road to Bristoe Station*, 24-5; Hard, *Eighth Illinois*, 269; *OR* 27, pt. 3, 827-28, 830-32, 835.

8. *OR* 51, pt. 2, 748-50; Henderson, *The Road to Bristoe Station*, 25-27.

9. Henderson, *The Road to Bristoe Station*, 27-28.

10. *OR* 29, pt. 2, 700, 701, 709; Dowdey and Manarin, *The Wartime Papers of R. E. Lee*, 595. Much of James Longstreet's First Corps left Richmond on September 14 and participated in the Confederate victory at Chickamauga on September 20, 1863. Moving these men required 16 different railroads and a trip of more than 835 miles. Clifford Dowdey, *A History of the Confederacy* (New York: Barnes and Noble, 1992), 295.

11. *OR* 29, pt. 2, 158-59, 719-20.

12. Tighe, *The Bristoe Campaign*, 39-40.

13. H. B. McClellan, *I Rode with J. E. B. Stuart* (Bloomington, IN: Indiana University Press, 1958), 372-73. The visitor was Dr. Hudgins, a resident of Jeffersonton, who had previously served as the surgeon of the 9th Virginia Cavalry.

14. *OR* 29, pt. 2, 158, 184-85; Meriwether Lewis, "Samuel Ruth and General R. E. Lee: Disloyalty and the Line of Supply to Fredericksburg, 1862-1863," *Virginia Magazine of History and Biography*, 71 (1963), 104; Meriwether Lewis, "Of Spies and Borrowed Names: The Identity of Union Operatives in Richmond Known as the Phillipses Discovered," *Virginia Magazine of History and Biography*, 89 (1981), 312; Henderson, *The Road to Bristoe Station*, 31-33.

15. Frank Moore, ed. *The Rebellion Record: A Diary of American Events* (New York: D. Van Nostrand, 1864), vol. 7, 503-04; William N. McDonald, *A History of the Laurel Brigade: Originally the Ashby Cavalry of the Army of Northern Virginia and Chew's Battery*. (Baltimore: Johns Hopkins University Press, 2002), 171-72; Henderson, *The Road to Bristoe Station*, 35-36; Trout, *After Gettysburg*, 125. It appears that a portion of McIntosh's brigade crossed the Hazel River at Starke's Ford. Trout, *After Gettysburg*, 145, note 40.

16. Jeffry D. Wert, *Cavalryman of the Lost Cause: A Biography of J. E. B. Stuart* (New York: Simon & Schuster, 2008), 309-10; McClellan, *I Rode with J. E. B. Stuart*, 372-73; Moore, ed., *The Rebellion Record*, vol. 7, 503. There is a dearth of specific information on this action from a Confederate perspective. A welcome exception is an anonymous account published in the *Rebellion Record*. Dated September 14, 1863, the account provides a fairly good accounting of the various regimental activities during the early part of the fight. It also contains some Northern accounts of the fight. Moore, ed., *The Rebellion Record*, vol. 7, 504-05. Most of the Federal accounts suggest there was little active Confederate resistance until they approached Brandy Station.

17. *OR* 29, pt. 1, 123-24; Trout, *After Gettysburg*, 126-27.

18. *OR* 29, pt. 1, 120; Henderson, *The Road to Bristoe Station*, 35.

19. Henderson, *The Road to Bristoe Station*, 38.

20. Grimsley, *Battles in Culpeper County, Virginia*, 16-17; *OR* 29, pt. 1, 118-19, 129-31; Moore, ed., *The Rebellion Record*, vol. 7, 502.

21. *OR* 29, pt. 1, 120.

22. *OR* 29, pt. 1, 118-21, 126-27; Willard W. Glazer, *Three Years in the Federal Cavalry* (New York: R. H. Ferguson and Co., 1873), 320-22; Tighe, *The Bristoe Campaign*, 45; Moore, ed., *The Rebellion Record*, vol. 7, 504. As so often happened during this war, various units claimed credit for the capture of enemy cannon, and the fight at Culpeper was no

exception. Several members of the 1st Pennsylvania (Taylor's brigade) claimed they captured the guns before continuing their advance against the enemy, and when they returned found the artillery in the hands of Custer's men. However, Gen. Pleasonton reported that the guns were captured by Custer's men. *OR* 29, pt. 1, 112; H. S. Thomas, *Some Personal Reminiscences of Service in the Cavalry* (Philadelphia: L. R. Hammersley & Co., 1889), 15.

23. Henderson, *The Road to Bristoe Station*, 40; *OR* 29, pt. 2, 118-21, 126-29.

24. Tighe, *The Bristoe Campaign*, 45-47; Henderson, *The Road to Bristoe Station*, 41.

25. *OR* 29, pt. 2, 114-16, 120-21, 131-32; Henderson, *The Road to Bristoe Station*, 40-41.

26. *OR* 29, pt. 1, 112, 134-35; *Richmond Whig*, September 16, 1863; Trout, *After Gettysburg*, 130-31.

27. *OR* 29, pt. 2, 176, 181.

28. *OR* 29, pt. 2, 176, 729.

29. Hard, *Eighth Illinois*, 271-72; Charles D. Page, *History of the Fourteenth Regiment, Connecticut Vol. Infantry* (Meridian, CT: Horton Printing Co., 1906), 182; Henderson, *The Road to Bristoe Station*, 42; Moore, ed., *The Rebellion Record*, vol. 7, 505. The skirmish on September 14 involved an attack by the 6th Virginia Cavalry, which drove back the 6th Ohio Cavalry until the 1st Maryland Cavalry arrived to provide assistance. *OR* 29, pt. 1, 116-17; Moore, ed., *The Rebellion Record*, vol. 7, 505.

30. Henderson, *The Road to Bristoe Station*, 44-45; *OR* 29, pt. 2, 191.

31. *OR* 29, pt. 2, 187; Williams, *Lincoln and His Generals*, 285-86.

32. *OR* 29, pt. 2, 196-98; Henderson, *The Road to Bristoe Station*, 47.

33. William C. Davis, *The Confederate General*, 6 vols. (n.p.: National Historical Society, 1991), vol. 3, 50-51, vol. 4, 65.

34. Josiah Favill, *The Diary of a Young Officer* (Chicago: R. R. Donnelley & Sons, 1909), 261.

35. *OR* 29, pt. 2, 201-02, 206-07; Trout, *After Gettysburg*, 153.

36. *OR* 29, pt. 2, 196-98; Henderson, *The Road to Bristoe Station*, 47, 49.

37. *OR* 29, pt. 2, 213-14.

38. *OR* 29, pt. 1, 140; Trout, *After Gettysburg*, 156-57.

39. *OR* 29, pt. 1, 141; Trout, *After Gettysburg*, 156; Walter Clark, *Histories of the Several Regiments and Battalions From North Carolina: In The Great War 1861-'65*, 5 vols. (Wilmington, NC:

Broadfoot Publishing, 1996), vol. 1, 448, hereafter cited as *North Carolina Regiments*; McDonald, *A History of the Laurel Brigade*, 175; H. B. McClellan, *Life and Campaigns of Stuart's Cavalry* (Richmond: J. W. Randolph and English, 1885), 374; Wert, *Cavalryman of the Lost Cause*, 310. Jack's Shop is now called Roncelle.

40. *OR* 29, pt. 1, 141-42.

41. McDonald, *A History of the Laurel Brigade*, 175; Henderson, *The Road to Bristoe Station*, 55-56; *OR* 29, pt. 1, 141-42.

42. Clark, *North Carolina Regiments*, vol. 3, 572-73; Glazer, *Three Years in the Federal Cavalry*, 325-28; Daniel Branson Coltrane, *The Memoirs of Daniel Branson Coltrane* (Raleigh, NC: Edwards and Broughton Co., 1956), 20.

43. Henderson, *The Road to Bristoe Station*, 58; *OR* 29, pt. 1, 141-43.

44. Robert G. Carter, ed., *Four Brothers in Blue; or Sunshine and Shadow of the War of the Rebellion, a Story of the Great Civil War, from Bull Run to Appomattox* (Austin, TX: University of Texas Press, 1978), 352; Henderson, *The Road to Bristoe Station*, 60, 63.

45. Tighe, *The Bristoe Campaign*, 65-66; Emory M. Thomas, *Bold Dragoon: The Life of J. E. B. Stuart* (New York: Harper & Row, 1986), 264.

46. Henderson, *The Road to Bristoe Station*, 64-67; Howard K. Beale, ed., *Diary of Gideon Welles*, 3 vols. (New York: W. W. Norton, 1960), vol. 1, 438-40; *OR* 29, pt. 1, 147-48; pt. 2, 220, 239.

47. *OR* 29, pt. 2, 227, 234, 236, 239, 285; Meade, *Life and Letters*, vol. 2, 152.

48. Henderson, *The Road to Bristoe Station*, 69-70; *OR* 29, pt. 2, 746, 759, 780; vol. 51, pt. 2, 772; Dowdey and Manarin, *Wartime Papers of R. E. Lee*, 604, 606-07; Walter H. Taylor, *Four Years with General Lee* (New York: Bonanza Books, 1962), 90.

Map Set 3: Approach to Bristoe Station
(October 6 - October 20, 1863)

1. Henderson, *The Road to Bristoe Station*, 69-70.

2. *OR* 29, pt. 2, 251, 406-08, 439-40, 445, 457-58, 460, 462-63; Ken Wiley, *Norfolk Blues: The Civil War Diary of the Norfolk Light Artillery* (Shippensburg, PA: Burd Street Press, 1997), 93; William Walker to brother, October 7, 1863, John K. Walker papers, Perkins Library, Duke University.

3. Henderson, *The Road to Bristoe Station*, 71-72, 74; *OR* 29, pt. 1, 407, 410; Tighe, *The Bristoe Campaign*, 79-80.

4. David W. Lowe, ed., *Meade's Army: The Private Notebooks of Lt. Col. Theodore Lyman* (Kent, OH: Kent State University, 2007), 48; Dowdey and

Manarin, *The Wartime Papers of R. E Lee*, 612; A. L. Peel Diary, October 9, 1863 entry, copy in the Fredericksburg and Spotsylvania National Military Park; Edwin C. Fishel, *The Secret War for the Union* (New York: Houghton Mifflin, 1996), 542.

5. *OR* 29, pt. 2, 268-76; Henderson, *The Road to Bristoe Station*, 75, 77.

6. *OR* 29, pt. 1, 347-48; Trout, *After Gettysburg*, 210; Robert J. Driver, Jr. *First and Second Maryland Cavalry* (Charlottesville, VA: Howell Press, Inc., 1999), 63.

7. *OR* 29, pt. 1, 230, 380, 384; Henderson, *The Road to Bristoe Station*, 78-81.

8. Henderson, *The Road to Bristoe Station*, 84-85, 216; Tighe, *The Bristoe Campaign*, 106-07; J. F. J. Caldwell, *History of a Brigade of South Carolinians* (Philadelphia: King and Baird, Printers, 1866), 114.

9. Robert J. Driver, *First and Second Maryland Infantry* (Bowie, MD: Willow Bend Books, 2003), 225.

10. *OR* 29, pt. 1, 253, 310; pt. 2, 280-84; Tighe, *The Bristoe Campaign*, 104-05.

11. Tighe, *The Bristoe Campaign*, 116.

12. *OR* 29, pt. 2, 278-79.

13. *OR* 29, pt. 2, 286-87; Tighe, *The Bristoe Campaign*, 116, 118.

14. Tighe, *The Bristoe Campaign*, 134-35, 152; Henderson, *The Road to Bristoe Station*, 103-04; LeRoy to father, October 11, 1863 (copy in Chatham House Library, Fredericksburg and Spotsylvania National Military Park).

15. Dowdey, *A History of the Confederacy*, 607, 611; Tighe, *The Bristoe Campaign*, 152.

16. *Richmond Daily Dispatch*, October 19, 1863.

17. *OR* 29, pt. 1, 347-48; Hard, *Eighth Illinois*, 120; Tighe, *The Bristoe Campaign*, 120-21. Adrian Tighe believes the orders to retreat were probably dated midday on October 10, but the messenger carrying them probably had trouble crossing the Rapidan River and/or in locating Buford.

18. *OR* 29, pt. 1, 348-49; Trout, *After Gettysburg*, 214-25; Grimsley, *Battles in Culpeper County, Virginia*, 19-20; Tighe, *The Bristoe Campaign*, 123.

19. *OR* 29, pt. 1, 385, 440-41, 455, 460.

20. James Harvey Kidd, *Personal Recollections of a Cavalryman with Custer's Michigan Brigade in the Civil War* (Ionia, MI: Sentinel Printing Co., 1908), 61; Coltrane, *The Memoirs of Daniel Branson Coltrane*, 22.

21. Tighe, *The Bristoe Campaign*, 151.

22. Henderson, *The Road to Bristoe Station*, 121-22; Freeman, *Lee's Lieutenants*, vol. 3, 239-40; Freeman, *R. E. Lee*, vol. 3, 174-75; Caldwell, *History of a Brigade of South Carolinians*, 114. Douglas Freeman shows a different route than does Henderson. I have chosen to use the latter's account.

23. *OR* 29, pt. 2, 291-92, 296; Henderson, *The Road to Bristoe Station*, 123-24.

24. *OR* 29, pt. 1, 356, 365, 456.

25. Grimsley, *Battles in Culpeper County, Virginia*, 24; *OR* 29, pt. 1, 444-45. Heth's division camped for the night by the Rappahannock River, while Anderson's and Wilcox's divisions ended their march near Amissville. Tighe, *The Bristoe Campaign*, 157.

26. *OR* 29, pt. 1, 236, 311; pt. 2, 294, 298-99.

27. *OR* 29, pt. 2, 304-06; Henderson, *The Road to Bristoe Station*, 140.

28. *OR* 29, pt. 1, 236-37; pt. 2, 304-05, 312; Tighe, *The Bristoe Campaign*, 198-99.

29. *OR* 29, pt. 1, 410, 447; Tighe, *The Bristoe Campaign*, 195. According to Tighe, "the halt at Warrenton, however essential for the needs of the army, would seal the fate of Lee's campaign." Henderson, *The Road to Bristoe Station*, 143; Clarence R. Geier, Joseph W. A. Whitehorne, Alyson Wood, Eric Troll, and Kimberly Tinkham, "The Civil War Engagements at Auburn, Virginia, October 13, 14, 1863: A Historical-Archeological Analysis," http://www.jenningsgap.com/auburn archaeology.html, 47-49. Historians have hypothesized that Stuart could have escaped if he had moved out after the III Corps had passed, but Stuart reasoned that a night ride was too hazardous. Freeman, *Lee's Lieutenants*, vol. 3, 255-56; Geier, et. al., "The Civil War Engagements at Auburn, Virginia, October 13, 14, 1863, 52-53.

30. *OR* 29, pt. 1, 447; Coltrane, *The Memoirs of Daniel Branson Coltrane*, 22; Clark, *North Carolina Regiments*, vol. 3, 578-79. Stuart's hiding place during the night of October 13-14 was a small valley with an entrance covered by woods. Freeman, *Lee's Lieutenants*, vol. 3, 255. Tighe, *The Bristoe Campaign*, 206.

31. *OR* 29, pt. 1, 237; *Treasured Reminiscences Collected by the John K. McIver Chapter United Daughters of the Confederacy* (Columbia, SC: The State Co. Printers, 1911), 48; John Pearson, personal communication. The village of Auburn was described by soldiers as being composed of a mill, post office, blacksmith shop, and a few houses. John D. Smith, *The History of the Nineteenth Regiment of Maine Volunteer Infantry, 1862-1865* (Minneapolis: Great Western Printing Co., 1909), 106.

32. *OR* 29, pt. 1, 253-54, 271, 368; Francis Walker, *History of the Second Army Corps* (New York: Charles Scribner's Sons, 1887), 338; Geier, et. al., "The Civil War Engagements at Auburn, Virginia," 52-53; John Pearson, personal communication. The soldiers used the name "Coffee Hill" because the men of Caldwell's division prepared coffee on the higher ground while waiting for the rest of the II Corps to pass.

33. Preston, *History of the Tenth Regiment of Cavalry New York State Volunteers*, (New York: D. Appleton and Co., 1892), 147-48; *OR* 29, pt. 1, 368. The roads over which Ewell's divisions marched are unclear. Henderson has Rodes' division marching along Dumfries Road and Early's on Double Poplar. Historian Tighe believed it was the reverse. I have followed Henderson's convention. Henderson, *The Road to Bristoe Station*, 151-52, 161-62; Tighe, *The Bristoe Campaign*, 212-13.

34. Henderson, *The Road to Bristoe Station*, 155-56; Coltrane, *The Memoirs of Daniel Branson Coltrane*, 24; Robert J. Trout, *Galloping Thunder: The Stuart Horse Artillery Battalion* (Mechanicsburg, PA: Stackpole Books, 2002), 374; *OR* 29, pt. 1, 238, 258, 307-08; Levi J. Fritz letter in the *Montgomery Ledger*, November 24, 1863. According to one of Stuart's cavalrymen, "Not a word was allowed except in whispers, not a spark of fire could be struck, while through the long night we stood there listening to the sounds of that mighty column of armed foes passing near by us." Clark, *North Carolina Regiments*, vol. 3, 579.

35. *OR* 29, pt. 1, 239. The direction of Ewell's approach to the battlefield is the subject of debate. Henderson, *The Road to Bristoe Station*, 159-60, believed that Rodes' and Johnson's divisions approached on Rogues' (Dumfries) Road and Early's traveled on Double Poplar Road. Unfortunately, he failed to cite convincing references or evidence to support this contention. Henderson probably relied heavily on a map prepared by Gen. Warren for his report of the campaign (*OR* 29, pt. 1, 1,018) because he reprinted it in his overview of the action on page 154 of his book. Others, such as Tighe, *The Bristoe Campaign*, 213, and John Pearson, who has extensively studied the battle, believe that all three of Ewell's divisions approached on Double Poplar Road. I have followed this latter interpretation because a close examination of the literature supports this contention. Brigadier General Armistead Long, in *OR* 29, pt. 1, 417, reported that Ewell's Corps marched in one

column from Warrenton and upon its approach to Auburn, split up, with Rodes on the right, Early on the left, and Johnson in the middle. In his autobiography, Jubal Early noted that "Rodes' division formed line in front . . . while I moved with my division and Jones' battalion of artillery to the left across the creek above the mill, and around to get in the enemy's rear." Jubal Early, *Lieutenant General Jubal Anderson Early, CSA: Autobiographical Sketch and Narrative of the War Between the States* (Wilmington, NC: Broadfoot Publishing Co., 1989), 304. According to Capt. William Seymour of the Louisiana Tigers (Hays' brigade, Early's division), "our Brigade was carried to the extreme left of the Corps and formed inline of battle. . . . We advanced some distance . . . when the enemy fell back under cover of his artillery, of which he had a powerful force." Terry L. Jones, ed., *The Civil War Memoirs of Captain William Seymour* (Baton Rouge, LA: LSU Press, 1991), 87. One of those cannoneers, Lt. Charles Brockway of Ricketts' battery noted that his gunners were ordered to swivel their pieces 180 degrees to take on the enemy behind them, which suggests that Rodes' men were marching on Double Poplar Road. Richard A. Sauers and Peter Tomasak, *Ricketts' Battery: A History of Battery F, 1st Pennsylvania Light Artillery* (n.p.: Luzerne National Bank, 2001), 119-20.

36. *OR* 29, pt. 1, 299-304; Arabella M. Willson, *Disaster, Struggle, Triumph: The Adventures of 1000 Boys in Blue* (Albany, NY: Argus Publishers, 1870), 214; Geier, et. al., "The Civil War Engagements at Auburn, Virginia," 56.

37. Clark, *North Carolina Regiments*, vol. 3, 581; Cadwallader Iredell to Mattie, October 23, 1863, Iredell Papers, University of North Carolina; *Charlotte Western Democrat*, November 10, 1863; Todd S. Berkoff, "Botched Battle at Bristoe," *America's Civil War*, September, 2003, 26.

38. *OR* 29, pt. 1, 239.

39. *OR* 29, pt. 1, 254-55, 261, 271, 307, 308, 418, 421, 423, 428; Sauers and Tomasak, *Ricketts' Battery*, 119-20; Charles Brockway letter, *Columbia Democrat*, October 17, 1863; Henderson, *The Road to Bristoe Station*, 160.

40. *OR* 29, pt. 1, 239.

41. *OR* 29, pt. 1, 239, 255, 268, 308; Henderson, *The Road to Bristoe Station*, 162; Geier, et. al., "The Civil War Engagements at Auburn, Virginia," 59; Thomas M. Aldrich, *The History of Battery A: First Regiment Rhode Island Light Artillery in the War to Preserve the Union* (Providence, RI: Snow and Farnham Printers, 1904), 250.

42. Henderson, *The Road to Bristoe Station*, 161-62; *OR* 29, pt. 1, 448.

43. *OR* 29, pt. 1, 255.

Map Set 4: The Battle of Bristoe Station
(October 14, 1863)

1. *OR* 29, pt. 1, 426; Henderson, *The Road to Bristoe Station*, 165-66; Tighe, *The Bristoe Campaign*, 224.

2. *OR* 29, pt. 1, 333, 335. According to the historian of the 27th North Carolina, "the campfires of the enemy still burning and evident signs of their departure in haste [from Greenwich]. . . . Guns, knapsacks, etc., strewn along the road showed that the enemy was moving in rapid retreat . . . It was almost like boys chasing a hare." Clark, *North Carolina Regiments*, vol. 2, 440.

3. *OR* 29, pt. 2, 213; Tighe, *The Bristoe Campaign*, 245, 247.

4. Richard F. Miller, *Harvard's War: A History of the Twentieth Massachusetts Volunteer Infantry* (Hanover, NH: University Press of New England, 2005), 295; *OR* 29, pt. 1, 241.

5. J. Michael Miller. "The Battles of Bristoe Station," *Blue and Gray Magazine*, vol. XXVI, issue 2 (2009), 43-44; *OR* 29, pt. 1, 426; Henderson, *The Road to Bristoe Station*, 167-70.

6. *OR* 29, pt. 1, 426, 430; William W. Hassler, *A. P. Hill: Lee's Forgotten General* (Chapel Hill, NC: University of North Carolina Press, 1957), 176; Monroe F. Cockrell, ed., *Gunner with Stonewall* (Jackson, TN: McCowat-Mercer Press, Inc., 1957), 79-80; Tighe, *The Bristoe Campaign*, 256-57; Henderson, *The Road to Bristoe Station*, 172; Miller, "The Battles of Bristoe Station," 60.

7. Janet Hewitt, ed., *Supplement to the Official Records of the Civil War*, 100 volumes (Wilmington, NC: Broadfoot Publishing Co., 1999), vol. 5, 599; *OR* 29, pt. 1, 430; Miller, "The Battles of Bristoe Station," 44; Berkoff, "Botched Battle at Bristoe," 28. Walker's Brigade was a consolidated unit composed of what had been Brockenbrough's and Archer's brigades. Several regiments from the latter brigade had been detached and so did not fight with Walker during this action. *OR Supplement*, vol. 5, 433-34.

8. Henderson, *The Road to Bristoe Station*, 171; *OR* 29, pt. 1, 277, 300; Tighe, *The Bristoe Campaign*, 265.

9. *OR* 29, pt. 1, 430.

10. Clark, *North Carolina Regiments*, vol. 2, 440-41; *OR* 29, pt. 1, 277, 281. The threat to Heth's division was noted by the men of the 46th

North Carolina, which formed the right flank. Its commander, Col. Edward Hall sent three messages to Heth, and when no assistance was received, he arbitrarily pivoted his command to face the II Corps along the railroad. This was short-lived and Hall returned the regiment to its original position facing Broad Run. Hewitt, ed., *OR Supplement*, vol. 5, 600.

11. Martha D. Perry, ed. *Letters from a Surgeon of the Civil War* (Boston: Little, Brown, and Co., 1906), 110; *OR* 29, pt. 1, 277.

12. *OR* 29, pt. 1, 281, 435.

13. Clark, *North Carolina Regiments*, vol. 2, 440-41; John A. Sloan, *Reminiscences of the Guilford Grays, Company B, 27th N.C. Regiment* (Washington: R. O. Polkinhorn, Printer, 1883), 68. One of the soldiers in Cooke's brigade wrote that the advance was "very rapid not a straggler left the ranks of our regiment, every man seeming in earnest and confident in the belief that we would soon overtake and capture a portion of the Federal army before us with their wagon train." Louis H. Manarin and Weymouth T. Jordan Jr., ed., *North Carolina Troops, 1861–1865, A Roster*, 17 vols. (Raleigh, NC: State Dept. of Archives and History, 1966), vol. 8, 440.

14. Rhodes, *The History of Battery B, First Rhode Island Light Artillery in the War to Preserve the Union, 1861-1865*, (Providence, RI: Snow & Farnham, Printers, 1894), 247-249; *OR* 29, pt. 1, 281. According to Maj. Edmund Rice, the 19th Massachusetts's movements were also interrupted by a battery dashing through its lines. *OR* 29, pt. 1, 284.

15. *OR* 29, pt. 1, 305-06; Sloan, *Reminiscences of the Guilford Grays*, 67.

16. *OR* 29, pt. 1, 242, 277, 281, 283.

17. Rhodes, *The History of Battery B, First Rhode Island Light Artillery*, 247-48; *OR* 29, pt. 1, 307-09; Sauer and Tomasak, *Ricketts' Battery*, 124.

18. *OR* 29, pt. 1, 285, 433; Cockrell, ed., *Gunner with Stonewall*, 79; Tighe, *The Bristoe Campaign*, 263-64; Henderson, *The Road to Bristoe Station*, 176.

19. Henderson, *The Road to Bristoe Station*, 175; Earl J. Hess, *Lee's Tar Heels: The Pettigrew-Kirkland-MacRae Brigade* (Chapel Hill, NC: University of North Carolina Press, 2002), 189; *OR* 29, pt. 1, 300.

20. Hess, *Lee's Tar Heels*, 189.

21. *OR* 29, pt. 1, 433; Henderson, *The Road to Bristoe Station*, 176. Gen. Walker's report is confusing. While he indicates that he had trouble making contact with Kirkland's brigade (which made its wheel to face the enemy), he acknowledges that his brigade crossed Broad Run

in line of battle. (He later recrossed in an effort to join in the fighting.) Why did Walker cross the stream in the first place if he saw Kirkland's men wheeling into action on its west side (and thus pulling farther away from his own right flank?) The only explanation is that Walker did not see Kirkland's wheel and believed that the rest of the attacking column had already crossed Broad Run.

22. Jack D. Welsh, *Medical Histories of Confederate Generals* (Kent, OH: Kent State University Press, 1995), 47, 127. Colonel Hall's rise to brigade command was not relished by the men under his command. According to one, it was "quite a fall to come down from General C to such a man as Col Hall." H. A. Butler to family, October 31, 1863, Elizabeth P. Huckaby Collection, Fredericksburg and Spotsylvania National Military Park.

23. *OR* 29, pt. 1, 427, 436-37.

24. Willson, *Disaster, Struggle, and Triumph*, 217; John Haskell, *The Haskell Memoirs: The Personal Narrative of a Confederate Officer* (New York: G. P. Putnam's Sons, 1960); 61-62; Henderson, *The Road to Bristoe Station*, 180; William S. Long to Family, October 15, 1863. Breckinridge Long Papers, Manuscript Division, Library of Congress; *Columbia Democrat*, October 17, 1863; *OR* 29, pt. 1, 435. The alignment of Kirkland's right flank is difficult to unravel. I have used Tighe's convention of the 26th North Carolina on the right flank. Tighe, *The Bristoe Campaign*, 275, rather than other representations.

25. *OR Supplement*, vol. 5, 600.

26. *OR* 29, pt. 1, 242.

27. *OR* 29, pt. 1, 277, 280-85, 289, 300-03; Clark, *North Carolina Regiments*, vol. 1, 743; vol. 3, 26-27, 93, 242; Perry, ed. *Letters from a Surgeon*, 112; Smith, *The History of the Nineteenth Regiment of Maine Volunteer Infantry*, 109; Miller, "The Battles of Bristoe Station," 48; Rob Orrison, personal communication.

28. *OR* 29, pt. 1, 286, 300, Miller, "The Battles of Bristoe Station," 47; Walker, *History of the Second Army Corps*, 352.

29. Walker, *History of the Second Army Corps*, 352.

30. Hess, *Lee's Tar Heels*, 189; Henderson, *The Road to Bristoe Station*, 181; Clark, *North Carolina Regiments*, vol. 1, 593; Todd S. Berkoff, "Botched Battle at Bristoe," http://bristoe.1stminnd.org/history.html.

31. *OR* 29, pt. 1, 287, 289-90, 294. There is disagreement about the direction of Smyth's movement. According to Col. Smyth's report of the action, "An order was received from General Hays to move forward through the wood and charge the column of the enemy on their right flank." *OR* 29, pt. 1, 294. Since Cooke's brigade was to Smyth's right, it would require an oblique movement. Some historians believe that Smyth's advance was parallel to the railroad, but this would have caused his troops to march past Cooke's men.

32. Mary E. Lewis, "The Life and Times of Thomas Bailey," 47th North Carolina File, Gettysburg National Military Park; *North Carolina Regiments*, vol. 1, 743; Ezra Simons, *A Regimental History of the One Hundred and Twenty-Fifth New York State Volunteers* (New York: Ezra D. Simons, 1888), 158; Miller, "The Battles of Bristoe Station," 48; Randy Bishop, *The Tennessee Brigade* (Bloomington, IL: Authorhouse, 2005), 267-68; *OR* 29, pt. 1, 433-34.

33. *OR* 29, pt. 1, 436-37.

34. *OR* 29, pt. 1, 294, 428, 434; Hess, *Lee's Tar Heels*, 192; Walker, *History of the Second Army Corps*, 353-54; Tighe, *The Bristoe Campaign*, 275; Berkoff, "Botched Battle at Bristoe," http://bristoe. 1stminnd.org/history .html; Mark R. Terry, "The Mystery Flags of Bristoe Station" (provided by Todd Berkoff), 5-6.

35. *OR* 29, pt. 1, 249.

36. *OR* 29, pt. 1, 278, 437-38; Ernest Linden Waitt, *History of the Nineteenth Regiment Massachusetts Volunteer Infantry, 1861-1865* (Salem, MA: n.p., 1906), 270; Miller, "The Battles of Bristoe Station," 48. According to the historians of Ricketts' Federal battery, the unit "simply annihilated the [Confederate] battery [McIntosh's], their fire producing high casualties among men and horses. Sauer and Tomasak, *Ricketts' Battery*, 124.

37. *OR* 29, pt. 1, 294; Zack C. Waters and James C. Edmonds, *A Small but Spartan Band: The Florida Brigade in Lee's Army of Northern Virginia* (Tuscaloosa, AL: University of Alabama Press, 2010), 96; Thomas D. Cockrell and Michael B. Ballard, eds., *A Mississippi Rebel in the Army of Northern Virginia* (Baton Rouge, LA: LSU Press, 1995), 212-13; *A Historical Sketch of the Quitman Guards* (New Orleans: Isaac T. Hinton, Printer, 1866), 95-96. The alignment of Perry's and Posey's brigades during the march and subsequent deployment has traditionally been listed with Perry first in line and on the left of the line of battle. However, credible evidence suggests the reverse. James Johnson Kilpatrick's diary entry of October 14, 1863, specifically notes that Carnot Posey's brigade led Anderson's march to Bristoe. Robert G. Evans, *The 16th Mississippi Infantry: Civil War Letters and Reminiscences* (Jackson, MS: University of

Mississippi Press, 2002), 209. Less compelling is Anderson's report, which puts Posey first and Perry second. *OR 29*, pt. 1, 429. Finally, the quote listed below from a member of the 5th Florida clearly indicates that the 2nd and 8th Florida regiments flanked the enemy, which could only occur if the Floridians were on the right side of the battle line.

The late advance of Richard Anderson's brigades offers yet another uncanny parallel to Gettysburg where, on July 3, 1864, a pair of brigades under Cadmus Wilcox and Edward Perry (the same Perry who advanced at Bristoe Station) advanced after the main attack against Cemetery Ridge had been defeated. Their intent was to support George Pickett's exposed right flank. Just as at Bristoe Station, however, they arrived too late to be of any help.

38. Waters and Edmonds. *A Small but Spartan Band*, 96.

39. *OR 29*, pt. 1, 249, 428; Davis, *The Confederate General*, vol. 5, 51. Posey died on November 13, 1863.

40. Henderson, *The Road to Bristoe Station*, 189; *OR 29*, pt. 1, 289-290, 359, 361.

41. Tighe, *The Bristoe Campaign*, 299.

42. *OR 29*, pt. 1, 255.

43. *OR 29*, pt. 1, 255; Miller, "The Battles of Bristoe Station," 50.

44. Early, *Autobiographical Sketch and Narrative*, 305-06; Donald C. Pfanz, *Richard S. Ewell: A Soldier's Life* (Chapel Hill, NC: University of North Carolina Press, 1998), 339. Unfortunately, none of Ewell's Second Corps officers filed reports on their activities at Bristoe Station. In his memoirs, the normally loquacious Brig. Gen. John Gordon discussed other campaigns with which he was not associated (e.g., Chickamauga and Vicksburg) instead of commenting on Bristoe Station. His silence speaks volumes about how he viewed his actions that day. John B. Gordon, *Reminiscences of the Civil War* (New York: Scribners, 1903).

45. *OR 29*, pt. 1, 243-44, 361; Miller, "The Battles of Bristoe Station," 50; St. Clair Agustin Mulholland, *The Story of the 116th Regiment, Pennsylvania Infantry in the War of the Rebellion* (Philadelphia: F. M. Manus, Jr., and Co., 1909), 162; Page, *History of the Fourteenth Regiment Connecticut Vol. Infantry*, 196-97; Andrew E. Ford, *The Story of the Fifteenth Regiment, Massachusetts Volunteer Infantry in the Civil War, 1861-1865* (Clinton: MA: Press of W. J. Coulter, 1898), 300-01.

46. *OR 29*, pt. 2, 313; Tighe, *The Bristoe Campaign*, 309-10.

47. Henderson, *The Road to Bristoe Station*, 192.

48. Armistead Lindsay Long, *Memoirs of Robert E. Lee* (Secacus, NJ: Blue and Gray Press, 1983), 311; Jones, ed., *The Civil War Memoirs of Captain William Seymour*, 88-89; *OR 29*, pt. 1, 427.

49. W. G. Bean, *Stonewall's Man, Sandie Pendleton* (Chapel Hill, NC: University of North Carolina Press, 2000), 149.

50. R. Lockwood Tower, ed., *Lee's Adjutant: The Wartime Letters of Colonel Walter Herron Taylor, 1862-1865* (Columbia, SC: University of South Carolina Press, 1995), 77. The *Charleston Mercury* viewed the Bristoe Station affair as an indictment against Lee's two top lieutenants. "His [Lee's] plans are admirably conceived, that which ended with the ugly affair at Bristoe, was all that could be desired, but he was compelled to entrust the execution of them to his Lieutenants, and we have no Jackson now. The truth is we want a new cut, shuffle and deal in Lieutenant Generals. Ewell's great physical sufferings have impaired his efficiency; he seems to lack decision; but he had Early and Rhodes [sic], men of excellent judgment. A. P. Hill has not risen to the requirements of a corps commander." *Charleston Mercury*, November 21, 1863.

51. Austin C. Dobbins, *Grandfather's Journal: Company B, Sixteenth Mississippi Infantry Volunteers Harris' Brigade Mahone's Division Hill's Corps A.N.V.* (Dayton, OH: Morningside Press, 1988), 164.

Map Set 5: General Lee Gives Up the Offensive (October 15 - 19, 1863)

1. *OR 29*, pt. 1, 411; pt. 2, 323-26; Henderson, *The Road to Bristoe Station*, 193-94; Alfred Scales to wife, October 20, 1863, Chatham House Library, Fredericksburg and Spotsylvania National Military Park. One-legged Dan Sickles, former commander of Federal III Corps, appeared at General Meade's headquarters in mid-October asking to resume command of his former corps. Meade did not have to think long and hard about his answer. Sickles recalled that Meade, "expressed his disinclination on account of his doubts as to my physical ability to meet the exigencies of the position of a corps commander." This falsehood was probably a better route than the truth for such a political general as Sickles. United States, *Report of the Joint Committee on the Conduct of the War.* (Millwood, NY: Kraus Reprint Collection, 1977), 303.

2. *OR 29*, pt. 1, 350, 449.

3. *OR 29*, pt. 1, 449-50.

4. OR 29, pt. 1, 450-51; Henderson, *The Road to Bristoe Station*, 196-97; Tighe, *The Bristoe Campaign*, 353.

5. OR 29, pt. 2, 326.

6. OR 29, pt. 2, 332-36; Henderson, *The Road to Bristoe Station*, 198-99; Meade, ed., *Life and Letters of George Gordon Meade*, vol. 2, 154. The exchanges between Meade and Halleck grew increasingly heated until the former once again replied, "I take this occasion to repeat what I have before stated, that if my course, based on my own judgment, does not meet with approval, I ought to be, and I desire to be, relieved from command." *OR 29*, pt. 2, 346.

7. OR 29, pt. 1, 382, 451, 998; Glazer, *Three Years in the Federal Cavalry*, 344.

8. OR 29, pt. 2, 349; Freeman, *R. E. Lee*, vol. 3, 186; Taylor, *Four Years with General Lee*, 224; Tighe, *The Bristoe Campaign*, 352.

9. OR 29, pt. 1, 382, 391, 451; McClellan, *I Rode with Jeb Stuart*, 393; Susan Blackford, *War Years with Jeb Stuart* (Baton Rouge, LA: Louisiana State University, 1993), 241.

10. Kidd, *Personal Recollections of a Cavalryman*, 212-15.

11. OR 29, pt. 1, 451.

12. OR 29, pt. 1, 382, 387, 391; Trout, *After Gettysburg*, 250.

13. Henderson, *The Road to Bristoe Station*, 202-03; OR 29, pt. 1, 387, 451; Chris Hartley, "The Bristoe Campaign." www.jebstuart.org/articles.cfm?ID=52.

14. OR 29, pt. 1, 451, 461.

15. Stephen Fonzo, "A Documentary and Landscape Analysis of the Buckland Mills Battlefield" (Washington: National Park Service, American Battlefield Protection Program, 2008), 23.

16. Kidd, *Personal Recollections of a Cavalryman*, 212-15; OR 29, pt. 1, 391.

17. Moore, ed., *The Rebellion Record*, vol. 7, 563-64; OR 29, pt. 1, 391-92.

18. OR 29, pt. 1, 232; Coltrane, *The Memoirs of Daniel Branson Coltrane*, 25.

19. Tighe, *The Bristoe Campaign*, 378-79.

PART 2: THE MINE RUN CAMPAIGN

Map Set 6: Prelude to Mine Run
(October 18 - November 7, 1863)

1. OR 29, pt. 2, 368, 405; Andrew A. Humphreys, Gettysburg to the Rapidan: The Army of the Potomac, July, 1863, to April, 1864 (New York: Charles Scribner's Sons, 1883) 35.

2. OR 29, pt. 2, 358-59, 361-62; Sparks, ed., *Inside Lincoln's Army*, 298. Meade's cautious nature is revealed in an October 30 letter to his wife: "I was most anxious to do so [fight Lee], but I would not do so with all the advantages on his side, and the certainty that if the battle went against me I could not extricate the army from its perilous position. I don't suppose I shall ever get credit for my motives except with the army." Meade, *Life and Letters*, vol. 2, 154-55.

3. George R. Agassiz, ed., *Meade's Headquarters 1863-1865: Letters of Colonel Theodore Lyman from the Wilderness to Appomattox* (Boston: Massachusetts Historical Society, 1922), 36-7; Williams, *Lincoln and His Generals*, 288; Meade, *Life and Letters*, vol. 2, 154.

4. OR 29, pt. 2, 375; Martin F. Graham and George F. Skoch, *Mine Run: A Campaign of Lost Opportunities* (Lynchburg, VA: H. E. Howard, 1987), 5.

5. OR 29, pt. 2, 811.

6. Trout, *After Gettysburg*, 257-58; OR 29, pt. 1, 343, 454; and pt. 2, 382. Although Jeb Stuart and his cavalry had performed well during this campaign, they again came under criticism. The *Richmond Whig* complained that too many Yankees were being captured, and according to Southern hospitality, the "visitors" had to be fed first. An editorial noted that "if the prisoners keep on coming; the meal tub and the flour barrel will soon give out." *Richmond Whig*, October 17, 1863.

7. Freeman, *Lee's Lieutenants*, vol. 3, 264; Freeman, *R. E. Lee*, vol. 3, 188; OR 29, pt. 1, 611, 631; Graham and Skoch, *Mine Run: A Campaign of Lost Opportunities*, 6.

8. Sparks, ed., *Inside Lincoln's Army*, 296; Agassiz, ed., *Meade's Headquarters*, 128-29; Jeffry D. Wert, *The Sword of Lincoln* (New York: Simon & Schuster, 2005), 317.

9. Charles N. Walker and Rosemary Walker, eds., *Diary of the War by Robt. S. Robertson* (Fort Wayne, IN: Allen County-Fort Wayne Historical Society, 1965), 137; Gregory J. Acken, ed., *Inside the Army of the Potomac: The Civil War Experience of Captain Francis Adams Donaldson* (Mechanicsburg, PA: Stackpole Books, 1998), 377-78.

10. Graham and Skoch, *Mine Run: A Campaign of Lost Opportunities*, 5.

11. Dowdey and Manarin, *Wartime Papers of R. E Lee*, 615.

12. Meade, *Life and Letters*, vol. 2, 154; Freeman Cleaves, *Meade of Gettysburg* (Norman, OK: University of Oklahoma Press, 1960), 202.

13. Graham and Skoch, *Mine Run: A Campaign of Lost Opportunities*, 8-9; OR 29, pt. 2, 409, 412; Coughenour, "The Mine Run Campaign," 28.

14. Agassiz, ed., *Meade's Headquarters 1863-1865*, 31.

15. OR 29, pt. 2, 425-26.

16. OR 29, pt. 2, 426-28; Coughenour, "The Mine Run Campaign," 41.

17. OR 29, pt. 1, 555, 575, 587; Salvatroe G. Cilella, Jr., *Upton's Regulars: The 121st New York Infantry in the Civil War* (Lawrence, KS: University of Kansas Press, 2009), 244-45.

Map Set 7: The Affair at Rappahannock Station (November 7, 1863)

1. Earl J. Hess, *Field Armies and Fortifications in the Civil War* (Chapel Hill, NC: University of North Carolina Press, 2005), 290-91; Graham and Skoch, *Mine Run: A Campaign of Lost Opportunities*, 6-7.

2. Jones, ed., *The Civil War Memoirs of Captain William Seymour*, 90; OR 29, pt. 1, 589, 627. According to Graham and Skoch, the 7th and 8th Louisiana were "deployed along a ridge about a quarter of a mile from their fortifications." However, Hays's report stated that the 8th Louisiana was "to the left of the Ninth Regiment, about a quarter of a mile *in advance . . .*" This suggests that the regiments were in front of the defenses, not in them, at this time. Graham and Skoch, *Mine Run: A Campaign of Lost Opportunities*, 17; OR 29, pt. 1, 627. The Louisiana troops captured the crest of Cemetery Hill on the night of July 2, only to retreat when no reinforcements arrived to solidify the advantage. Hays's brigade replaced the Stonewall Brigade in the Rappahannock Station defenses. Jones, ed., *The Civil War Memoirs of Captain William Seymour*, 90-91.

3. OR 29, pt. 1, 611, 618-20.

4. Jones, ed., *The Civil War Memoirs of Captain William Seymour*, 91; Graham and Skoch, *Mine Run: A Campaign of Lost Opportunities*, 15-16; Richard Elliott Winslow III, *General John Sedgwick: The Story of a Union Corps Commander* (Novato, CA: Presidio Press, 1982), 122; OR 29, pt. 1, 574-80; Robert W. Iobst and Louis H. Manarin, *The Bloody Sixth: The Sixth North Carolina Regiment, Confederate States of America* (Durham, NC: Christian Printing Company, 1965), 163.

5. OR 29, pt. 1, 620-21, 627; *Early, Autobiographical Sketch and Narrative*, 309.

6. Jones, ed., *The Civil War Memoirs of Captain William Seymour*, 91; OR 29, pt. 1, 621, 627; Iobst

and Manarin, *The Bloody Sixth*, 159. According to Gen. Hays, the Federal line advanced about 2:30 p.m. and he gradually pulled his regiments back into the defenses about this time before his skirmishers fell back to the road about 3:00 p.m. OR 29, pt. 1, 627.

7. OR 29, pt. 1, 613.

8. OR 29, pt. 1, 585; A. S. Daggett, "Carried by Assault: The Story of the Union Victory at Rappahannock," *Philadelphia Weekly Times*, April 9, 1887.

9. Robert S. Westbrook, *History of the 49th Pennsylvania Volunteers* (Altoona, PA: *Altoona Times*, 1898), 168-169; Larry B. Maier, *Rough & Regular: A History of Philadelphia's 119th Regiment of Pennsylvania Volunteer Infantry* (Shippensburg, PA: Burd Street Press, 1997), 113; OR 29, pt. 1, 588, 594; Isaac O. Best, *History of the 121st New York State Infantry* (Chicago: Lt. James Smith, 1921), 101; Cilella, *Upton's Regulars*, 239.

10. OR 29, pt. 1, 585-86. In his report of the action, Gen. Russell claimed that he was the one to request permission to charge the enemy works. Another account, written by Sedgwick's chief of staff, has all three generals involved in the decision-making process as there was an impromptu cancel of war. All three seemed reluctant, but Russell seemed most assured that an attack would be successful. OR 29, pt. 1, 588; Martin T. McMahon, "From Gettysburg to the Coming of Grant," *Battles and Leaders of the Civil War*, vol. 4, 86.

11. Graham and Skoch, *Mine Run: A Campaign of Lost Opportunities*, 21.

12. OR 29, pt. 1, 589, 599; Cilella, *Upton's Regulars*, 236; Maier, *Rough and Regular*, 115-16; Jones, ed., *The Civil War Memoirs of Captain William Seymour*, 93.

13. OR 29, pt. 1, 588-89, 597-99; Jones, ed., *The Civil War Memoirs of Captain William Seymour*, 93.

14. Terry L. Jones, *Lee's Tigers: The Louisiana Infantry in the Army of Northern Virginia* (Baton Rouge, LA: LSU Press, 1987), 183; OR 29, pt. 1, 621-22.

15. Westbrook, *History of the 49th Pennsylvania*, 168.

16. OR 29, pt. 1, 588.

17. Westbrook, *History of the 49th Pennsylvania*, 168; Maier, *Rough and Regular*, 118; OR 29, pt. 1, 589, 601.

18. James P. Gannon, *Irish Rebels, Confederate Tigers: A History of The 6th Louisiana Volunteers* (Mason City, IA: Savas Publishing Co., 1998), 214.

19. OR 29, pt. 1, 601; Maier, *Rough and Regular*, 118-19; James S. Anderson, *Fifth Wisconsin Reunion*

Pamphlets: Report of Proceedings of the 5th Wisconsin Volunteer Association Annual Reunions (Madison, WI: n.p., 1900, 1901, 1903), 34.

20. Clark, *North Carolina Regiments*, vol. 1, 319; vol. 3, 417; *OR 29*, pt. 1, 630.

21. George W. Bicknell, *History of the Fifth Maine Volunteers* (Portland, ME: H. L. Davis, 1871), 266-67; *OR 29*, pt. 1, 589, 601.

22. A. S. Daggett, "The Battle of Rappahannock Station, Virginia," MOLLUS, Maine, vol. 4, 195; *OR 29*, pt. 1, 592, 594. According to the historian of the 5th Maine, his regiment was in a single line of battle, while the 121st New York was in "close column by divisions," resulting in a much more compact line of battle. Bicknell, *History of the Fifth Maine*, 268. According to some historians, the men stacked arms, kindled fires, and prepared supper close to the enemy works. Cilella, *Upton's Regulars*, 239. This appears unlikely according to other historians, such as Mike Block (personal communication with the author).

23. *OR 29*, pt. 1, 592; Cilella, *Upton's Regulars*, 239.

24. Bicknell, *History of the Fifth Maine*, 270; Best, *History of the 121st New York State Infantry*, 101; *OR 29*, pt. 1, 592, 594; *Memorial and Letters of Rev. John R. Adams* (n.p: privately printed, 1890), 131-32; William Morse Diary, November 7, 1863 entry, (Androscroggin Historical Society, Auburn, ME).

25. Stephen E. Ambrose, *Upton and the Army* (Baton Rouge, LA: LSU Press, 1964), 25; Peter S. Michie, *The Life and Letters of Emory Upton, Colonel of the Fourth Regiment of Artillery, and Brevet Major-General, U.S. Army* (New York: Arno Press, 1979), 83-5; Best, *History of the 121st New York State Infantry*, 101; Clark, *North Carolina Regiments*, vol. 3, 417; Gannon, *Irish Rebels*, 214.

26. Davis, "Archibald Campbell Godwin," in *The Confederate General*, vol. 2, 201; *OR 29*, pt. 1, 622-23.

27. *OR 29*, pt. 1, 623; Graham and Skoch, *Mine Run: A Campaign of Lost Opportunities*, 26.

28. Jones, *Lee's Tigers*, 184.

29. Albert A. Batchelor to his father, December 21, 1863, Albert A. Batchelor papers, Louisiana State University; Camille Baquet, *History of the First Brigade, New Jersey Volunteers, from 1861-1865* (Trenton, NJ: MacCrellish & Quigley, 1910), 102.

30. *OR 29*, pt. 1, 622; Samuel D. Buck, *With the Old Confeds: Actual Experiences of a Captain in the Line* (Baltimore: H. E. Houck and Co., 1925), 94-98; Iobst and Manarin, *The Bloody Sixth*, 168.

31. *OR 29*, pt. 1, 629, 630; Jones, *Lee's Tigers*, 185-86; Diary of Isaiah Fogelman, November 7, 1863 entry (Chatham House Library, Fredericksburg and Spotsylvania National Military Park). The Confederate captives began their march to Washington on the morning of November 8. They reached Warrenton Junction later that day and were put on trains. Upon reaching Washington, they were marched to the docks on the Potomac River where they boarded the steamer *John Brooke* bound for Point Lookout Prison, which they reached on November 10. Iobst and Manarin, *The Bloody Sixth*, 166.

32. *OR 29*, pt. 1, 559; Graham and Skoch, *Mine Run: A Campaign of Lost Opportunities*, 28; Clark Baum to wife, November 10, 1863 (copy in Chatham House Library, Fredericksburg and potsylvania National Military Park).

33. Clark, *North Carolina Regiments*, vol. 1, 320. Peter W. Hairston, a staff officer, recorded the following exchange in his diary: "When we were drawn up in line of battle near Culpepper Genl. Lee rode up to him [General Hays] & said 'Genl. This is a sad affair, how do you feel to day?' 'I feel sir, as well as a man can feel who has lost so many men.' Well [it] is all over now and can not be helped the only thing is to try to get even with them today.'" Peter W. Hairston Diary, Southern Historical Collection, University of North Carolina; Iobst and Manarin, *The Bloody Sixth*, 168.

Map Set 8: Confederate Defeat at Kelly's Ford (November 7, 1863)

1. *OR 29*, pt. 1, 631. Rodes wrote in his official report of the engagement: "At Kelly's Ford the bluffs are on the enemy's side, close to the river, and encircle the ground which my outpost force was compelled to occupy. On our side the land for a mile or more from the river bank is cleared and slopes gently to the river. It is necessary to notice these facts to account properly for the losses of the two regiments mentioned." *OR 29*, pt. 1, 631.

2. *OR 29*, pt. 1, 631; Darrell L. Collins, *Major General Robert E. Rodes of the Army of Northern Virginia: A Biography* (El Dorado Hills, CA: Savas Beatie LLC, 2008), 323; Hewitt, ed., *OR Supplement*, vol. 5, 609.

3. Hewitt, ed., *OR Supplement.*, vol. 5, 610; Collins, *Rodes*, 322-23. Cox would have the dubious distinction of being wounded eleven times during the war. Ezra Warner, *Generals in Gray: Lives of the Confederate Commanders* (Baton Rouge, LA: LSU Press, 1959), 64. In his report of the action, Lt. Col. Walter Stallings claimed that he sent a dispatch

directly to General Rodes. Hewitt, ed., *OR Supplement*, vol. 5, 610.

4. *OR* 29, pt. 1, 566-67, 574; Graham and Skoch, *Mine Run: A Campaign of Lost Opportunities*, 12; Regis de Trobriand, *Four Years with the Army of the Potomac* (Boston: Tickner and Co., 1889), 548.

5. *OR* 29, pt. 1, 632-33; Clark, *North Carolina Regiments*, vol. 2, 502.

6. de Trobriand, *Four Years with the Army of the Potomac*, 548.

7. George Lewis, *The History of Battery E, First Regiment Rhode Island Light Artillery in the War of 1861 and 1865, to Preserve the Union* (Providence, RI: Snow and Farnham, 1892), 239; Heinz K. Meier, ed., *Memoirs of a Swiss Officer in the American Civil War* (Bern, Switzerland: Herbert Lang and Co., 1972), 129.

8. Graham and Skoch, *Mine Run: A Campaign of Lost Opportunities*, 12; Charles A. Stevens, *Berdan's United States Sharpshooters in the Army of the Potomac, 1862–1865* (St. Paul, MN: Price McGill Co., 1892), 368-79; Hewitt, ed., *OR Supplement*, vol. 5, 610-11.

9. de Trobriand, *Four Years with the Army of the Potomac*, 549.

10. de Trobriand, *Four Years with the Army of the Potomac*, 549; Hewitt, ed., *OR Supplement*, vol. 5, 611; Stevens, *Berdan's United States Sharpshooters*, 679.

11. *OR* 29, pt. 1, 561, 632.

12. *OR* 29, pt. 1, 633; Gary W. Gallagher, *Stephen Dodson Ramseur: Lee's Gallant General* (Chapel Hill, NC: University of North Carolina Press, 1985), 86.

13. Graham and Skoch, *Mine Run: A Campaign of Lost Opportunities*, 15; *OR* 29, pt. 1, 632.

14. Taylor, *Four Years with General Lee*, 116; Bean, *Stonewall's Man*, 151.

Map Set 9: Lee Withdraws Below the Rapidan River (November 8 - 27, 1863)

1. Winslow, *General John Sedgwick*, 124; *OR* 29, pt. 2, 443; Meade, *Life and Letters*, vol. 2, 443; Coughenour, "The Mine Run Campaign," 42.

2. Graham and Skoch, *Mine Run: A Campaign of Lost Opportunities*, 30-31.

3. Clark, *North Carolina Regiments*, vol. 5, 186.

4. Robert E. Park, "War Diary of Captain Robert Emory Park," *Southern Historical Society Papers (SHSP)*, vol. XXVI, 23; *OR* 29, pt. 1, 614.

5. *OR* 29, pt. 2, 434. V Corps was on the road to Kelly Ford at 4:00 a.m. Humphreys, *Gettysburg to the Rapidan*, 47.

6. *OR* 29, pt. 1, 563.

7. *OR* 29, pt. 2, 435.

8. de Trobriand, *Four Years with the Army of the Potomac*, 550.

9. *OR* 29, pt. 2, 438-39; Sparks, ed., *Inside Lincoln's Army*, 304; Agassiz, *Meade's Headquarters*, 45.

10. Graham and Skoch, *Mine Run: A Campaign of Lost Opportunities*, 34.

11. Graham and Skoch, *Mine Run: A Campaign of Lost Opportunities*, 29, 36; Worsham, *One of Jackson's Foot Cavalry*, 184; LeRoy Edwards to father, November 10, 1863. (Copy in Chatham House Library, Fredericksburg and Spotsylvania National Military Park).

12. Harlan Cross, Jr. "Civil War Letters." (Copy in Chatham House Library, Fredericksburg and Spotsylvania National Military Park); Graham and Skoch, *Mine Run: A Campaign of Lost Opportunities*, 36.

13. Humphreys, *Gettysburg to the Rapidan*, 49-50, 53.

14. George Skoch, "The Man Who Fed the South," *Civil War Times Illustrated*, November 1983, Vol. XXII, 44; *OR* 29, pt. 2, 830, 832-33.

15. John D. Chapla, *42nd Virginia Infantry* (Lynchburg, VA: H. E. Howard, 1983), 39-40.

16. *OR* 29, pt. 2, 832.

17. *OR* 29, pt. 2, 449, 454, 459-61; Winslow, *General John Sedgwick*, 125.

18. Graham and Skoch, *Mine Run: A Campaign of Lost Opportunities*, 38-40; *OR* 29, pt. 1, 1, 13, 677; *OR* 29, pt. 2, 474.

19. *OR* 29, pt. 1, 11.

20. Coughenour, "The Mine Run Campaign," 52, 54.

21. Sparks, ed., *Inside Lincoln's Army*, 311; *OR* 29, pt. 1, 13-14. Judson Kilpatrick's cavalry division (now under Brig. Gen. George Custer) would guard the fords while John Buford's cavalry division (now under Brig. Gen. Wesley Merritt) guarded the field trains. The infantrymen carried eight days of rations and another ten days were hauled in the wagons. Only half of the ambulances and ammunition wagons accompanied the marching men. This meant that each man carried only 30 additional rounds per man. *OR* 29, pt. 1, 229; Coughenour, "The Mine Run Campaign," 56-57.

22. Humphreys, *Gettysburg to the Rapidan*, 50; Coughenour, "The Mine Run Campaign," 57.

23. *OR* 29, pt. 1, 14, 694, 794.

24. Winslow, *General John Sedgwick*, 126; *OR* 29, pt. 1, 736-38, 760-61, 768.

25. Humphreys, *Gettysburg to the Rapidan*, 53.

26. *OR* 29, pt. 1, 827; Graham and Skoch, *Mine Run: A Campaign of Lost Opportunities*, 47.

27. *OR* 29, pt. 1, 677, 823; Ella Lonn, *Desertion During the Civil War* (New York: Century, 1928), 151-52, 233.

28. Graham and Skoch, *Mine Run: A Campaign of Lost Opportunities*, 48; Caldwell, *History of a Brigade of South Carolinians*, 118; Freeman, *R. E. Lee*, vol 3, 195.

29. *OR* 29, pt. 1, 495-96.

30. Humphreys, *Gettysburg to the Rapidan*, 55.

31. *OR* 29, pt. 1, 730-31, 838-39; Humphreys, *From Gettysburg to the Rapidan*, 56.

32. *OR* 29, pt. 1, 794, 806-07, 898-99; N. D. Preston, "With Gregg at Mine Run." *Philadelphia Weekly Times*, July 1, 1882.

33. *OR* 29, pt. 2, 499-500; Adolfo Cavada Diary, November 27 entry, Philadelphia Historical Society.

34. *OR* 29, pt. 2, 500.

35. *OR* 29, pt. 1, 29, 761; Graham and Skoch, *Mine Run: A Campaign of Lost Opportunities*, 51; Davis, "The Bristoe and Mine Run Campaigns," 497.

36. *OR* 29, pt. 2, 501; Sparks, ed., *Inside Lincoln's Army*, 314.

37. *OR* 29, pt. 1, 897.

38. Graham and Skoch, *Mine Run: A Campaign of Lost Opportunities*, 49.

39. Early, *Autobiographical Sketch and Narrative*, 319; *OR* 29, pt. 1, 876-77.

Map Set 10: Encounter at Payne's Farm (November 27, 1863)

1. *OR* 29, pt. 1, 761-62, 846; Graham and Skoch, *Mine Run: A Campaign of Lost Opportunities*, 53.

2. *OR* 29, pt. 1, 846, 862.

3. Warner, *Generals in Gray*, 158.

4. Stewart Sifakis, *Who Was Who In the Civil War* (New York: Facts on File, 1988), 524.

5. *OR* 29, pt. 2, 500.

6. Theodore P. Savas, "The Musket Balls Flew Very Thick: Holding the Line at Payne's Farm," *Civil War: The Magazine of the Civil War Society* (Vol. X, No. 3, Issue 25), 23; Theodore Savas, "Decision at the Crossroads: The Battle of Payne's Farm, November 27, 1863," unpublished manuscript, personal collection of Theodore Savas, 8-11; *OR* 29, pt. 1, 762-63.

7. *OR* 29, pt. 1, 742, 750, 763.

8. Savas, "The Musket Balls Flew Very Thick," 23.

9. *OR* 29, pt. 1, 862-63.

10. Savas, "The Musket Balls Flew Very Thick," 22; *OR* 29, pt. 1, 766; Savas, "Decision at the Crossroads," 12.

11. *OR* 29, pt. 1, 846, 862. Johnson indicated in his report that John M. Jones's brigade reached Locust Grove by noon. This is probably too early by at least one hour and perhaps two.

12. Gregg S. Clemmer, *Old Alleghany: The Life and Wars of General Ed Johnson* (North Potomac, MD: Hearthside Pub. Co., 2004), 512; Lee A. Wallace, *5th Virginia* (Lynchburg, VA: H. E. Howard, 1988), 52; John D. Chapla, *48th Virginia Infantry* (Lynchburg, VA: H. E. Howard, 1989), 63; Worsham, *One of Jackson's Foot Cavalry*, 187.

13. *OR* 29, pt. 1, 863, 869-70.

14. *OR* 29, pt. 1, 742, 777.

15. John D. Chapla, *50th Virginia Infantry* (Lynchburg, VA: H. E. Howard, 1997), 81; John D. Chapla, *48th Virginia Infantry*, 63; Alexander Baird to mother, December 13, 1863 (Chatham House Library, Fredericksburg and Spotsylvania National Military Park); Clark, *North Carolina Regiments*, vol. 1, 198; *OR* 29, pt. 1, 850, 857, 866, 868, 875; Worsham, *One of Jackson's Foot Cavalry*, 187.

16. Clemmer, *Old Alleghany*, 512-13; *OR* 29, pt. 1, 847; Savas, "Decision at the Crossroads," 13.

17. Robertson, Jr., *The Civil War Letters of General Robert McAllister*, 364; *OR* 29, pt. 1, 846.

18. *OR* 29, pt. 1, 870.

19. *OR* 29, pt. 1, 852. The commander of the 33rd Virginia, Lt. Col. Abraham Spengler, also reported that his men had thrown up light works, but it was at their own volition. *OR* 29, pt. 1, 855.

20. William B. Colston Memoir, Virginia Historical Society; *OR* 29, pt. 1, 849, 850; Robert K. Krick, *Lee's Colonels: A Biographical Register of the Field Officers of the Army of Northern Virginia* (Dayton, OH: Morningside Bookshop, 1984), 83; Savas, "Decision at the Crossroads," 12-13; Chaplain Abner C. Hopkins Diary, October 27, 1863 entry, Virginia Historical Society. Lieutenant Colonel Raleigh Colston's left leg was amputated, and although he rallied for a time, he died of pneumonia in a Charlottesville hospital on December 23, 1863.

21. *OR* 29, pt. 1, 781.

22. Henri Le Fevre Brown, *History of the Third Regiment, Excelsior Brigade, 72d New York, 1861-1865* (Jamestown, NY: Journal Publishing Co., 1902), 120-21.

23. *OR* 29, pt. 1, 847.

24. *OR* 29, pt. 1, 863.

25. *OR* 29, pt. 1, 870.

26. *OR* 29, pt. 1, 777, 780.

27. *OR* 29, pt. 1, 849; Lowell Reidenbaugh, *33rd Virginia Infantry* (Lynchburg, VA: H. E. Howard, 1987), 74. Walker is mistaken in his recollection. In fact, the woods at that point were no deeper than perhaps 300 yards.

28. Worsham, *One of Jackson's Foot Cavalry*, 187; *OR* 29, pt. 1, 871.

29. *OR* 29, pt. 1, 870.

30. Savas, "Decision at the Crossroads," 15; Clark, *North Carolina Regiments*, vol. 1, 198; Walter Clark, "Letters to Home" (copy in Chatham House Library, Fredericksburg and Spotsylvania National Military Park).

31. *OR* 29, pt. 1, 866-68; Savas, "Decision at the Crossroads," 16.

32. *OR* 29, pt. 1, 863.

33. Savas, "Decision at the Crossroads," 19; *OR* 29, pt. 1, 849, 852-53.

34. *OR* 29, pt. 1, 856, 859.

35. Savas, "Decision at the Crossroads," 16-17; *OR* 29, pt. 1, 768, 773, 866, 869; Robertson, *The Civil War Letters of General Robert McAllister*, 364. Lieutenant Colonel Robert Bodine of the 26th Pennsylvania wrote in his report, "my regiment was then advanced and became warmly engaged until some troops on the left gave way, when it was forced to retire, to prevent being outflanked and captured." *OR* 29, pt. 1, 769; Savas, "The Musket Balls Flew Very Thick," 53; Thomas E. Merchant, *Eighty-Fourth Regiment Pennsylvania Volunteers* (Philadelphia: Sherman & Co., 1889), 72.

36. *OR* 29, pt. 1, 865.

37. Charles W. Turner, *Ted Barclay, Liberty Hall Volunteers: Letters from the Stonewall Brigade* (Berryville, VA: Rockbridge Publishing Co., 1992), 117; *OR* 29, pt. 1, 853; Hewitt, ed., *OR Supplement*, vol. 5, 627.

38. *OR* 29, pt. 1, 871, 873.

39. Worsham, *One of Jackson's Foot Cavalry*, 187; *OR* 29, pt. 1, 871.

40. *OR* 29, pt. 1, 856. Jones survived the battle, but both he and his good friend and fellow brigade commander Leroy Stafford would meet their end six months later at the battle of the Wilderness in early May 1864. Davis, *The Confederate General*, vol. 3, 205, vol. 5, 195.

41. *OR* 29, pt. 1, 755.

42. Agassiz, ed., *Meade's Headquarters*, 266; Stephen R. Taaffe, *Commanding the Army of the Potomac* (Lawrence, KS: University of Kansas Press, 2006), 181-82.

43. *OR* 29, pt. 1, 772, 866-67. Ward's brigade was deployed behind the guns as his men watched the enemy approach. The historian of

the 124th New York wrote: "our battery was handled in a masterly manner—its rapid discharges of grape told with fearful effect on that portion of the enemy's charging line in our immediate front, which soon broke and fled; and then . . . the Union troops who had been giving ground took courage and with a shout started forward on a countercharge, and all that portion of the Confederate line in front . . . fell back a considerable distance." Charles H. Weygant, *History of the One Hundred and Twenty-fourth NYSV: The Orange Blossom Regiment* (Newburgh, NY: Journal Publishing House, 1877), 239.

44. *OR* 29, pt. 1, 865.

45. Willie Walker Caldwell, *Stonewall Jim: A Biography of General James A. Walker, C.S.A.* (Elliston, VA: Northcross House, 1990), 94; Savas, "Decision at the Crossroads," 20.

46. *OR* 29, pt. 1, 847; Savas, "Decision at the Crossroads," 25.

47. *OR* 29, pt. 1, 871.

48. *OR* 29, pt. 1, 859; Savas, "Decision at the Crossroads," 25.

49. *OR* 29, pt. 1, 867; Savas, "Decision at the Crossroads," 15-16; Savas, "The Musket Balls Flew Very Thick," 53.

50. *OR* 29, pt. 1, 768, 865, 867, 869; Savas, "Decision at the Crossroads," 15-16; Savas, "The Musket Balls Flew Very Thick," 53.

51. Jones, *Lee's Tigers*, 187-88; *OR* 29, pt. 1, 871, 874-875; Savas, "Decision at the Crossroads," 24; Gen. Stafford conspicuously galloped up and down his line, seemingly oblivious to enemy bullets whizzing past him. What most of the men did not know was that Stafford's horse was badly spooked, and the only way he could control it was by keeping it in motion. Jones, *Lee's Tigers*, 187-88.

52. Worsham, *One of Jackson's Foot Cavalry*, 187.

53. *OR* 29, pt. 1, 750.

54. E. M. Haynes, *A History of the Tenth Regiment, Vermont Volunteers* (Lewiston, ME: Tenth Vermont Regimental Association, 1870), 50; Weygant, *History of the One Hundred and Twenty-fourth NYSV*, 239; *OR* 29, pt. 1, 780; William B. Jordan, Jr., *Red Diamond Regiment: The 17th Maine Infantry, 1862-1865* (Shippensburg, PA: White Mane Publishing Co., 1996), 101; Ruth L. Silliker, *The Rebel Yell & the Yankee Hurrah: The Civil War Journal of a Maine Volunteer* (Camden, ME: Down East Books, 1985), 129.

55. *OR* 29, pt. 1, 759; D. G. Crotty, *Four Years Campaigning in the Army of the Potomac* (Grand Rapids, MI: Dygert Brothers and Co., 1874), 113; A. G. Feather, "The Mine Run Campaign." *Philadelphia Weekly Times*, August 6, 1887.

56. Edward Hagerty, *Collis' Zouaves: The 114th Pennsylvania Volunteers in the Civil War* (Baton Rouge, LA: LSU Press, 1997), 274.

57. OR 29, pt. 1, 849, 856, 871-72.

58. OR 29, pt. 1, 783-84; Savas, "Decision at the Crossroads," 21-22; "Highly Interesting Letter from the 87th Pennsylvania," *The Republican Compiler (Gettysburg)*, December 14, 1863.

59. OR 29, pt. 1, 837.

60. OR 29, pt. 1, 681-82.

61. Helena A. Howell, *Chronicles of the Hundred and Fifty-First New York Volunteer Infantry* (n.p., n.d.), 49.

Map Set 11: Confrontation at Mine Run (November 27 - December 2, 1863)

1. Coughenour, "The Mine Run Campaign," 64-65; Humphreys, *Gettysburg to the Rapidan*, 60.

2. Lowe, ed., *Meade's Army*, 73; Humphreys, *Gettysburg to the Rapidan*, 61; OR 29, pt. 1, 695. Warren's move shoved back Brig. Gen. John Gordon's Confederate brigade and captured a number of his Georgians. His reference to Ewell is evidence the Union high command did not realize that Jubal Early was leading Ewell's Second Corps during the Mine Run Campaign.

3. OR 29, pt. 1, 15-16, 695.

4. Freeman, *R. E. Lee*, 195-96; Park, "War Diary " 24; OR 29, pt. 1, 828-29, 904.

5. Humphreys, *Gettysburg to the Rapidan*, 63; Coughenour, "The Mine Run Campaign," 65.

6. Agassiz, ed., *Meade's Headquarters*, 55; OR 29, pt. 1, 16; *Western Sun*, December 19, 1863.

7. Cross, "Civil War Letters" (Chatham Library, Fredericksburg and Spotsylvania National Military Park).

8. Winslow, *General John Sedgwick*, 128; OR 29, pt. 1, 829, 834, 848, 896.

9. Robertson, *Civil War Letters of General Robert McAllister*, 367.

10. Robertson, *Civil War Letters of General Robert McAllister*, 367; Thomas Francis Galway, *The Valiant Hours: An Irishman in the Civil War* (Mechanicsburg, PA: Stackpole Books, 1961), 173.

11. OR 29, pt. 1, 696.

12. OR 29, pt. 1, 16; Humphreys, *Gettysburg to the Rapidan*, 64; Graham and Skoch, *Mine Run: A Campaign of Lost Opportunities*, 70.

13. Humphreys, *Gettysburg to the Rapidan*, 64.

14. Graham and Skoch, *Mine Run: A Campaign of Lost Opportunities*, 71; OR 29, pt. 1, 807-808; Humphreys, *Gettysburg to the Rapidan*, 69.

15. Robertson, *Civil War Letters of General Robert McAllister*, 365.

16. OR 29, pt. 1, 696; Galway, *The Valiant Hours*, 173.

17. Graham and Skoch, *Mine Run: A Campaign of Lost Opportunities*, 71-72; OR 29, pt. 1, 807, 829, 899-900.

18. OR 29, pt. 1, 697; Walker, *History of the Second Army Corps*, 379.

19. OR 29, pt. 1, 16.

20. Coughenour, "The Mine Run Campaign," 67.

21. Laura Elizabeth Lee, *Forget-Me-Nots of the Civil War: A Romance, Containing Reminiscences and Original Letters of Two Confederate Soldiers* (St. Louis: A. R. Fleming Printing Co., 1909), 101.

22. Worsham, *One of Jackson's Foot Cavalry*, 189.

23. Graham and Skoch, *Mine Run: A Campaign of Lost Opportunities*, 74-75; Luvaas Nye, "The Campaign That History Forgot," 32; Mason W. Tyler, *Recollections of the Civil War* (New York: G. P. Putnam Sons, 1912), 127.

24. Bradley M. Gottfried, *Stopping Pickett: The History of the Philadelphia Brigade* (Shippensburg, PA: White Mane Publishing Company, 1999), 188; Robertson, *Civil War Letters of General Robert McAllister*, 367-68; Robert E. Bigbee, "More About Mine Run," *National Tribune*, July 26, 1883; William Landon, "Prock's Last Letters to the Vincennes Western Sun," *Indiana Magazine of History*, Vol. 35, No. 1 (March, 1939), 77.

25. Charles Edward Davis to Father, December 3, 1863 (Civil War Collection, Brown University Library); H. S. Stevens, "Those Slips of Paper: Another Graphic Account," *National Tribune*, July 12, 1883.

26. Robertson, *Civil War Letters of General Robert McAllister*, 368.

27. OR 29, pt. 1, 698; Taylor, *Gouverneur Kemple Warren* 160-61; Adolpho Cavada Diary, November 30, 1863 entry.

28. Sparks, ed., *Inside Lincoln's Army*, 317.

29. Thomas L. Livermore, *Days and Events, 1860-1866* (Boston: Houghton Mifflin Co., 1920), 303; Coughenour, "The Mine Run Campaign," 69-70. Coughenour hypothesized that Meade waited a couple of hours to visit Warren so he could compose himself.

30. Graham and Skoch, *Mine Run: A Campaign of Lost Opportunities*, 79; OR 29, pt. 2, 929.

31. Leroy Edwards to father, November 29, 1863, Leroy Edwards Papers, Randolph Macon College.

32. Coughenour, "The Mine Run Campaign," 70-71; OR 29, pt. 2, 530-31.

33. *OR* 29, pt. 2, 530-31.

34. *OR* 29, pt. 1, 896; Robert E. Lee, *Recollections and Letters of General Robert E. Lee* (Garden City, NY: Doubleday, Page & Co., 1924), 116.

Map Set 12: Winter Interlude, 1863 -1864
(December 2, 1863 - March 1864)

1. Dowdey and Manarin, *Wartime Papers of R. E. Lee*, 630-31.

2. *OR* 29, pt. 2, 858-59.

3. Edward Steer, *The Wilderness Campaign* (Harrisburg, PA: The Stackpole Company, 1960), 30-31; *OR* 29, pt. 2, 866.

4. Gary Gallagher, "Our Hearts are Full of Hope: The Army of Northern Virginia in the Spring of 1864," in *The Wilderness Campaign*, Gary Gallagher, ed. (Chapel Hill, NC: University of North Carolina Press, 1997), 42-43; Dowdey and Manarin, *Wartime Papers of R. E. Lee*, 647, 698.

5. Gallagher, "Our Hearts are Full of Hope," 43.

6. Freeman, *R. E. Lee*, vol. 3, 241.

7. Freeman, *R. E. Lee*, vol. 3, 208; Pfanz, *Richard S. Ewell*, 349. Freeman, *Lee's Lieutenants*, vol. 3, 325-30; *OR* 33, 1,095; *OR* 29, pt. 2, 861. Brigadier General William Averell's cavalry raid into the Allegheny Mountains toward the vital Virginia and Tennessee Railroad gave General Lee an opportunity to test Early in an independent capacity. The campaign got off to a poor start when Early ordered his main cavalry force in the wrong direction, allowing Averell to slip away unscathed.

8. *OR* 33, 460-62.

9. Carter, ed., *Four Brothers in Blue*, 375, 378.

10. John J. Hennessy, "I Dread the Spring: The Army of the Potomac Prepares for the Overland Campaign," in *The Wilderness Campaign*, 67-68; *OR* 29, pt. 2, 598.

11. Hennessy, "I Dread the Spring," 67-68; Daniel M. Holt, *A Surgeon's Civil War: The Letters and Diary of Daniel M. Holt, M.D.*, ed. James M. Grenier, Janet L. Coryell, and James R. Smither (Kent, OH: Kent State University Press, 1994), 160-61; Agassiz, ed., *Meade's Headquarters*, 58-59.

12. Bradley M. Gottfried, *Kearny's Own: The History of the First New Jersey Brigade in the Civil War* (New Brunswick, NJ: Rutgers University Press), 151-55.

13. *OR* 33, 717-18, 722-23; Hennessy, "I Dread the Spring," 81-86.

Map Set 13: The Affair at Morton's Ford
(February 6-7, 1864)

1. Meade, *Life and Letters*, 165; Graham and Skoch, *Mine Run: A Campaign of Lost Opportunities*, 84-85.

2. *OR* 33, 506-07; Humphreys, *Gettysburg to the Rapidan*, 72-73; Page, *History of the Fourteenth Regiment, Connecticut Vol. Infantry*, 216-17.

3. *OR* 33, 519; Wayne Mahood, "Tiger at Morton's Ford." *Civil War Times Illustrated*, vol. 41, No. 7 (February 2003), 25.

4. Humphreys, *Gettysburg to the Rapidan*, 72-73.

5. *OR* 33, 119-20, 123; W. D. Taylor, "Morton's Ford, Va.," *National Tribune*, September 18, 1890.

6. *OR* 33, 127; Willson, *Disaster, Struggle, Triumph*, 235.

7. Mahood, "Tiger at Morton's Ford," 27; *OR* 33, 127, 133; Graham and Skoch, *Mine Run: A Campaign of Lost Opportunities*, 88; Simons, *A Regimental History of the One Hundred and Twenty-Fifth New York State Volunteers*, 190-91; Willson, *Disaster, Struggle, Triumph*, 235; Galway, *The Valiant Hours*, 188.

8. *OR* 33, 142. The affair at Morton's Ford was briefly reported by Robert E. Lee and artillery battalion commander H. E. Cabell. No other reports seem to have been filed. Cabell erroneously reported that the works were initially defended by two regiments from Doles's brigade and two from Ramseur's (Johnson's division) and were later reinforced by Steuart's brigade. This error was repeated by Graham and Skoch (*Mine Run: A Campaign of Lost Opportunities*, 88). In fact, no organized Confederates were in the works when Owen's men made their initial advance. William Meade Dame, *From the Rapidan to Richmond* (Baltimore: Green-Lucas Company, 1920), 41; Robert Stiles, *Four Years Under Marse Robert* (New York: Neale Publishing Company, 1903), 235-36; Pfanz, *Richard S. Ewell*, 353.

9. Dame, *From the Rapidan to Richmond*, 41.

10. *OR* 33, 524.

11. Welsh, *Medical Histories of Confederate Generals*, 65; Pfanz, *Richard S. Ewell*, 353; Freeman, *Lee's Lieutenants*, vol. 3, 334.

12. Pfanz, *Richard S. Ewell*, 353.

13. Robert Grier Stephens, Jr., ed., *Intrepid Warrior: Clement Anselm Evans, Confederate General from Georgia* (Dayton, OH: Morningside, 1992), 347-48; G. W. Nichols, *A Soldier's Story of His Regiment (61st Georgia) and Incidentally of the Lawton-Gordon-Evans Brigade* (Kennesaw, GA: Continental Book Company, 1961), 132-33; Pharris DeLoach Johnson, *Under the Southern Cross: Soldier Life with*

Gordon Bradwell and the Army of Northern Virginia (Macon, GA: Mercer University Press, 1999), 148.

14. OR 33, 127, 133; Simons, *A Regimental History of the One Hundred and Twenty-Fifth New York State Volunteers*, 192.

15. Page, *History of the Fourteenth Regiment, Connecticut Vol. Infantry*, 217-18.

16. OR 33, 115.

17. Stephens Jr., ed., *Intrepid Warrior*, 349-50.

18. Page, *History of the Fourteenth Regiment, Connecticut Vol. Infantry*, 219-21.

19. OR 33, 121, 122; Humphreys, *Gettysburg to the Rapidan*, 73-4.

20. Graham and Skoch, *Mine Run: A Campaign of Lost Opportunities*, 94; Nichols, *A Soldier's Story of His Regiment*, 135.

21. Fitzhugh Lee, *General Lee: A Biography of Robert E. Lee* (New York: Da Capo Press, 1994), 323; Freeman, *R. E. Lee*, vol. 3, 334.

Summation

1. Coughenour, "The Mine Run Campaign," 25-26.

Bibliography

Archival Sources

Androscroggin Historical Society (Auburn, Maine)
William Morse Diary

Brown University Library
Civil War Collection

Fredericksburg National Military Park Library
H. A. Butler letters
Walter Clark, "Letters to Home"
Harlan Cross, Jr. "Civil War Letters"
Leroy Edwards letters

Gettysburg National Military Park
Mary E. Lewis, "The Life and Times of Thomas Bailey" (47th North Carolina File)

Library of Congress
Breckinridge Long Papers

Navarro College, Corsicana, Texas
Pearce Civil War Collection

Philadelphia Historical Society
Adolfo Cavada Diary

Savas, Theodore Peter Collection
"Decision at the Crossroads: The Battle of Payne's Farm, November 27, 1863." Unpublished Manuscript.

Southern Historical Collection, University of North Carolina, Chapel Hill
Lyon Papers
Richard W. Waldrop Papers

Virginia Historical Society (Richmond)
William B. Colston Memoir

Newspapers

Charleston Mercury, November 21, 1863
Charlotte Western Democrat, November 10, 1863
Columbia Democrat, October 17, 1863
Montgomery Ledger, November 24, 1863

Richmond Daily Dispatch, August 11, 1863 and October 19, 1863
Richmond Enquirer, August 7, 1863
Richmond Whig, September 16, 1863 and October 17, 1863

Official Documents

Hewitt, Janet, ed. *Supplement to the Official Records of the Civil War*, 100 Volumes. Wilmington, NC: Broadfoot Publishing Co., 1999.

United States. *Report of the Joint Committee on the Conduct of the War*. Millwood, NY: Kraus Reprint Collection, 1977.

United States War Department. *The War of the Rebellion: A Compilation of the Official Records of the Union and Confederate Armies*, 128 Volumes. Washington, DC: U.S. Government Printing Office, 1880-1901.

Books

Acken, Gregory J., ed. *Inside the Army of the Potomac: The Civil War Experience of Captain Francis Adams Donaldson*. Mechanicsburg, PA: Stackpole Books, 1998.

Agassiz, George R. ed. *Meade's Headquarters 1863-1865: Letters of Colonel Theodore Lyman from the Wilderness to Appomattox*. Boston: Massachusetts Historical Society, 1922.

Aldrich, Thomas M. *The History of Battery A: First Regiment Rhode Island Light Artillery in the War to Preserve the Union*. Providence, RI: Snow and Farnham Printers, 1904.

Ambrose, Stephen E. *Upton and the Army*. Baton Rouge, LA: LSU Press, 1964.

Anderson, James S. *Fifth Wisconsin Reunion Pamphlets: Report of Proceedings of the 5th Wisconsin Volunteer Association Annual Reunions*. Madison, WI: np, 1900, 1901, 1903.

Baquet, Camille. *History of the First Brigade, New Jersey Volunteers, from 1861-1865*. Trenton, NJ: MacCrellish & Quigley, 1910.

Basler, Roy P., ed. *The Collected Works of Abraham Lincoln*. Eight Volumes. New Brunswick, NJ: Rutgers University Press, 1953.

Beale, Howard K., ed. *Diary of Gideon Welles*. Three Volumes. New York: W. W. Norton, 1960.

Bean, W. G. *Stonewall's Man, Sandie Pendleton*. Chapel Hill, NC: University of North Carolina Press, 2000.

Best, Isaac O. *History of the 121st New York State Infantry*. Chicago: Lt. James Smith, 1921.

Bicknell, George W. *History of the Fifth Maine Volunteers*. Portland, ME: H. L. Davis, 1871.

Bishop, Randy. The Tennessee Brigade. Bloomington, IL: Authorhouse, 2005.

Blackford, Susan. *War Years with Jeb Stuart*. Baton Rouge, LA: Louisiana State University, 1993.

Brown, Henri Le Fevre. *History of the Third Regiment, Excelsior Brigade, 72d New York, 1861-1865*. Jamestown, NY: Journal Publishing Co., 1902.

Buck, Samuel D. *With the Old Confeds: Actual Experiences of a Captain in the Line*. Baltimore: H. E. Houck and Co., 1925.

Busey, John W. and David G. Martin. *Regimental Strengths and Losses at Gettysburg*. Hightstown, NJ: Longstreet House, 2005.

Caldwell, J. F. J. *History of a Brigade of South Carolinians, Known First As "Gregg's" and Subsequently As "McGowan's Brigade."* Philadelphia: King and Baird, Printers, 1866.

Caldwell, Willie Walker. *Stonewall Jim: A Biography of General James A. Walker, C.S.A.* Elliston, VA: Northcross House, 1990.

Carter, Robert G., ed. *Four Brothers in Blue; or, Sunshine and Shadow of the War of the Rebellion, a Story of the Great Civil War, from Bull Run to Appomattox*. Austin, TX: University of Texas Press, 1978.

Chapla, John D. *42nd Virginia Infantry*. Lynchburg, VA: H. E. Howard, 1983.

———. *48th Virginia Infantry.* Lynchburg, VA: H. E. Howard, 1989.

———. *50th Virginia Infantry.* Lynchburg, VA: H. E. Howard, 1997.

Cilella Jr., Salvatroe G. *Upton's Regulars: The 121st New York Infantry in the Civil War.* Lawrence, KS: University of Kansas Press, 2009.

Clark, Walter. *Histories of the Several Regiments and Battalions from North Carolina: In the Great War 1861-'65.* Five Volumes. Wilmington, NC: Broadfoot Publishing Co., 1996.

Cleaves, Freeman. *Meade of Gettysburg.* Norman, OK: University of Oklahoma Press, 1960.

Clemmer, Gregg S. *Old Alleghany: The Life and Wars of General Ed Johnson.* North Potomac, MD: Hearthside Pub. Co., 2004.

Cockrell, Monroe F., ed. *Gunner with Stonewall: Reminiscences of William Thomas Poague.* Jackson, TN: McCowat-Mercer Press, Inc., 1957.

Cockrell, Thomas D. and Michael B. Ballard, eds. *A Mississippi Rebel in the Army of Northern Virginia: The Civil War Memoirs of Private David Holt.* Baton Rouge, LA: LSU Press, 1995.

Coddington, Edwin B. *The Gettysburg Campaign: A Study in Command.* New York: Charles Scribner's Sons, 1968.

Collins, Darrell. *Major General Robert E. Rodes of the Army of Northern Virginia: A Biography.* New York, NY: Savas Beatie LLC, 2008.

Coltrane, Daniel Branson. *The Memoirs of Daniel Branson Coltrane.* Raleigh, NC: Edwards and Broughton Co., 1956.

Couture, Richard T., ed. *Charlie's Letters: The Correspondence of Charles E. Denoon.* n.p., 1982.

Crotty, D. G. *Four Years Campaigning in the Army of the Potomac.* Grand Rapids, MI: Dygert Brothers and Co., 1874.

Crowninshield, Benjamin W. *A History of the First Regiment of Massachusetts Cavalry Volunteers.* Boston: Houghton Mifflin and Co., 1891.

Dame, William Meade. *From the Rapidan to Richmond and the Spottsylvania Campaign A Sketch in Personal Narration of the Scenes a Soldier Saw.* Baltimore: Green-Lucas Company, 1920.

Dana, Charles A. *Recollections of the Civil War.* D. Appleton and Co., 1902.

Davis, William C. *The Confederate General.* Six Volumes. n.p.: National Historical Society, 1991.

de Trobriand, Regis. *Four Years with the Army of the Potomac.* Boston: Tickner and Co., 1889.

Dobbins, Austin C. *Grandfather's Journal: Company B, Sixteenth Mississippi Infantry Volunteers, Harris' Brigade, Mahone's Division, Hill's Corps, ANV.* Dayton, OH: Morningside Bookshop, 1988.

Dowdey, Clifford and Louis H. Manarin. *The Wartime Papers of R. E. Lee.* New York: Bramhall House, 1961.

———. *A History of the Confederacy.* New York: Barnes and Noble, 1992.

Driver Jr., Robert J. *First and Second Maryland Cavalry.* Charlottesville, VA: Howell Press, Inc., 1999.

———. *First and Second Maryland Infantry.* Bowie, MD: Willow Bend Books, 2003.

Early, Jubal. *Lieutenant General Jubal Anderson Early, CSA: Autobiographical Sketch and Narrative of the War Between the States.* Wilmington, NC: Broadfoot Publishing Co., 1989.

Evans, Robert G. *The 16th Mississippi Infantry: Civil War Letters and Reminiscences.* Jackson, MS: University of Mississippi Press, 2002.

Favill, Josiah. *The Diary of a Young Officer. Serving With the Armies of the United States During the War of the Rebellion.* Chicago: R. R. Donnelley & Sons, 1909.

Fishel, Edwin C. *The Secret War for the Union. The Untold Story of Military Intelligence in the Civil War.* New York: Houghton Mifflin, 1996.

Ford, Andrew E. *The Story of the Fifteenth Regiment, Massachusetts Volunteer Infantry in the Civil War, 1861-1865.* Clinton, MA: Press of W. J. Coulter, 1898.

Freeman, Douglas Southall. *R. E. Lee: A Biography.* Four Volumes. Charles Scribner's Sons, 1951.

———. *Lee's Lieutenants: A Study in Command.* Three Volumes. Scribner, 1944.

Gallagher, Gary W. *Stephen Dodson Ramseur—Lee's Gallant General.* Chapel Hill, NC: University of North Carolina Press, 1985.

———, ed. *The Wilderness Campaign,* Chapel Hill, NC: University of North Carolina Press, 1997.

Galway, Thomas Francis. *The Valiant Hours: An Irishman in the Civil War*. Mechanicsburg, PA: Stackpole Books, 1961.

Gannon, James P. *Irish Rebels, Confederate Tigers: A History of the 6th Louisiana Volunteers, 1861-1865*. Mason City, IA: Savas Publishing Co., 1998.

Glatthaar, Joseph T. *General Lee's Army: From Victory to Collapse*. New York: Free Press, 2008.

Glazer, Willard W. *Three Years in the Federal Cavalry*. New York: R. H. Ferguson and Co., 1873.

Gordon, John B. *Reminiscences of the Civil War*. New York: Scribner, 1903.

Gottfried, Bradley M. *Stopping Pickett: The History of the Philadelphia Brigade*. Shippensburg, PA: White Mane Publishing Company, 1999.

————. *Kearny's Own: The History of the First New Jersey Brigade in the Civil War*. New Brunswick, NJ: Rutgers University Press, 2005.

Graham, Martin F. and George F. Skoch. *Mine Run: A Campaign of Lost Opportunities*. Lynchburg, VA: H. E. Howard, 1987.

Grimsley, Daniel A. *Battles in Culpeper County, Virginia, 1861-1865, and Other Articles (1900)*. Culpeper, VA: Raleigh Travers Green, 1900.

Hagerty, Edward. *Collis' Zouaves: The 114th Pennsylvania Volunteers in the Civil War*. Baton Rouge, LA: LSU Press, 1997.

Hard, Abner. *History of the Eighth Cavalry Regiment, Illinois Volunteers*. Dayton, OH: Morningside Bookshop, 1986.

Haskell, John. *The Haskell Memoirs: The Personal Narrative of a Confederate Officer*. New York: G. P. Putnam's Sons, 1960.

Hassler, William W. *A. P. Hill: Lee's Forgotten General*. Chapel Hill, NC: University of North Carolina Press, 1957.

Haynes, E. M. *A History of the Tenth Regiment, Vermont Volunteers*. Lewiston, ME: Tenth Vermont Regimental Association, 1870.

Henderson, William D. *The Road to Bristoe Station: Campaigning With Lee and Meade, August 1- October 20, 1863*. Lynchburg, VA: H. E. Howard, 1987.

Hess, Earl J. *Lee's Tar Heels: The Pettigrew-Kirkland-MacRae Brigade*. Chapel Hill, NC: University of North Carolina Press, 2002.

————. *Field Armies and Fortifications in the Civil War*. Chapel Hill, NC: University of North Carolina Press, 2005.

Hinton, Isaac T. *A Historical Sketch of the Quitman Guards: Company E, Sixteenth Mississippi Regiment, Harris' Brigade: from its organization in Holmesville, 21st April . . . of Northern Virginia, 9th April, 1865*. New Orleans: 1866.

Holt, Daniel M. *A Surgeon's Civil War: The Letters and Diary of Daniel M. Holt, M.D.*, James M. Grenier, Janet L. Coryell, and James R. Smither, eds. Kent, OH: Kent State University Press, 1994.

Howell, Helena A. *Chronicles of the Hundred and Fifty-First New York Volunteer Infantry*. n.p., n.d.

Humphreys, Andrew A. *Gettysburg to the Rapidan: The Army of the Potomac, July, 1863, to April, 1864*. New York: Charles Scribner's Sons, 1883.

Iobst, Robert W. and Louis H. Manarin. *The Bloody Sixth: The Sixth North Carolina Regiment, Confederate States of America*. Durham, NC: Christian Printing Company, 1965.

Johnson, Pharris DeLoach, ed. *Under the Southern Cross: Soldier Life with Gordon Bradwell and the Army of Northern Virginia*. Macon, GA: Mercer University Press, 1999.

Johnson, Robert U., and Buell, Clarence C. *Battles and Leaders of the Civil War*. Four Volumes. New York: Thomas Yoseloff, 1956.

Jones, Terry L. *Lee's Tigers: The Louisiana Infantry in the Army of Northern Virginia*. Baton Rouge, LA: LSU Press, 1887.

————, ed. *The Civil War Memoirs of Captain William Seymour*. Baton Rouge, LA: LSU Press, 1991.

Jordan Jr., William B. *Red Diamond Regiment: The 17th Maine Infantry, 1862-1865*. Shippensburg, PA: White Mane Publishing Co., 1996.

Jordan Jr., Weymouth T. and Louis H. Manarin, eds. *North Carolina Troops, 1861-1865, A Roster*, 17 vols. Raleigh, NC: State Dept. of Archives and History, 1966.

Kidd, James Harvey. *Personal Recollections of a Cavalryman with Custer's Michigan Brigade in the Civil War*. Ionia, MI: Sentinel Printing Co., 1908.

Krick, Robert K. *Lee's Colonels: A Biographical Register of the Field Officers of the Army of Northern Virginia*. Dayton, OH: Morningside Bookshop, 1984.

Lee, Fitzhugh. *General Lee: A Biography of Robert E. Lee*. New York: Da Capo Press, 1994.

Lee, Laura Elizabeth. *Forget-Me-Nots of the Civil War: A Romance, Containing Reminiscences and Original Letters of Two Confederate Soldiers*. St. Louis: A. R. Fleming Printing Co., 1909.

Lee, Robert E. *Recollections and Letters of General Robert E. Lee*. Garden City, NY: Doubleday, Page & Co., 1924.

Lewis, George. *The History of Battery E, First Regiment Rhode Island Light Artillery in the War of 1861 and 1865, to Preserve the Union*. Providence, RI: Snow and Farnham, 1892.

Livermore, Thomas L. *Days and Events, 1860-1866*. Boston: Houghton Mifflin Co., 1920.

Long, Armistead Lindsay. *Memoirs of Robert E. Lee*. Secacus, NJ: Blue and Gray Press, 1983.

Longstreet, James. *From Manassas to Appomattox: Memoirs of the Civil War in America*. Bloomington, IN: Indiana University Press, 1960.

Lonn, Ella. *Desertion During the Civil War*. New York: Century, 1928.

Lowe, David W., ed. *Meade's Army: The Private Notebooks of Lt. Col. Theodore Lyman*. Kent, OH: Kent State University, 2007.

McClellan, H. B. *Life and Campaigns of Stuart's Cavalry*. Richmond: J. W. Randolph and English, 1885.
———. *I Rode with J. E. B. Stuart*. Bloomington, IN: Indiana University Press, 1958.

McDonald, William N. *A History of the Laurel Brigade: Originally the Ashby Cavalry of the Army of Northern Virginia and Chew's Battery*. Baltimore: Johns Hopkins University Press, 2002.

Maier, Larry B. *Rough & Regular: A History of Philadelphia's 119th Regiment of Pennsylvania Volunteer Infantry, The Gray Reserves*. Shippensburg, PA: Burd Street Press, 1997.

Meade, George Gordon. *The Life and Letters of George Gordon Meade*, 2 Volumes. Charles Scribner's Sons, 1913.

Meier, Heinz K., ed. *Memoirs of a Swiss Officer in the American Civil War*. Bern, Switzerland: Herbert Lang and Co., 1972.

Memorial and Letters of Rev. John R. Adams. np: privately printed, 1890.

Merchant, Thomas E. *Eighty-Fourth Regiment Pennsylvania Volunteers*. Philadelphia: Sherman & Co., 1889.

Michie, Peter S. *The Life and Letters of Emory Upton, Colonel of the Fourth Regiment of Artillery, and Brevet Major-General, U.S. Army*. New York: Arno Press, 1979.

Miller, Richard F. *Harvard's War: A History of the Twentieth Massachusetts Volunteer Infantry*. Hanover, NH: University Press of New England, 2005.

Moore, Frank, ed. *The Rebellion Record: A Diary of American Events*. 12 Volumes. New York: D. Van Nostrand, 1864.

Mulholland, St. Clair Agustin. *The Story of the 116th Regiment, Pennsylvania Infantry in the War of the Rebellion*. Philadelphia: F. M. Manus, Jr., and Co., 1909.

Neese, George M. *Three Years in the Confederate Horse Artillery*. New York: Neale Publishing Co., 1911.

Nichols, G. W. *A Soldier's Story of His Regiment (61st Georgia) and Incidentally of the Lawton-Gordon-Evans Brigade*. Kennesaw, GA: Continental Book Company, 1961.

Page, Charles D. *History of the Fourteenth Regiment, Connecticut Vol. Infantry*. Meridian, CT: Horton Printing Co., 1906.

Perry, Martha D., ed. *Letters from a Surgeon of the Civil War*. Boston: Little, Brown, and Co., 1906.

Pfanz, Donald C. *Richard S. Ewell: A Soldier's Life*. Chapel Hill, NC: University of North Carolina Press, 1998.

Powell, William H. *Fifth Army Corps*. G. P. Putnam Sons, 1896.

————. *History of the Tenth Regiment of Cavalry New York State Volunteers*. New York: D. Appleton and Co., 1892.

Raymer, Jacob Nathaniel. *Confederate Correspondent: The Civil War Reports of Jacob Nathaniel Raymer, Fourth North Carolina*. E. B. Munson, ed. Jefferson, NC: McFarland, 2009.

Reidenbaugh, Lowell. *33rd Virginia Infantry*. Lynchburg, VA: H. E. Howard, 1987.

Rhodes, John H. *The History of Battery B: First Rhode Island Light Artillery in the War to Preserve the Union, 1861-1865*. Providence, RI: Snow & Farnham, Printers, 1894.

Robertson, Jr., James I. *The Civil War Letters of General Robert McAllister*. Harrisburg, PA: The Archive Society, 1997.

Sauers, Richard A. and Peter Tomasak. *Ricketts' Battery: A History of Battery F, 1st Pennsylvania Light Artillery*. n.p.: Luzerne National Bank, 2001.

Sifakis, Stewart. *Who Was Who in the Civil War*. New York: Facts on File, 1988.

Silliker, Ruth L. *The Rebel Yell & the Yankee Hurrah: The Civil War Journal of a Maine Volunteer*. Camden, ME: Down East Books, 1985.

Simons, Ezra. *A Regimental History of the One Hundred and Twenty-Fifth New York State Volunteers*. New York: Ezra D. Simons, 1888.

Sloan, John A. *Reminiscences of the Guilford Grays, Company B, 27th N.C. Regiment*. Washington: R. O. Polkinhorn, Printer, 1883.

Smith, John D. *The History of the Nineteenth Regiment of Maine Volunteer Infantry, 1862-1865*. Minneapolis: Great Western Printing Co., 1909.

Sparks, David S., ed. *Inside Lincoln's Army: The Diary of Marsena Rudolph Patrick, Provost Marshal General, Army of the Potomac*. New York: Thomas Yoseloff, 1964.

Steer, Edward. *The Wilderness Campaign*. Harrisburg, PA: Stackpole Books, 1960.

Stephens Jr., Robert Grier, ed. *Intrepid Warrior: Clement Anselm Evans, Confederate General from Georgia*. Dayton, OH: Morningside Bookshop, 1992.

Stevens, Charles A. *Berdan's United States Sharpshooters in the Army of the Potomac, 1861-1865*. St. Paul, MN: Price-McGill Co., 1892.

Stiles, Robert. *Four Years Under Marse Robert*. New York: Neale Publishing Co., 1903.

Taaffe, Stephen R. *Commanding the Army of the Potomac*. Lawrence, KS: University of Kansas Press, 2006.

Taylor, Emerson G. *Gouverneur Kemple Warren: The Life and Letters of an American Soldier, 1830-1882*. Boston: Houghton Mifflin and Co., 1932.

Taylor, Walter H. *Four Years with General Lee*. New York: Bonanza Books, 1962.

Thomas, Emory M. *Bold Dragoon: The Life of J.E.B. Stuart*. New York: Harper & Row, 1986.

Thomas, H. S. *Some Personal Reminiscences of Service in the Cavalry*. Philadelphia: L. R. Hammersley & Co., 1889.

Tighe, Adrian G. *The Bristoe Campaign: General Lee's Last Strategic Offensive with the Army of Northern Virginia, October 1863*. XLibris: n.p., 2011.

Tower, R. Lockwood, ed. *Lee's Adjutant: The Wartime Letters of Colonel Walter Herron Taylor, 1862-1865*. Columbia, SC: University of South Carolina Press, 1995.

Treasured Reminiscences Collected by the John K. McIver Chapter United Daughters of the Confederacy. Columbia, SC: The State Co. Printers, 1911.

Trout, Robert J. *After Gettysburg: Cavalry Operations in the Eastern Theater, July 14, 1862 to December 31, 1862*. Hamilton, MT: Eagle Editions, Ltd., 2011.

————. *Galloping Thunder: The Stuart Horse Artillery Battalion*. Mechanicsburg, PA: Stackpole Books, 2002.

Turner, Charles W. *Ted Barclay, Liberty Hall Volunteers: Letters from the Stonewall Brigade*. Berryville, VA: Rockbridge Publishing Co., 1992.

Tyler, Mason W. *Recollections of the Civil War*. New York: G. P. Putnam Sons, 1912.

Waitt, Ernest Linden. *History of the Nineteenth Regiment Massachusetts Volunteer Infantry, 1861-1865*. Salem, MA: n.p., 1906.

Walker, Charles N. and Rosemary Walker, eds. *Diary of the War by Robt. S. Robertson*. Fort Wayne, IN: Allen County-Fort Wayne Historical Society, 1965.

Walker, Francis. *History of the Second Army Corps*. New York: Charles Scribner's Sons, 1887.

Wallace, Lee A. *5th Virginia*. Lynchburg, VA: H. E. Howard, 1988.

Warner, Ezra. *Generals in Gray: Lives of the Confederate Commanders*. Baton Rouge, LA: LSU Press, 1959.

——. *Generals in Blue: Lives of the Union Commanders*. Baton Rouge, LA: LSU Press, 1959.

Waters, Zack C. and James C. Edmonds. *A Small but Spartan Band: The Florida Brigade in Lee's Army of Northern Virginia*. Tuscaloosa, AL: University of Alabama Press, 2010.

Welsh, Jack D. *Medical Histories of Confederate Generals*. Kent, OH: Kent State University Press, 1995.

Wert, Jeffry D. *Cavalryman of the Lost Cause: A Biography of J.E.B. Stuart*. New York: Simon & Schuster, 2008.

——. *A Glorious Army: Robert E. Lee's Triumph 1862-1863*. New York: Simon & Schuster, 2011.

——. *The Sword of Lincoln*. New York: Simon & Schuster, 2005.

Westbrook, Robert S. *History of the 49th Pennsylvania Volunteers*. Altoona, PA: Altoona Times, 1898.

Weygant, Charles H. *History of the One Hundred and Twenty-fourth NYSV: The Orange Blossom Regiment*. Newburgh, NY: Journal Publishing House, 1877.

Wiley, Ken. *Norfolk Blues: The Civil War Diary of the Norfolk Light Artillery*. Shippensburg, PA: Burd Street Press, 1997.

Williams, T. Harry. *Lincoln and His Generals*. New York: Alfred A. Knopf, 1952.

Willson, Arabella M. *Disaster, Struggle, Triumph: The Adventures of 1000 Boys in Blue*. Albany, NY: Argus Publishers, 1870.

Winslow III, Richard Elliott. *General John Sedgwick: The Story of a Union Corps Commander*. Novato, CA: Presidio Press, 1982.

Worsham, John H. *One of Jackson's Foot Cavalry*. New York: Neale Publishing Co., 1912.

Articles and Essays

Berkoff, Todd S. "Botched Battle at Bristoe." *America's Civil War*, September 2003, 22-29, 70-71.

Bigbee, Robert E. "More About Mine Run." *National Tribune*, July 26, 1883.

Coughenour, Lt. Col. Kavin L. "The Mine Run Campaign: An Operational Analysis of Major General George G. Meade." Study Project, U.S. Army War College, March 1, 1990.

Daggett, A. S. "Carried by Assault: The Story of the Union Victory at Rappahannock." *Philadelphia Weekly Times*, April 9, 1887.

——. "The Battle of Rappahannock Station, Virginia," *MOLLUS*, Maine. Portland, ME: Lefavor-Tower Company, 1915, vol. 4, 190-199.

Davis, Lt. Col. George B. "The Bristoe and Mine Run Campaigns," in *Campaigns in Virginia, Maryland, and Pennsylvania, 1862-1863*. Boston: Griffith-Stillings Press, 1903, 470-502.

Feather, A. G. "The Mine Run Campaign." *Philadelphia Weekly Times*, August 6, 1887.

Fonzo, Stephen. "A Documentary and Landscape Analysis of the Buckland Mills Battlefield." Washington, DC: National Park Service, American Battlefield Protection Program, 2008.

Geier, Clarence R., Joseph W. A. Whitehorne, Alyson Wood, Eric Troll, and Kimberly Tinkham. "The Civil War Engagements at Auburn, Virginia, October 13, 14, 1863: A Historical-Archeological Analysis," http://www.jenningsgap.com/auburnarchaeology.html.

Landon, William. "Prock's Last Letters to the Vincennes Western Sun," *Indiana Magazine of History*, Vol. 35, No. 1 (March 1939), 76-94.

Lewis, Meriwether. "Of Spies and Borrowed Names: The Identity of Union Operatives in Richmond Known as the Phillipses Discovered." *Virginia Magazine of History and Biography*, 89 (1981), 308-327.

——. "Samuel Ruth and General R. E. Lee: Disloyalty and the Line of Supply to Fredericksburg, 1862-1863." *Virginia Magazine of History and Biography*, 71 (1963), 35-109.

Luvaas, Jay and Wilbur S. Nye. "The Campaign that History Forgot," *Civil War Times Illustrated*, vol. 8, (November 1969), 11-27, 30-42.

McMahon, Martin T. "From Gettysburg to the Coming of Grant," in *Battles and Leaders of the Civil War*. Four Volumes. New York: Thomas Yoseloff, 1956. Vol. 4, 81-94.

Mahood, Wayne. "Tiger at Morton's Ford." *Civil War Times Illustrated*, Vol. 41, Number 7 (February 2003), 24-31.

Miller, J. Michael. "The Battles of Bristoe Station," *Blue and Gray Magazine*, Vol. XXVI, Issue 2 (2009), 6-27, 40-50.

Park, Robert E. "War Diary of Captain Robert Emory Park," *Southern Historical Society Papers* (SHSP), Vol. XXVI (1898), 20-31.

Preston, N. D. "With Gregg at Mine Run." *Philadelphia Weekly Times*, July 1, 1882.

Savas, Theodore P. "The Musket Balls Flew Very Thick: Holding the Line at Payne's Farm." *Civil War: The Magazine of the Civil War Society*, Vol. X, no. 3, Issue 25, 1992.

Seeley, Charles S. "The Mine Run Campaign Commemorated Next Week." *Orange Review*, November 1964.

Skoch, George. "The Man Who Fed the South." *Civil War Times Illustrated*, Vol. XXII, (November 1983), 40-44.

Stevens, H. S. "Those Slips of Paper: Another Graphic Account." *National Tribune*, July 12, 1883.

Index

About the Author

Bradley M. Gottfried holds a Ph.D. in Zoology from Miami University. He has worked in higher education for more than three decades as a faculty member and administrator and is currently the President of the College of Southern Maryland.

An avid Civil War historian, Dr. Gottfried is the author of nine books, including *The Battle of Gettysburg: A Guided Tour* (1998); *Stopping Pickett: The History of the Philadelphia Brigade* (1999); *Brigades of Gettysburg* (2002); *Roads to Gettysburg* (2002); *Kearny's Own: The History of the First New Jersey Brigade* (2005), *The Maps of Gettysburg* (2007), *The Artillery of Gettysburg* (2008), and *The Maps of First Bull Run* (2009). He is currently (with co-editor Theodore P. Savas) completing *The Gettysburg Campaign Encyclopedia*.

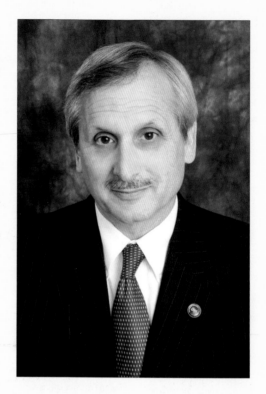